TRAINING FOR THE FUTURE
Handbook

Contents

INTRODUCTION

Florian Malzacher and Jonas Staal

Trainings, Trainers and Trainees

We face intersecting crises in the rise of authoritarian politics, economic precarization and environmental catastrophe, and as a result our culture has long taken a dystopian turn. To imagine the future today often means nothing but a worsening extension of the present in which libertarian geo-engineering and alt-right ecofascism will rule supreme. Right-wing and libertarian forces across the world operate through a web of think tanks and schools to ensure they maintain hegemony over our shrinking future.

We founded Training for the Future in 2018 to reclaim the future as a site of collective struggle. We sought to oppose the culture of dystopian normativity and create our own organizational infrastructure to train for alternate futurities and, consequently, alternate pasts and presents. In recognizing the need for structural organization and actionability in order to reclaim the means of production of the future, we chose the *training* as a method and the *training camp* as the common site of practice.

The notion of training suggests a particular hierarchy, namely that between trainer and trainee. This means that the trainer has a certain competence in reclaiming the future as a site of common struggle, which needs to be transferred to the trainee. Joining the training camp is to accept this temporary division of roles and power, and to follow instructions and exercises – even if one might not yet be familiar with the futurity their new competence might enable or whether one entirely agrees with the particular future proposed to them in the first place. To train then means to follow a proposal, a possibility, in which critical reflexes take the form of embodied practice first and verbal reflection second.

But this temporal division of roles only emphasizes their exchangeability. In our training camp, trainers also partake in other trainings as trainees. And if a training is executed successfully, a former trainee can then act as trainer. Therefore, the division of power and agency named through the trainer/trainee dichotomy is aimed at overcoming this very separation. At the end of each of our intensive training camps, if executed successfully, all participants are trainers for the future.

Though perhaps we should we say 'futures' in the plural? Our pasts differ, as do our presents, so how could we expect the future to be singular? We train for futures, and the training camp is a site of assembly for these alternate futurities. Together they make visible the possibility that dystopian normativity can be shattered; that there is a plurality of worlds to be struggled for and that we do not have to accept the world as it is simply because this is how it has been presented to us. We train to make worlds instead. And we train to seek commonalities and solidarities between this world of many worlds.

Training Camps: Faculty, Forms, Places

Throughout our different training camps, the training faculty changes. Trainers are art activists, protest choreographers, autonomists, zoöpologists, progressive hackers, data communalists, futurological herstoriographers, social interrogators, anal armies, care collectivists, emancipatory memologists and pan-socialist agitators. Each of them brings different embodied understandings, tactics and instructions to make common futures present and to transform present struggles into futurities.

The localities where our training camps are held matter. In 2018 and 2019 they took place amidst the industrial remnants of the Ruhr area in Germany – archaeologies of a future driven by a belief in industrial progress. This location embodies a history of proletarian consciousness and unionization, a history where humans recognized their agency in shaping future-history. But it equally forms a history of predatory class oppression, and of an extractivist industrial paradigm that denied agency to nonhuman comrades and burnt livable futures for all. The two training camps that we organized in these ruins of the future took the form of neo-constructivist landscapes, where hybrid training objects propagated fragmented slogans of the past as part of a collective exercise to train the future. As such, the location and the form of our camps together enacted a critical, dialogical and morphological solidarity.

Due to the Covid-19 pandemic, the locality of the 2021 training camp took a decentralized form, highlighting the way in which the pandemic further intensified dystopian normativity. Additionally, 'vaccine apartheid' has made the vast disparities in wealth and livability even more visible, exacerbating the unequal pasts, presents and futures we carry. This pandemic period showed staggering quarterly figures for trillion-dollar companies like Amazon, providing proof for all to see that our common crisis is the capital accumulation of the 0.1% that make up the ruling elite. The age of climate crisis-fueled pandemics – its beginning marked by Covid-19 – shows us the endgame of disaster capitalism, in which remnants of the future will remain the sole property of tech elites hiding in underground luxury bunkers in New Zealand or self-exiled to the terraformed backup planet Mars.

Yet in the face of disaster, questions of redistribution and collectivity gain additional urgency. This is why, under the title Collectives, Collectivity and Collectivizations, we organized parallel trainings in Argentina, Colombia, the United States, the Philippines, South Africa, Rojava (Western Kurdistan), Italy and Switzerland. Through developing a decentralized version of our training camp, we attempted to contribute to the reclaiming of futures as a commons – and to do so at exactly the moment when the commons is being stolen from us in the most violent manner.

The Covid-19 pandemic demanded each trainer to revisit the conditions within which collectivity was to be shaped in a moment of deep atomization and isolation. As such, each training proposed a methodology to redefine what it means to assemble and do collective work when the systems we inhabit and the catastrophes they produce fragment us so profoundly. The result of this decentralized training camp was a collective choreography across different geographies, and different pasts and presents, to map the possibility of shared futures and a biosphere for all.

Handbook, Manuals, Reflections

The handbook you are holding documents in text and image the training camps that took place from 2018 to 2021. It contains manuals from the 2021 camp, which enable you to exercise trainings or to organize camps of your own, and interviews with various trainers from the 2019 camp, in which they reflect on their methodologies and consider how to further the struggle toward reclaiming the means of production of the future. Assembled together, this handbook stands as a testimony to the manifold futures that agitate our present; the manifold futures that defy the culture of dystopian normativity and that ensure collective worlds of work, technology, care and intimacy are present right here and right now, for all those willing to train for and with them.

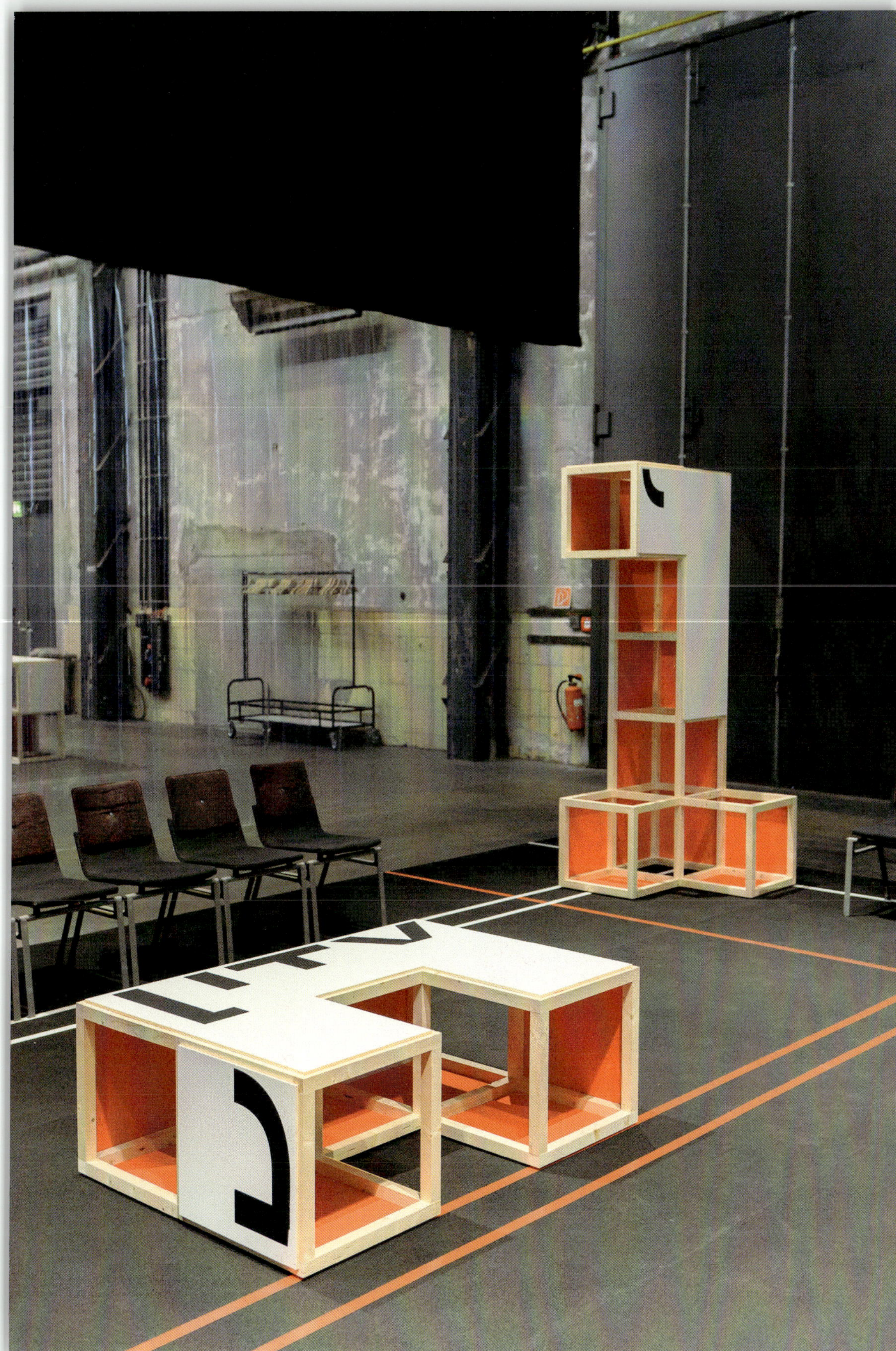

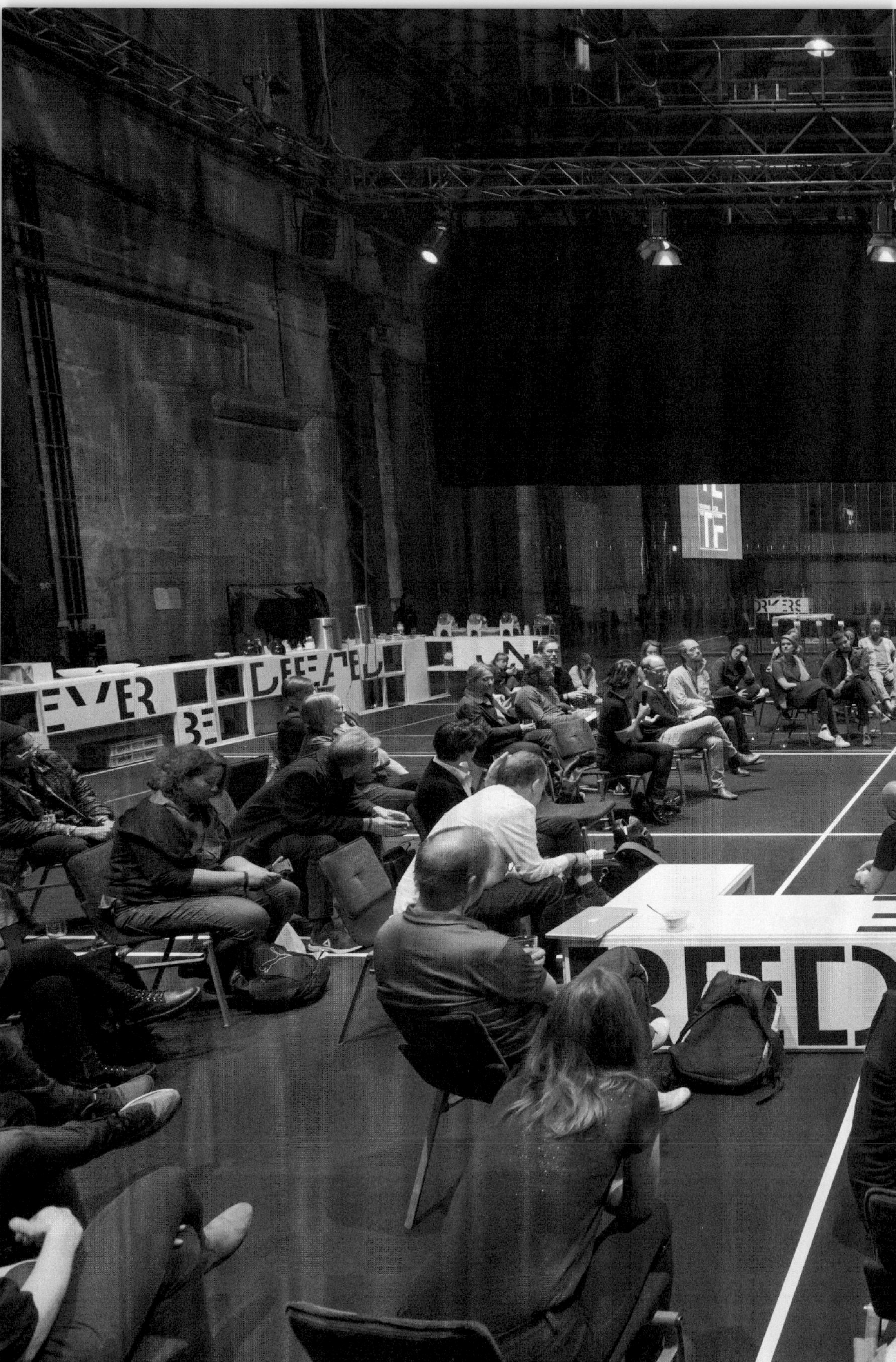
EVER

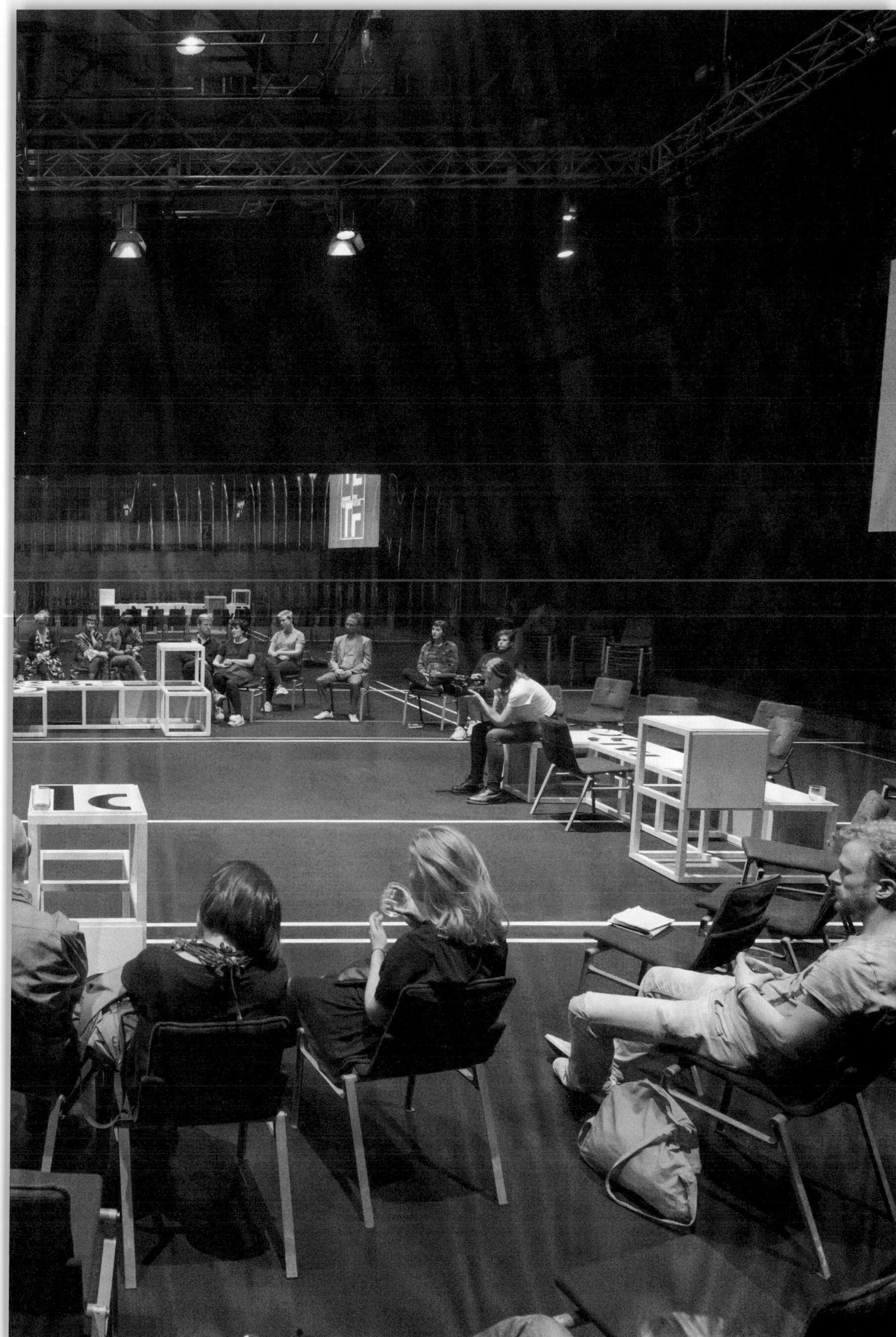

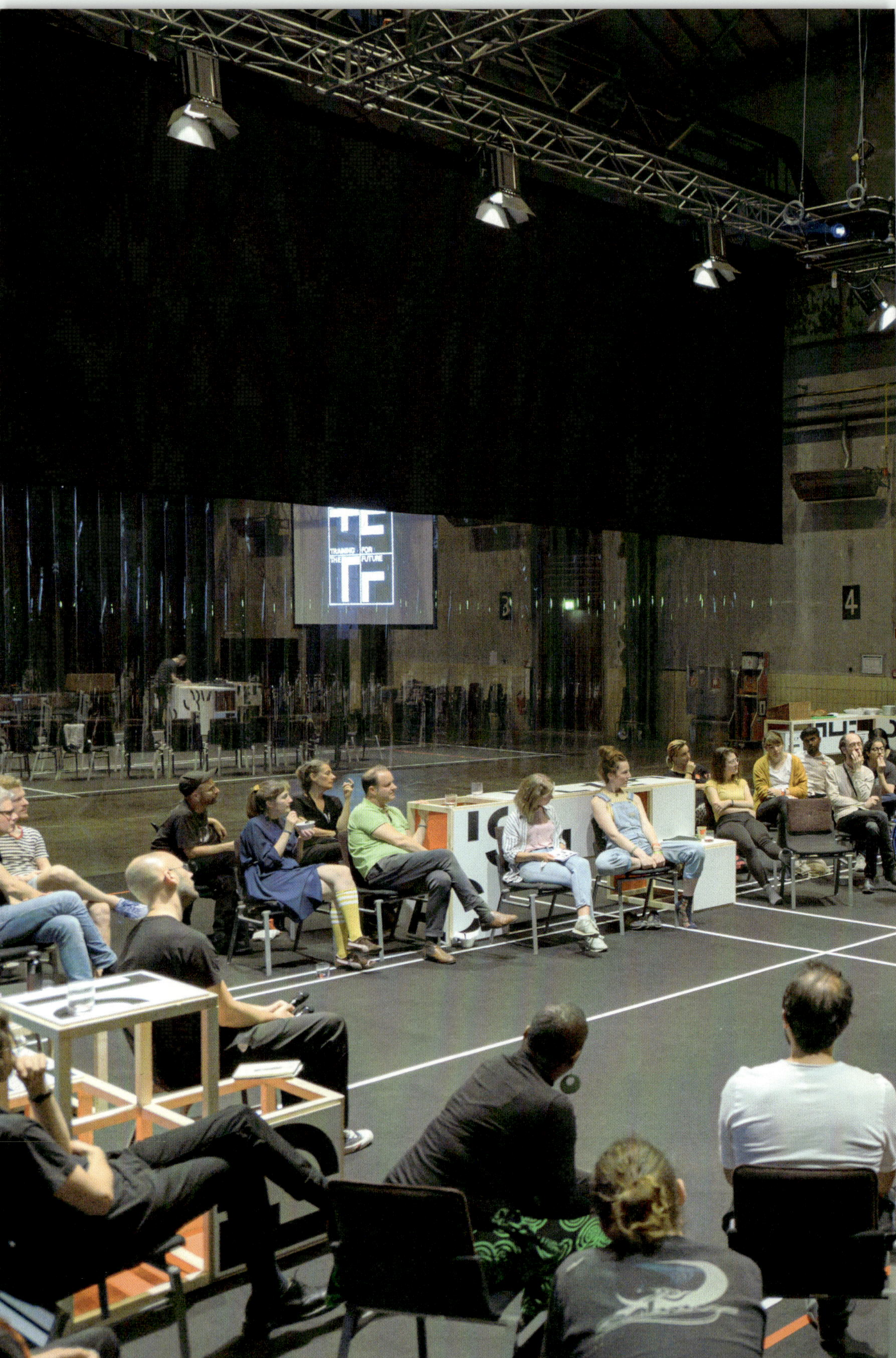

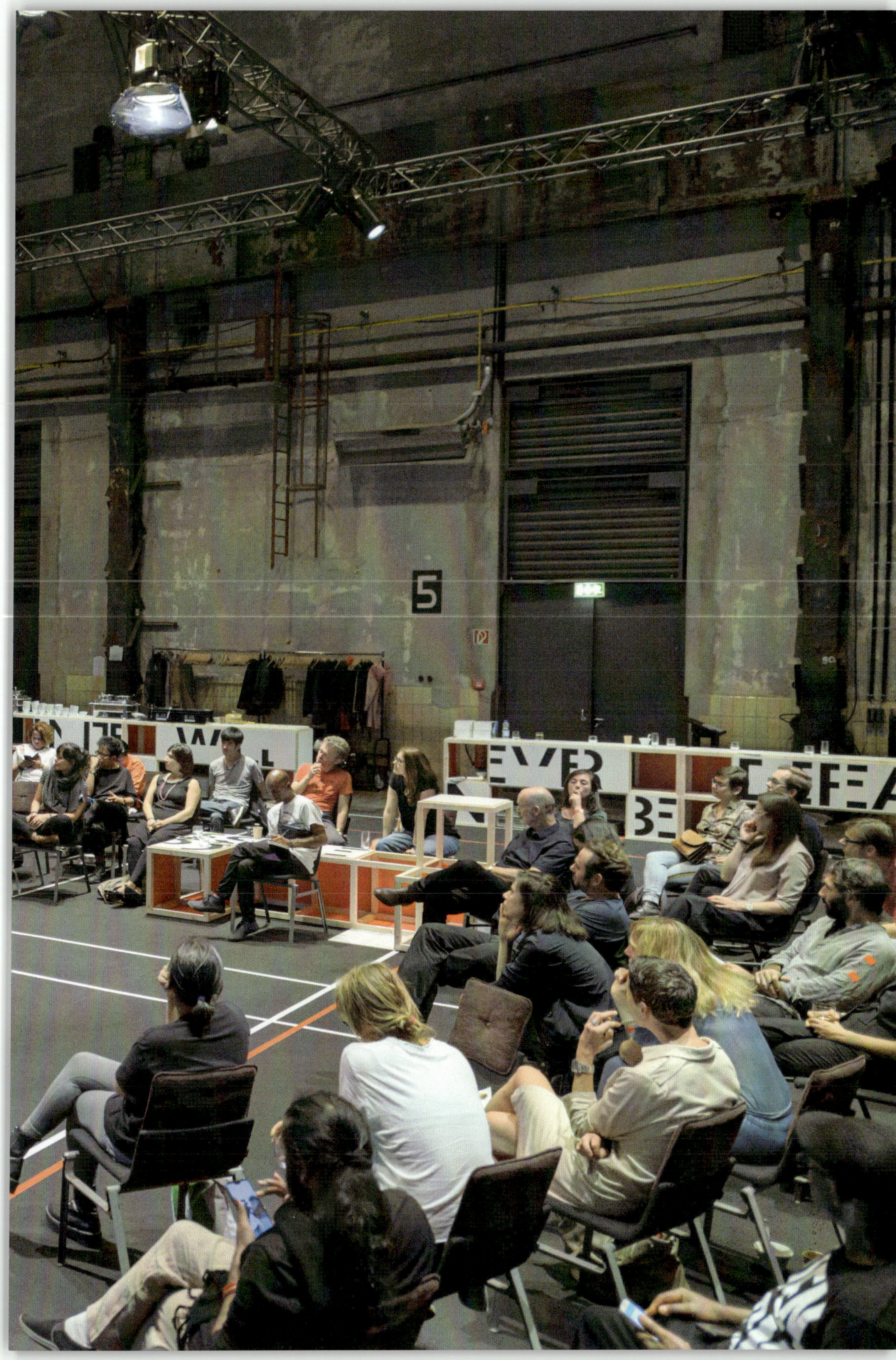
5

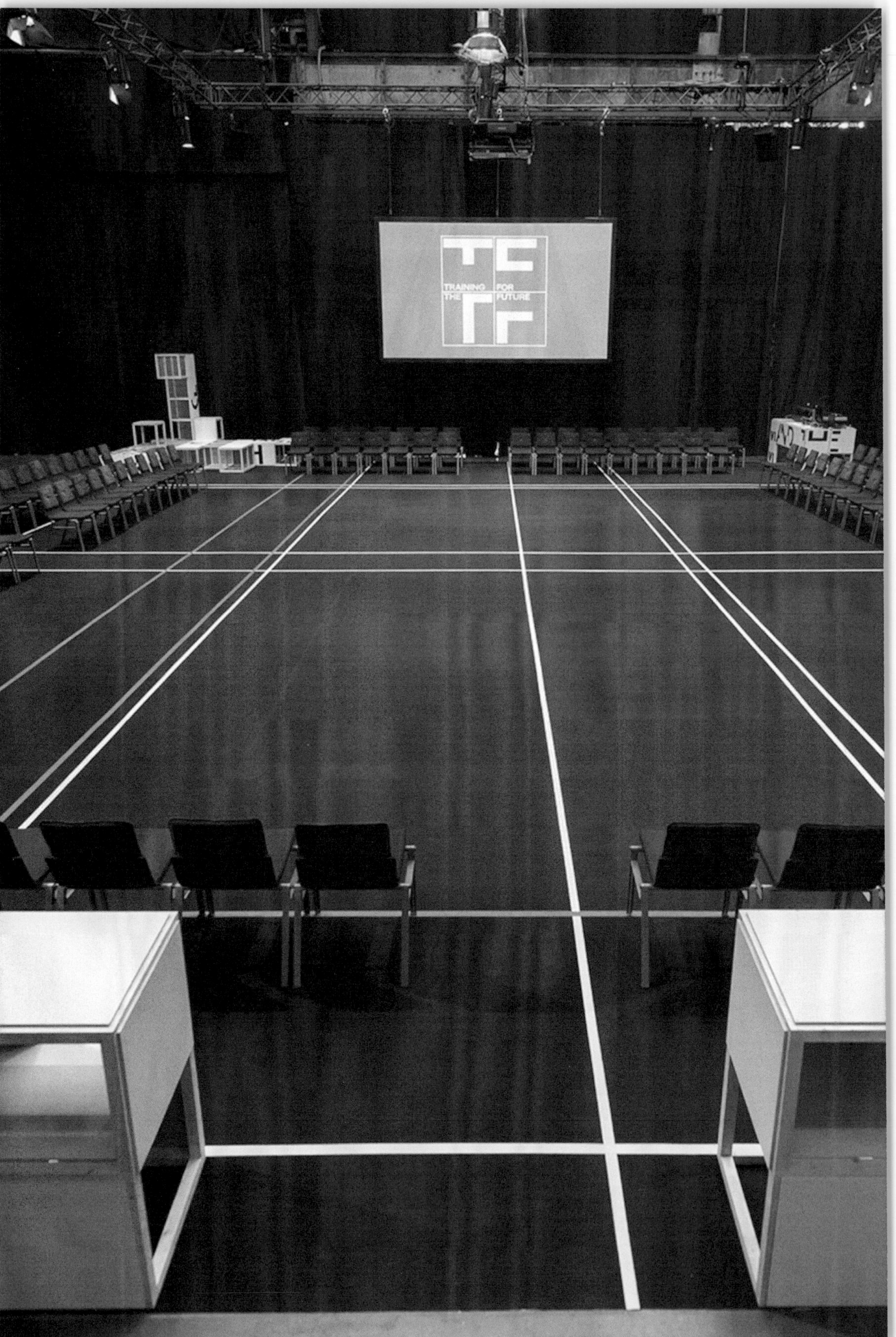
TRAINING FOR
THE FUTURE

TRAINING MANUALS

2021

Due to the Covid-19 pandemic, the 2021 edition of Training for the Future had a decentralized form, with trainings taking place in parallel across the world.

MARCH 6, 2021, BUENOS AIRES, ARGENTINA

Post-pandemic Errorist Training, Etcétera

Focused on art and activism, public interventions and performances in times of pandemic, this training works as a toolbox for social and cultural initiatives, artists, activists and collectives interested in collaborations between art and community. By using errorist methods, the training aims to develop a collection of diverse strategies for survival, collecting proposals for possible actions and interventions to respond to the challenges brought on by the upcoming world. Such actions are based in solidarity and commonality, paying special attention to the role of collective care.

Etcétera is a multidisciplinary collective founded in 1997 in Buenos Aires with the intention to bringing art to sites of immediate social conflict and to bring those social conflicts into arenas of cultural production. In 2005, they were part of the founding of the International Errorist movement – an international organization that proclaims error as a philosophy of life. Since 2007, co-founders Loreto Garin Guzman and Federico Zukerfeld have coordinated Etcétera's activities.

Visual documentation by Etcétera and the International Errorist movement. Pictures: Veronica Coman / Etcétera Archive

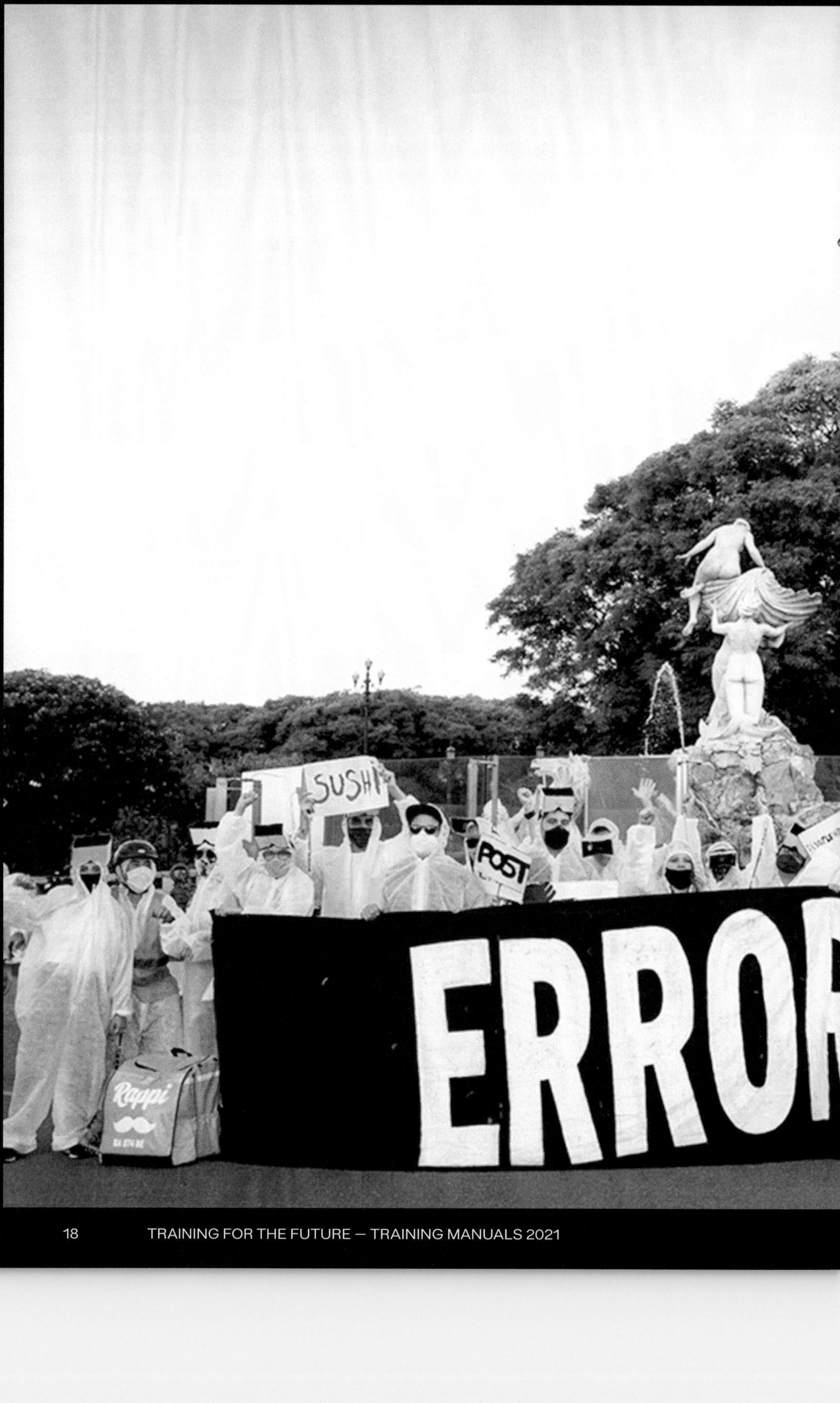
SUSHI
POST
ERROR
Rappi

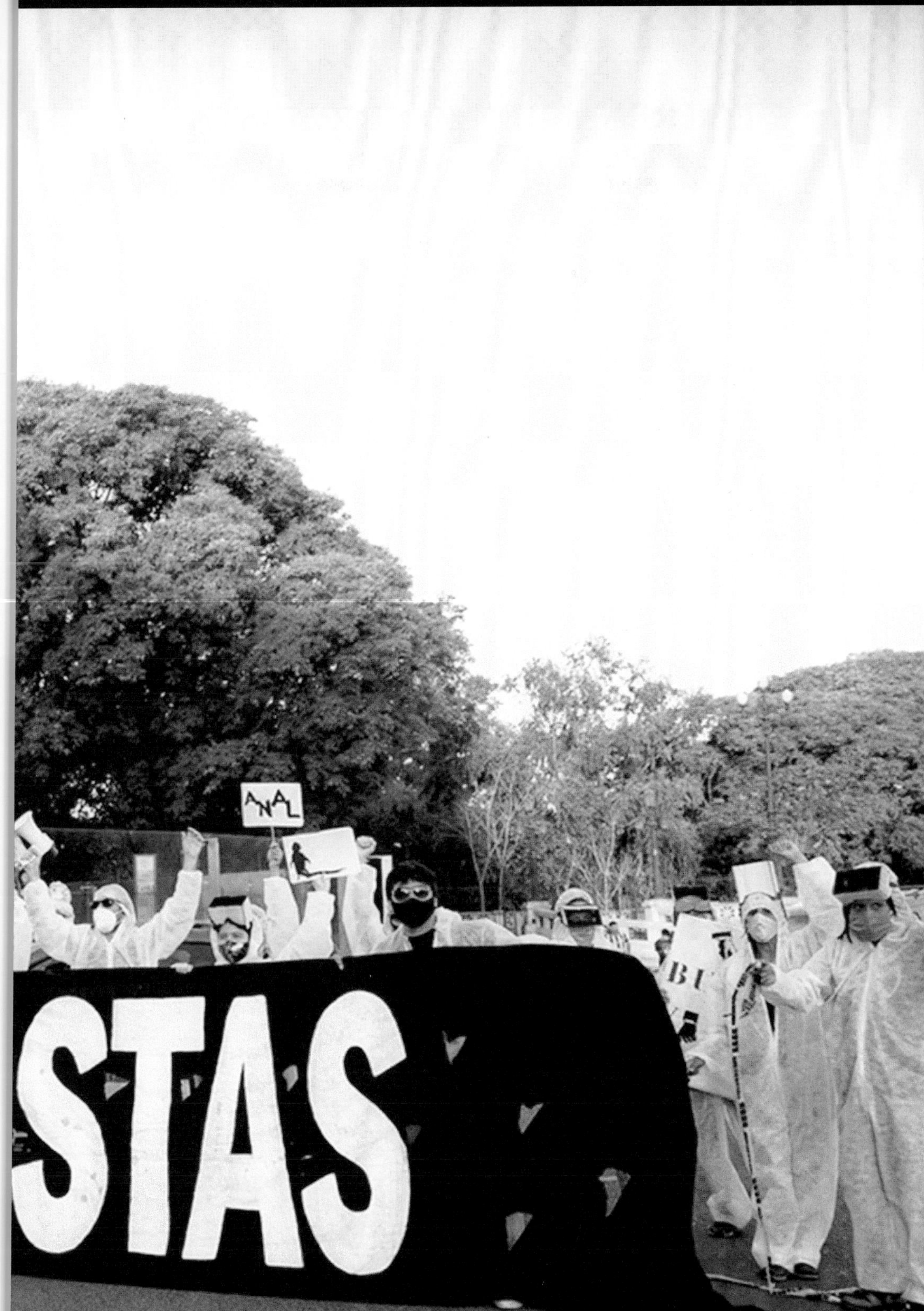
ANAL
STAS

ENTRENAMIENTO ERRORISTA POST-PANDEMICO

Errare Umanun Est

---

1. We are all errorists.
2. Errorism bases its action in error.
3. Errorism is a philosophically erroneous position,
a ritual of negation, a disorganized organization.
4. Errorism's field of action contains all practices
that aim at the liberation of the human being and of language.
5. Errorism sees failure as perfection and error as delight.
6. Errorism does not exist and exists.
One approximates and one removes.
One believes and one self-destroys.
One assumes in old and new forms.

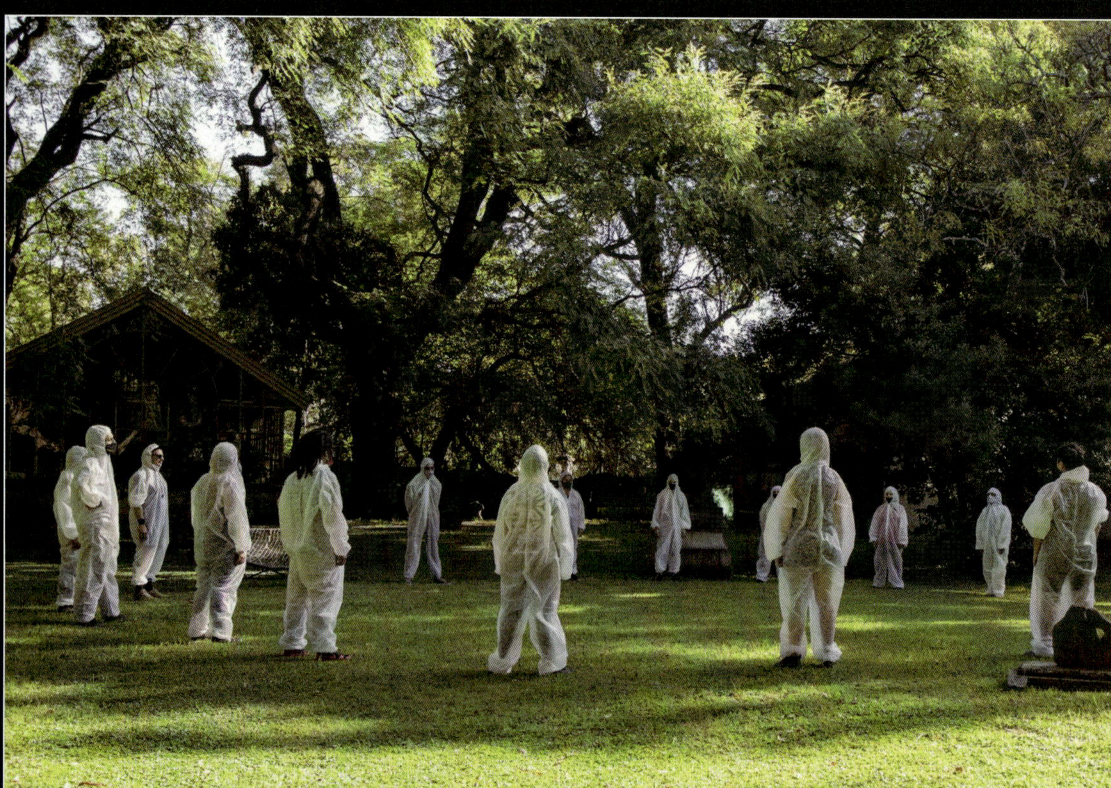

1. TERRITORY AND PROTOCOLS

Look for a public space that has some link with social conflicts or urgent questions: a space that can support you, help you in a context like the pandemic, that can comply with sanitary protocols and that respects diversity. It must have water, electricity, a bathroom and a place to hide objects. In case of a pandemic, the place should have a garden and many square meters with high ceilings. For example (see image), a public university with a nice, old museum dedicated to free public art education.

2. DRESSING PROTOCOL

A good wardrobe should serve to create a climate, an atmosphere. It should take us to another time and make us feel different, generating impact when many of us are using it. When we train, a good costume should make us feel comfortable and protected, it should make us feel other and be able to act. If you are going through the waves of a global pandemic, and you are going to develop physical exercises, think about costumes that allow people who do not know each other to feel the confidence to touch each other or to be close for many hours, sometimes even losing the social distance. Think that this group will go out into the street where others will also be present.

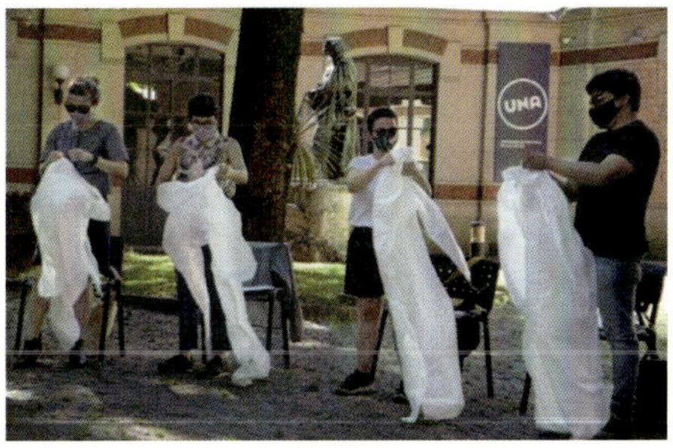

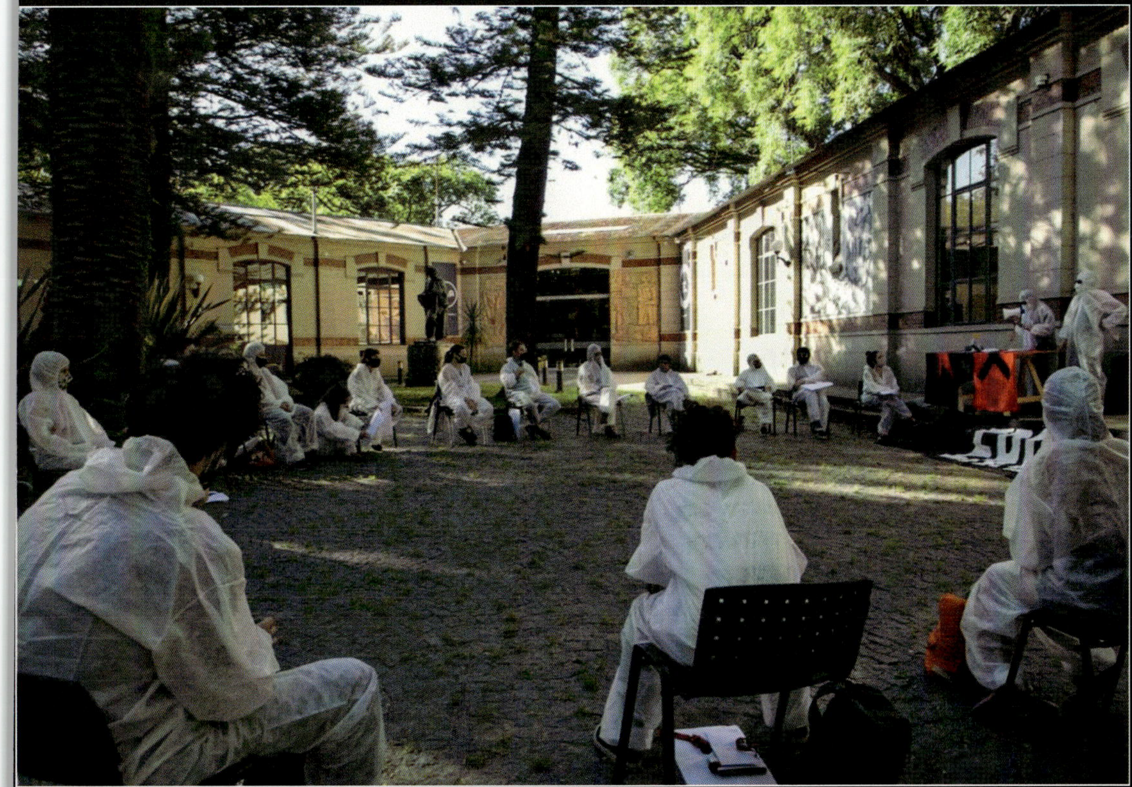

3. ASSEMBLY PARTICIP-ATION

For a good errorist training, the assembly is a fundamental tool for the collectivization of ideas, decision-making and carrying out actions. When we talk about participation, we must think precisely about what it means in each context. For these trainings, it's important to reverse the model of cultural bureaucratization and produce other alternative models of resource distribution, such as contributing financially to the participants of the training or allowing autonomy in the management of resources and ways of life.

We must remember that collective social imagination is different to participation. Today the notion of participation is a misleading concept that can be used to manipulate and instrumentalize social needs and collective desires so as to lead them to consumerism or the ballot box. That is why it is important to use all resources, creative and imaginative, to stimulate social interaction and to produce new (non-passive) audiences.

To do this, errorism is a key method as it proposes a contextual displacement that transforms meaning and encourages the taking of (wrong) positions. The errorist trainings work on the common, the collective and collectivization as well as on how to develop emancipatory practices, the meaning of social participation and artistic activism.

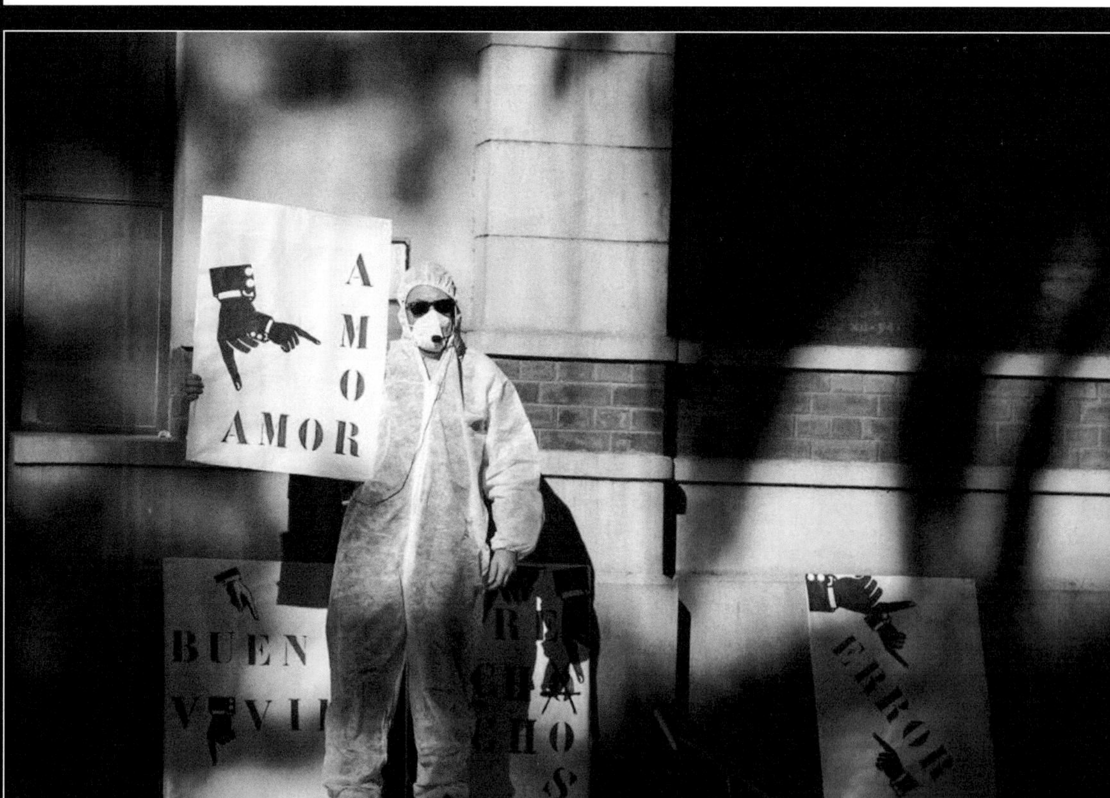

4. CONCEPTS AND CONFLICTS

Develop the training by looking for key concepts, problems or conflicts and collective needs or desires. Starting with identifying these concepts, develop collective exercises that then put the words into action. For example, in our trainings we use double banners with concepts on either sides: work/error, rights/good living, education/housing, etc.

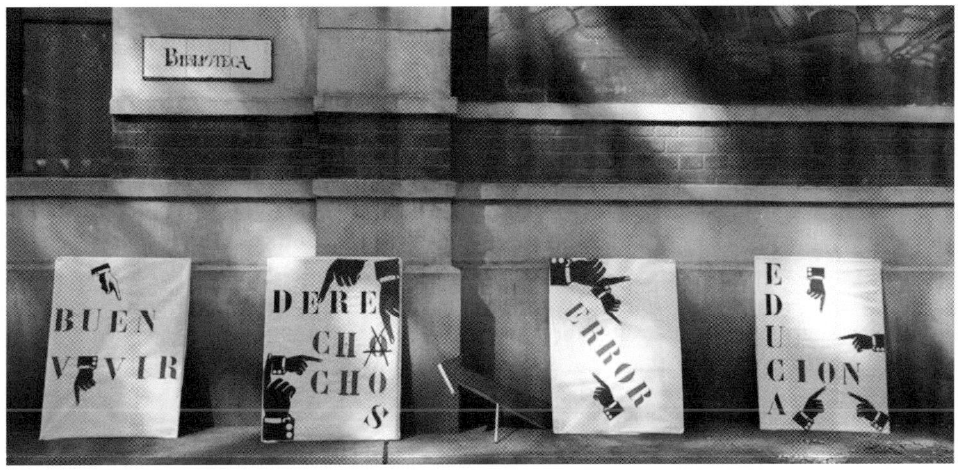

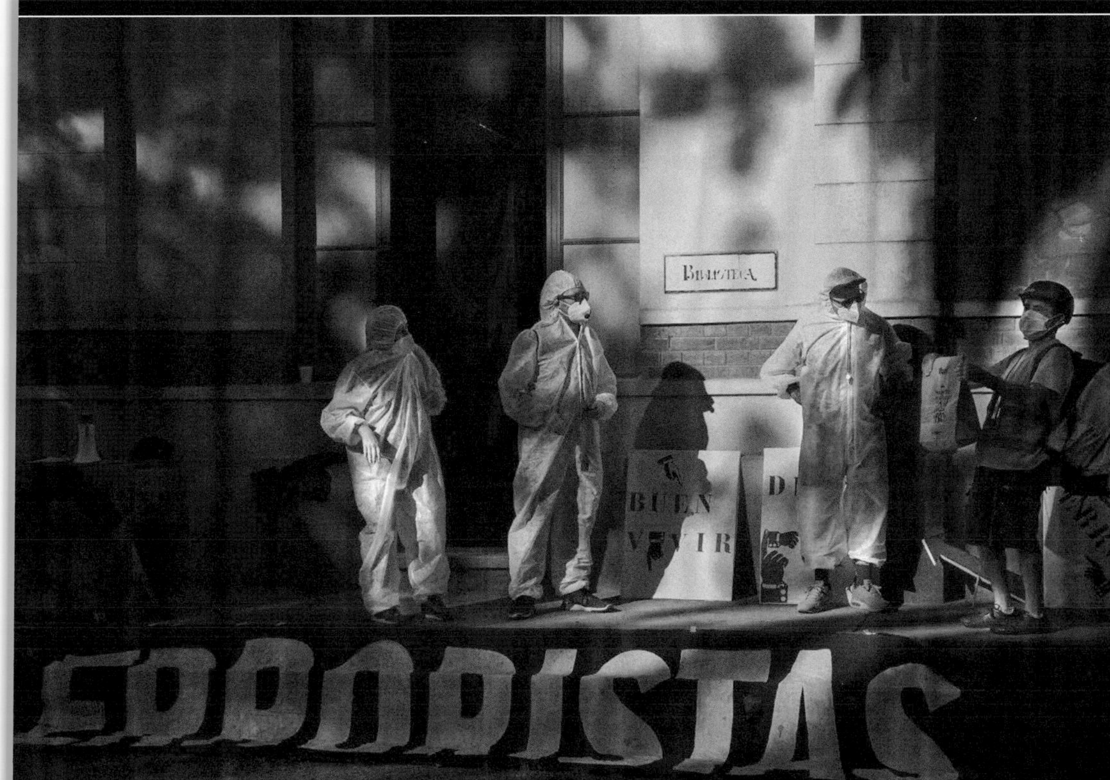

5. COMRADES, DE-ALIENATED ALLIES

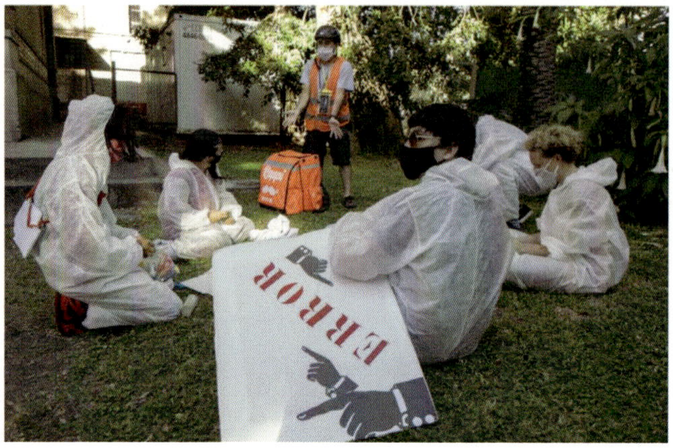

Think about your allies to generate physical and mental trainings. For example, a performance artist that performs flowing exercises where we move like birds, we are all leaders and we let ourselves be guided by our companions. These are exercises that generate collectivization and confidence in oneself and in the collective. You could also invite an 'infiltrated' trainer, such as a worker from a recovered factory, who due to the precariousness of their labor has a less classic job that evidences new forms of precarious labor. An infiltrated trainer will help as a spiritual guide to understand the post-pandemic labor situation.

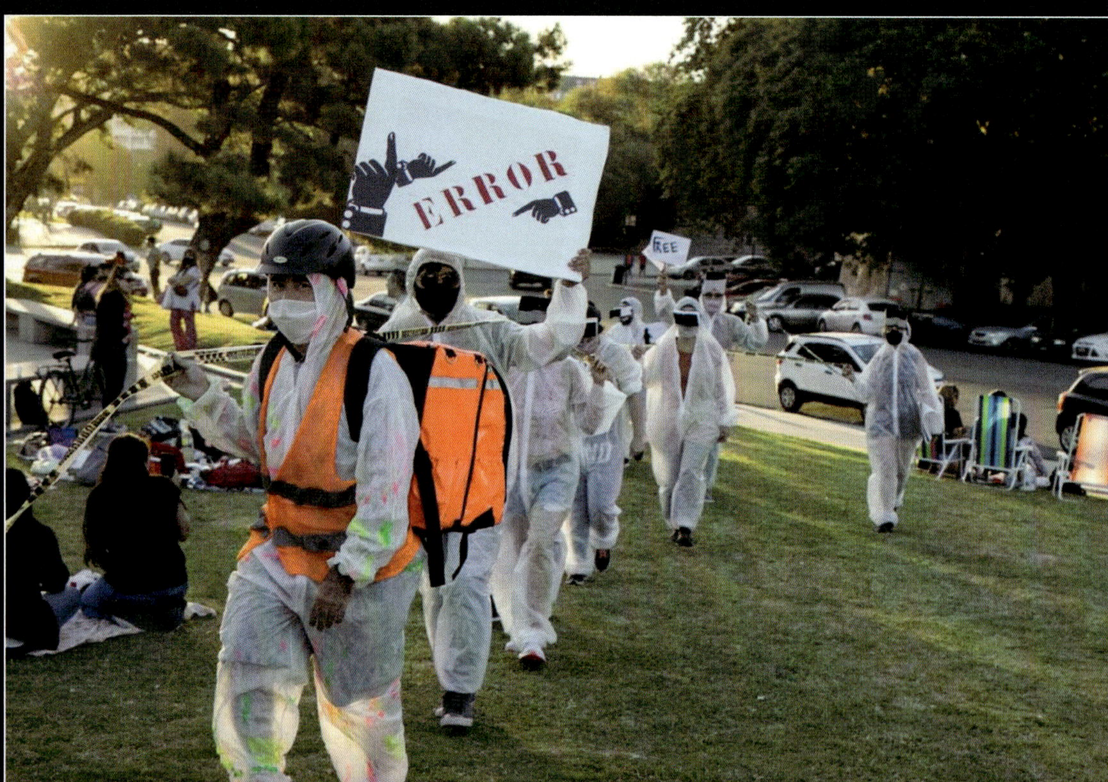

6. ERRORISM BASES ITS ACTION IN ERROR

Take the training for what it is: an exercise or a game. In that sense, never start with psychoanalyzing subjectivities. In quarantine we have had a lot of time to be involved in such processes, and we have had a lot of time isolated, thinking about ourselves. Conversely, help the trainees to forget their individuality for a few hours, let them escape from their subjectivities, let the experience help them escape preconceptions. Make them imagine an extreme context, one where we are facing the end of an era and we must act collectively, finding common objectives quickly. Even if these objectives seem banal, we embrace them together and give ourselves to error. *Errare humanum est!* Move to direct action as a tool to collectivize erroristly. If there are errors that result in someone feeling violated in their subjectivity, they can decide to not participate or to instead return to subsequent debates at a later stage when we make an evaluation.

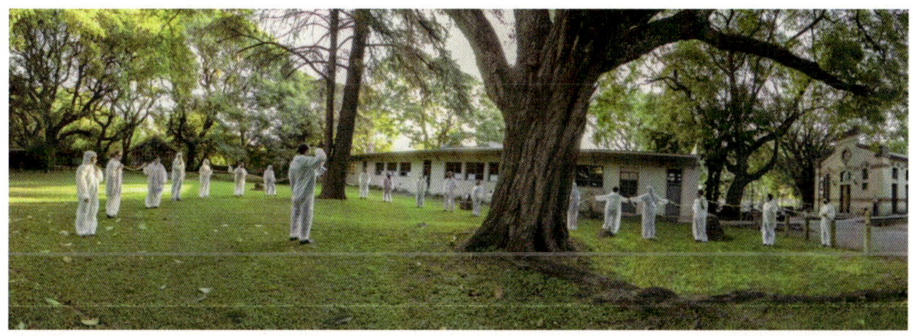

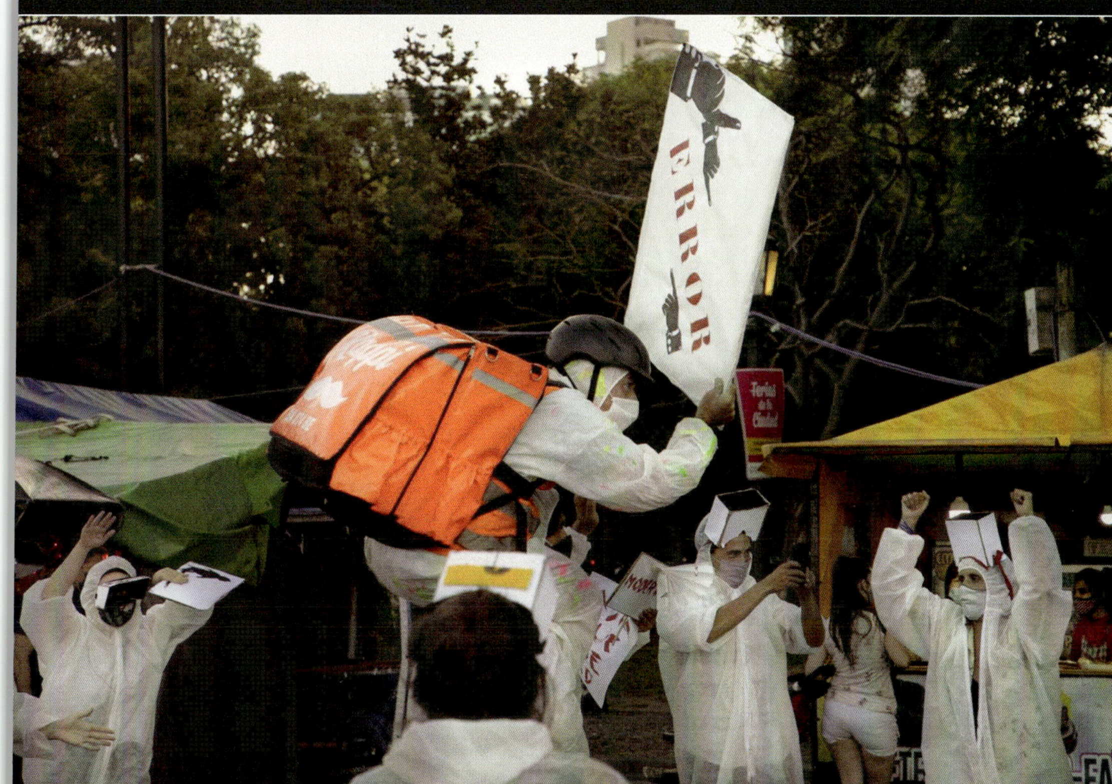

7. FOR ERRORISM POLITICS = LIFE

Play with utopia and dystopia in a dialectical way, as if both are part of a whole. Choose some topics to develop, but before think about the group you are going to train and choose concepts especially dedicated to them. They can be based on questions or slogans. For example: Education or pedagogies? Can we escape from the labor pandemic? Where will we live? What is good living? What rights will be gained and what rights will be lost? Love/error? Where did the collective body go? Where is the collective body?

8. A COMMON ERROR

Separate the participants into working groups in which they will develop an action strategy around some of the topics. Each of these groups will be responsible for communicating this action to all the trainees. Those who do not wish to participate have the right to do so. The realization of this action in public space will then be a collective challenge, so try to break any feelings of competition that may arise.

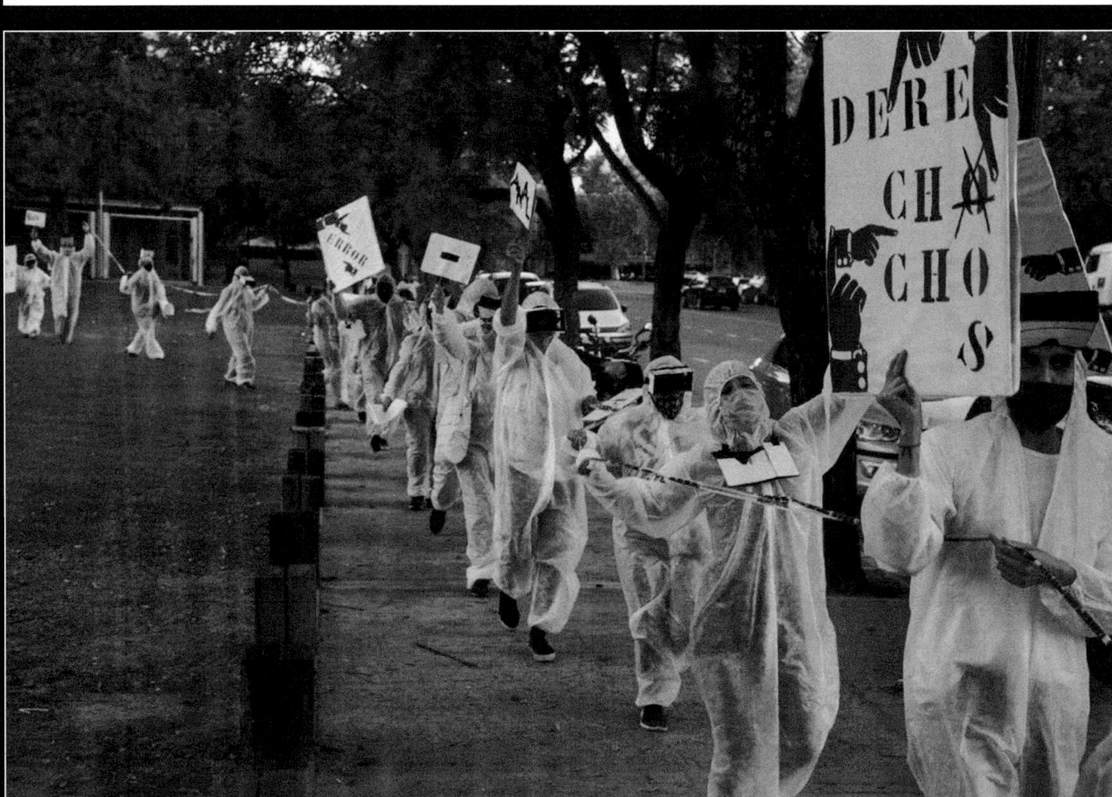

9. USE TOOLS FROM ERRORIST THEATER

There are two important categories:

1. **Actor-cides** are actors and actresses that fall within the International Errorist movement (or not) and that surrender, as if martyrs, to the theatrics of the experience. They jump into the void or explode and they don't fear death, because errorist theater is death and life at the same time.

2. **Spect-actors** are subjects or multitudes that see themselves interlaced in the theatrics of errorist action, yet not only as spectators but also as participating actors in the scenic performance. The spect-actors are trapped by the actor-cides in the magic play of errorist theater.

The 'Dramaturgy of Error' developed by actor-cides and spect-actors constitutes itself as the central drama of the work. Confusion and surprise, lapses and failed acts are the most precious arms of errorist theater. From the outset, it does not matter who acts and who observes as actor-cides and spect-actors coincide in a living cell of errorist theater that then interacts with the social scenery.

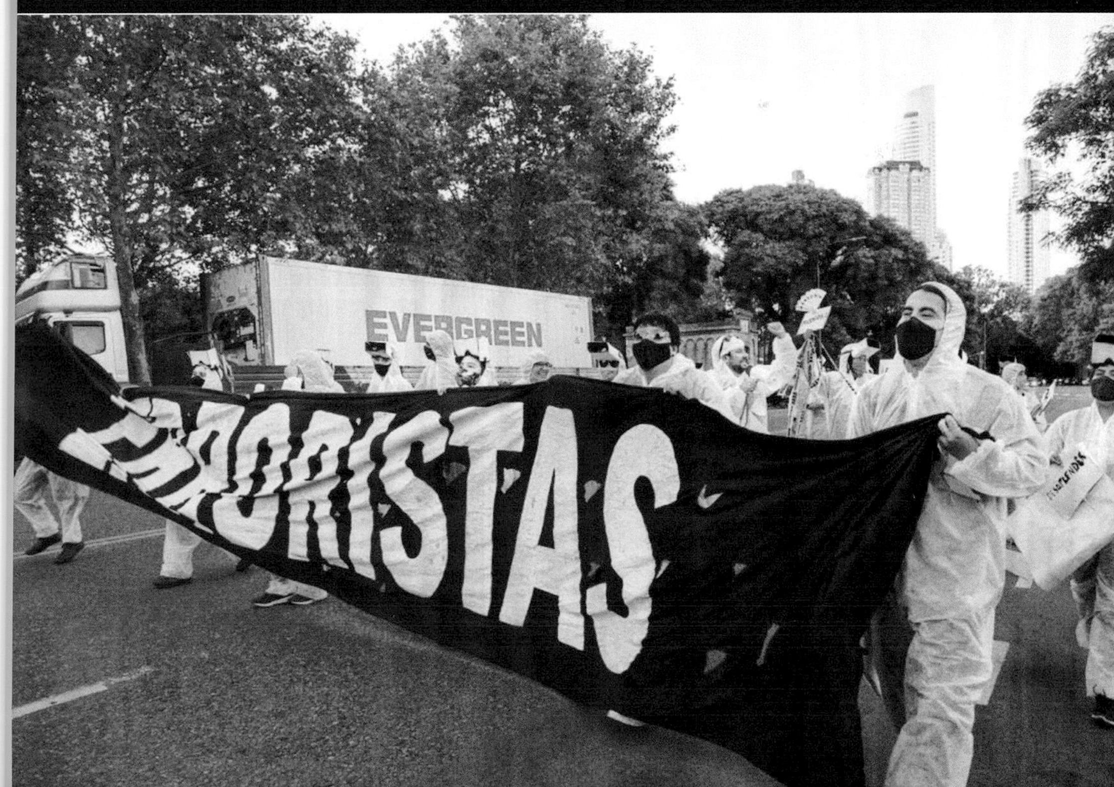

10. THE MYSTICS OF ACTION

Before the energy falls, the errorist must go out into the streets with force. For this, it is essential that one of the errorist trainers shake the group, creating a feeling of absolute confidence. For this we use errorist mantras, hymns and songs. The trainees must transition from being sleeper cells into active participants ready to err at any moment. In shaking the group awake, we diminish the fear to err.

11. GO TO THE STREETS!

A poetics of errorist theater do not invent fictitious scenarios or unilateral conventions. It looks for social scenarios and appropriates them violently, infiltrating the scene. Dramaturgy is being created by the succession and simultaneity of errors. Here, there is no question: the dramatic action results from error. Therefore, we do not charge entrance fees and we do not have entrances. Whoever wants to enter can enter. If we decide to enter the scene, we will do it. This process of spontaneity forms part of the 'errorist spectacle.'

POST-PANDEMIC ERRORIST TRAINING

Coordinated by Etcétera

Date: March 6, 2021
Location: Museo La Carcova, Universidad Nacional de las Artes, Buenos Aires, Argentina
Trainers: Etcétera (Loreto Garin Guzman and Federico Zukerfeld)
Guest Trainers: Fernando Castillo (textile worker, trade unionist of recovered factory and actor) and Augusto Zaquetti (artist and cultural activist)
Documentation: Verin Comán

Participants: Lina Angel, Rico Arancibar, Ofelia Arrigo, Ximena Astudillo Delgado, Juliana Beltrán, Francisco Benvenutti, Amalia Boselli, Romina Cariola, Julia Cossani, Maria Alejandra Fauquie Wefer, Nico Hache, Cecilia Leiva, Luciana Mastromauro, Sofia Medici, Emilia Molina, Ana Isabel Orozco, Johanna Palmeyro, Sebastián Pardo, Nico Rodríguez Sosa and Javier Sandoval Velasquez

Thanks to Goethe-Institut Buenos Aires, Museo La Carcova, Universidad Nacional de las Artes, Fiorella Cominetti and Patricia Moreira

MARCH 6–7, 2021, BOGOTÁ, COLOMBIA

Open the Hole So the World Gets Inside, House of Tupamaras

In this training, through movement-thought exercises, the notions of the 'penetrable' and the 'impenetrable' are explored in order to reshape mental, social and disciplinary structures through change and experimentation.

Since 2017, House of Tupamaras has created divergent pieces that involve dance, performance and the visual arts. House of Tupamaras has had a particular interest in developing nightly encounters between the LGBTQIA+ community and the local context in order to build safe and inclusive dance floors based on mutual respect.

Visual documentation by Juan Diego Muñoz

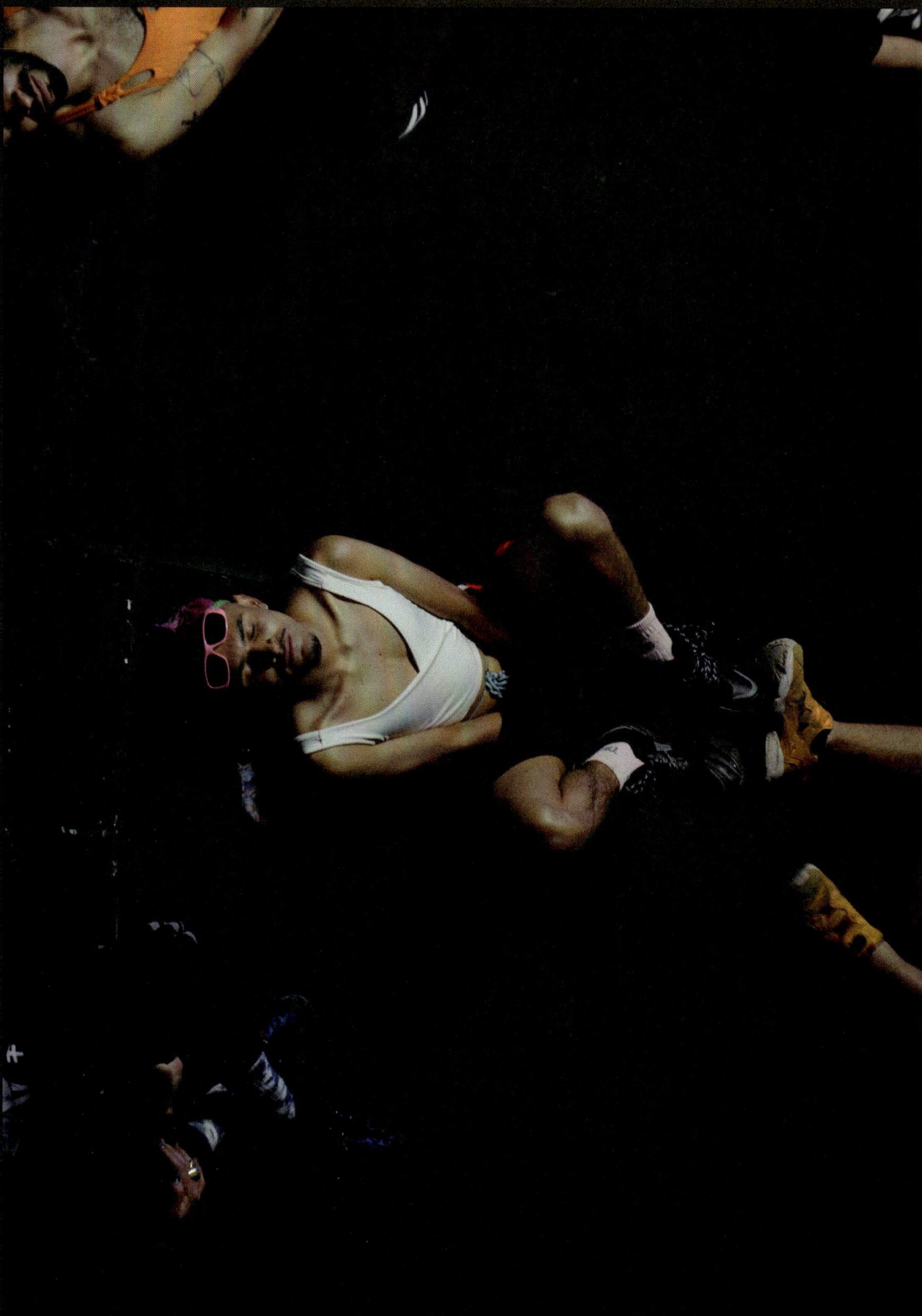

OPEN THE HOLE SO THE WORLD
GETS INSIDE

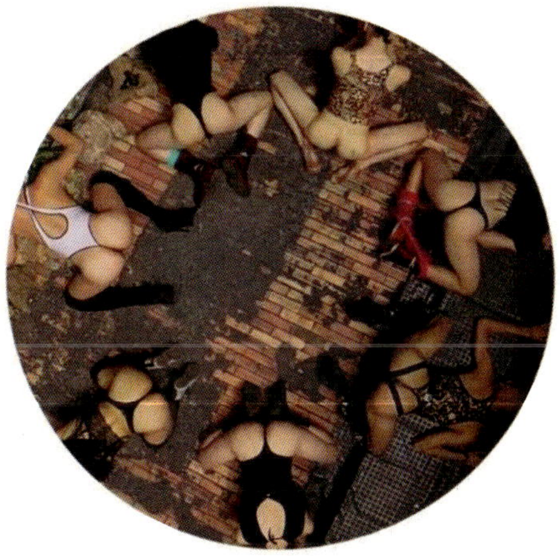

HOUSE OF
TUPAMARAS

Take a position on the ground and have someone read these images to you, visualize them.

Play with these images as you like. use them to your liking they are yours now.

Imagine that you are urinating and you stop urinating, being aware of which muscles you use to stop it.

As you inhale, imagine that the anus absorbs a noodle.

As you exhale imagine that the anus is sending a kiss to the world.

Imagine that the anus is an eye, when you inhale it closes the eyelid, when you exhale you open it.

Imagine that the anus is independent of your entire pelvis and it moves with its own consciousness.

Allow yourself to feel the anus with touch, to reconcile with it

Present the anus to the world.

Project the anus to the sun.

It grows from the pelvic floor.

Exhale in stasis and imagine that the anus is a submachine gun.

Exhale and while the pelvis goes back as if pulled with a thread.

Inhale and the ass sucks, while the pelvis tries to look at the face, forming a c with the back.

REPEAT AS MUCH AS YOU WANT AND WHERE YOU WANT

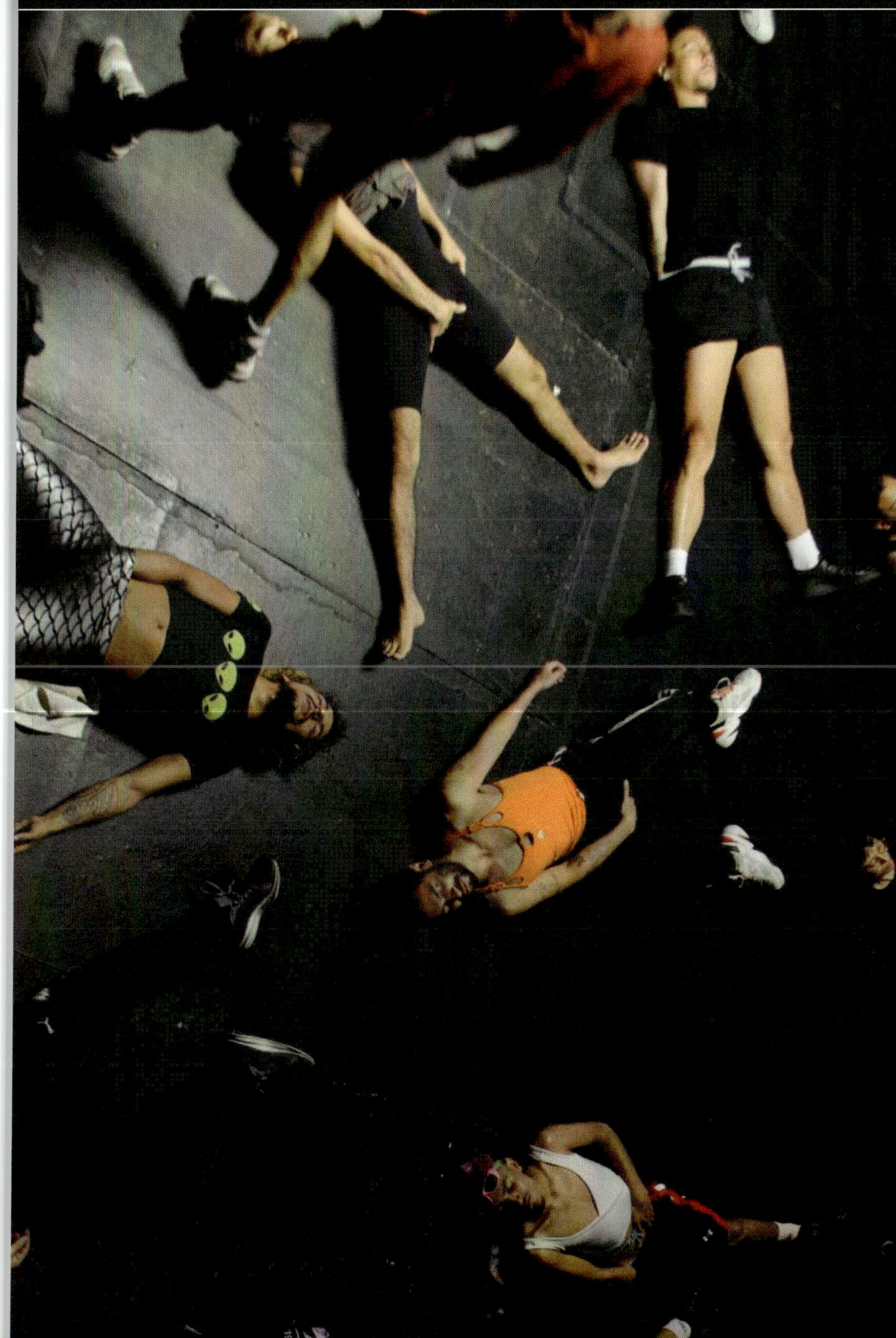

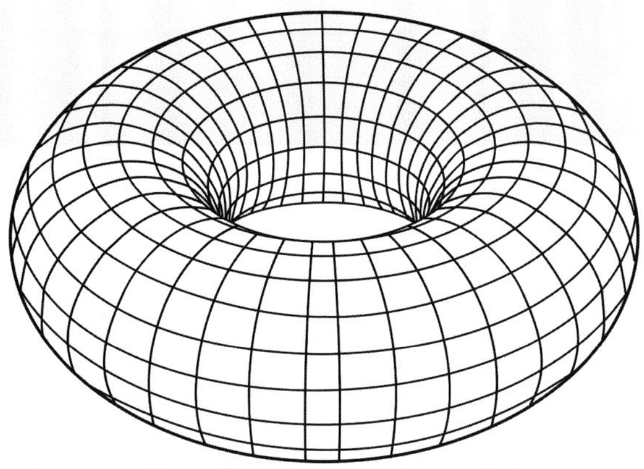

we are a donut

"Part of the contemporary myth about the "individual" is built around the idea of a complete being, closed in on itself, a separate and autonomous unit. In fact, the etymology of individual means precisely that, that it cannot be divided. We are not going to enter here into the division of psychoanalysis, which directly contradicts this idea (the subject would be precisely something divided from its foundation, an entity separated from the real by language, and whose identity is founded on the other). Here we are going to study the human creature as mere corporeality. These two holes, the anus and its overrated companion the mouth, show us that the human body (and that of all animals) is not a closed and complete entity, but quite the opposite, it is something open, but also open in a very special way.

The topology has described this type of surface as a torus. We are not referring to that animal that represents racial and masculine Spain, but a figure that we can quickly describe as a donut. Or, if you want, imagine a bottle where the mouth and the ass will communicate. In reality, the torus itself is a "closed" species in the sense that all its points communicate continuously. That is, the central hole of the donut is there, but it does not interfere with the continuity of the surface of the torus. Continuing with our analogy, the human body can be described as a closed surface, but with a structural hole, which is the digestive system. This contradicts the image we have of our own body, intuitively: when we ingest something, we say that we put it "inside" the body, but in reality we are throwing it "out". We do not "put" anything in, we are passing it through a hole. When we put a dildo up our ass, the same. "

JAVIER SÁEZ, SEJO CARRASCOSA, Por el culo. Políticas anales, Egales, 2011

By changing this topological image of the body, we present ourselves to the world and the world itself presents itself as something where there is no exterior or interior, therefore, the world is no longer impenetrable or penetrable.

1. Go out into the world with this image of the torus, get lost in it, walk for no reason and aimlessly, stop in a certain place and look around you, bring something (thing, image, object, text or idea) that gives an account of your reflection.

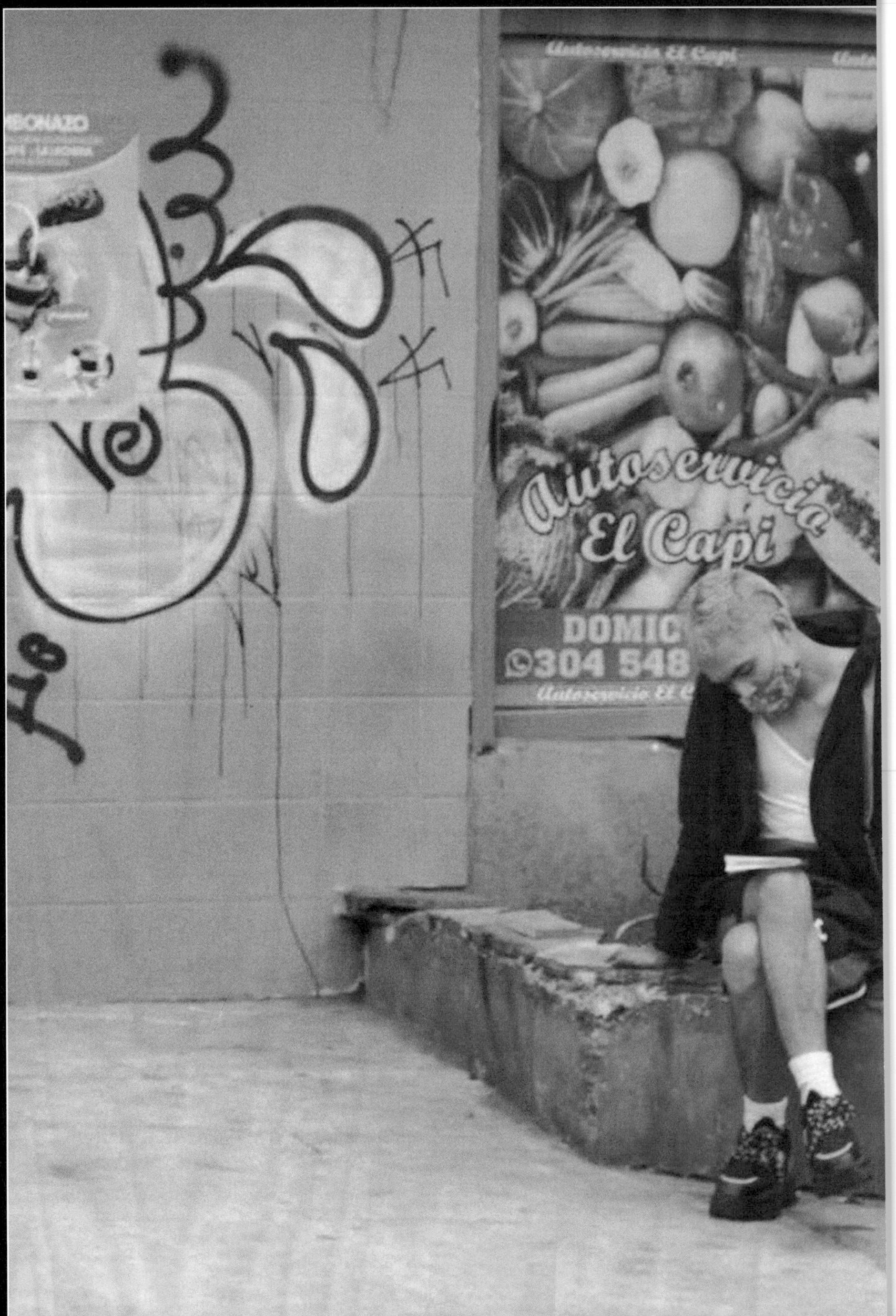
Autoservicio El Capi
DOMIC
©304 548

instructions for a possible anal army

is a southern ass grease bounce,
Shake your bum bum bum!!!!
Migra asses, asses that their power is in fat, size and volume.
My ass is a machine gun
Why is that?
Because I'm passive and I give bullet
I'm passive and I give bullet
Traaa-traaa- traaa- traaa
Shake your bum bum bum bum!!!!
I don't play games anymore
If you invade my space I'll give you a bullet...
If you mess with me and my friends
I'll shoot you out....
Shake your bum bum bum bum!!!!
Cause I'm a badass, cause I'm a badass, cause I'm a badass, cause I'm a badass
My ass is aggressive and it's violent, I'm passive and I'm very violent
My revolution is fighting,
My ass is my revolution
My ass is my weapon and the rebound is my ammunition
Because we are the kind of people who put our asses out
Without fear of anything.
Southern asses, southern marikas and bounce coming from the south.
Shake your bum bum bum bum!!!!

My Ass Is a Machine Gun

Spread your legs
Bend your knees
Stick your ass out as far as you can
Start to drive your hips back and forth
Then as if your two buttocks want to clap against each other, you're going to move the fat,
Start to feel the bounce of the buttocks as you flex
And straighten your knees.

Do it repeatedly until you get your ass loose and bullet.
Play whatever music you want and do constant repetitions.
Feeling like your ass is a machine gun.

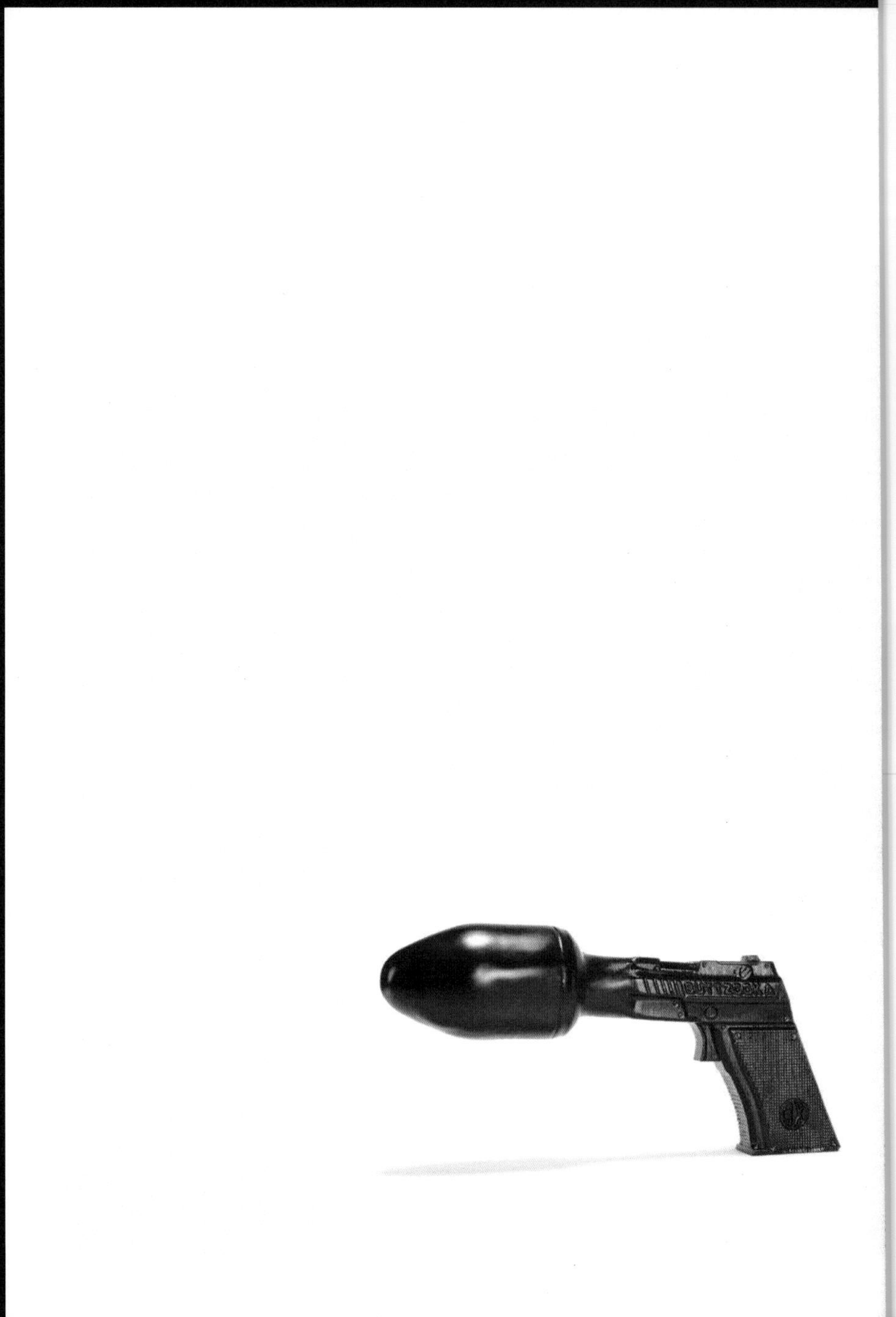

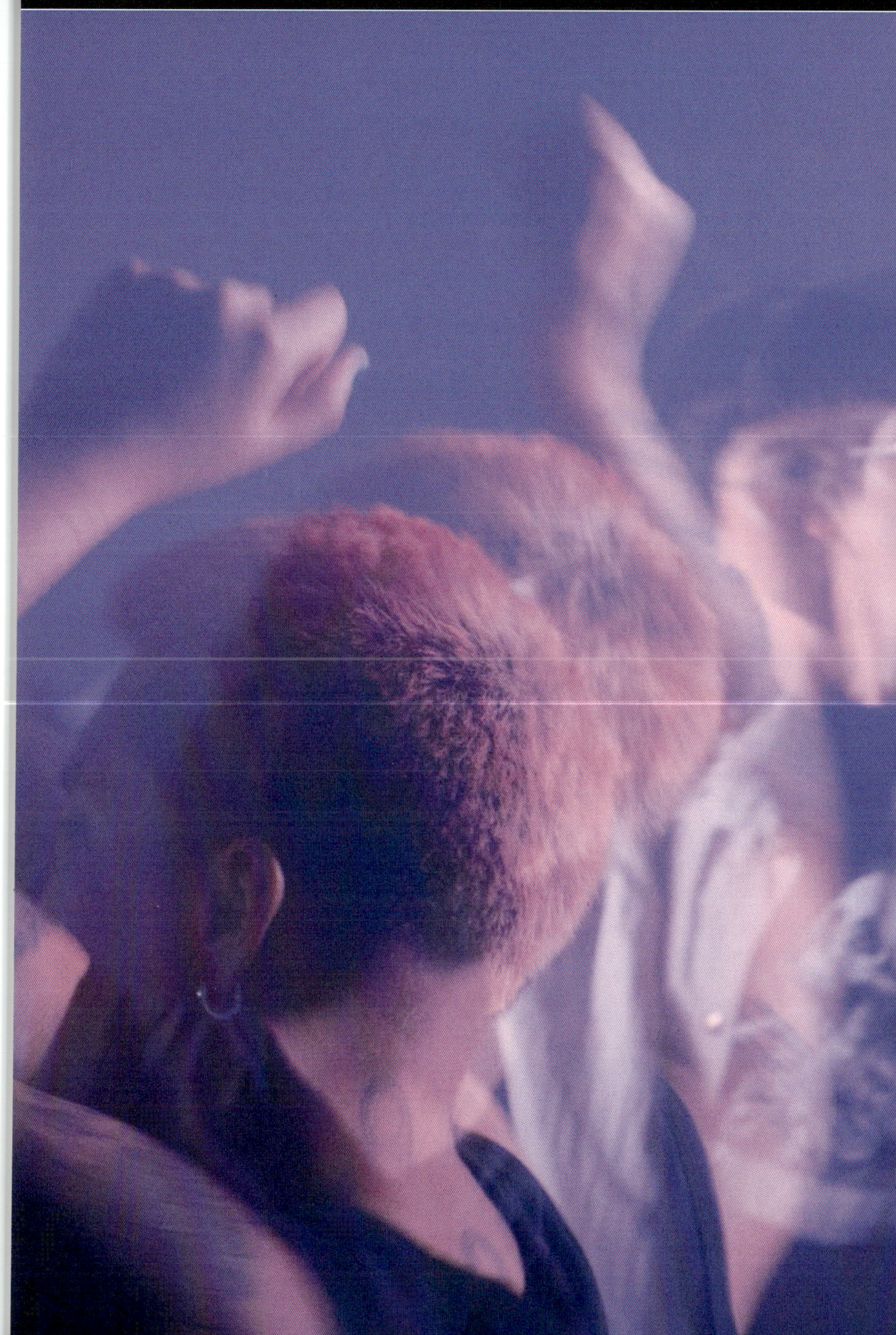

Dance
Dance from the anus
Dance from the fat
Dance
Dance
Dance
Dance with the light off
Dance like you're in the club
make your space your own club.

Eu Sou Passiva, Mas Meto Bala

Eu sou passiva
Mas meto bala
Se vier tapar meu cu
Com a sua bíblia
Eu meto bala
Silas Malafaia
Ama o gay como ao bandido
Então ele me ama em dobro
Que sou gay e sou bandida
Eu sou gay e sou bandida
Mas não transo o Malafaia
Não dou bola pro fascismo
Não tolero homofobia
E se vier mexer comigo
(Barulho de tiros)
Eu sou passiva
Mas meto bala
Se vier tapar meu cu
Com a sua bíblia
Eu meto bala
Infeliciano
Diz que bichice tem cura
Mas se vier me curar
Ele é quem vai tomar uma curra
Sou passiva
Violenta
Tô armada
E meto bala
Se vier tapar meu cu
Com a sua bíblia
Eu meto bala
Essa é uma declaração de guerra
Das bichas do terceiro mundo

SI NO PODEMOS SER VIOLENTA NO ES NUESTRA REVOLUCIÓN

Eu sou passiva
Mas meto bala
Se vier tapar meu cu
Com a sua bíblia
Eu meto bala
Jair Bolsonaro
Fala mal das prostitutas
Mas se tranca no motel
E vai beber água de chuca
Vai, Edir Macedo, deixa de ser recalcada
Vai, viado, se liberta
Abre o edi
E vem pra festa
Eu sou passiva
Mas meto bala

k-trina erratik
MC Katrina
Monstra Errática
Natown, Brazil
https://soundcloud.com/popguerrilha

THE DANCE OF THE FUTURE HAVE NO FORM.

DANCE

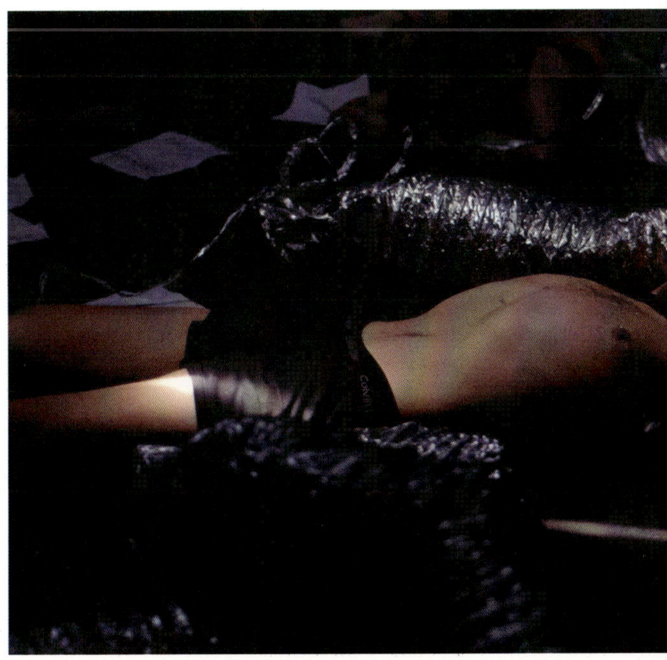

Now get on 4 points, direct the anu
towards the sky, like a sunflower tha
seeks to feed, this position is ideal fo
reading, peel off the text and water i
on the ground, so you can find yoursel
better with it.
The sentences are going to choose you,
the words are the ones that will choose
to be read by you.

Disorderly reading of "anal terror" by
Beatriz Preciado.

Party relationship, communication, self-experimentation and passion

Once upon a time there was an anus.

In the 70s

Make love with the trees

The politics of the anus are invented

Anus: hole that ends the digestive tract and through which the stool is excreted

Thus, a form of political action different from the one proposed at the time is emerging.

Let the anus rebel.

The homosexual anus speaks and produces for the first time a knowledge about itself.

Use of injury

Get ready to play

How then to define the practices of anal love?

How do you know if you still have a anus

Revolutions also build their own margins

We are in great need of allie

The anal revolution will be slow

Do you actually know what an anus is

Anus the and mouth the

It's about everyone's anus

Oedipus had an anus

Heterosexual feminism is afraid of the anal revolution.

Fear of the anal revolution

Be suspicious of visual and linguistic evidence

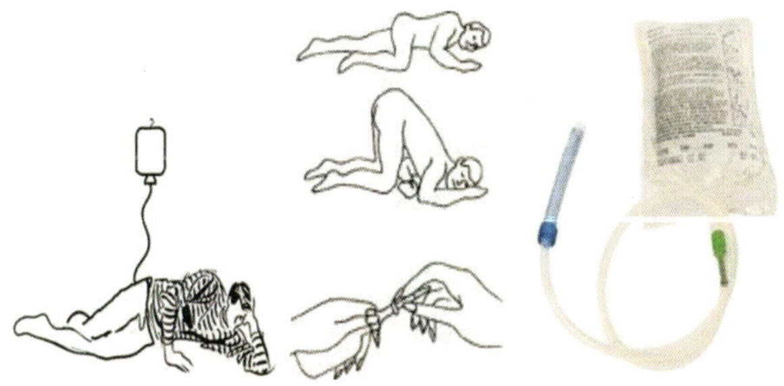

INSTRUCTIONS FOR ENEMAS

Read full instructions before starting
CONTRAINDICATIONS

- Intestinal inflammation
- peritonitis
- Abdominal trauma
- Postoperative of abdominal surgeries

It is important to defecate before doing the enema.

- 1500 ml enema bag empty
- 3 tablespoons of organic coffee
- Cloth strainer
- Vaseline or lubricant
- 1 tablespoon of baking soda
- Disinfectant (sodium hypochlorite) to wash the bag at the end of the enema

Instructions

- Add 1.5 liters of water in a container and bring it to boil adding 3 tablespoons of organic coffee, once it boils lower the heat and let it boil for 5 to 10 minutes, strain it with a cloth strainer and let it cool to room temperature or ideally 37 degrees.

- Add the tablespoon of baking soda. It is very important not to do the enema when the coffee is hot, it can cause serious burns in the digestive tract.
- Store a towel or mat in the bathroom so that you can lie on the floor comfortably.
- Before applying the enema, discard the blue ring on the hose and the protective lining that comes with the bag.
- Raise the key of the bag until it is comfortable for the moment to open it while lying down.
- Close the tap and fill the bag with the enema (the coffee before prepared, at the temperature of 37 degrees).
- Hang the bag in a high place.
- Put petroleum jelly or lubricant on the end of the hose
- Lie on the right lateral ulna or fetal position.
- Insert the hose into the anus and remove the lock.

- Once the coffee has gone down and entered your intestinal tract, remove the hose.
- hold for 12-15 minutes.
- make changes of position especially at times when it is difficult to retain.
- If you breathe deeply before making the change of position, the sensation of
evacuation will disappear. This will help to keep retaining.
- If you find it very difficult to retain the enema, that is almost impossible, use half that is 750 ml, and try to increase each enema until you reach 1500 ml.
- Once the 12 or 15 minutes have passed and you are sitting in the toilet, evacuate the enema, it is ideal to perform an abdominal massage and in the liver area accompanied by deep breathing.
- It is possible that after the first three enemas your abdomen feels swollen because it does not evacuate completely.

STERILIZING THE BAG

- Wash the bag with hot soapy water.
- Insert the hose into the same bag
- Pour the chlorine inside, move the bag looking for the chlorine to reach all the internal parts of the bag.
- Let stand for 5 minutes.
- Throw away the bleach and rinse the bag, then it will be ready to use again.

RECOMMENDATIONS

- It is recommended that the next meal be light, it can be a potato broth and an orange juice.
- Perform the enema once a week, for a month, observing what reactions the body has.
- It is important not to perform the enemas so often as the intestinal flora must be taken care of.

HOUSE OF TUPAMARAS
WWW.TUPAMARAS.COM

PVSSY DIVX
LAIKATAMARA
COBRA TAMARA
PXNNY TAMARA
DEMONIA TAMARA
LADY HUNTER
BARETAMARA
HONEY VERGONY
ROXXY TAMARA

PHOTOS: JUAN DIEGO MUÑOZ
SPECIAL THANKS: ANGELA MARCIALES

Goethe-Institut Kolumbien
Training for the future 2021

Bogotá - Colombia

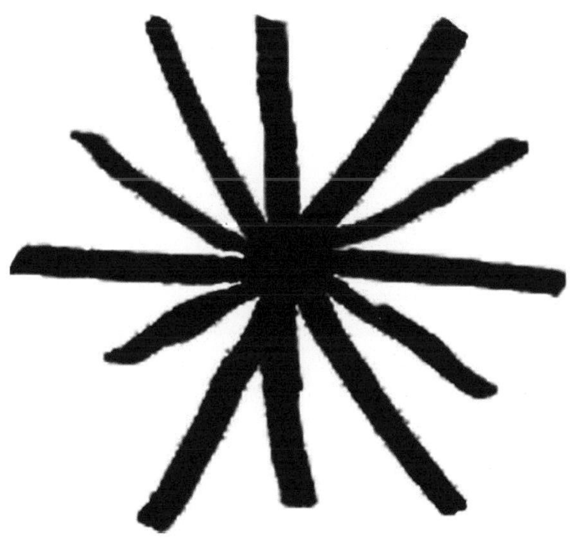

MARCH 6, 2021, NEW YORK CITY, UNITED STATES

Start in a Place Together, Savitri D and Reverend Billy & The Stop Shopping Choir

This training begins in the Meadowlands, on the edge of New York City on a rock formation known as the Tonnele Jut. The Meadowlands is a fragmented habitat in the middle of the biggest distribution center on the East Coast. Materials move in and out twenty-four hours a day. This land has survived more than 200 years of industry and development; it is the site of extraction, pollution, abuse and trauma. The training begins a process of remediation and resistance with the Tonnele Jut as teacher.

The Stop Shopping Choir is a radical performance community based in New York City. They are a highly diverse group of people with skills in many areas including science, social work, creative production, farming and the healing arts. They share a love of singing and a commitment to justice and the earth. Savitri D and Reverend Billy have made direct actions, long-term campaigns and spectacles with many kinds of communities and groups in fields, rivers, apartments, television studios, weapons factories, prisons, libraries, churches, universities, elections, banks and in every imaginable retail space on earth.

Visual documentation by Matt Liu and Savitri D

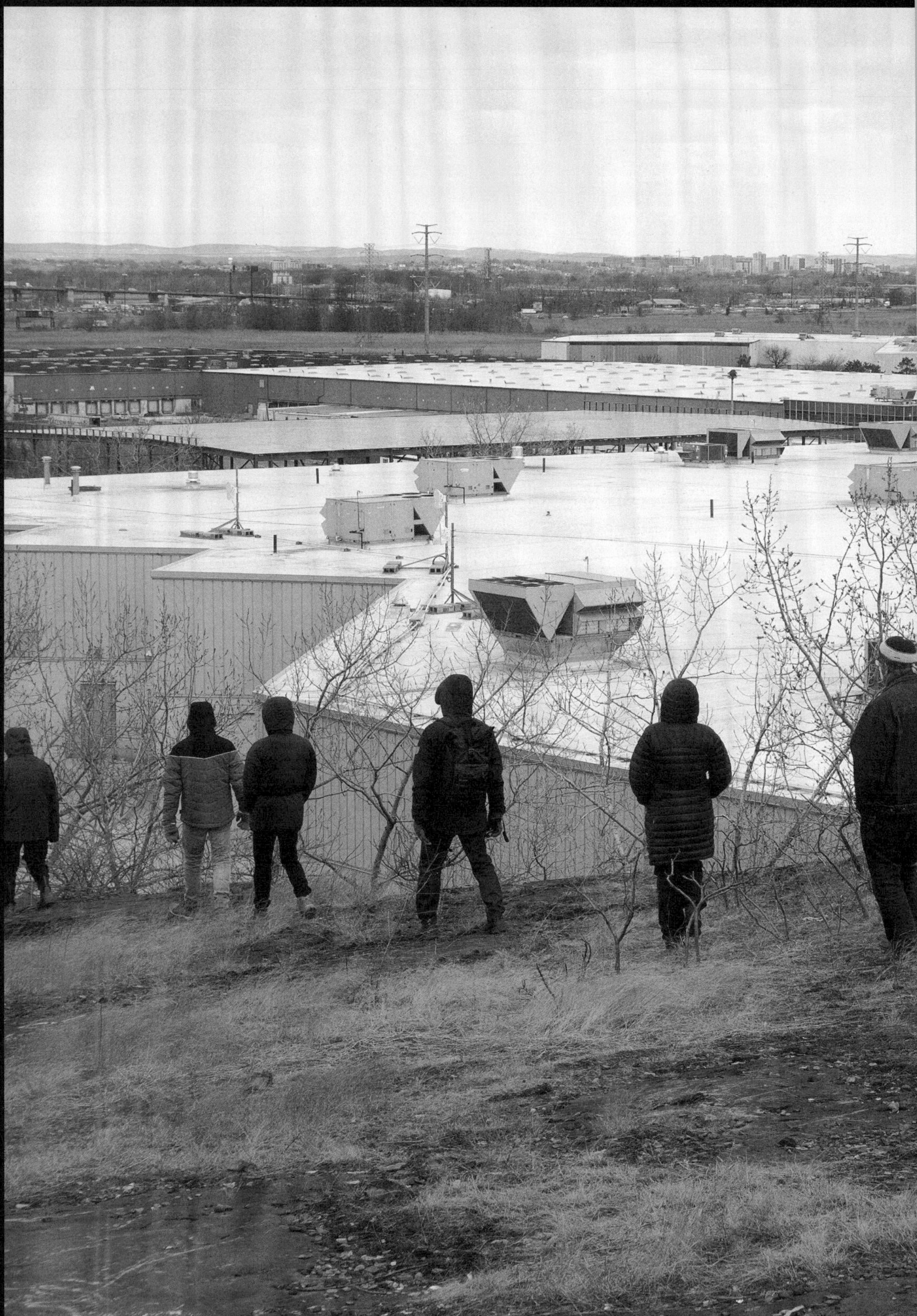

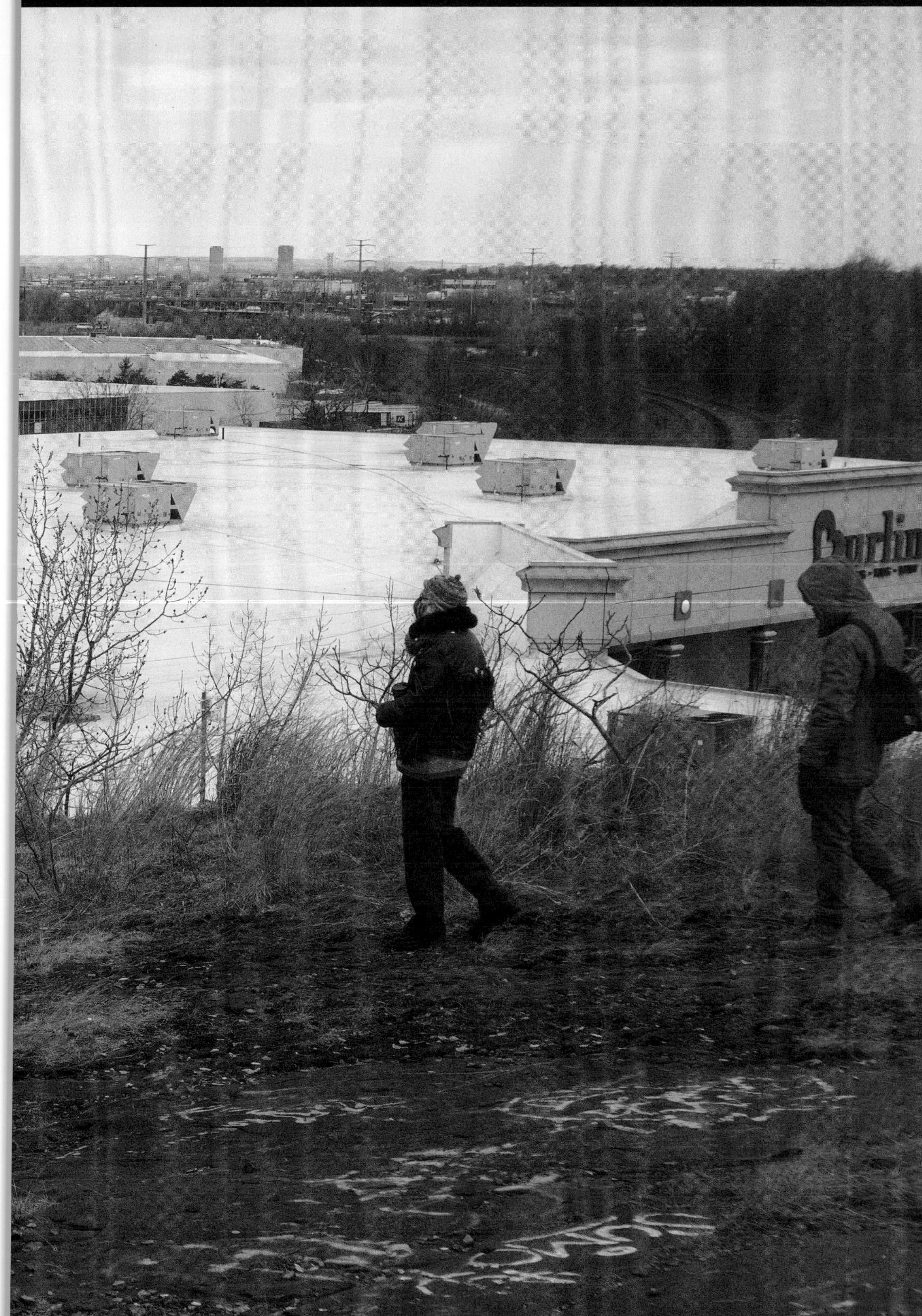

Welcome to the Meadowlands

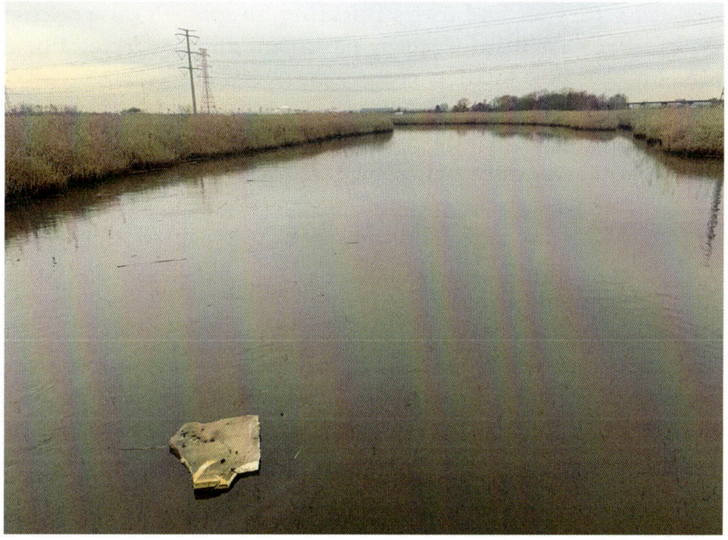

We begin in the Meadowlands, on the edge of New York City (NYC) on a rock formation known as the Tonnele Jut. It is a short drive to New Jersey from NYC, through the Lincoln or Holland Tunnel and then north through Hoboken to Bergen. The area is dense, heavily paved, cut up, bisected. The logic of grids and urban planning does not exist because it is an old place, and because it sits on the edge of a wetland which is constantly encroaching and being encroached upon. The Meadowlands is a fragmented habitat in the middle of the biggest distribution center on the East Coast of the United States, and it has been a critical hub of industrial development since colonization. This is Lenni-Lenape land, Unami Dialect Hackensack Band, Algonquin Nation, Turtle Clan. The land was 'sold' on January 30, 1658, along with every territory that now makes up northern Hudson County. It was sold to Peter Stuyvesant for eighty fathoms of wampum, twenty fathoms of cloth, twelve brass kettles, six guns, one double-brass kettle and half a barrel of strong beer.

Materials move in and out twenty-four hours a day, as do commuters, trucks, trains, bodies, goods, raw materials, commodities and luxury wholesale and retail goods. There are recycling centers and scrap shops, trash depots and waste terminals. Everywhere one looks people are working. Occasionally one encounters food, a restaurant, a bar, rundown fast-food joints and the local ethnic cuisine – Chinese, Cambodian, jerk chicken, a spread which changes as immigrant communities move on. Once in a while there is a bus stop and someone sitting there, waiting for a bus that rarely comes. But no one is ever walking, and there are no sidewalks.

The so-called Tonnele Jut is a large, flat, upthrust serpentinite rock that emerges from the marshy and impenetrable wetlands and sits between a Burlington Coat Factory and a Lowe's Building Supply – two working-class retail giants. Its edges are reinforced by pavement and concrete. The rock formed approximately 200 million years ago.

Species documented so far include 260 plus birds (thirty-three of which are state-listed as endangered, threatened or declining), twenty-two mammals, fifty-one-plus fish, fifty-one bees and 420 plants. Wetlands make up roughly 7,800 acres of the Meadowlands, and they include brackish and freshwater marshes dominated by the common reed as well as cordgrass spartina marshes and hardwood swamps. This is a critical wildlife corridor shared by peregrine falcons, snowy owls, bald eagles, American coots, black skimmers, diamondback terrapins, red foxes, meadow voles, black-crowned night herons, northern harriers, muskrats, red-winged blackbirds, marsh wrens, common yellowthroats, willow flycatchers and swamp sparrows.

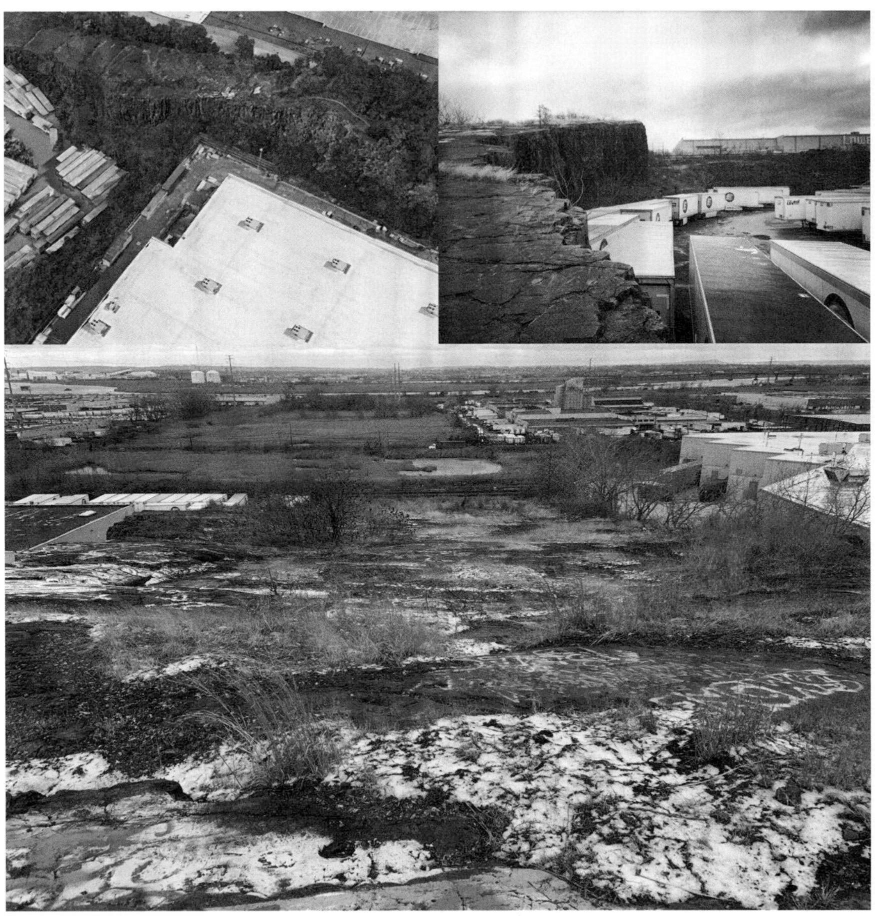

Towards a Solidarity with Place

Stripped of persona, disoriented, we find ourselves revealed by a shared experience of an unknown place. This is the slow work of undoing human chauvinism, or how to not take a selfie. When we arrive at a place we have never been, when we are disoriented, our natural response is, Where am I? Instead, our first questions will be: What is this place? What is happening here? What has happened here? The question 'Where am I?' only comes as a response to the place itself.

This is a series of steps, a procedure towards a solidarity with place. It can be applied anywhere and it can take a moment or hours. Contemplate a world in which you do not know which role you will play. This is the position and perspective we hope you can bring to this teaching.

Begin this journey as nobody, as an every person. Forget who you are and forget who you know. Exist as strangers. Know nothing about others. Make no assumptions. Dispense with identity and cliquishness. Perhaps come as someone else, with a new name. Unknow. We begin this process by abandoning ourselves to the future.

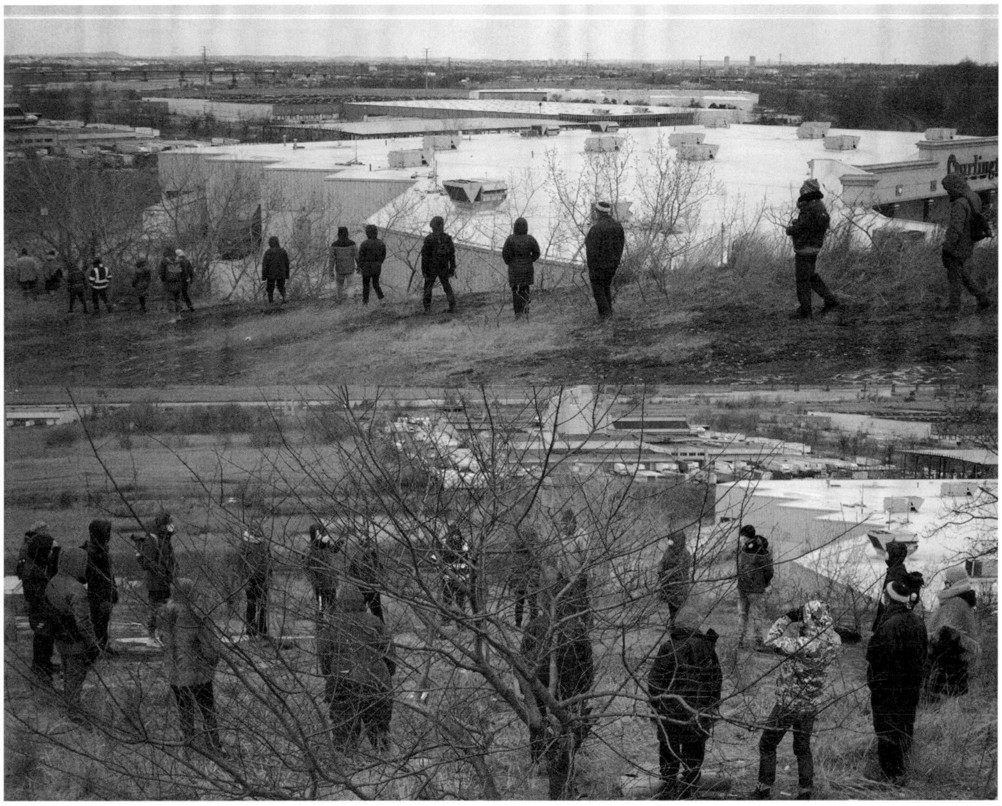

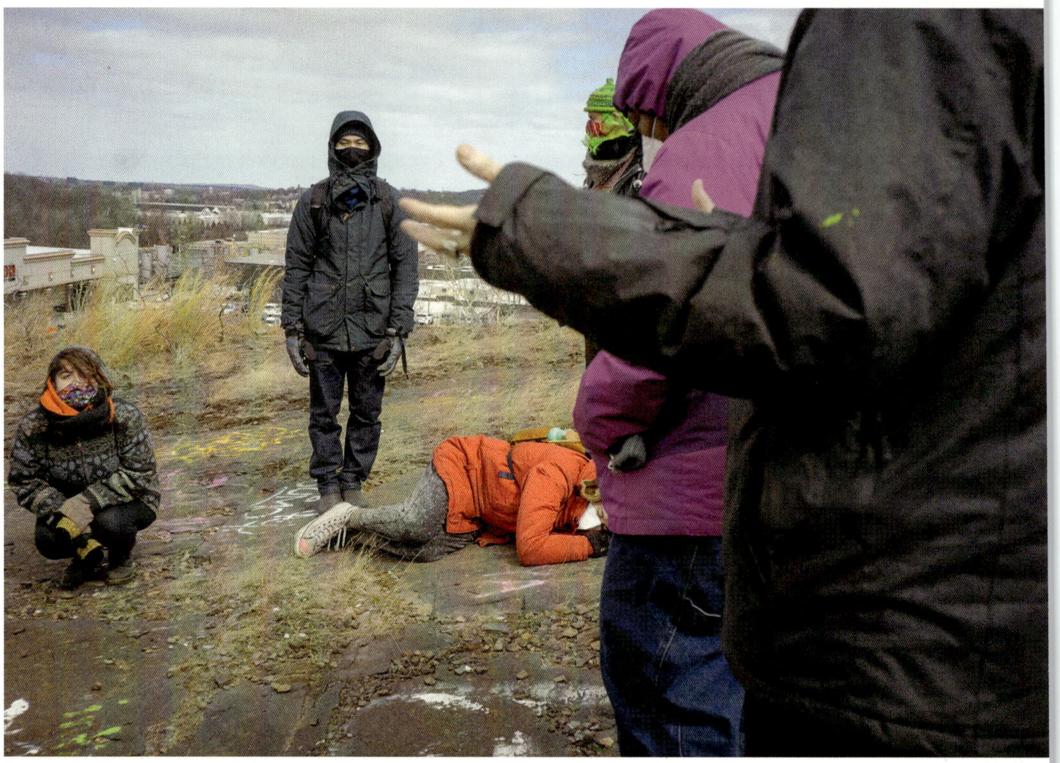

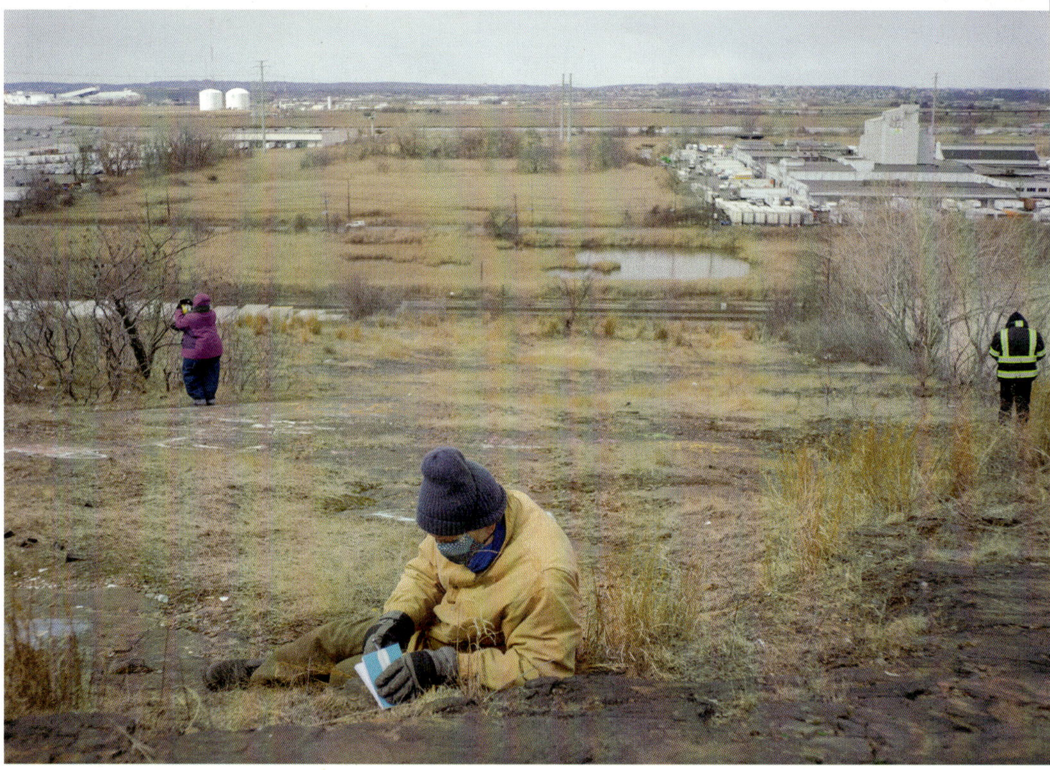

Start in a Place Together

Instructions:

ARRIVE at the body. Find your legs and feet, open your eyes, awaken your senses, listen, observe, sound out.

ASSESS perimeters and boundaries. Where does the place stop and start? What makes the place the place?

OBSERVE what is here, what is not here, who was here, what was here, when it was here, what happens here.

REFLECT in order to develop a response alone or in small groups. Write, think, process.

ASSEMBLE and ensure that the whole group decides what to do using the information gathered to make decisions. Is there meaning? Should it be shared? What can we do now?

DEPART

The Story of the Place

We can tell the story of the place without us in it.
We can tell the story of the place with us in it.
The story can be about us.
The story can not be about us.
We can commit to a way of telling the story, with each of us saying to whom we will tell the story.
We can keep the story private and personal or make it public and performative.
This story-making is creative and not bound by any rules except those that the group decides on.

For example:

I will tell the story to my sister, my kid's teacher, at least one stranger and in a letter to my isolated aunt.

For example:

The story is a tree, and we tell the story as a tree would grow, branching out from a trunk. How big is the tree?

For example:

We create a list of ONLY facts and ONLY fictions and see how long they can coexist.

Considerations

The ontological reset: reorienting, depositioning and uncentering to generate collective awareness from a nonhuman position. Can I see the place without me in it? Can we see the place without us in it? Can we care if no one knows we care? The community makes decisions together, of any shape and size so as to grow shared pathways, neurally, practically and muscularly. Try not to disturb anyone else's habitat. Leave no trace and pick up trash.

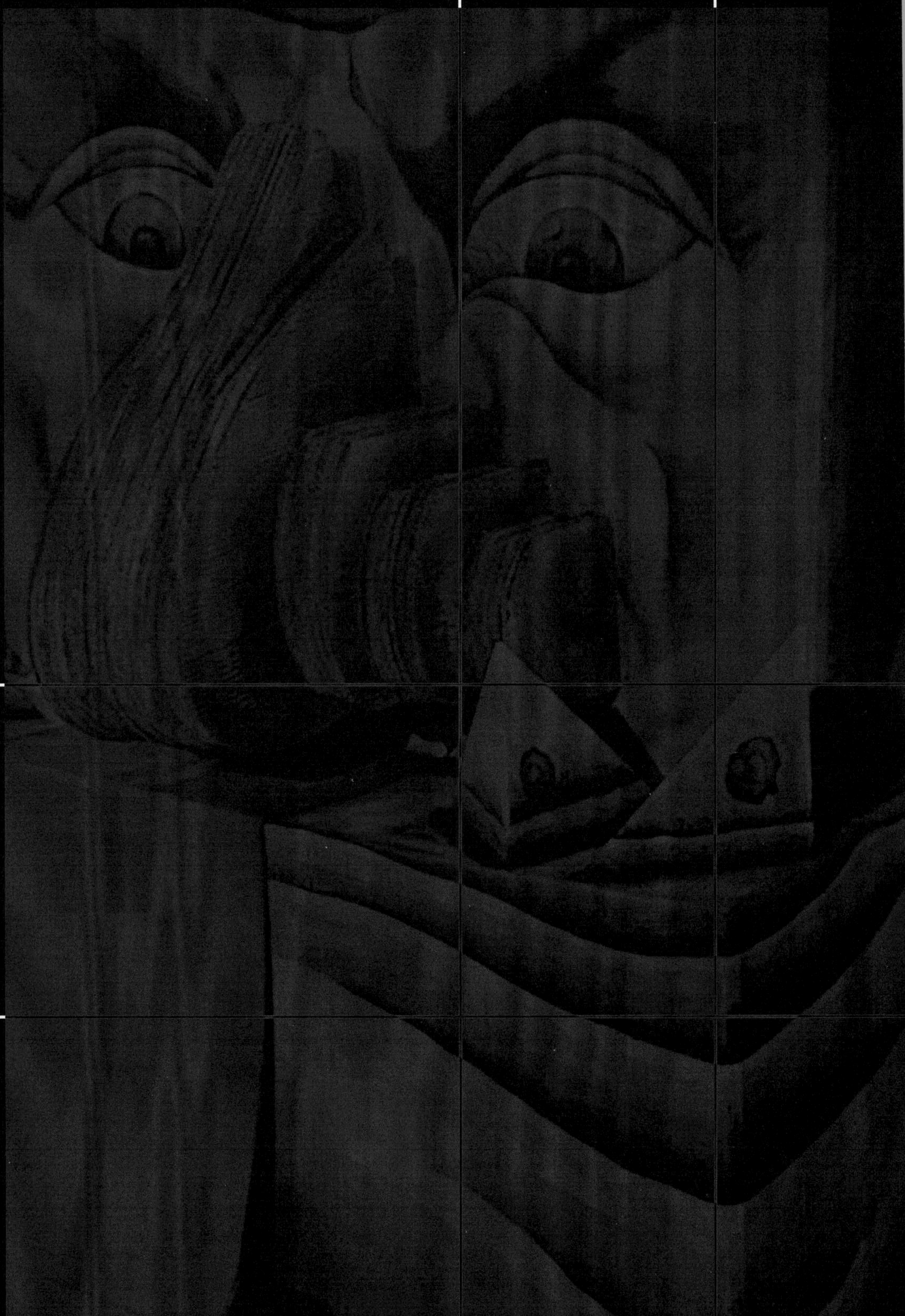

MARCH 6–30, 2021, MANILA, THE PHILIPPINES

Draft for a Manual on Collective Work, UGATLahi Art Collective and Concerned Artists of the Philippines

For this training, cultural workers of Philippine mass movements come together to draft a manual that guides the production of materials for the cultural movement using redistributive and regenerative principles of collective work. The participants share experience in organizing effigy production – a process involving multiple lines of work and intensive collaboration among participants. The participants consult literature on principles of collective work such as *Araling Aktibista* [Activist Studies] and other texts produced by mass movements.

UGATLahi Artist Collective is an organization of visual artists based in the Philippines. The group was established in the early 1990s and work together to create images of protest. Since 2001, they have created effigies (protest puppetry) of the Philippine president for each State of the Nation Address. The group is also active in performance and installation art.

Concerned Artists of the Philippines is a Philippine artists and cultural workers' organization committed to advancing freedom of expression and the people's movement for justice, nationalism and democracy. It traces its beginnings to the Free the Artist, Free the Media movement of February 1983 – an anti-state censorship campaign that united over 500 artists and media workers against plans by the dictatorial government of President Ferdinand Marcos to expand the powers of the Board of Censors.

Visual documentation by Concerned Artists of the Philippines and UGATLahi

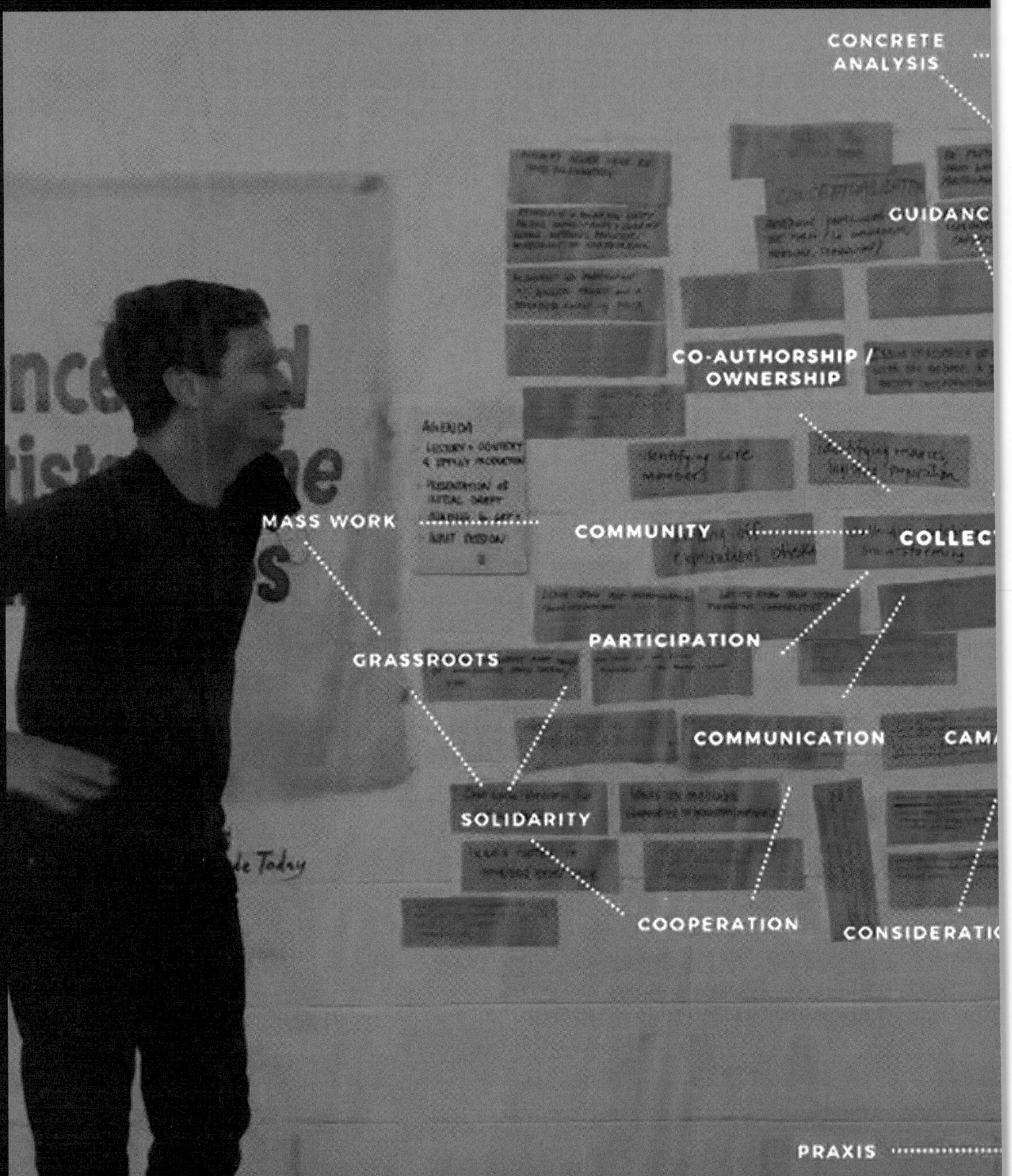
CONCRETE ANALYSIS
CO-AUTHORSHIP / OWNERSHIP
MASS WORK
COMMUNITY
PARTICIPATION
GRASSROOTS
COMMUNICATION
SOLIDARITY
COOPERATION
PRAXIS

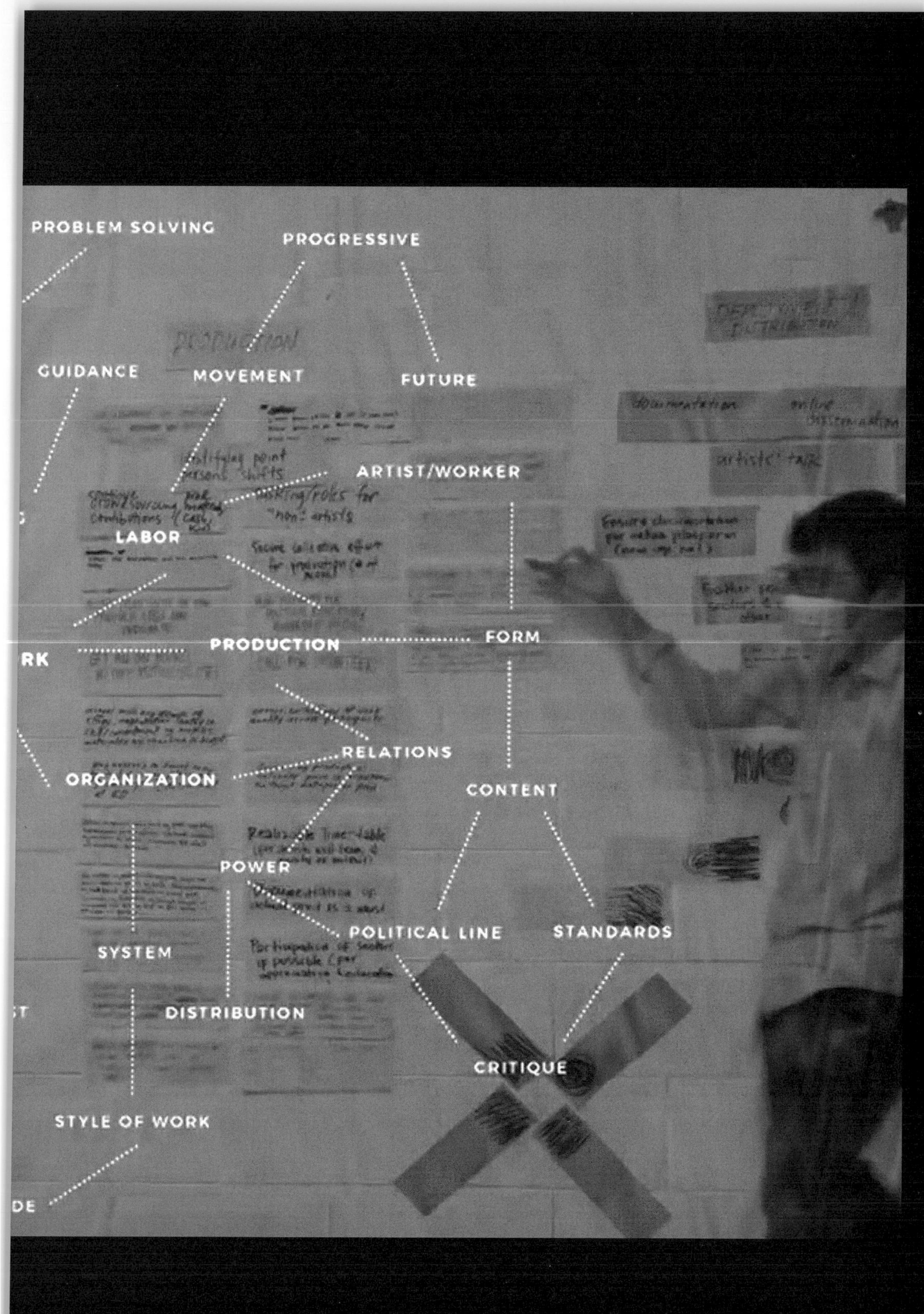
PROBLEM SOLVING
PROGRESSIVE
GUIDANCE
MOVEMENT
FUTURE
ARTIST/WORKER
LABOR
RK
PRODUCTION
FORM
RELATIONS
ORGANIZATION
CONTENT
POWER
POLITICAL LINE
STANDARDS
SYSTEM
DISTRIBUTION
CRITIQUE
STYLE OF WORK
DE

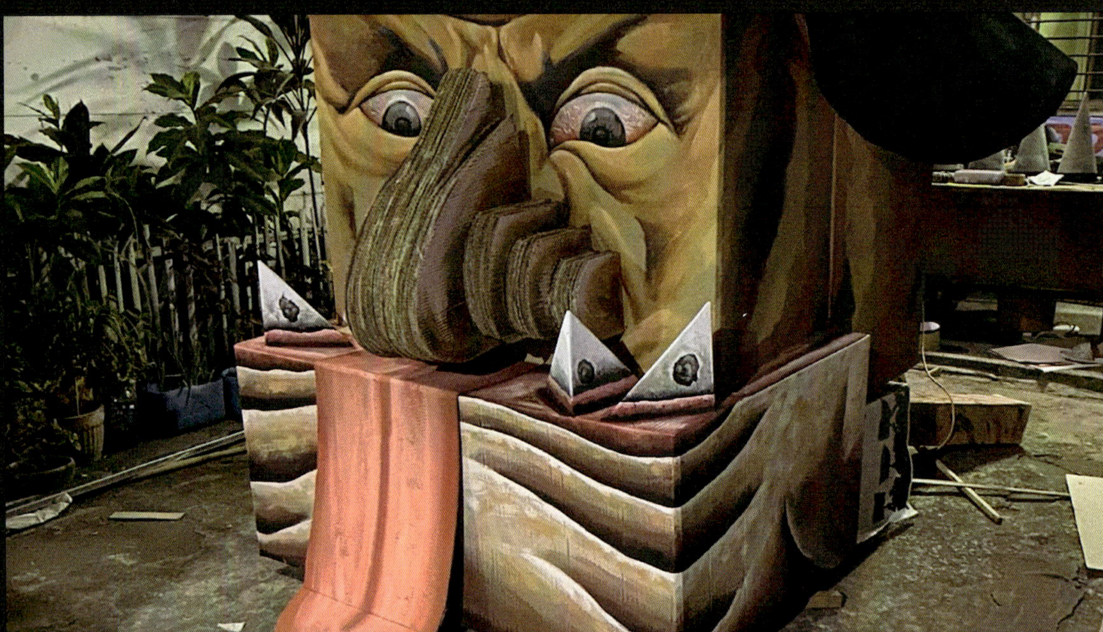

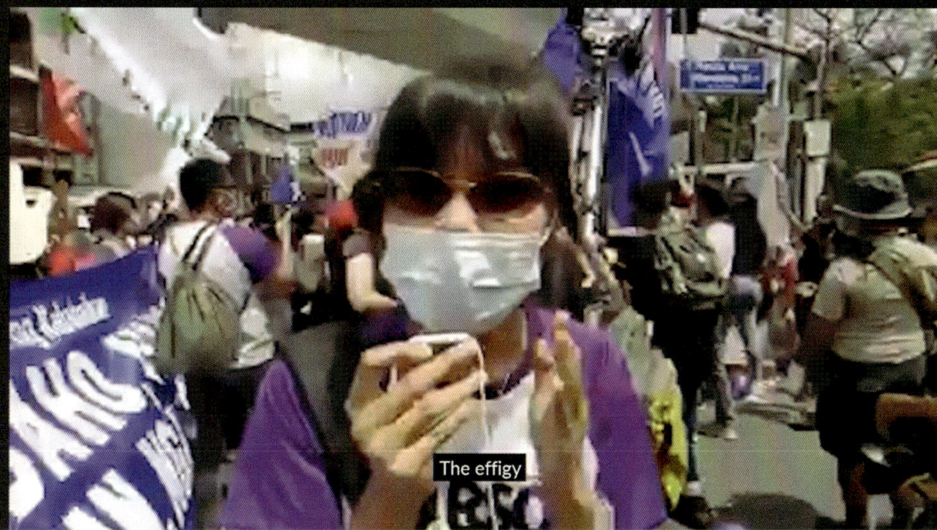
The effigy

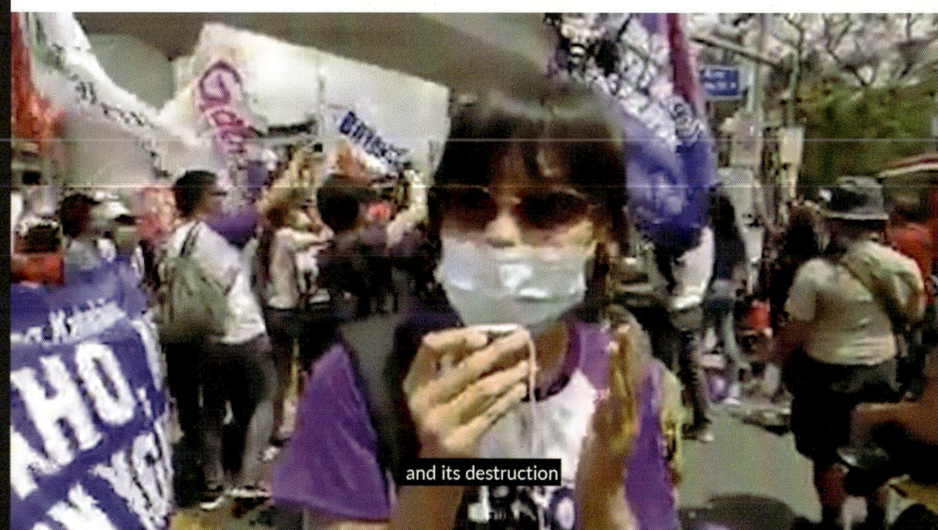
and its destruction

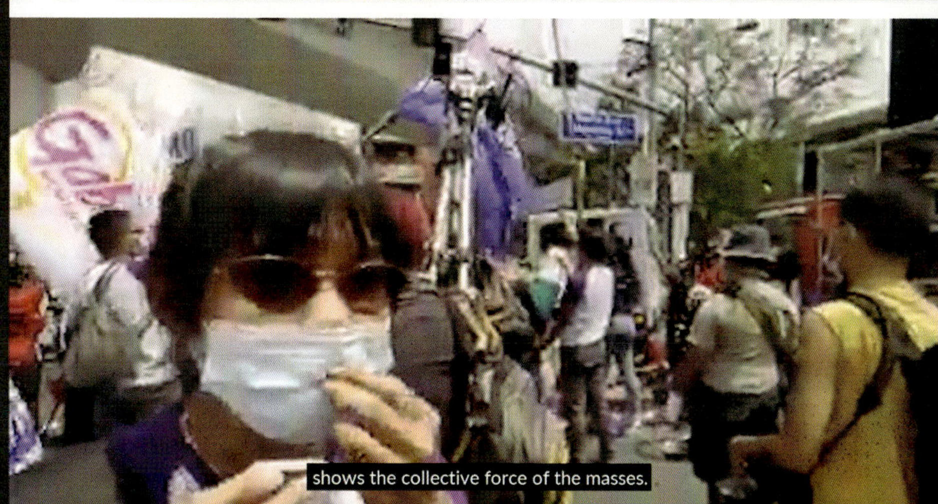
shows the collective force of the masses.

DRAFT MANUAL FOR COLLECTIVE WORK

PREPARED BY

CONCERNED ARTISTS OF THE PHILIPPINES
RESEARCH AND EDUCATION COMMITTEE

For Neil

TABLE OF CONTENTS

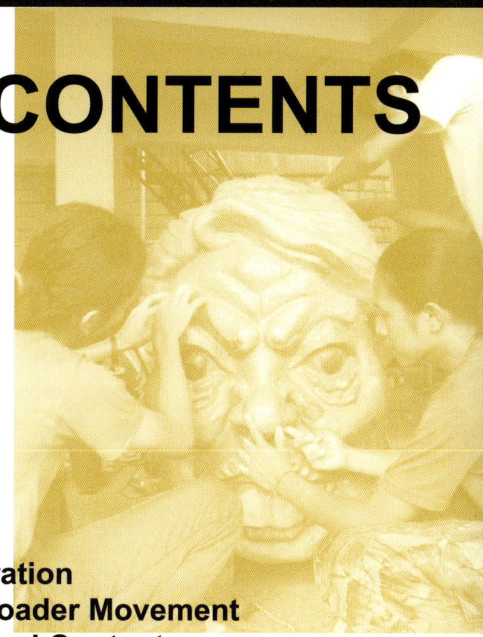

INTRODUCTION

The Concerned Artists of the Philippines (CAP) and UGATLahi Artist Collective are happy to share the collaborative work done towards preparing this 'Draft Manual for Collective Work.' Collective work is a principle embraced by both organizations, where many self-identify as cultural workers who are part of larger social movements. Both organizations also share a rich history of coming together to collaborate on different productions, exhibits and mobilizations. Today, however, we find ourselves at a point where distance and isolation is the norm. The realities we lived with before the pandemic – the imbalance of power and resources present between the 1% and 99% – are the same, and the conditions of which are definitely getting worse. Covid-19 confirmed but also reversed a lot of notions about how we learn, work and live as communities. Hence, there is the increasingly urgent need to reflect on how we continue to affirm the value of the collective, whether through labor, learning or in continuing dissent.

As cultural workers, our context is the Philippines, which is maybe as far as 10,000 kilometers away, depending on where you are now. Our practice is in solidarity with communities facing the pandemic and political repression, where the stakes are very real and the sacrifices many. We are currently working to survive two things: both Covid-19 and a toxic administration. This is a president who last year passed an anti-terrorism law, shut down the largest media network and displayed an embarassing subservience to Chinese and US economic interests over those of our country, our resources and the people. We have lost at least 23,000 to Covid-19 and more due to continuing state neglect and human rights abuses, such as the killings of activists and President Duterte's 'war against illegal drugs,' which targeted suspected or accused users among the poor. The latter is being acted on by the International Criminal Court, which Duterte refuses to recognize in his public statements. The Covid-19 lockdown imposed a year ago was widely criticized for its use of force, which resulted in human rights violations, and the vaccine rollout is the slowest in the Asian region. Next year is a national election year where our choices will mostly be determined by a history of dynastic and patronage politics.

There is a lot that artists and cultural workers can do in the face of such neglect and injustice. Even while remaining a critical and necessary voice in society, many of the arts and culture industries here have been most affected by unemployment or underemployment, patronage politics and cooptation. The fragmentation brought on by the pandemic also manifests in cultural production, dissemination and criticality, seeping into consciousness itself. The 'Draft Manual for Collective Work' was therefore conceptualized as a modest contribution to responding to this situation in a self-reflexive way.

'Collective work' is a broad term, so we started with looking at the effigy as a case study to discuss how works are produced with and for people's movements in the country. CAP's Research and Education Committee began with a focus group discussion and workshop on the effigy as a protest art form. This was organized in collaboration with past and present members of UGATLahi artist collective, which has been involved in important effigy works since the late 1990s. We took off from both oral history/sharing and art historical research, situating how the form started in 1964 along with the rise of nationalist and political ferment in the region, how it was among the forms of creative dissent before and after the fall of the dictatorship and how its production significantly progressed alongside the development of artist collectives. It was important to address history, theory and current practice and production. The participants had to combine both physical and online meetings, and the effort coincided with the production of an actual effigy for International Working Women's Day on March 8. Soon after this, the country again went into lockdown following a sharp rise in cases. As such, we had to combine synchronous and asynchronous ways of discussing and working.

For several weeks, the training team distilled resources on the value and process of collective work through discussions, readings and the sharing of practice. The resulting draft text was presented in a face-to-face session, but its redrafting was put on hold due to the lockdown the week after, however will certainly be picked up again and included in further educational discussions. CAP and UGATLahi worked with colleagues from different disciplines based in Manila, Quezon City and Baguio, all who were part of artist collectives meeting through digital channels when face-to-face was not possible. Production on other works and activities, physical or online, continued alongside this.

We know that time is doubly precious these days. By giving cultural workers in the network a temporary space or interruption of time to commit to memory, the training project is less an abstract rendering of a theoretical model and more a living draft, crafted from the exchange of theory and action in response to the crisis. It is important to note that the effigy is not the end product of the training, but the start of a conversation and commitment to collectivization – it gives form to this attempt to constellate. The shape of communal work can take on many forms, from a Google document to an effigy being set on fire.

In the end, the process of communing and crafting was as important as the output, editing and the text itself. It continued well beyond the physical meetings, generating new inputs and dialogues along the way. The collaborative nature of the document, though stilled temporarily, becomes its afterlife and authorship continues to be altered in the process of picking it up, using it and responding to it. As opposed to training as a singular activity imparted from one specialized person to another, the process was comparatively arduous as you got input from different people and different perspectives and disciplines.

The key points discussed in the draft manual include the processes of conceptualization, production and deployment in the public sphere. Each section stresses the need of organizing, ideological development and propaganda in varying degrees. The flow of the draft starts from the need to carve out a space and lines for collaboration in order to unite in both form and content, in organizing production in such a way as to ensure participation, consolidation and learning among collaborators and lastly in engaging the public sphere through protest mobilizations, documentation and discourse. Overall, the process strives towards regeneration, creating a feedback loop of both theory and practice through which we learn and affirm values on how we exist, resist and forge the future collectively.

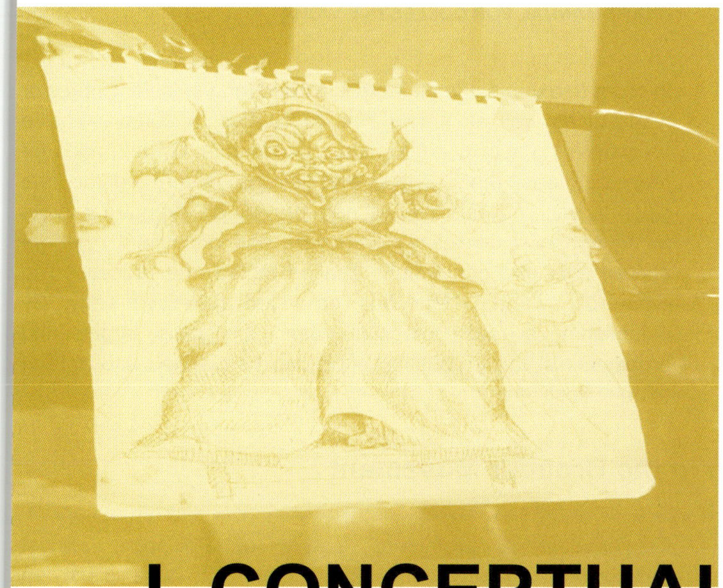

I. CONCEPTUALIZATION

1. Establishing a Platform for Collaboration

Conceptualizing the effigy begins by establishing a conducive space or platform for collaboration through which objectives and goals are set and clarified, and through which ideas for production may be constructively exhausted, debated and refined. This conceptualization of the production effort should also espouse room for education and establish processes that foster collective work.

The collaborators are often a composite of cultural workers and political organizers who should acknowledge each other as capable propagandists employing different practices to similar ends. It is counterproductive to the conceptualization process and overall collectivity for collaborators to resort to a division of labor between intellectual and practical fields. This will help establish a collective acknowledgement of the variety of methods, materials and resources at the group's disposal. The collaborators in the conceptualization process should not be limited to either spearheading the production of the effigy or planning the mobilization. There should be an active effort to involve other allied organizations and groups in the conceptualization and production efforts.

In order to exhaust ideas, there is a need for a sufficient space or platform as well as ample time to conduct a comprehensive brainstorming activity among the collaborators. Ground rules for respecting each other's inputs and being considerate of the time given to each collaborator will help provide an avenue for ideas to flourish and be refined with care and consistency; where agreements and contentions can be tabled and processed to arrive at a sharp, firm and grounded collective unity. By establishing a space for collaboration, the goals, targets and processes of the production effort can be clarified and agreed upon collectively.

2. Situating Production in the Broader Movement

Effigies are a prominent feature of Philippine protest mobilizations, which, more often than not, take place on 'red-letter days' or public holidays (e.g. Labor Day, the State of the Nation Address, Bonifacio Day). Thus, effigy conceptualization and production should, as much as possible, be planned well in advance of these dates. Of course, there are cases when effigies might be needed as a response to an emergent issue and organizers and production groups will have to respond or adjust quickly and flexibly in such circumstances. Over and above the timing of these mobilizations, we must acknowledge that they inevitably set the direction for the effigy's conceptualization.

Depending on the theme of the mobilization, the collaborators should be aware of the pertinent campaigns in order to achieve collective unity on said issues and to help them decide on the design. This can be achieved by engaging collaborators to participate in educational discussions as part of the production process. Presenting a situationer geared towards the campaign or issue will cover the fundamentals and any recent developments of the particular campaign to be addressed by the production effort. This will ensure that the collaborators are working within the same understanding and will also prevent the conceptualization process from being monopolized by the protest organizers alone, which is counterintuitive to collective work. Conversely, situating the effigy within the broader campaign also emphasizes that the effigy production is only part of the larger, more intricate and interdependent effort of staging a mass mobilization.

Ultimately, the work of producing an effigy is not merely a collaboration between artists and political organizers. Insofar as any effigy is situated in and responds to the needs of people's campaigns and struggles, it cannot but consider the political circumstances and history of those struggles as simultaneously shaping its processes and constituting part of its materials. The collective engaged in production is thus always also engaged in a collaboration with history. This is a humbling perspective that renders the production effort a more profound and painstaking enterprise.

3. Working Toward the Unity of Form and Content

The following are guiding principles for collectively conceptualizing with a mind for unity of form and content during the process.

First, in order for the collective to unite, and for the final material to have unity and harmony in a specific and concise form, the collaborators should educate themselves on the ideological underpinnings of the campaign and mobilization for which the effigy is to be produced. This will help them arrive at an appropriate visual peg and ideological thrust for a working draft or creative study. The team can then review the creative studies, briefs, maquettes and the like in order to test the feasibility of the concept. Also, depending on the form, the collaborators should research further into the mechanisms, materials and symbolisms that will be used for the effigy. Overall, the team should ensure that the visual form and symbolism of the effigy design simultaneously historicizes and particularizes the message of the campaign it is meant for.

It is important to ensure clarity in the overall design by avoiding over-elaborate forms and compounded symbolisms that may not lend themselves to reception in the span of a mobilization or distract from the primary message appropriate to the mobilization. Secondly, during the conceptualization of the effigy and the logistical planning of its production, the collaborators should determine the time and resources needed by assessing and synthesizing the scope of the concept and the production methods against the degree to which the collaborating organizations will directly participate in production. They should also account for the planned conduct of the mobilization. These assessments will determine and dictate the concrete horizons of the work's propaganda capabilities.

It is only practical that the design drafted by the collaborators be kept flexible enough to leave space for improvisation and modification, as may become necessitated by circumstance or made available or possible by the participants themselves. It should be able to accommodate the ideas, skills and artistic persuasions of those participants who will be working on the effigy. This flexibility in the ideas should also include the processes and materials to be used in production. The group should also consider the modularity of the design during the conceptualization period since this will facilitate ease of deployment or dismantling.

Lastly, the team of collaborators should make sure that the process and all stages of the production are accounted for when establishing the concept and design. This means that they should consider the design from the production phase (e.g. construction of the armature, painting, sculpting, finishing) to its deployment (e.g. transportation, presentation, reception and burning).

These guiding principles ensure that the conceptualization of the design is rooted in the campaign's and the mobilization's political demands and practical requirements. It will also help to sharpen the design insofar as it considers the mass's struggles, the mobilization's form and the movement's capacity for production. The collaborative process of these ideas can be consolidated in a visual and ideological mood or peg board, which will aid all collaborators in leveling-off during the production process.

.

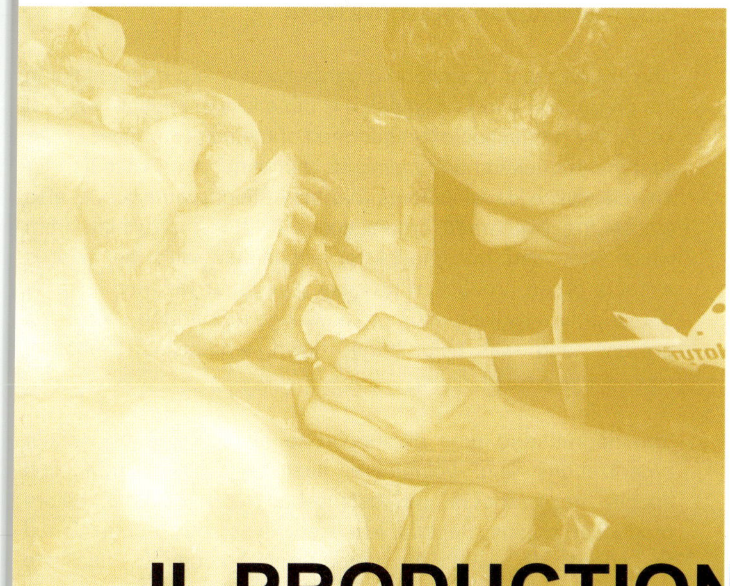

II. PRODUCTION

At the end of the conceptualization phase, a design and concept for the effigy is determined and decided upon. The production phase involves executing and realizing the design. The process of production is a multi-component effort that expands well beyond the physical construction of the effigy or managing the resources required. Production should be approached as a platform for learning, organizing, and fostering collectivity.

1. Avenues of Collaboration

The production process of the effigy should be situated within the broader organizing goals of the organization and the campaign for which the effigy is being made. It is important that the production is a collective and collaborative process, involving participants from different sectors and organizations.

At the start of the production process, the possible involvement of people outside the organization must be assessed. Specifically, it is important to consider which sectors are directly involved in the campaign (e.g. peasants, labor unions, women) and to identify the specific groups from those sectors who will be involved in the production process as partners.

The involvement of sectoral organizations with a direct stake in the production effort's campaign is beneficial in multiple ways. It keeps the production effort informed of the considerations of the sector/s in question and maintains a channel of coordination for any campaign developments that may affect production. It also places the concerned organizations in closer proximity, from which they can become better acquainted with the various aspects of the production process. The latter will help towards the long-term redistribution of knowledge around the production process and will help break down tendencies toward a client-service relationship.

The degree and type of support to be provided by partner organizations (e.g. volunteers, financial support, production space, etc.) should be established and clarified before production begins. Sectoral representatives should be assigned to coordinate with the production group to facilitate communication between organizations. Additional support from other organizations and allies should be welcomed and maximized. Identify which aspects of production require additional support and establish lines of collaboration or assistance accordingly.

Before production starts, an assessment of the number of participants needed must be made based on the design. Then a call for volunteers must be disseminated across organizations and networks. Open calls are an opportunity for broadening the number of backgrounds and knowledges involved in production as well as helping to expand the networks and membership of the organizations involved. However, security must also be kept in mind and the call must adjust accordingly. It should be considered that there are situations where a call should only be distributed through allied organizations and not made public.

A point person for alliance work within the production team must be assigned when working with multiple organizations. They will serve as a liaison for campaign meetings and communicating with partner organizations. It is important to note that the person assigned to this will be involved in many decision-making processes. Thus, they should have the capacity to speak for the production team while still keeping in mind that the production is a collective effort. Finally, a point person within the production group must also be identified to serve as an official channel to the partner organizations. This helps facilitate clarity of communication between organizations.

2. Division of Tasks

Effigy production is an effort across multiple disciplines, which may be hard to manage without an organizational structure. A main production head must be appointed to oversee the entire production team. The different tasks involved in executing the design can then be divided among a number of subheads (e.g. armature, painting, logistics, etc.).

Keep in mind that production heads are coordinators among peers and facilitators of participation instead of bosses or supervisors. The designated heads for the production team are in charge of ensuring that the participants have all the resources and skills needed to complete the daily production goals. They should also coordinate with the participants so that they may collectively establish a consistency in form. The designated heads for the production team are in charge of ensuring that daily production goals are being met or, if not, making the necessary adjustments to address delays. They should also assist in establishing and maintaining consistency of quality among the participants' contributions. It should be noted that in the context of the organization between productions, these leadership roles should ideally be rotated so as to foster growth among the membership.

The primary tasks to be accomplished should be identified by the heads to maximize the production effort. It is important for the production team's heads to get to know the participants so as to become acquainted with their capabilities and limitations. This will help them guide the participants toward the tasks that build on their strengths and facilitate their need for growth and learning. But ultimately, members should be free to choose the roles that they will take responsibility for. The commitment and readiness of participants to undertake particular tasks should be factored into the production plan and adjusted accordingly.

3. Production Plan and Timetable

Key to the process of production is laying out a production plan. At the outset, the difficulty of the effigy's design must be assessed against the production team's capacity to execute it. This is based on the available skill sets of the participants (carpentry, painting, sculpting, etc.), the available resources and the time frame allotted for production.

The effigy's design must also be reviewed to determine the materials that need to be acquired for its production. This must be done while considering the budget for the entire project and the feasibility of procuring those materials. In the event that the projected expenses exceed the budget, then the production team must think of alternative materials or processes for production. The design can also be reviewed to see where adjustments can be made. Participation in deciding on adjustments should be open to the whole production team and representatives from partner organizations. This helps maintain a shared ownership of the effort and maximizes the broad skills and knowledges available to the group. There must also be an accessible sourcebook for schematics, plan documents, meeting minutes and the like, so team members can refer to them easily should the need arise.

A timetable for production should be drafted detailing daily targets from pre-production to post-production. This calendar should be constantly updated and detailed as the process of production progresses or changes. It is important to create a timetable that is realistic for both the well-being of the participants and the quality of the output.

Each production day should have information on that day's goals available. Having detailed information serves to guide the production better and illustrations for each day's target output may even be included. This should be evaluated at the end of each day so that the overall schedule may be adjusted accordingly.

The timetable must also consider the possible ebb and flow of the volume of participants. The availability of participants with specialized skills must also be taken into consideration as their knowledge may be vital for the project to progress at certain points. These should be incorporated into the timetable to maximize the participants' involvement at any given point and to minimize wasted time. An example of this would be to schedule labor-intensive tasks on days where a high volume of participants is expected. Shifting days should also be considered so as not to burnout the participants.

4. Collective Education in and through Production Work

Besides the construction of the effigy itself, one of the production's main considerations is the education of the participants through collective work. This involves gaining awareness of the organizational, ideological and political goals of producing the effigy. By means of participating in production, participants should become acquainted with the broader political landscape in which the effigy production is situated, gain a better understanding of the processes of production and familiarize themselves with the culture of collective work.

It is important to plan a program for political education that may be conducted simultaneously with production. The planning of a curriculum should consider the particular campaign for which production is geared as well as participants' varying degrees of political awareness and education. In line with this, a coordinator of education should be assigned and volunteers from the production team and partner organizations should be readied to instruct the participants. It is important to try and rotate instructor duties so that the tasks of reviewing study materials and preparing sessions can be distributed among the group instead of overburdening a particular individual, as this limits their ability to participate in other aspects of production and prevents others from learning by way of teaching.

Another aspect of education in the production process is the sharing and transfer of practical skills and knowledge. At the outset and at every stage of production, orientations should be conducted to familiarize the team with each step or process they will be participating in. Heads should be cognizant of the capabilities and limitations of the team so that they may help in creating opportunities for them to learn and expand their capabilities. Conversely, team members should not hesitate to share any familiarity with the materials or processes involved that may help the overall effort. It should be noted that the process of production may become compartmentalized due to how the production team and the division of tasks are organized. Team members should encourage each other to try their hand at different aspects of the production process.

Production heads should facilitate regular disposition checks to maintain unity of purpose and keep everyone on the same page. Through this process, team members get to know more about each other, their backgrounds, motivations, general moods and any specific circumstances they are facing that might require the group's attention and assistance. Disposition checks might seem formal or awkward to some in the beginning, but they need not be consistently marked off as a specific process within production. The process of keeping up with team members' dispositions can be integrated into the whole production process. Meals, in particular, are a good avenue for getting acquainted and checking on each other. Keeping lines of communication open between team members helps keep the group consolidated overall.

Regular assessments are a crucial part of facilitating learning throughout the production process. By means of assessment, team members become more aware of how the different practices employed toward production contribute to successes or setbacks in the overall process. Sessions for criticism and self-criticism should also be integrated into assessments so as to identify and resolve any concerns that might be affecting particular team members or the production effort in general. Assessments should be conducted daily in order to centralize experience, collectively learn and jointly decide how to proceed with work.

Particular effort should be made to document the different aspects of production throughout the process. Point persons should be assigned to see to this particular task depending on their availability at different stages of the process. The documentation should be collated regularly and can be used to aid assessments and media work. Comprehensive documentation ensures that the production process will serve the organization's future education efforts and propaganda work.

5. Logistics

Logistics work is an important part of the production process as there are many components that need to be maintained and managed. A point person for logistics should be assigned to coordinate the practical needs of the production team.

One aspect is the procurement and utilization of the materials needed for the effigy. These need to be maintained within the budget and kept available. This requires knowledge of the rate at which the production team's resources are being used. Toward this, cleaning and inventory should be conducted at the end of each production day. Logistics will then assess the remaining supplies against production needs and immediately ensure the procurement of further supplies if necessary. Guidelines for cleanliness and order in the workspace should also be established to help keep track of materials and minimize losses or delays.

Feeding the production team also falls within the responsibility of those assigned to logistics work. Dietary restrictions are important to consider given the varying physiological needs and cultural backgrounds of the participants. Planning meals and coordinating their preparation will help minimize costs and ensure that the production team receives nutritious food.

The security of participants and the production space is also a primary concern. Logistics heads should ensure that the work environment is safe from surveillance and intrusion by state agents. A buddy system whereby each team member is assigned to keep track of another can be created to bolster individual security and cultivate a sense of responsibility for one another. A paralegal team may also be assigned for the production process if deemed necessary.

Managing media presence also falls under the responsibilities of logistics work. Media practitioners seeking to document the production process or interview team members must be managed so as to minimize interruption to the flow of work.

6. Aktitud

Aktitud is a term in the activist vernacular that encompasses the characteristics needed for comradeship and collectivity. It is used to denote the right attitude to activism, work and comradeship. A guide to proper aktitud is essential to the production process as it also serves to direct participants on how they should approach collective work. In general, there is aktitud that involves the collective and there is aktitud that pertains to individual dispositions or habits of thinking and working. Also included here is an adaptation of the section 'Combat Liberalism' from *Araling Aktibista* [The Activist Study], which enumerates forms of liberalism that are anathema to fostering the principled unity that underpins collectivity.

a. Group Dynamics

The group should keep in mind the principle of 'Unite, Struggle, Unite.' This refers to the organizing principle for forming alliances that stresses the need to establish common ground for unity, address and resolve differences in a principled manner and thereby arrive at further unity.

The obverse principle of 'Struggle, Unite, Struggle' should also be adhered to. This permutation refers to the cycle of criticism, resolution and acknowledgment of further room for improvement. The different individuals participating must learn to convey their ideas and listen to the ideas of others. The pride of the individual must be subordinated to the collective good. Criticism should be presented to the group through the correct channels such as assessments. These are avenues for improvement vital not only to the individual but to the collective as well. However, when there is a conflict of ideas, which is common in any collective endeavor, then the wisdom of the collective must be acknowledged.

If an individual or unit in the production group is experiencing consistent failures or weaknesses then the group should investigate or analyze the roots that lead to that deficiency and take necessary steps to address and improve the situation.

It must be kept in mind that the paramount goal of collective work is the political, ideological and organizational development of the participants, which supersedes the importance of creating the 'perfect output.'

Heads should consider the individual differences of the participants. Especially with new participants, given that they may not have the same level of commitment, aptitude or background for collective work, so imposing undue demands or expectations should be avoided. However, heads should not hesitate to encourage participants to work past their limitations. They should assess to what degree limitations can be overcome, then maximize what is available.

The varied knowledge, experience and training of team members should be harnessed and maximized. Different styles, skills and ways of approaching production problems should be acknowledged, studied and employed for the benefit of all. Conversely, production heads should avoid insisting only on familiar or established styles and approaches.

Due to the structure created for the division and distribution of work, there is a tendency for the production team to become compartmentalized into groups. The production team must strive to actively seek out opportunities to learn despite this. The environment of the workplace should be open to exploration and play even outside established styles or methods.

The tools and resources used for production must be regarded and cared for in common. Wastefulness and carelessness towards materials, tools and resources should be avoided and discouraged. Team members should be responsible for maintaining each other's capacity to work, which includes taking care of their physical and mental well-being.

b. Individual Dispositions

Production team members should take criticism constructively from fellow participants. However, they should be careful not to criticize others' failings if they stem from different physiological limitations or mental capacities. It is always better to inquire about a problem and its possible causes before criticizing someone for it.

It is important not to settle in production work, and to always maintain a drive to improve one's work. Humility and a willingness to learn is crucial to growth in collective work. Team members should be open to unfamiliar tasks and new responsibilities, including political and organizational work.

Team members should not hesitate to ask questions through fear of appearing ignorant. Inquiry is crucial to learning and building one's capacity to contribute to the collective effort.

Team members should maintain an openness to a broad array of cultural forms and ideas. They should trust in the capabilities of their peers and be open to the different perspectives they bring to the collective process.

Participants should situate any particular task within the broader goals of production. This will help keep the work from becoming mechanical and will foster a more comprehensive appreciation for the process.

Team members should make their ability to commit time to production clear to the group so as to help in the management of time and expected personnel.

Team members should be sensitive to the urgency of production and stay aware of the contingent character of the different tasks involved. Delays in one task can stall progress in another.

It is important for participants to be accountable for the responsibilities they take on.

Team members, especially heads, need to maintain their temper and compartmentalize emotional responses. While criticism should be centralized and collectively processed in appropriate platforms, team members should be mindful of circumstances where it is better to be open about issues or concerns during the production process as opposed to waiting for the post-production assessment.

Production heads should also avoid favoritism among participants.

c. Combat Liberalism in Collective Work

Liberalism manifests itself in various aspects of production. The following are a few principle types that can harm the process and goals of collective work.

1. To let things slide for the sake of peace and friendship when a person has clearly done wrong, and to refrain from principled argument because they are an old acquaintance, a fellow townsman, a schoolmate, a close friend, a loved one, an old colleague or old subordinate. Or to touch on the matter lightly instead of going into it thoroughly, so as to stay on good terms. The result is that both the organization and the individual are harmed.

2. To indulge in criticism in private instead of actively putting forward one's suggestions to the organization is irresponsible and overlooks the need for collective learning. To say nothing to people to their faces but to gossip behind their backs, or to say nothing at a meeting but to gossip afterwards. To show no regard at all for the principles of collective life but to follow one's own inclination.

3. To let things drift if they do not affect one personally. To say as little as possible while knowing perfectly well what is wrong. To be worldly-wise, to play safe and to seek only to avoid blame.

4. To not abide by the collective's decisions and instead give pride of place to one's own opinions. To demand special consideration from the collective but to reject its discipline.

5. To indulge in personal attacks, pick quarrels, vent personal spite or seek revenge instead of entering into an argument and struggling against incorrect views for the sake of unity, progress or getting the work done properly.

6. To hear incorrect views without rebutting them or to hear counterproductive remarks without bringing them to the attention of the group, instead taking them on calmly as if nothing had happened.

7. To be among the masses and fail to conduct propaganda and agitation or to be indifferent to the task of propaganda, forgetting that the production work does not end in the studio or production space, or insisting that one is an artist above propaganda work.

8. To see someone harming the interests of your fellow worker in the collective and yet not feeling indignant or dissuaded or stop them or reason with them, but instead allowing them to continue.

9. To work half-heartedly without a definite plan or direction. To work perfunctorily and muddle along – 'So long as one remains a monk, one goes on tolling the bell.' To be slipshod in work and slack in study.

10. To regard oneself as having rendered great service to the production effort. To pride oneself on being a veteran with superior skills. To disdain minor assignments while favoring major tasks.

11. To be aware of one's own mistakes and yet make no attempt to correct them, taking a liberal attitude toward oneself.

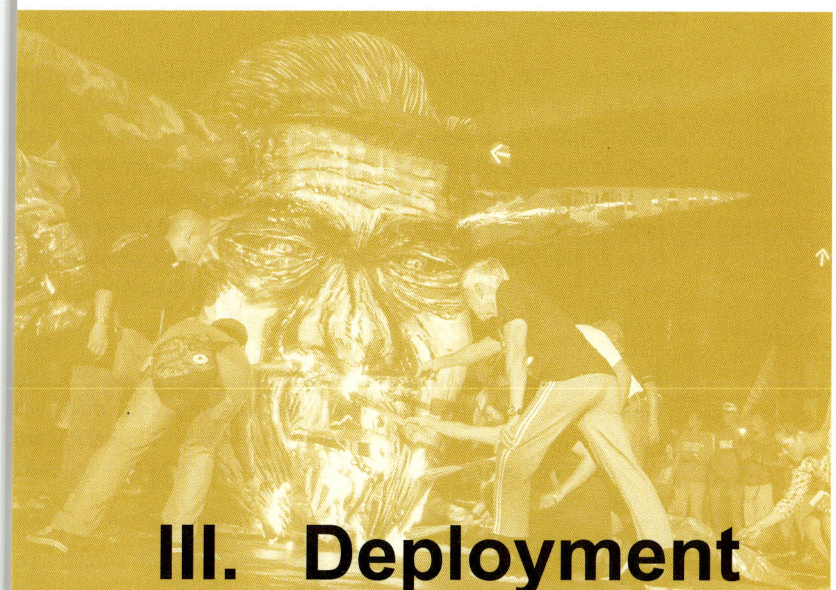

III. Deployment Distribution Reception

The deployment of the effigy production entails collective work traced across the following aspects: logistics, documentation, educational discussion opportunities and assessment. The public deployment of the effigy emphasizes the necessity of coordinating with the broader mobilization effort, the importance of documentation, the potential of the effigy to prompt discourse, education, and public engagement and the need to assess and measure the processes and impacts of production and deployment in preparation for future undertakings.

1. Logistics

The team involved in the production of the effigy and its deployment should practice foresight and preparation when it comes to the logistics. All members should be involved and have responsibilities for the effigy. It is important that the team account for the members and volunteers who can join the transfer of the effigy from its production site to the mobilization venue.

Due to its size, it is highly recommended that the effigy itself be modular so that it can be transported easily. The production team should plan its deployment by securing its transportation and preparations should be made on part of the team for making sure that there is enough manpower to help carry and transport the parts of the effigy and for its assembly in the venue. It should be brought early to the mobilization venue in a truck or vehicle that can accommodate its size in order to avoid the expected traffic congestion on the road and the truck ban.

Tasks are distributed to members and volunteers of the group to make sure that the transportation and unloading of the effigy will have a smooth transition. In the event that parts of the effigy are damaged en route, the team should be prepared to do a quick fix of the effigy.

Aside from assuring the venue of the effigy, the team should also know its part in the program. This would mean that it is important for the team to know the flow of the mobilization's program by coordinating with the organizers of the mobilization before the effigy's deployment. The possibility of having unforeseen changes in the program should also be considered and thus team members should stay involved and informed in order to be able to meet any emergent needs or situations. They should prepare to negotiate the effigy's placement within the program should there be changes they have not been consulted on.

In terms of security, the team should also make sure that there are marshalls assigned to ensure the safety of members and volunteers. Security protocols and fallbacks should be discussed and disseminated in advance.

These are the most common logistical concerns that might arise during the deployment of an effigy. The team should also carefully study the circumstances and adjust and plan accordingly.

2. Documentation

Members should note that the documentation of the effigy is valuable not only for archival posterity but for its potential contribution to the educational or programing needs of the organization. Active documentation of effigies mostly started around 2002–2003, and the learning curves of production groups have greatly benefitted from having access to the documentation materials. Care should be taken so that documentation includes not only its deployment but its production and conceptualization stages as well (e.g. sketches, drafts, campaign papers).

The archived documentation will be useful for the organization in exploring possibilities that create links between or cut across different instances of production. For example, it can be material used for an artists' talk, with members of the collective discussing their collaborative effort to create the effigy. In 2017, the exhibition Dissident Vicinities gathered these effigies, documentations of their production and other paraphernalia. These examples show the importance of the act of documentation in extending and creating new connections through the discourse of effigy production and collectivization. Additionally, the documentation and the archive that will be established can be a rich source for online dissemination and may be used as propaganda by the people's movement in the future.

It should be noted that this documentation is not limited to media files of the effigy and its production. It can also include data and other documentation, such as the tracking of materials, sources and pricing that may prove useful for future actions and productions.

3. Educational Discussion Opportunities

The deployment of an effigy within a mobilization presents opportunities for education. It is important to note that the moment the effigy is in the mobilization or public space, its ownership shifts to the public. This means that the effigy now becomes a shared entry point for discussions with the participants, other activists and the rest of the public through the media. They may start with questions about the figure portrayed, how long the production took, the material used and the number of people involved in the production. But the discourse can also be extended in order to accommodate new interpretations and understandings of the work depending on who views it. This public engagement can flesh out the attitudes and working methods of effigy production to popularize and emphasize the collective process in order to redistribute attention and credit toward the varied labor/ers involved in the process. This can lead to disabling the notion of the individual artist commonly espoused in capitalist frameworks of art-making. Corollary to this would be defetishizing the art object and its production as well as conventional ties to personal consumption.

There are times when the program of a mobilization might hit a lull or the position of the team in the crowd is not conducive to listening. This can be a chance to launch a group discussion in the middle of the mobilization. The organization can invite different speakers from sectors that can further the discourse about the issues and campaigns that are the focus of that mobilization. This is a good way to maximize their own presence in the mobilization.

4. Propaganda and Media Engagement

In terms of the propaganda work that the effigy can achieve, the production team can ensure that it will be far-reaching by preparing materials and assigning members of the team the task of facilitating the production's entry into public discourse. These materials could entail press releases, statements or other supplementary texts.

An assigned spokesperson on behalf of the organization should also be prepared to face the media and discuss the effigy. The spokesperson can relay the concept involved and the meaning of its imagery/form. Common questions that the spokesperson should be prepared to answer include details of its production such as its cost, the provenance of its budget, how long it took to construct the effigy, the number of people involved, etc. More importantly, the spokesperson should assiduously link the production effort with the mobilization's campaigns and direct the discourse toward the prevailing struggles being undertaken by the masses. It should be noted that the program committee of the mobilization usually coordinates such media engagement and so connecting early on with the committee would be most beneficial.

Since the work is proffered to the media and public, the spokesperson should be able to present pertinent points and interpretative cues without shutting the door on other possible interpretations. Instead, anticipate the potential counter-propaganda efforts and prepare accordingly. The media should not be approached or regarded as a monolithic entity.

Instead, the spokesperson should keep in mind the dynamics and the landscape of the political economy whenever engaging with them.

5. Assessment

During and after its deployment, it is important to gather feedback from sectors and participants of the mobilization. These can also come from other members and volunteers of the production team, the masses and other organizations and activists. Collecting these reactions and comments in connection to the effigy will be helpful for assessing the work's efficacy and measuring its fulfillment as a propaganda tool, which can enrich the development of the production efforts of the organizations involved. The feedback garnered can also be a useful tool in understanding how the public views effigies and mobilizations in general.

On the side of the members and volunteers involved in the production, the team should make sure that they are able to consolidate all those involved. Continue to maintain ties, deepen relationships and thereby encourage sustained participation in further collective work to be undertaken.

Another layer of this assessment would be among other artists and collaborators from other sectors. In the post-mobilization assessment with them, reactions and the discourses surrounding them should likewise be gathered. This is a way to discern their point of view in terms of effigy making. Do the organizers support the propaganda goals that the effigy can supply? Are there instances where the value of cultural work concedes to political exigencies? Is there an awareness of the effigy's contribution to the mobilization? These can be starting prompts for the assessment and will help strengthen collective work, not only for the team but for the other artists and collaborators of other sectors.

If there were other members of the group or organization that were not directly part of the effigy's production, it would still be beneficial to actively pursue their opinions and include them in the critical discourse since they may point toward the development and enrichment of these collective efforts.

Collecting their opinions and assessments would also mean acknowledging their involvement in the broader collective of the movement.

Finally, an assessment criteria that should be included is the exploration of methods of deployment and production with an eye for sustainability, both in terms of cost and environmental repercussions.

ACKNOWLEDGEMENTS

Concerned Artists of the Philippines Research and Education Committee
UGATLahi Artist Collective
Training for the Future
Goethe-Institut Philippinen

Luigi Almuena
Paolo Arago
Jeune Aramburo
Antares Gomez Bartolome
Franco P. Brobio
Avianna Castaño
Katsch Catoy
CJ Despuez
Boy Dominguez
Aldrich Brian Fang
Lisa Ito
Ides Macapanpan
Emil Mercado
Isis Molintas
Iggy Rodriguez
Rose Roque
Max Santiago
Christopher Heraldo Zamora

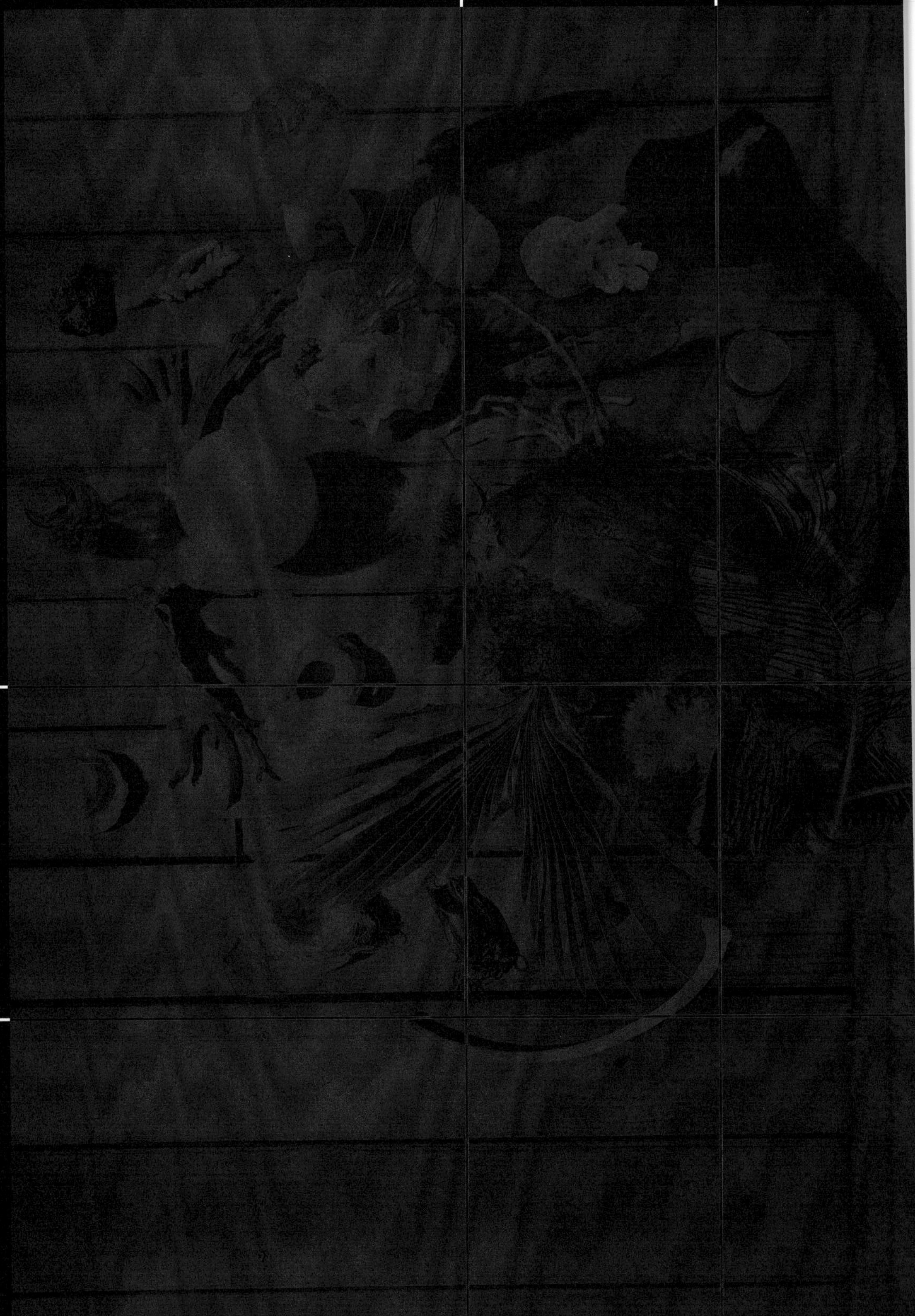

MARCH 6–7, 2021, CAPE TOWN DISTRICT, SOUTH AFRICA

AncientFutures, Zayaan Khan

The knowledge we inherit comes to us through many channels, informing how we navigate our survival in the places we reside. The Ancient-Futures training focuses on the collection of plants, seeds, land and sea to explore their ties to our collective memory and ecology. Participants join in collective exercises that range from cooking to an introduction to fibers. Through a discussion-based approach aimed at opening up the peri-pheries, various questions underpin the focus of this training, such as: How much of our survivorship is based on financialized means and systems? How might we unbind our consumption from neoliberal-ism and extractivism, and instead orient it toward something sovereign that nourishes our creativity? How might creativity encourage our survival?

Zayaan Khan is a local cultural practitioner, food activist and artist based in Cape Town. She focuses on the nuanced relationships between the ecological and urban lives that live in our city.

Visual documentation by Sara Lagardien Abdullah

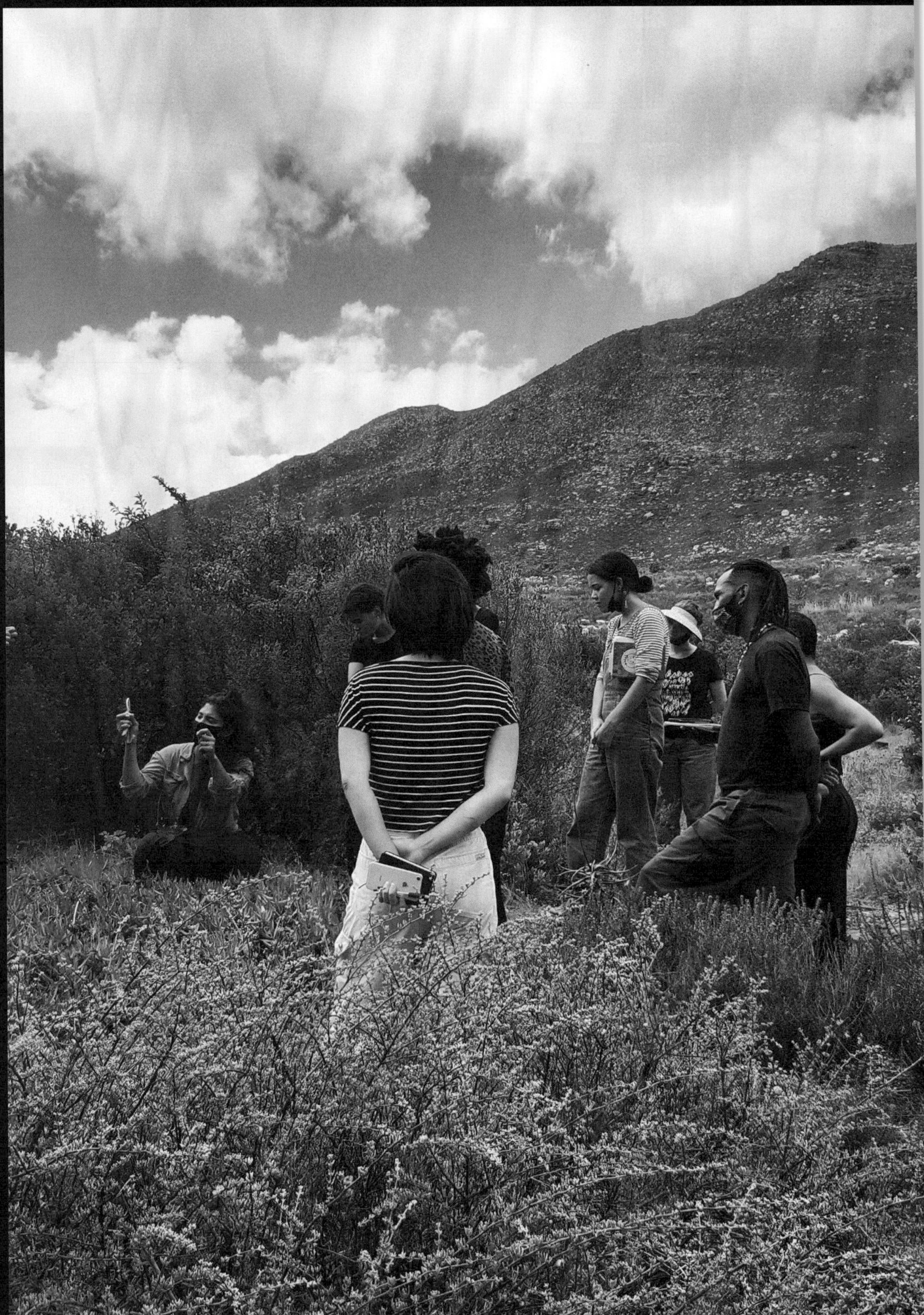

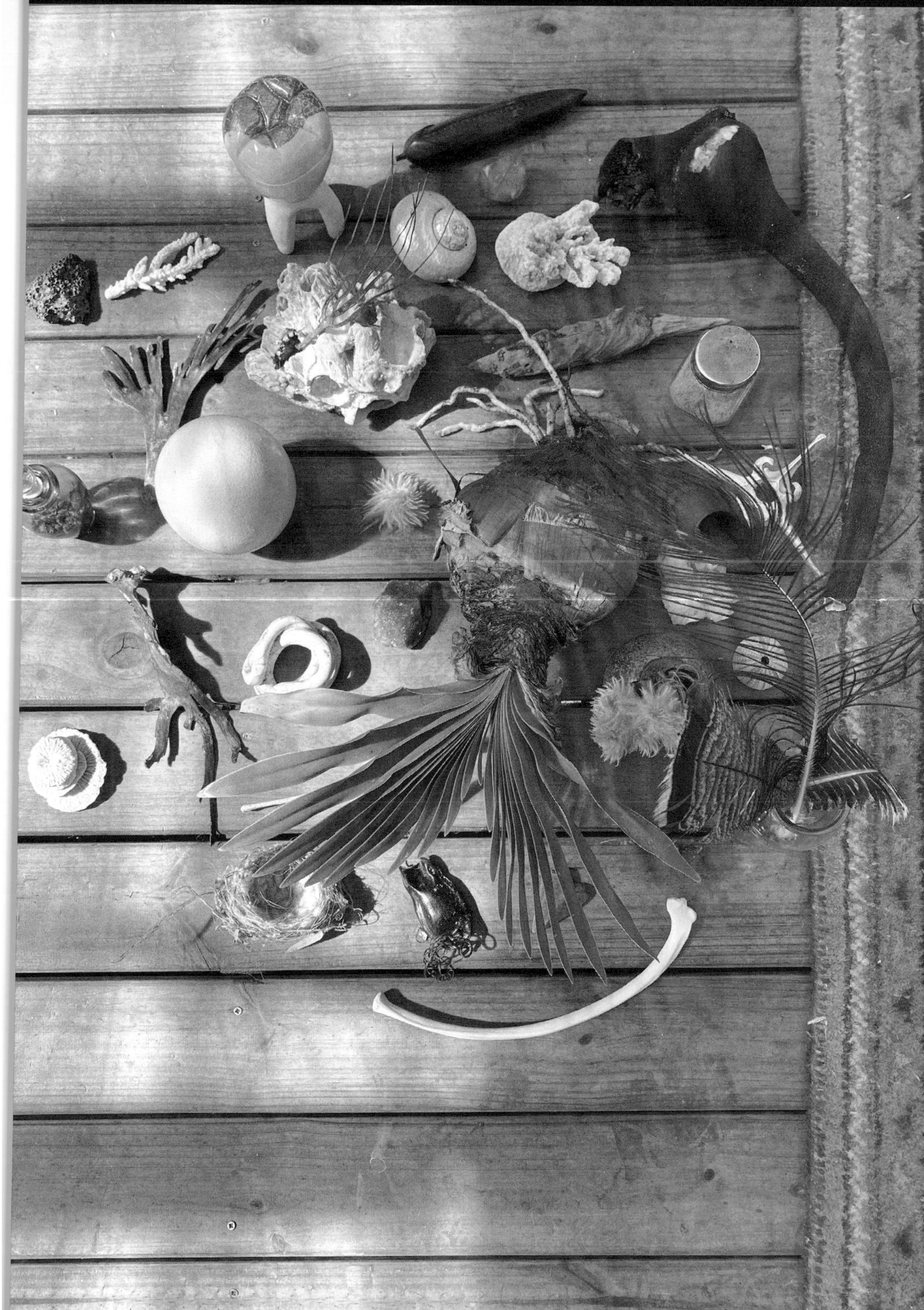

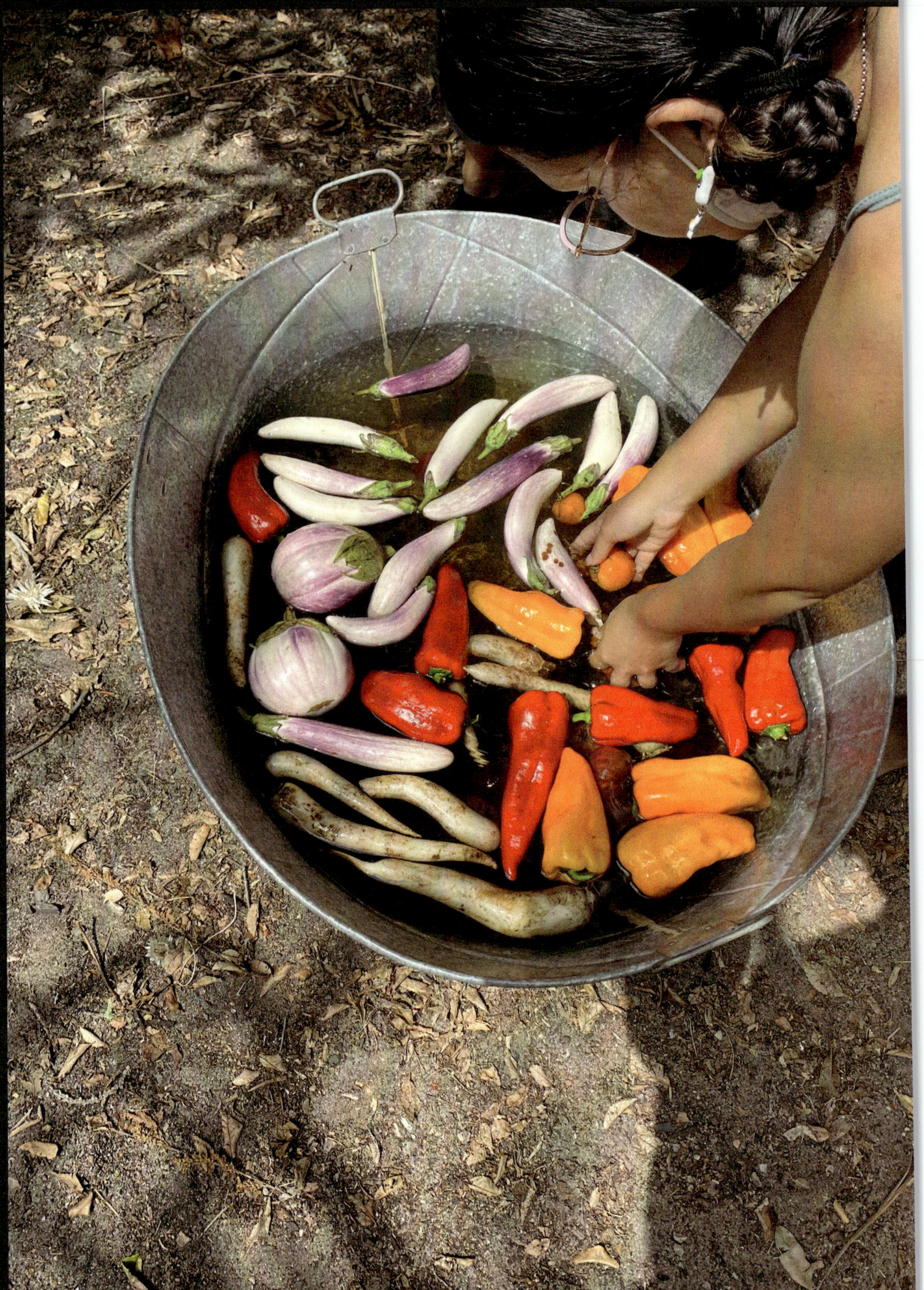

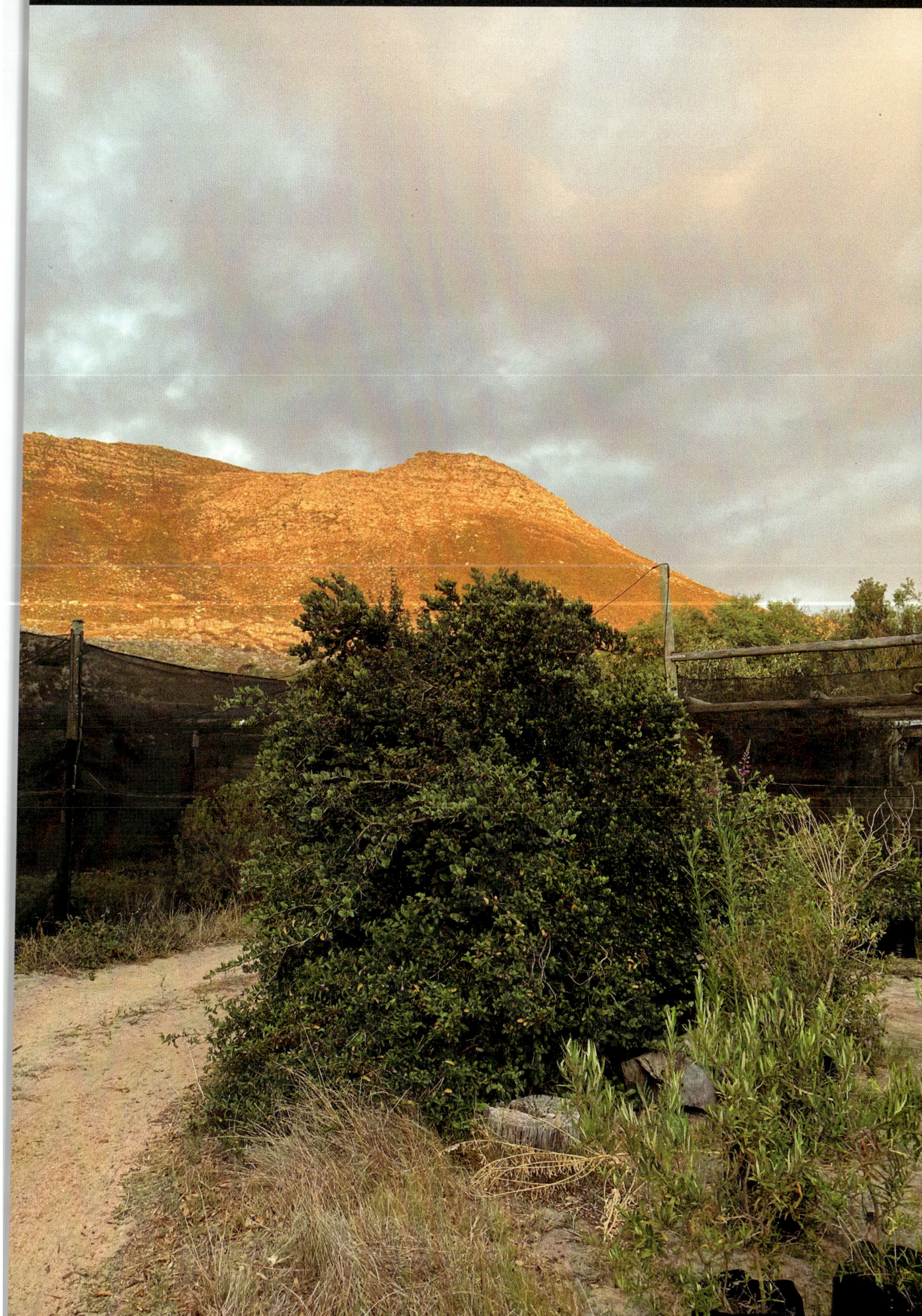

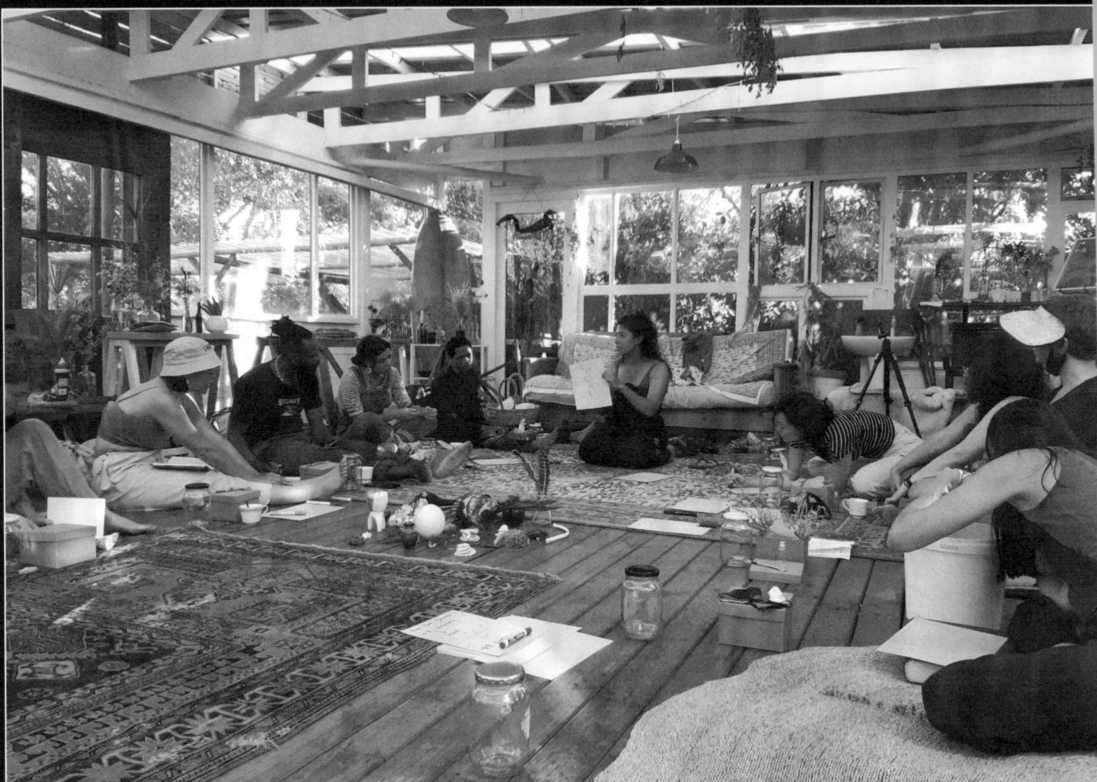

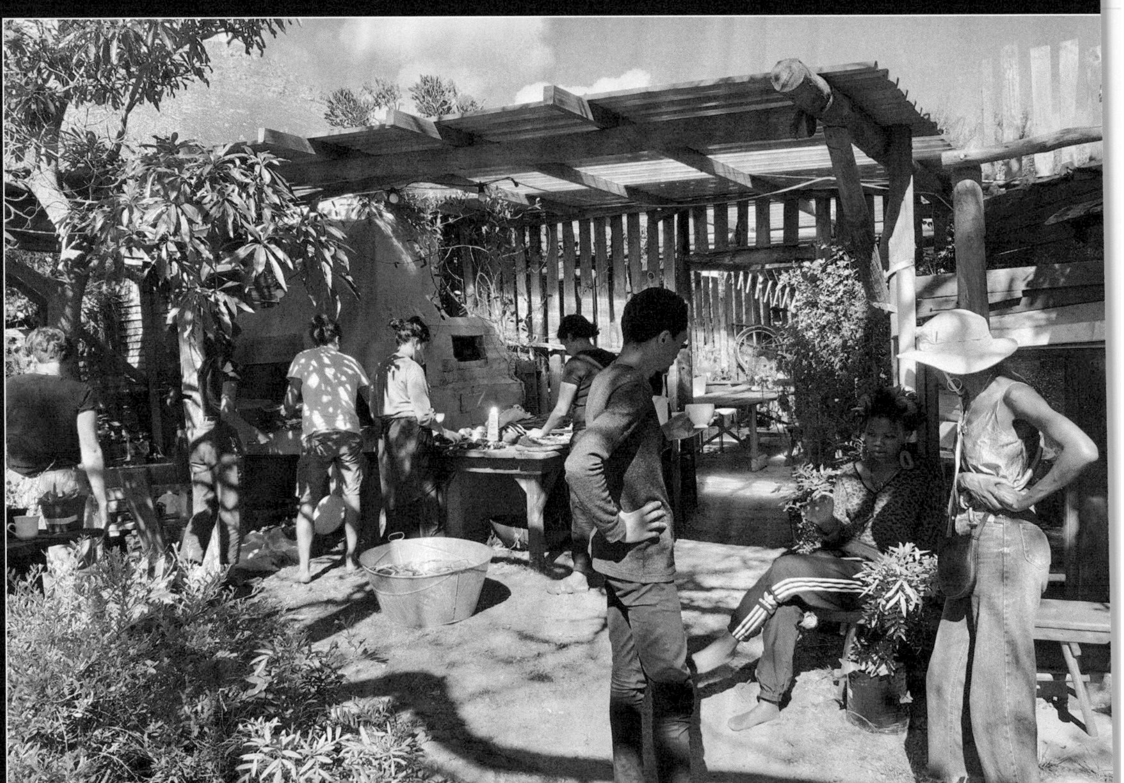

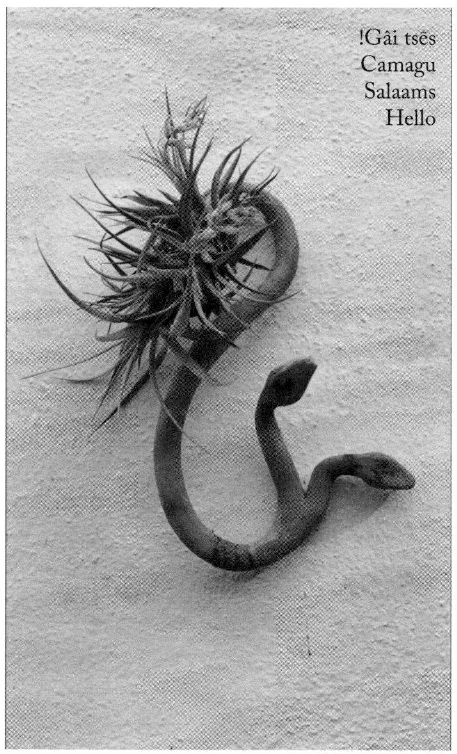

Welcome to
this
Training of
the Ancient
Future

Held by
Zayaan Khan

//Hui !Gaeb, Azania
Cape Town, South Africa

TRAINING FOR THE FUTURE

MY NAME IS……………………………………..

I AM FROM……………………………………

MY SUPERPOWER IS………………………...
……………………………………………………
……………………………………………………

I WISH MY SUPERPOWER WAS…………..
……………………………………………………
……………………………………………………

CONTENTS

With humble thanks to the trainees for their generosity.

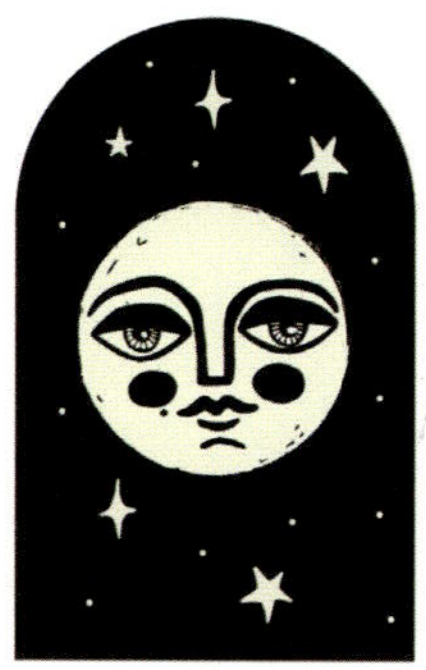

The Future, have you been there? Does it even exist? What a near and faraway place. Sometimes I remember time is infinite and there is time for everything that needs time. Other times I remember there is no time left.

Time is constructed through so many ways of knowing and being, measurements of moments held and inherited. Sometimes time is a circle, no beginning and no end, moving in a still way or moving constantly; sometimes passive, also active and of course passiveactive. Passiveactive can be stretchy like a blanket – this way works best when thinking about big space and deep time.

I have never met anyone who doesn't accept time. Every existence that cycles through existing abides by this continuum – water, dassies, seeds, salt, mountains, artificial intelligence, laws, buckets, microphones, even the first stars to ever exist.

Welcome to the Ancient Futures, our aim is to try make sense of the things we lost along the way like belonging, identity, our necessity to grieve and our knowings. Life may teach us that knowledge comes from the land and we understand the land to be everything the land holds including the seas, the soils, the plants, us and all the things at the edge of sight, like bacteria, mycelium and zooplankton.

The land is alive, as we are alive, as water is alive. The life/lives of the land have lived through a few billion years of being. The last hundreds of years have resulted in a lot of trauma and suffering.[1] This is buried in the land and the land is unable to process and release this trauma in the way it needs to. Metabolic processes are disrupted by intensive extractive methodologies of agriculture, mining, construction, wars, fracking, forced

[1] When things tense to this pressure of trauma, individuals and certain spaces becomes vessels of traumatic release. Feeling the trauma is a way to manifest its release, to grieve becomes release, moments of recognition held in the mourning, building a narrative of release which in turn creates more space for the potential of love/s. This is fine work, blade thin, as too much trauma and grieving of ancient pains may debilitate you.

removals, pollution and ecocides (the genocides of animals, peoples, insects, plants and bacteria).

We welcome you to grow your own superpowers, to dance around our ways of keeping time, of sun or moon or stars or space orbits. We could even measure time by heartbeats, of which each one is very different.

We trust you have many questions and so do we.

One question that comes up time and time again involves the concept of time management – the anxieties and stresses that arise when we feel as though we are 'running out of time.' I'd like to share with you some ways to perhaps overcome this feeling of being overwhelmed. To do this we need to trust our imagination and to be able to suspend belief and the rigid construction of conformed knowledge that is TIME.

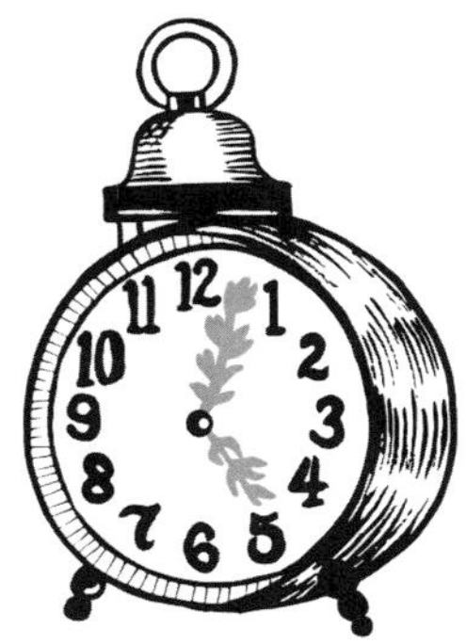

Here it helps to make yourself a cup of steaming hot thyme tea every morning. Use this as a daily reminder that time is a construct. Thyme is a great ally to build resistance in spaces we may feel weak, thyme traditionally is used to encourage a sense of courage – the root word of *Thymus vulgaris* is Greek for 'courage.' And of course when we suspend belief we make more space for magic and thyme can help us uncover time, reroute time, stretch time and shrink time. Making thyme for time and time for thyme.

Let me now tell a short story about this landscape we have gathered in, a segue to give us some deep time context as to how we got here, how much has changed and how very much has stayed the same.

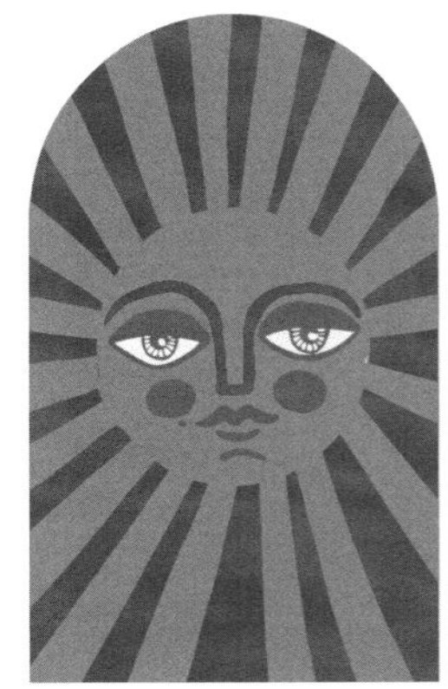

Illustrations by Amber Tak

Hoerikwaggo is the mountain that rises from the sea, especially if we look from Bloubergstrand, or Blue Mountain Beach, named, I assume, because from that vista point the mountain takes on a blue hue and looks as if it is rising from the sea.

This landscape has a rich history spanning from deep time and into antiquity, with the South West Cape being an origin of humanity and thus always a cosmopolitan place that has received countless visitors over the years.

Hoerikwaggo as a descriptive concept is also pertinent because we know that five million years ago this mountainscape was an island, with the feet of Hoerikwaggo dipping its toes into the cold ocean, with currents washing up from the icy south. So much life teems around these mountain feet, all the fish and all the algae, all the cephalopods and sea slugs, sea snails, urchins and limpets, lobsters and tubeworms, barnacles, mussels, birds, seals, penguins, dune vegetation, insects and all the animals that resided on this mountain island. This place is hyperdiverse, there is so much life that some of this life has the superpower of invisibility. Sometime later, the mountain emerged from the sea (or the sea retreated) and this same landscape on which we sit was reunited with the landscape of the African continental mass. Now more animals and insects and bacteria and peoples (eventually) could move through this land on foot. The mountain has a special connection with the waters it rises out from. This mountain is a huge sponge that always has the sweetest water trickling out, even in the deepest of droughts the mountain has sweet water in abundance.

Place of sweet waters is an indigenous name given to these riverways and *Camissa* refers to the people who settled along the riverbanks. And this City? //Hui !Gaeb – the place where the clouds gather. This land has always been wealthy in water, healing for everyone who ventures through here.

This land is known as one of the most biodiverse of the whole world and its abundance of life is a reason why humanity has succeeded here for millennia. This land and sea are not only abundant but generous in their abundance, where survival is akin to thriving and joy is an accessible way of life.

In more recent colonial histories, these waters were also a pull for European settlement and encouraging a new style of agriculture that required ownership of land. Even though foreign visitors had journeyed here many times before this and people were able to trade, engage, communicate (despite language differences) and help each other, these new settler stories dominated many of the indigenous stories because of the written word and erasure of oral histories past. Dark days arrived and the enslavement and genocide of people, animals and the land ensued.

Fast forward a few hundred years and our inheritance has been forced through an economic narrative where our survivorship, once closely linked with land and sea, is now embedded in financialized systems.

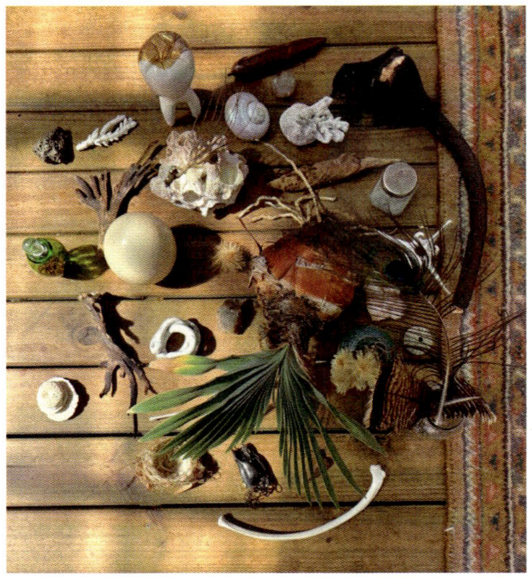

***Can it be that my own organs, thoughts and dreams have become entangled in the network of capital?
How could we unhinge ourselves from such a way of being to venture into a Future of delight and a deeper sense of knowing?***

Let us consider the sea as ***the original brine***, the saltwater goodness that allows our foods to thrive when we take them from an aerobic environment to an anaerobic environment (inside a jar). We can use seawater to ferment vegetables or fruits as it has a comfortable salt content (usually around 3.5%), but it must be specially (and easily) prepared.

Of course, the ocean is a complete saturation of everything that lives (and lives in different forms of life) in the deep time scale that the world is. Part of this saturation is the invisible zooplankton that are released by sea animals in their offerings of reproduction. This is important to consider if we are to use this seawater in a terrestrial ferment. Animal proteins that decompose on land have a very specific smell that may override our gentle aerobic nosebuds and may influence our ferments to go in a direction we do not want them to go (think über STANK!). It is also of utmost importance that the seawater we harvest is clean of any pollutants and away from large settlements or effluent that may flow into the sea.

HOW TO PREPARE SEAWATER FOR CULINARY USE:

1. Collect your seawater in buckets or bottles.
2. Place seawater on a rolling boil for three minutes (just wanting to kill any residual bacteria but also any plankton that may be within it) and let it cool so it is not dangerous to handle.
3. Sieve it through multiple layers of fine cloth or three coffee filters to rid of any microparticles we do not want, most especially sand.
4. Let this water cool thoroughly and it is ready to ferment with!

Please don't forget to taste this water though, as we are talking about the saltiness of the Atlantic or Pacific or Indian, not the high salt content of other seas like the Aegean Sea or the Salt Lake currently known as the Dead Sea. The seas around the south of here are roughly 3.5% salt to water.

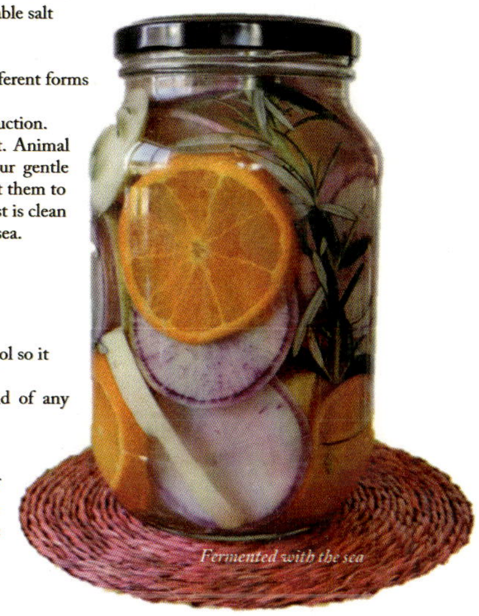

Fermented with the sea

The planet had a vastly different gaseous reality back in the days of roughly four billion years ago. The gases precipitated and created one vast ocean littered with continental islands. This ocean became saline as the earth's mineral salts saturated the future seas.

This salty waterscape became the first environment for life to burst into photosynthetic possibility through cyanobacteria that could convert sunlight into food, release oxygen, reproduce, thrive and die. Fast forward a couple billion years and here we are exploring, breathing, reproducing, consuming, dying; as if our bacterial inheritance laid out the blueprint.

And if we consider ourselves: there is much of us that is

water

salts

bacteria

Enough so that we may even consider these our ancient ancestors, rolled up in us and we cannot live without them.

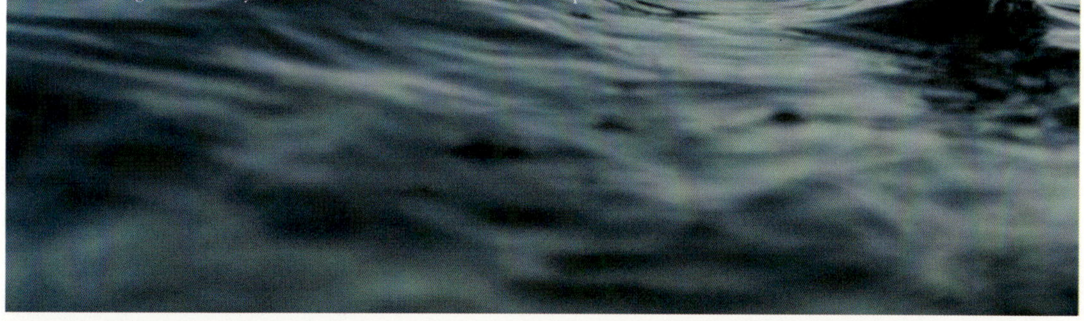

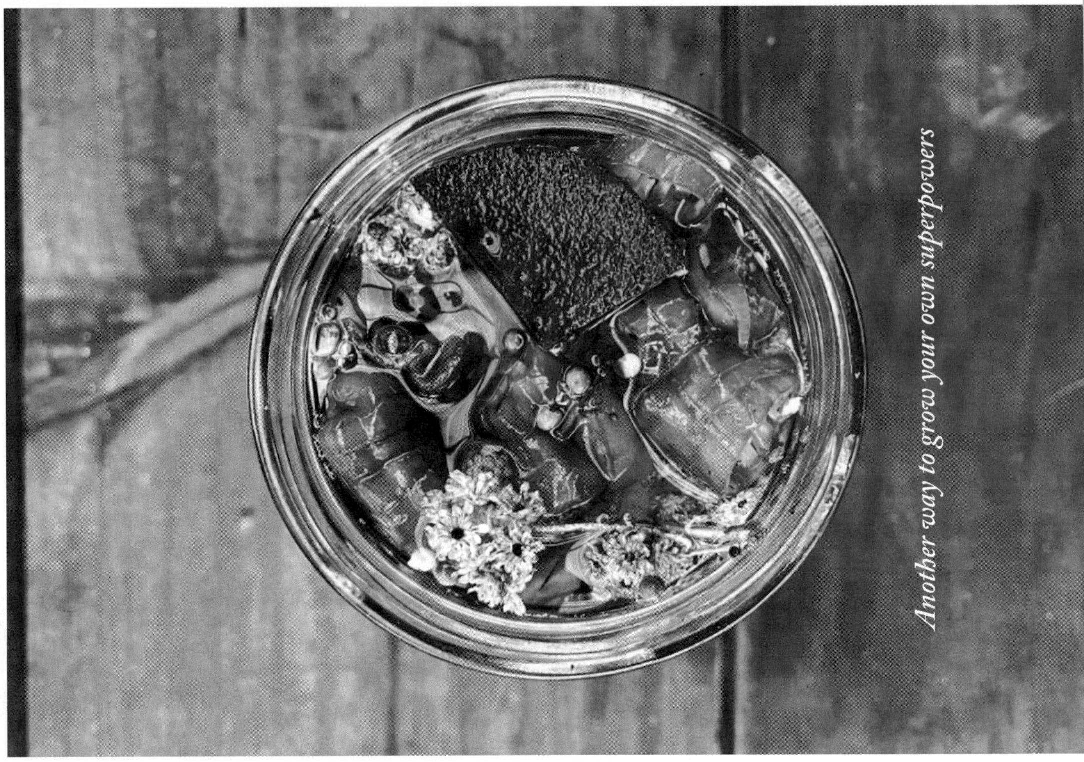

HOW TO FERMENT:

Fermentation is an enigmatic force. By simply creating the right environmental conditions you are transforming food in such a way that it is more alive than when you started. You are a custodian creating niche environments with seawater and produce, allowing microorganisms to proliferate. A simple gesture of salt and vegetables can create the most magical transformations.

1. Prepare your produce whether fruit or vegetable. Make sure it is clean and skin any areas that may be too bitter (like some carrot and beetroot skin as well as dense areas like the tops and bottoms).

2. Combine flavours you like. I like sweet and savoury so I like to add fruit to my vegetables, like pineapple or pear with cabbage or radish. Throw in some herbs and spices!

3. Cut the produce so it fits nicely into the jar and is easily removed with a fork when it is ready.

4. Fill your jar well so you utilise all the expensive real estate inside it.

5. Top up with your prepared seawater all the way to the top, and close tightly with your lid.

6. Place your jar in a shallow bowl or plate to catch any escaping brine as the contents bubble and ferment away.

7. Leave your jar in an obvious place so that you can keep an eye on it every day. Be sure to clean any overflow so it doesn't attract any fruit flies.

8. You know it's ready when it starts to change and show signs of life – smells may begin to waft, the clarity of the brine will fade and it will become cloudy, it will bubble and fizz and then you know the bacteria within are happy happy happy.

9. You are welcome to eat from it at any time, honestly, but best leave it without opening for at least a week to get that fermenty flavor funk. Let it ferment for a couple more weeks if you like, there's no right or wrong way here. The longer you leave it the more sour power you'll get (and a bigger microbial diversity).

10. Best to refrigerate once opened – it'll continue to ferment but just much slower.

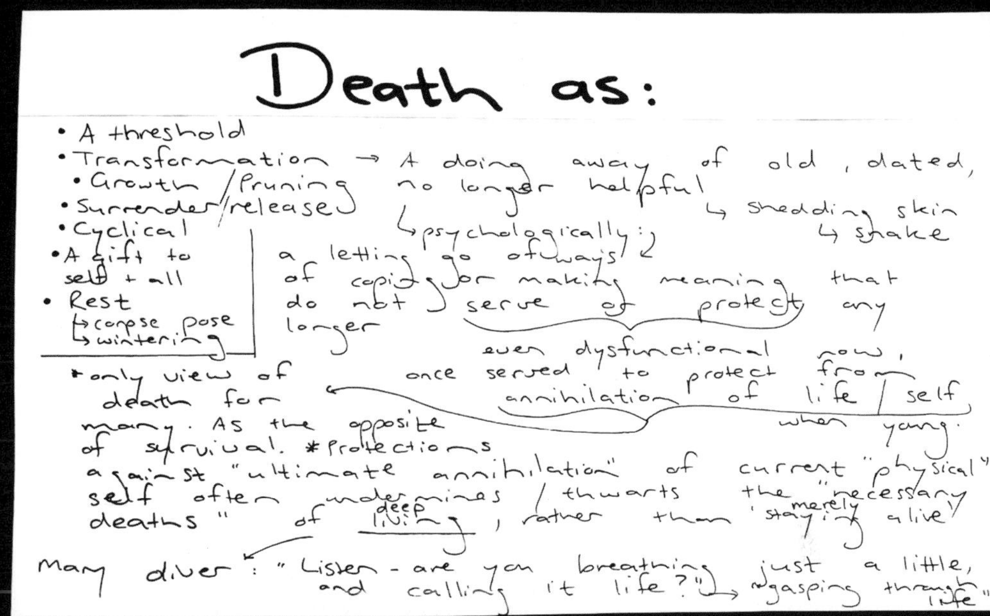

Death as:

- A threshold
- Transformation → A doing away of old, dated, no longer helpful ↳ shedding skin ↳ snake
- Growth / Pruning
- Surrender/release
  ↳ psychologically: a letting go of ways of coping or making meaning that do not serve or protect any longer
- Cyclical
- A gift to self + all
- Rest
  ↳ corpse pose
  ↳ wintering

even dysfunctional now, once served to protect from annihilation of life / self when young.

*only view of death for many. As the opposite of survival. *Protections against "ultimate annihilation" of current "physical" self often undermines / thwarts the "necessary deaths" of deep living, rather than merely 'staying alive'

Mary Oliver: "Listen - are you breathing just a little, and calling it life?" → "gasping through life"

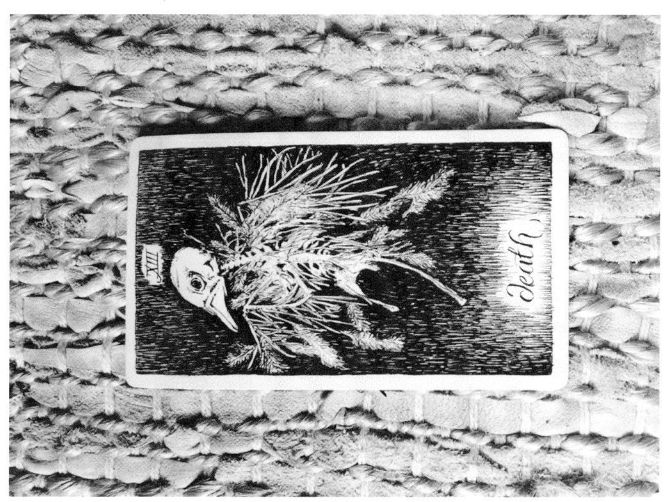

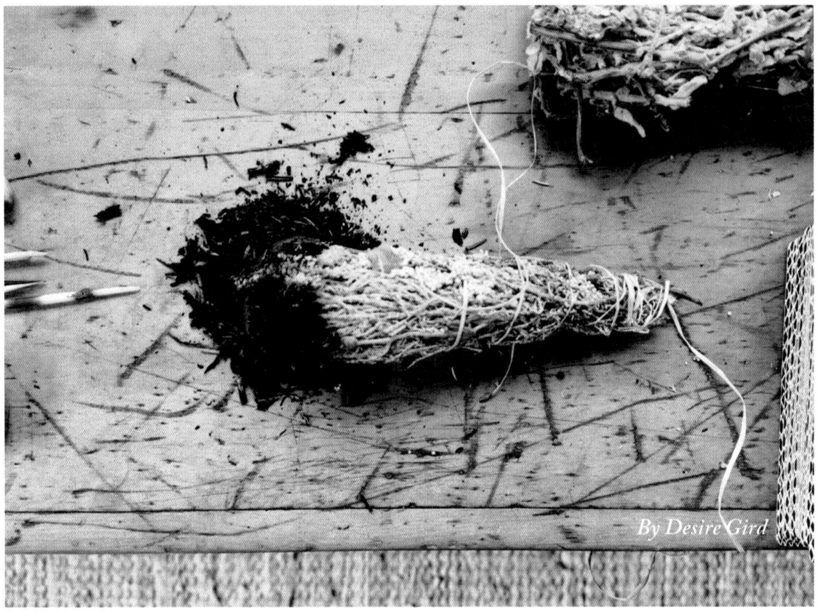

By Desire Gird

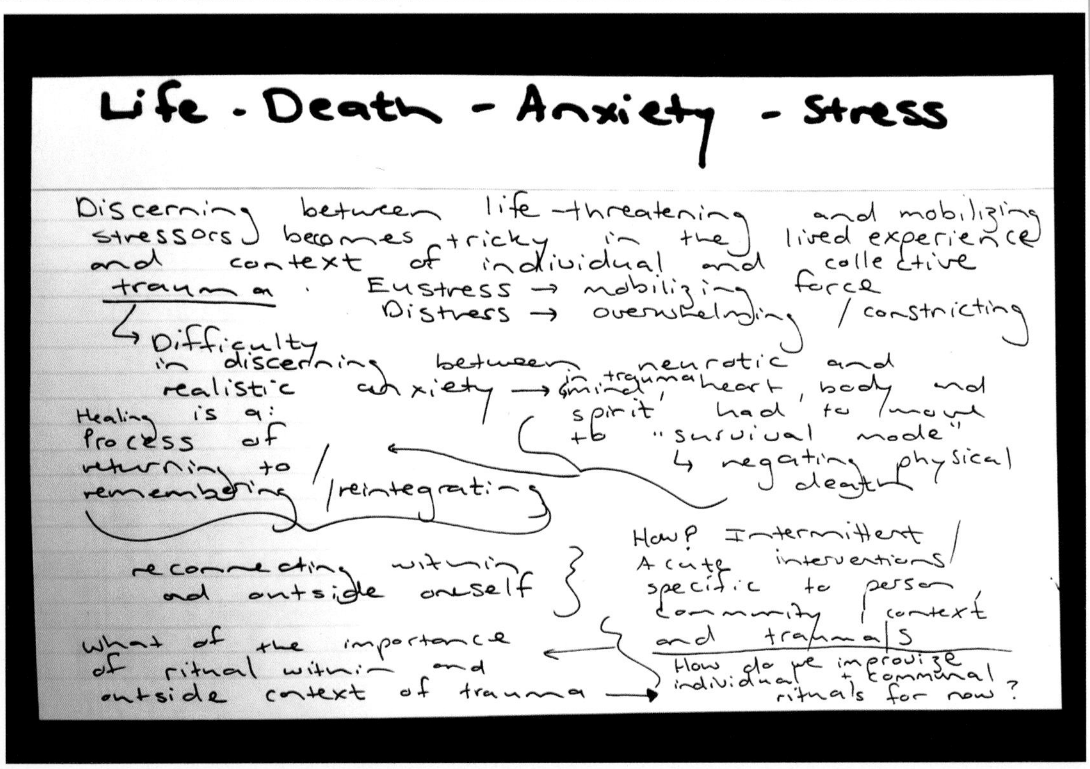

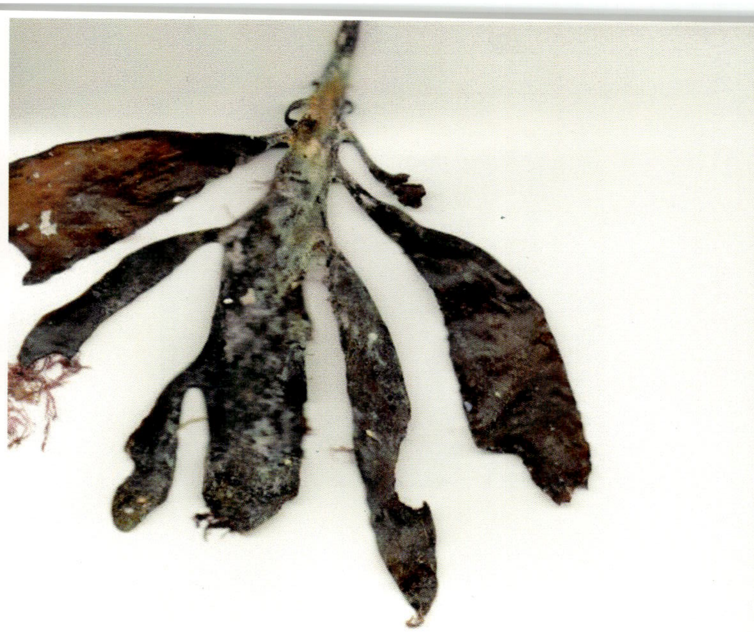

Getting to know everyone that lives around you may feel a daunting task, but don't worry, it just takes time. You may feel moved to learn the names of plants or algae or rocks in their Latin reckoning but it is not a must, this is just how things have been named for the past few hundred years and through a settler ideology. Naming is so important and while we do not negate or devalue the need for taxonomic status, we must pay respect for older and other classification (or non-classification) systems. Once you begin to learn everyone, you will learn who their community is too, the insects that depend on them, the animals, the waters, the people. Your eyes will begin to change too, they will see things in a new way, reaching for recipes or solutions for things that may ail you.

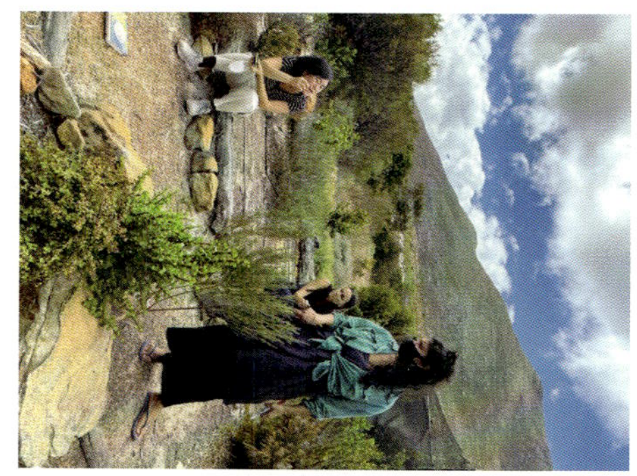

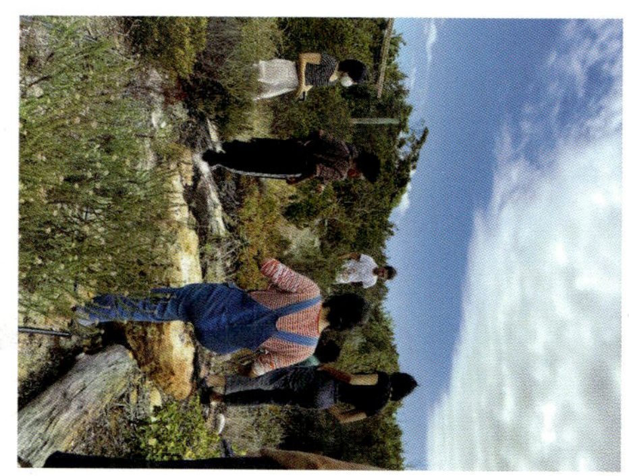

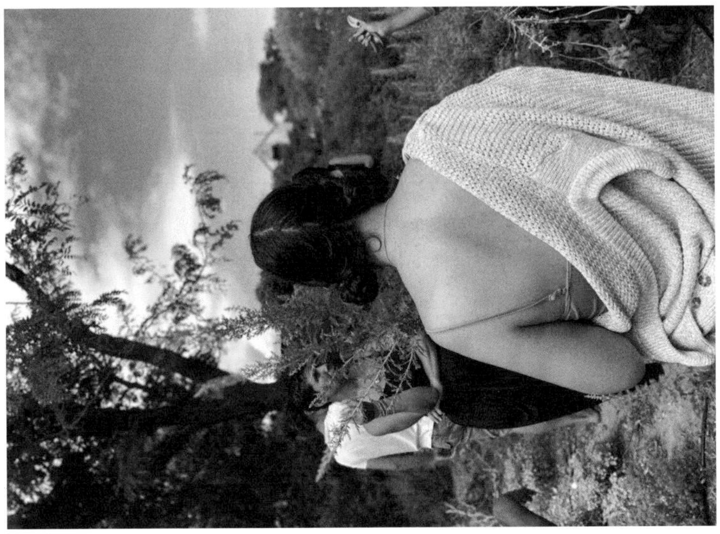

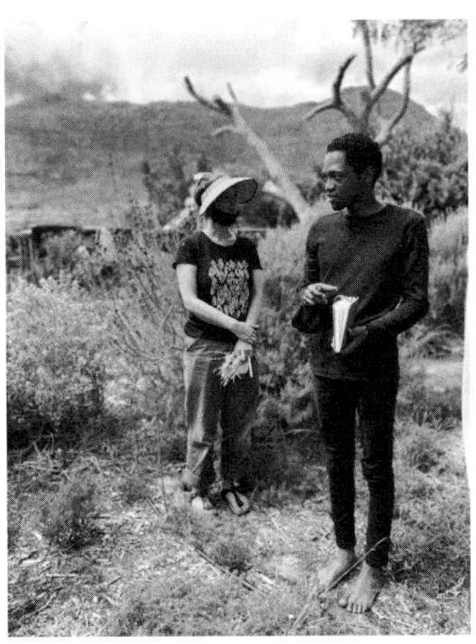

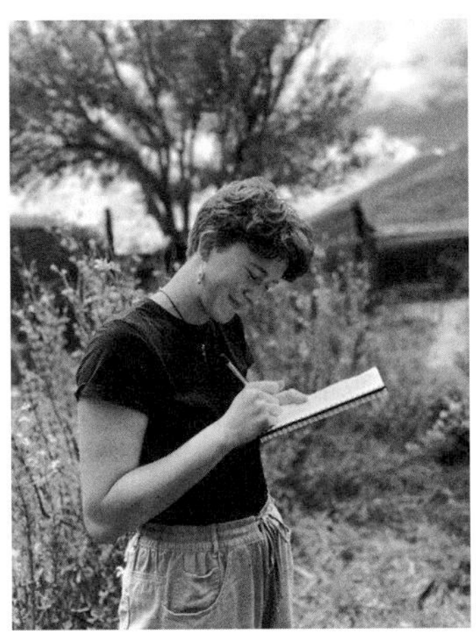

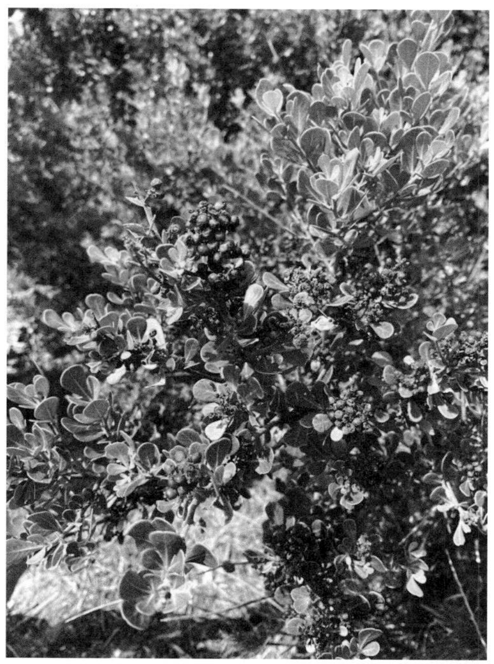

Images by Sara Lagardien Abdullah

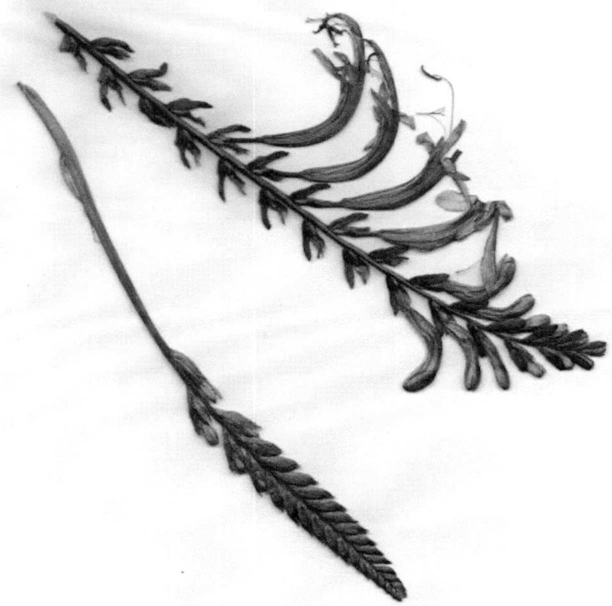

Learning plants means learning them throughout their seasons, as sometimes what you seek disappears completely outside of growing season. Here in the South West Cape growing season is wintertime. This might seem strange but of course this is when our rains come. Winter can be miraculous and a great time to pay attention to the bulbs that grow like potatoes around us. Learning to propagate them is also a future skill of custodianship. Learning plants means learning their parts too, their seeds and leaves and flowers and fruits and

OPEN-HANDED *(weaving time)*

Three words had been swirling around me after leaving your workshop on time and thyme: the generosity of land and nature, and being generous over generations.

Weaving is a form of journaling, a record of impressions, rhythms, thoughts and pattern flow in my heart and mind's eye. A meditation.

With love,
Sibabalwe

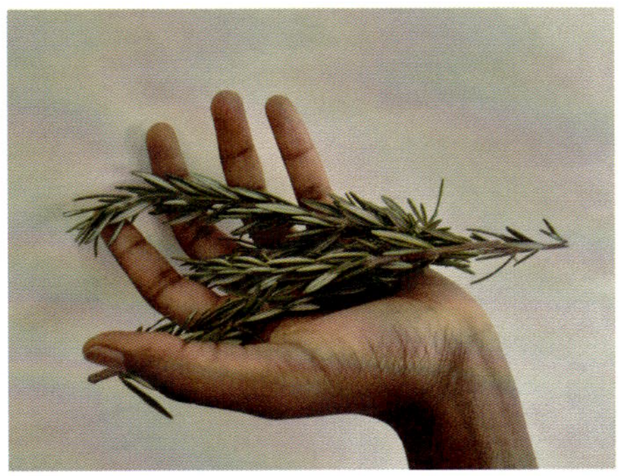

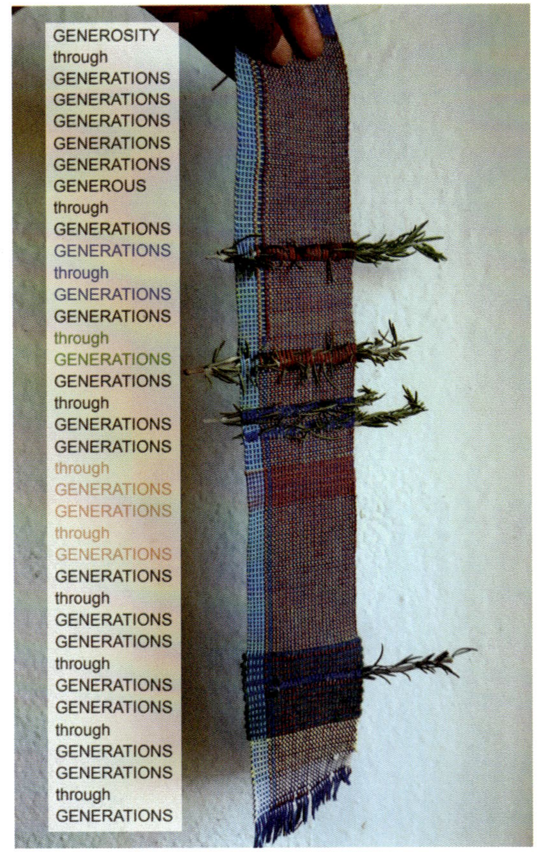

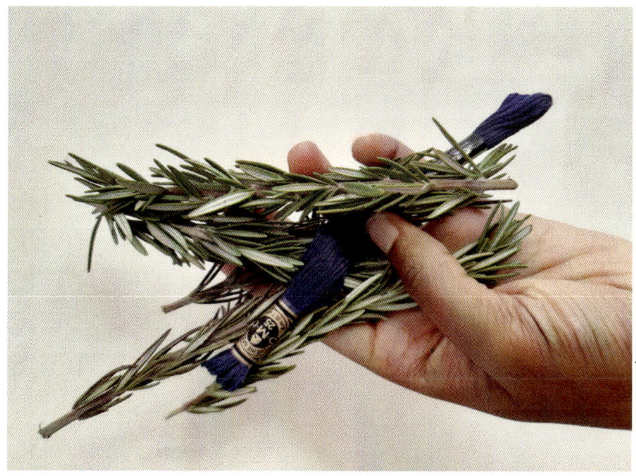

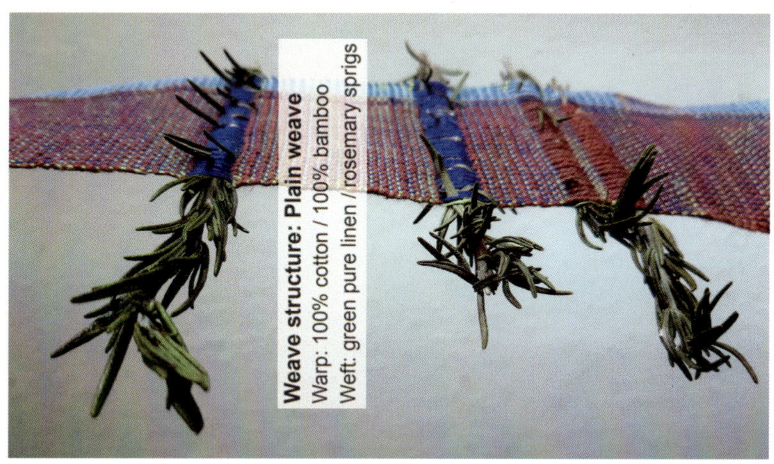
Weave structure: Plain weave
Warp: 100% cotton / 100% bamboo
Weft: green pure linen / rosemary sprigs

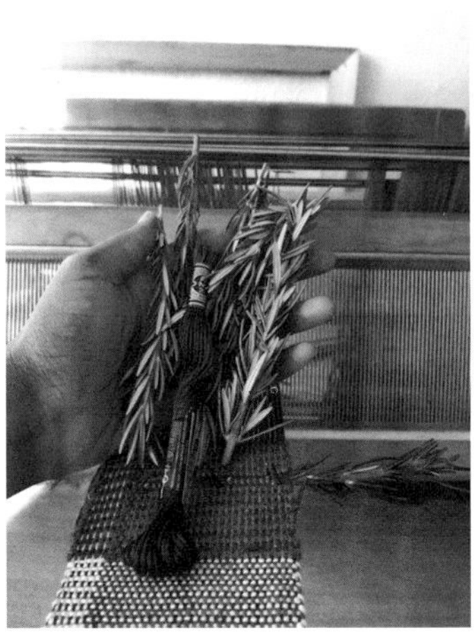

GENEROSITY
through
GENERATIONS
GENERATIONS
GENERATIONS
GENERATIONS
GENERATIONS
GENERATIONS
GENEROUS
through
GENERATIONS

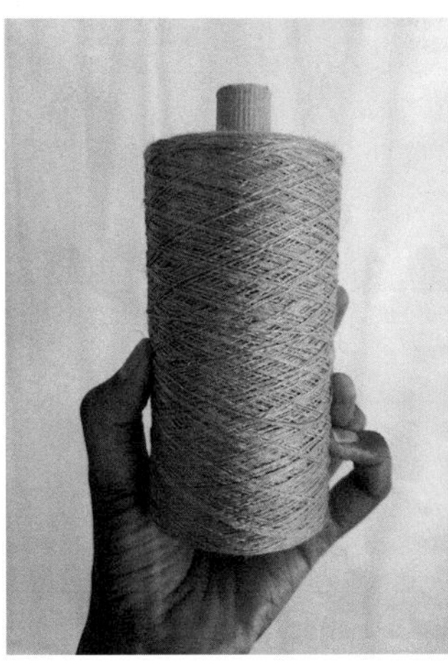

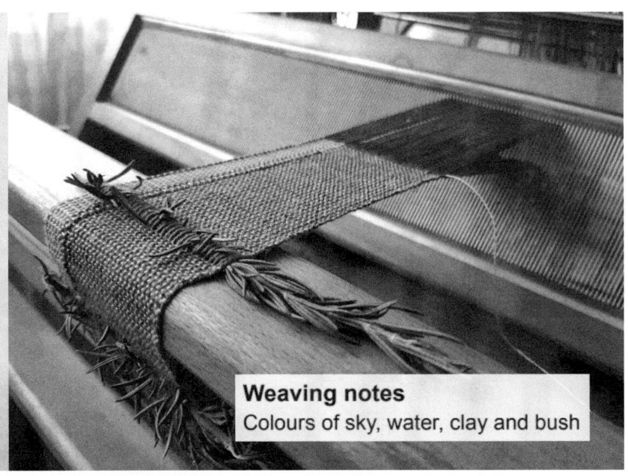

Weaving notes
Colours of sky, water, clay and bush

Definition of *generous*

1a : liberal in giving : openhanded a generous benefactor
b : marked by abundance or ample proportions wide overhangs and generous verandas— Lewis Mumford : copious a thin salt-and-pepper moustache interrupted by a generous nose— Richard Zabel
c : characterized by a noble or kindly spirit : magnanimous, kindly a generous heart
2 archaic : highborn

Definition of *generosity*

1a : the quality or fact of being generous a person of great generosity
b : a generous act
2 : abundance great generosity of spirit

Words woven by Sibabalwe Ndlwana

Merriam-Webster

Definition of *generation*
1a : a body of living beings constituting a single step in the line of descent from an ancestor
b : a group of individuals born and living contemporaneously the younger generation
c : a group of individuals having contemporaneously a status (such as that of students in a school) which each one holds only for a limited period
d : a type or class of objects usually developed from an earlier type first of the … new generation of powerful supersonic fighters— Kenneth Koyen
2a : the action or process of producing offspring : procreation
b : the process of coming or bringing into being generation of income
c : origination by a generating process : production especially : formation of a geometric figure by motion of another
3 : the average span of time between the birth of parents and that of their offspring

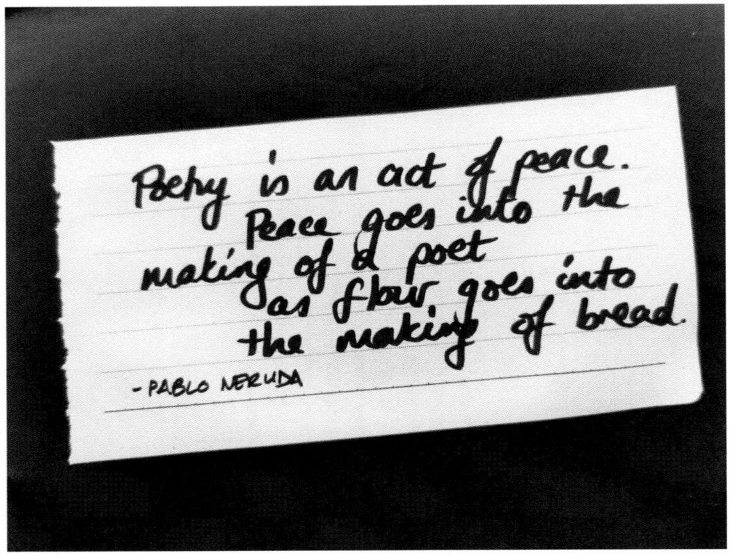

No booksellers, no books
No books, no learning
No learning, no knowledge
No knowledge, no wisdom
No wisdom, no ethics
No ethics, no conscience
No conscience, no community
No community, no bread.
— The Talmud

Bread baking is in my blood. It's one of those traditions that need to be passed down and passed on and shared. Sourdough is a collecting and a digesting and a gathering, and there are so many factors that will affect a bake: time, air temperature, the particular bacteria that live on the hands of the person mixing the dough, and dare I say it, the mood that flows through those hands. Each bread is unique and beautiful, and *each bread is a lesson.*

Without going too deeply into the science of it, a sourdough starter is a mixture of flour and water that invites wild yeasts in the air *to gather and feed and multiply*, and is the original yeast used in baking bread, before commercial yeasts became popularized to speed up bread production in our ever-quickening production-driven world. It's a living thing and it needs care and feeding, but it's not high maintenance.

There are many intimidating recipes floating around, but below you'll find a very friendly, low input, high reward recipe for sourdough bread.

To start a starter:

A good starter takes about a week to establish, feeding it daily. To start, mix ½ cup of good water with ½ cup white bread flour (I like to use an unbleached stoneground flour, but use what you have access to), and, if you have some handy, a teaspoon of good raw honey. I use a 1L glass jar, and I don't close the lid fully, because the yeasts in the air need an entry-point into the flour-water mixture.

For the next week, feed the starter ¼ cup water and ¼ flour daily, and mix well each time. If your jar is getting too full, you can pour out some of your starter to make room for the fresh flour and water.

Smell your starter and get familiar with how it changes as the week goes on. It will start smelling sweetly sour, a bit like beer, and it will start bubbling and growing.

Once it is established, you can start baking with it. If your first bake isn't too successful, don't give up. Sometimes your starter just needs a bit longer to establish more strongly, but the more you bake, the more active and strong your starter will become.

Maintaining your starter:

I normally keep my starter in the fridge when I am not baking. This slows down the fermentation, and lowers the active maintenance that you have to do. I'll take my starter out of the fridge and feed it about two hours before I bake, but that will also depend on outside temperature and how active my starter is at the time. If I haven't baked in a while, I might take it out and feed it a little bit, and then do a second feeding in a few hours time.

I'll feed it between ¼ and 1 cup of each flour and water, depending on how much I will be baking.

If you're not baking often, try and feed your starter at least once a week, and you can just feed it and then put it back in the fridge.

A Basic Medium Loaf of Sourdough Bread:

2 cups water
1/3 cup active starter
2 tsp salt
4 cups bread flour
(you can use straight white bread flour, or mix it with brown bread flour and/or rye flour)

Mix the water and the starter together until the starter has dissolved. Add in the salt and mix that up. Add the flour and mix until it's all incorporated, and there are no dry bits of flour left. I mix with my hands, but you can use a wooden spoon or any favorite utensil. This dough will be very sticky, but as it ferments it will become more manageable.

Cover your mixing bowl (I place mine inside a plastic bag and tie a knot) and leave it to ferment for 8-12 hours. If it is cooler, your fermentation will take longer. Sometimes in the heat of summer it could take as little as 6 hours. If you want to extend your fermentation time, you can leave your mixing bowl in the fridge, and take it out to ferment at ambient temperature for about 6 hours before shaping your loaf.

To shape your loaf, turn your dough onto a floured surface, and fold the sides into the centre in a sort of closed flower shape. I bake in a loaf tin, so I then roll the dough into a sausage shape and place it in an oiled tin with the seam side down. Leave the dough in its tin for 30 minutes to an hour, covered with a dishcloth.

Preheat your oven to 240-250°C. Once it is hot, place a small tray of water at the bottom of the oven to create steam. This helps make a good crust.

Score/cut the top of your loaf down the center and put it in the middle of your oven.

Bake for 45 minutes. Turn it out of the tin and tap on the bottom with your fingernails. If it sounds hollow, it's baked through. If not, put it back in the oven for a bit longer. Your crust should be beautifully browned.

When it's ready, remove it from the tin and leave it to cool on a wire rack. Allow it to cool for at least 45 minutes, as the inside is still baking as it cools. If you listen closely, you can hear the crust crackling as it cools down and contracts.

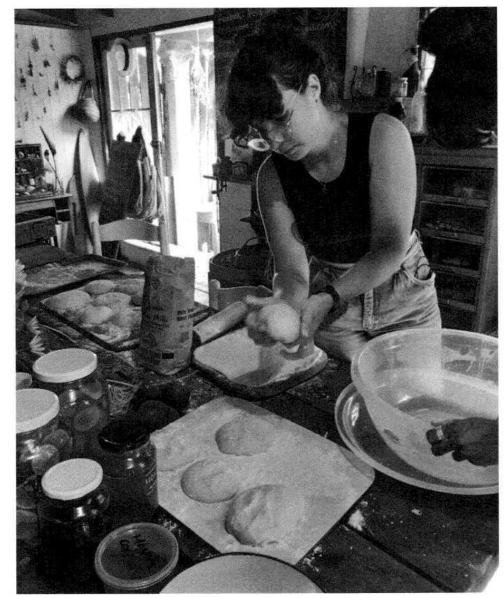

I find *there is a lot of intuition involved in baking bread*, and the more you bake, the more comfortable you become and the more adventurous you allow yourself to be. You *start listening to your dough*, and you might decide when mixing that on a certain day you need a little bit more flour or a little bit more water. *Your fluency in bread increases with every bake*, and sometimes it will surprise you and do something completely unexpected.

It's living and it sustains life. It is a vessel for other beautiful flavours. It is home.

With love,
Sivan

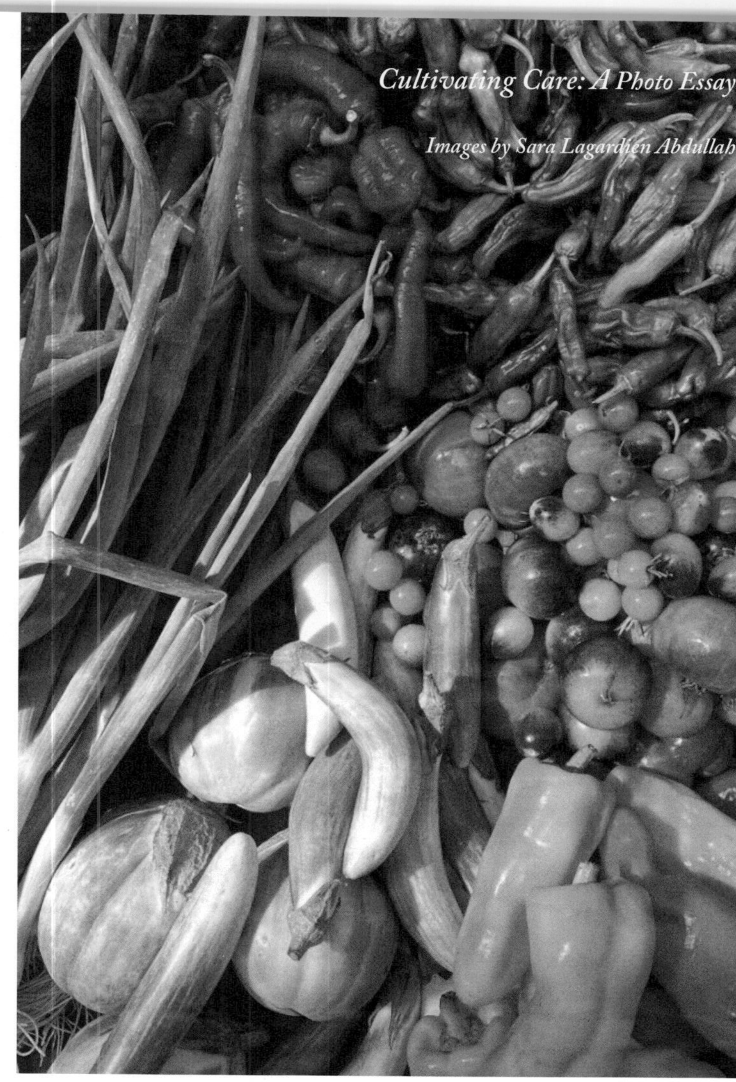

Cultivating Care: A Photo Essay

Images by Sara Lagardien Abdullah

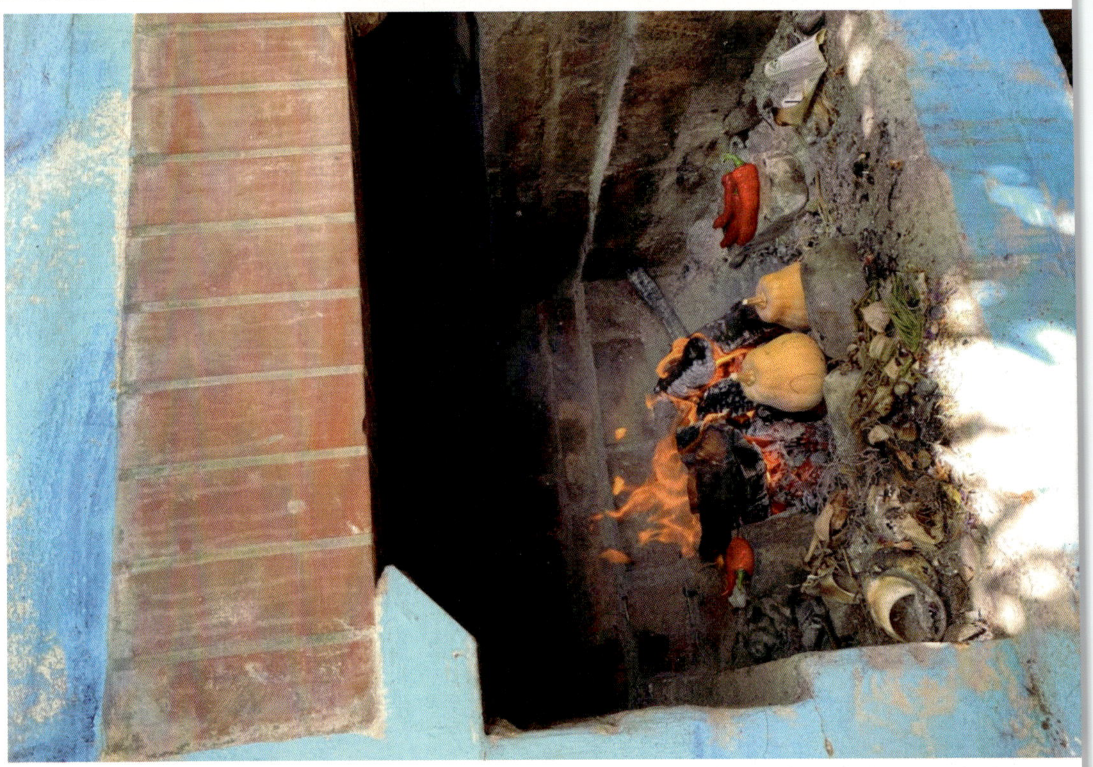

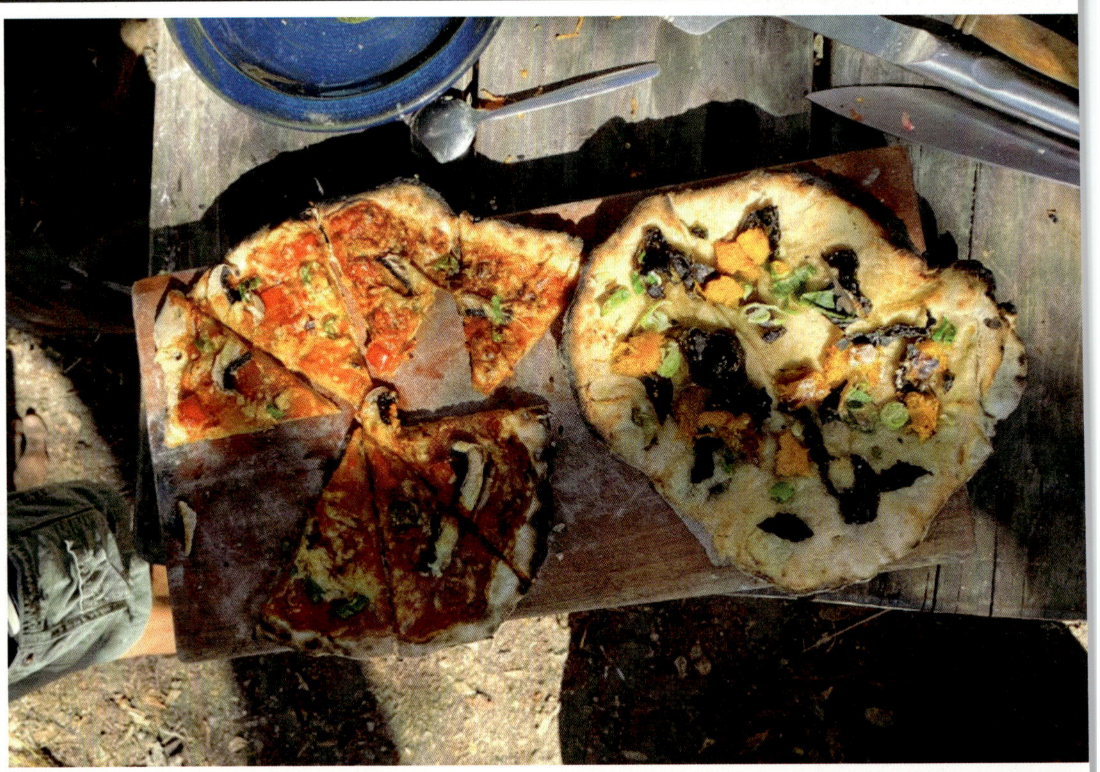

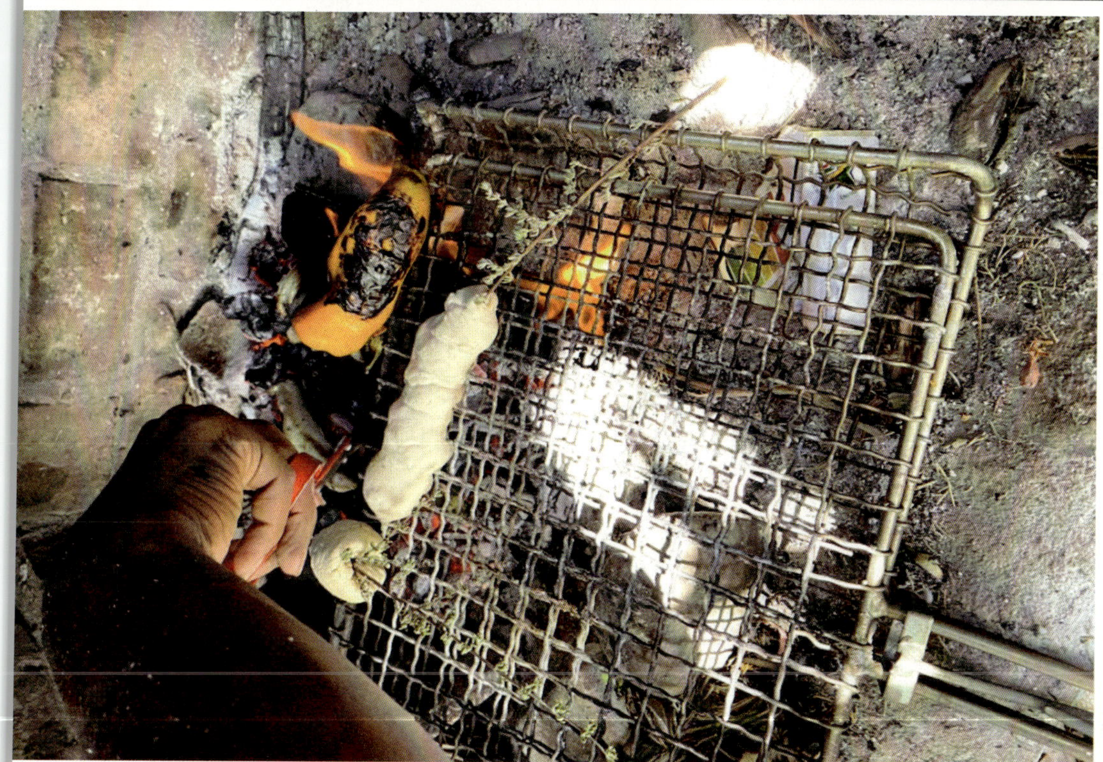

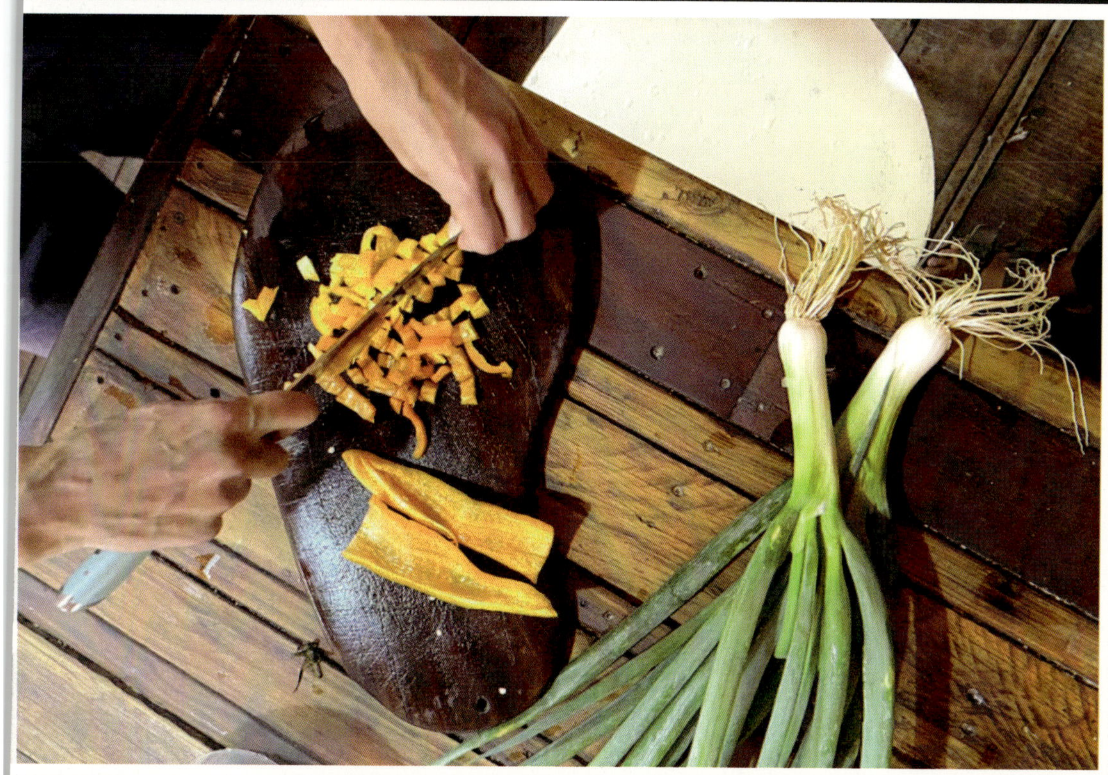

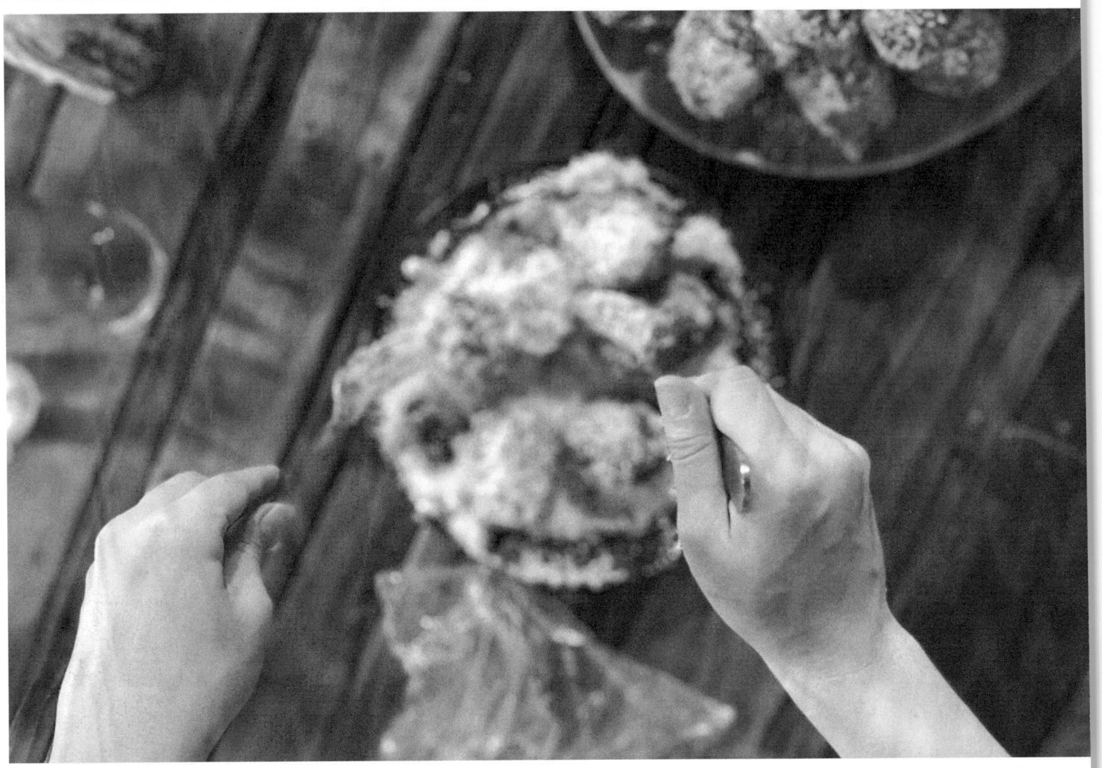

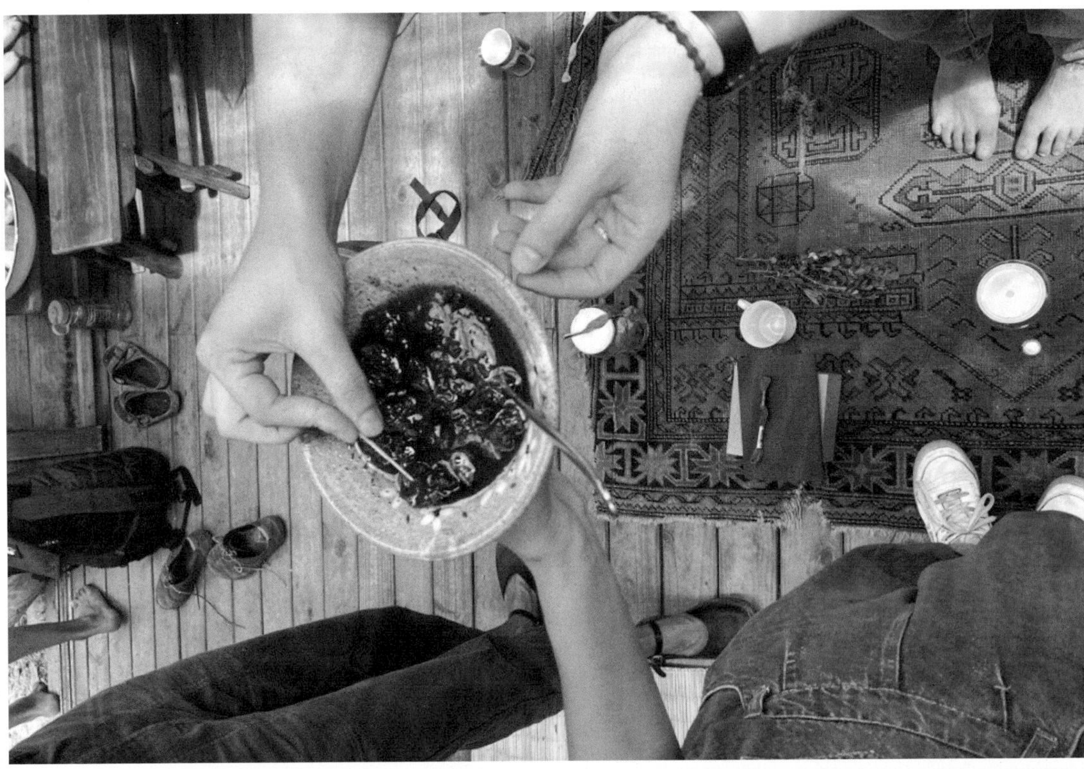

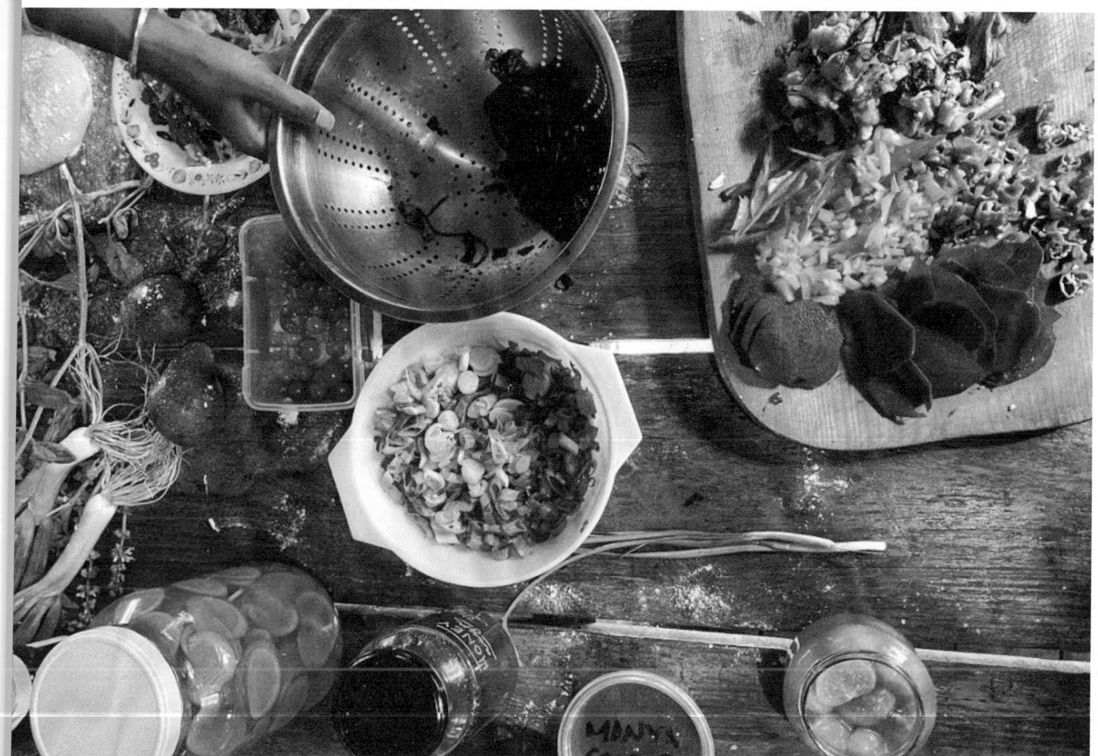

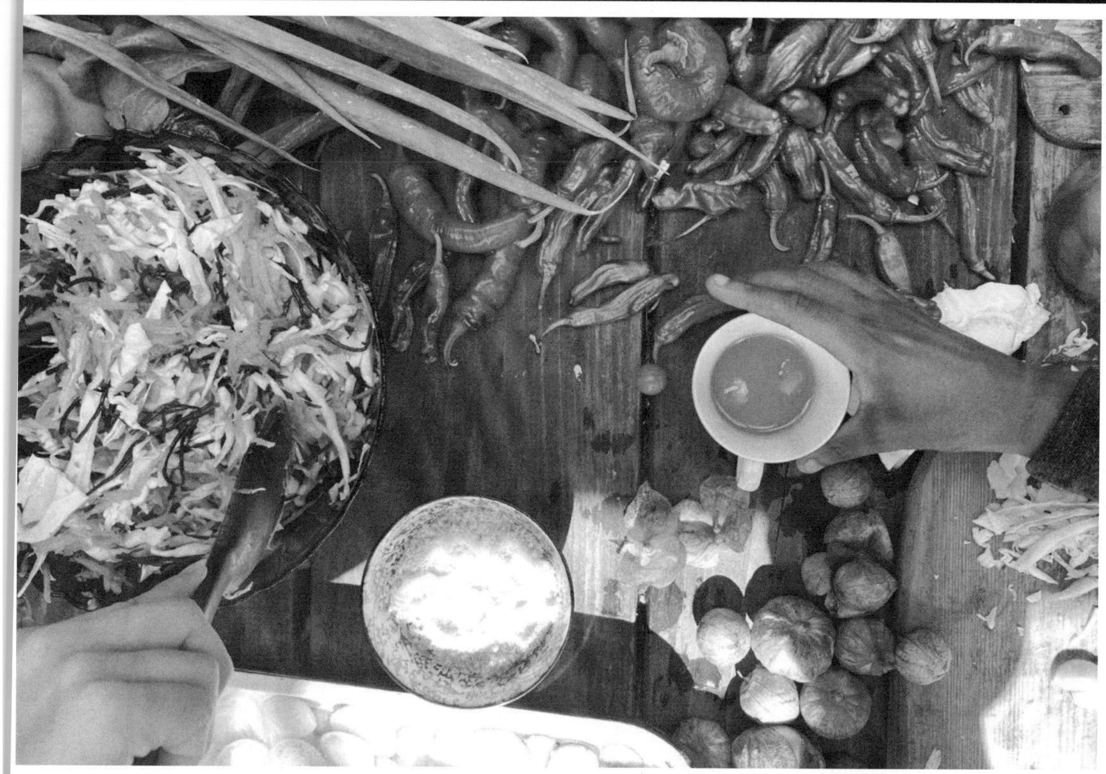

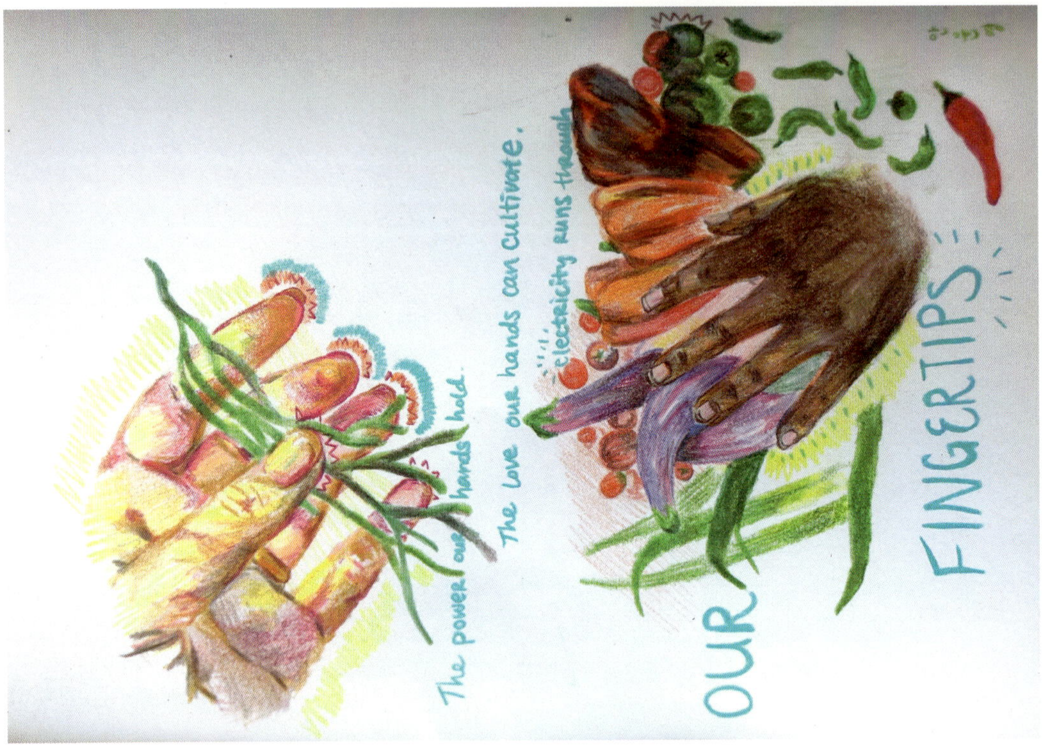
The power our hands hold.
The love our hands can cultivate.
electricity runs through
OUR FINGERTIPS

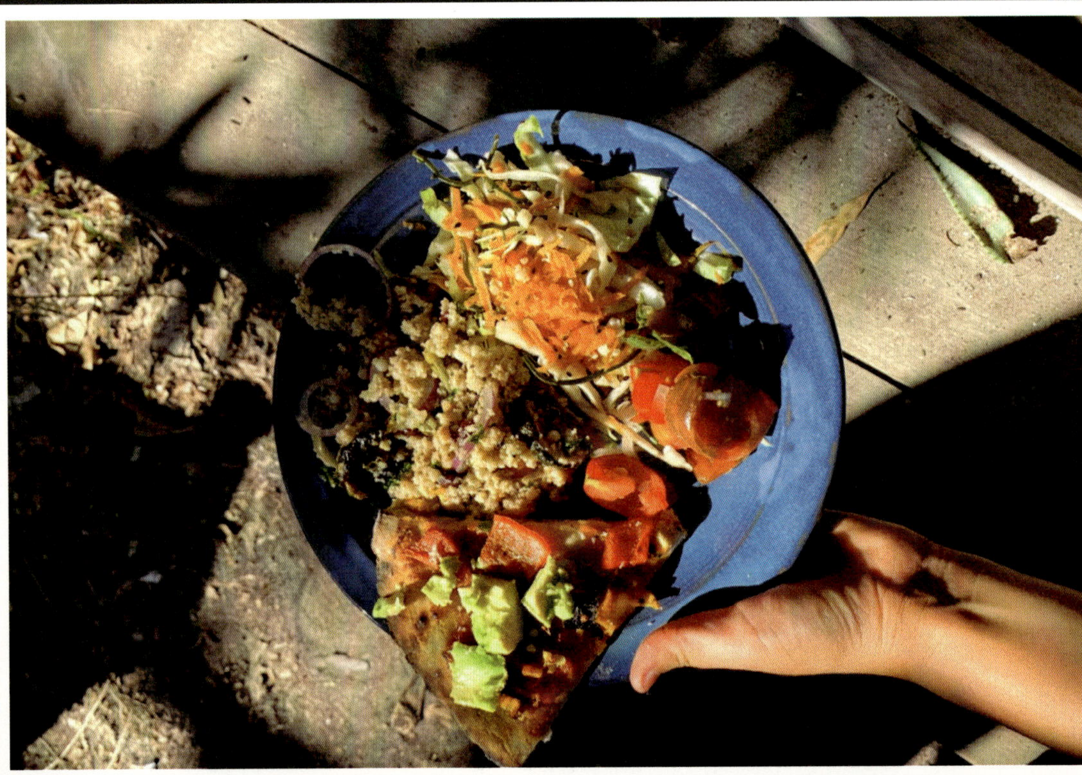

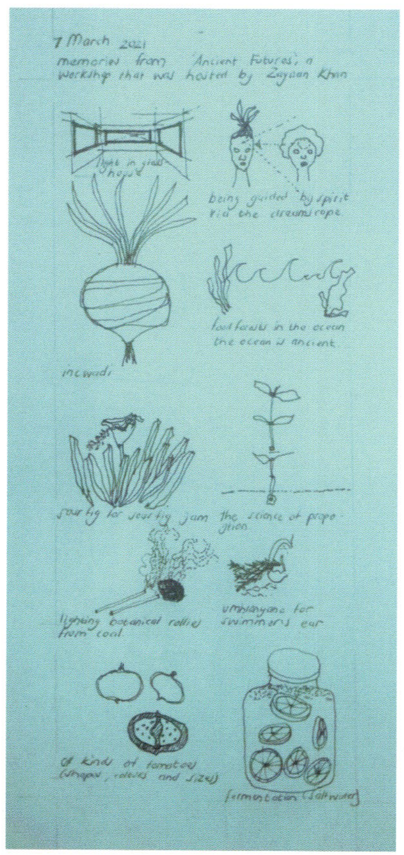

May the Future be an unfolding, generous place for us all.

My best,
Zayaan

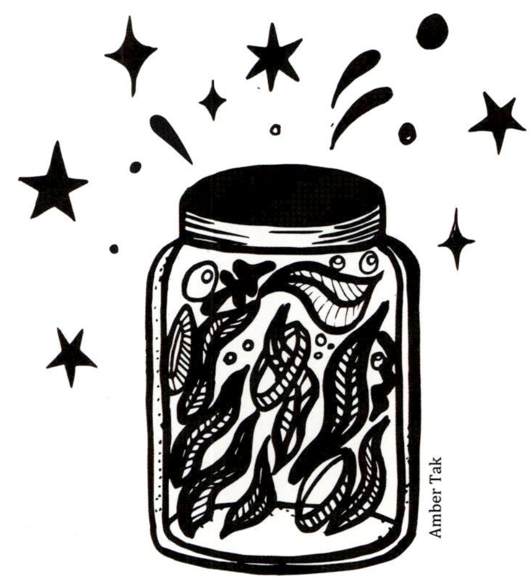

Amber Tak

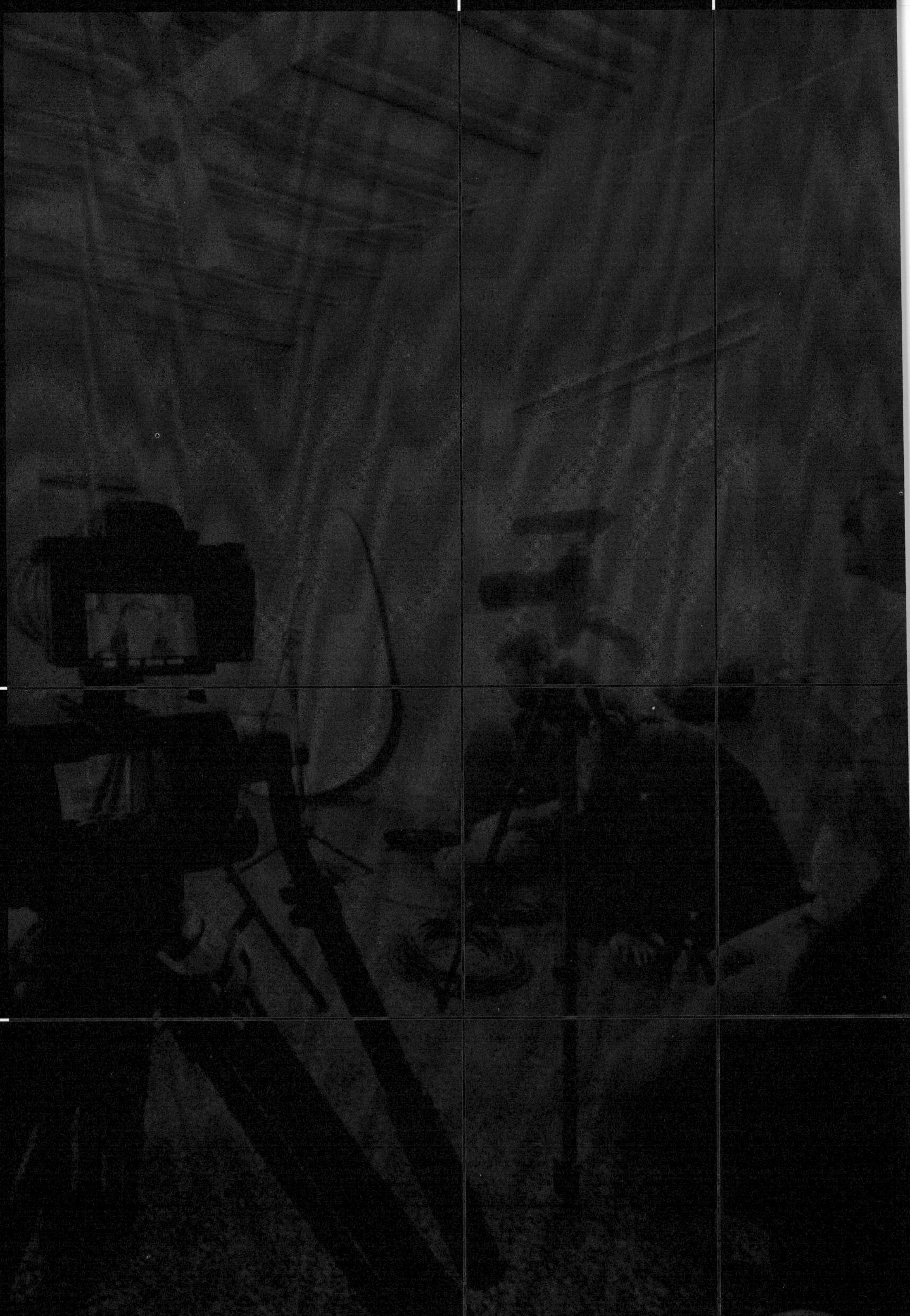

MARCH 6–APRIL 6, 2021, DÊRIK, ROJAVA

Communal Cinema of the Future-Past, Rojava Film Commune, Pargîn Chapter

In this month-long training, members of the Rojava Film Commune work with local communities in Rojava (Western Kurdistan/Northern Syria) to explore the role of cinema in reconstructing nomadic forms of stateless agriculture, language, music and poetry through film. Communal life forms of the past become possible models to communalize the future.

Rojava Film Commune is a cultural association founded in 2015 by local and international filmmakers under the umbrella of the Rojava Revolution. The commune creates and screens films, supports local filmmakers and trains new talents to return the culture of cinema to the region.

Visual documentation by Rojava Film Commune

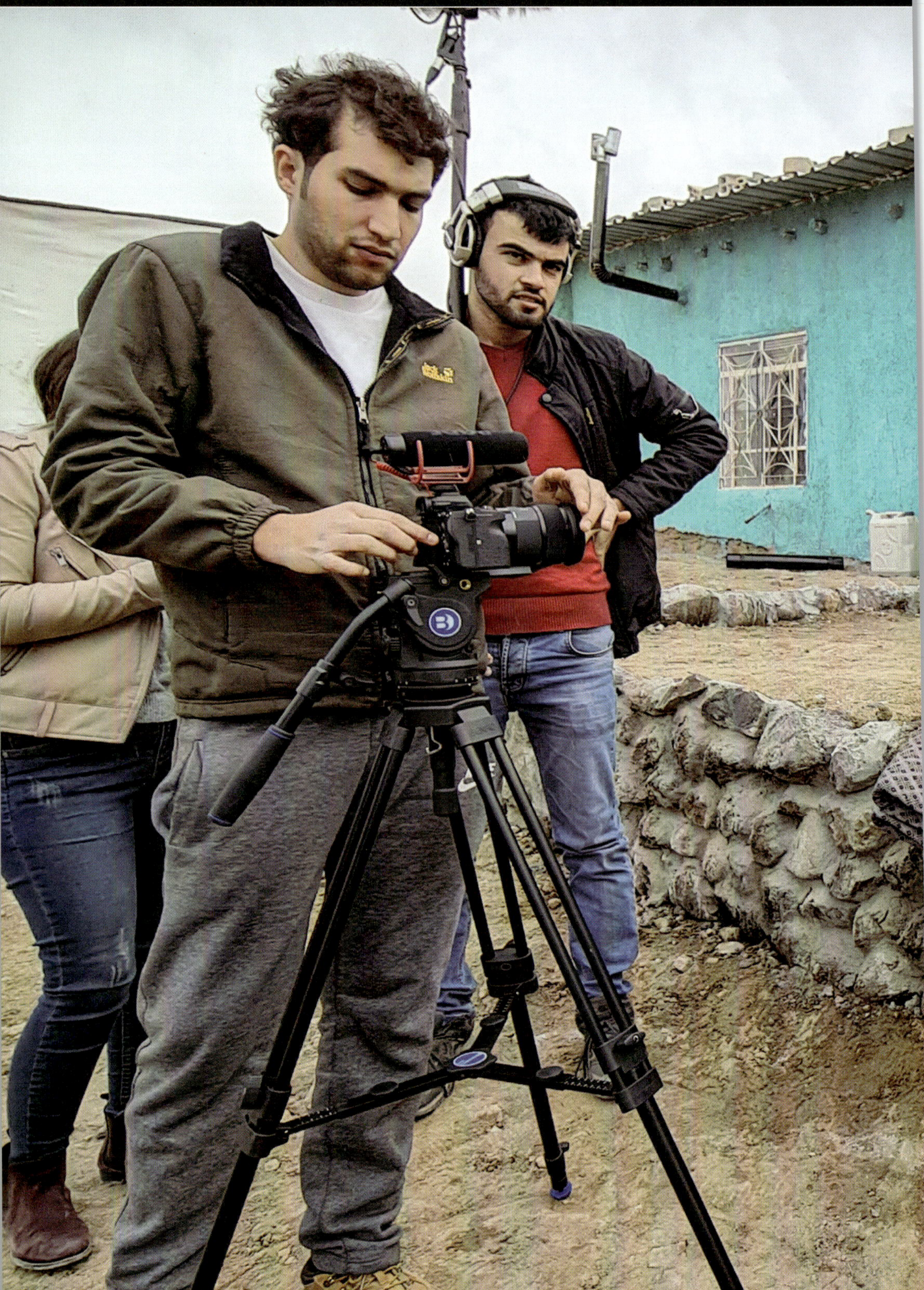

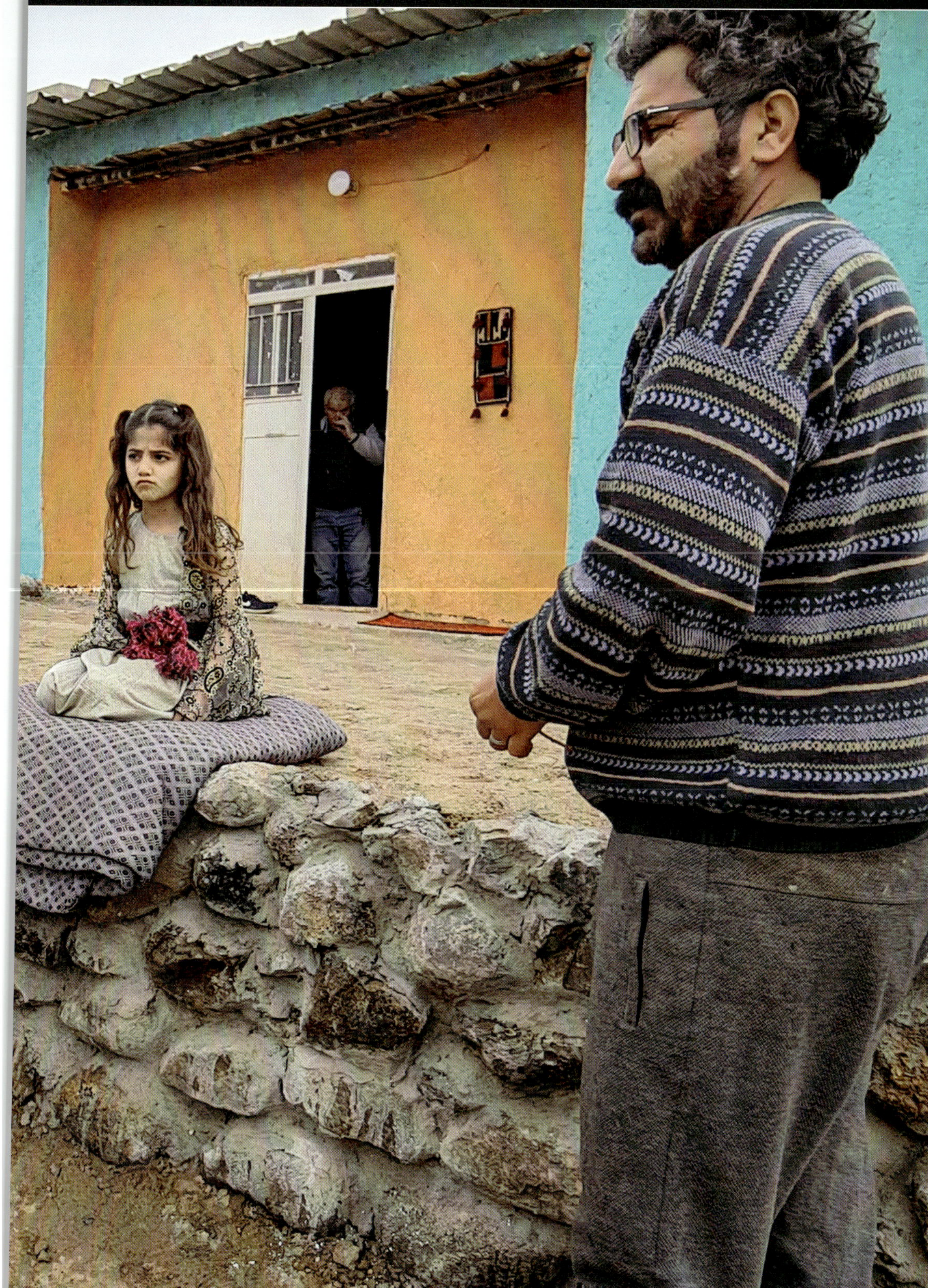

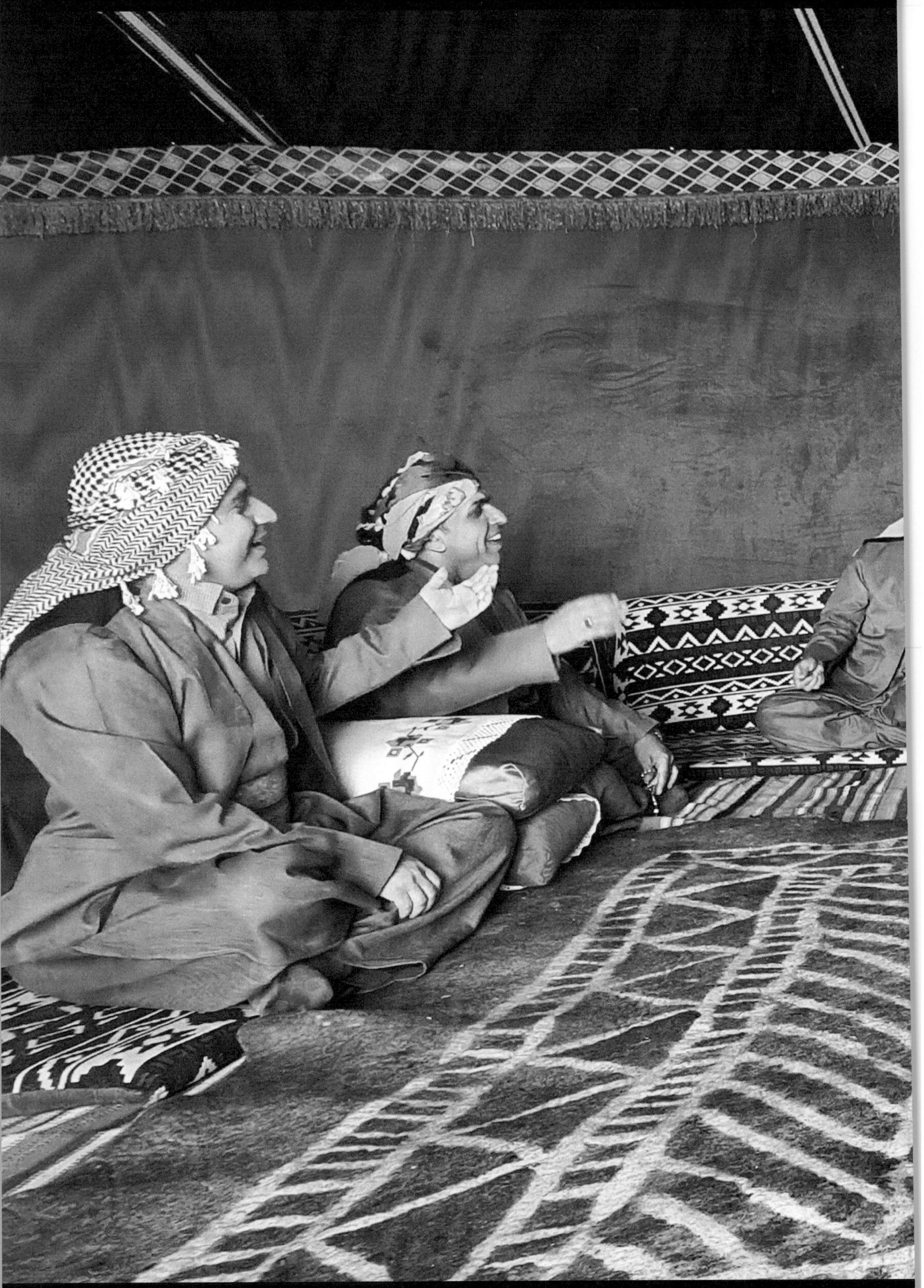

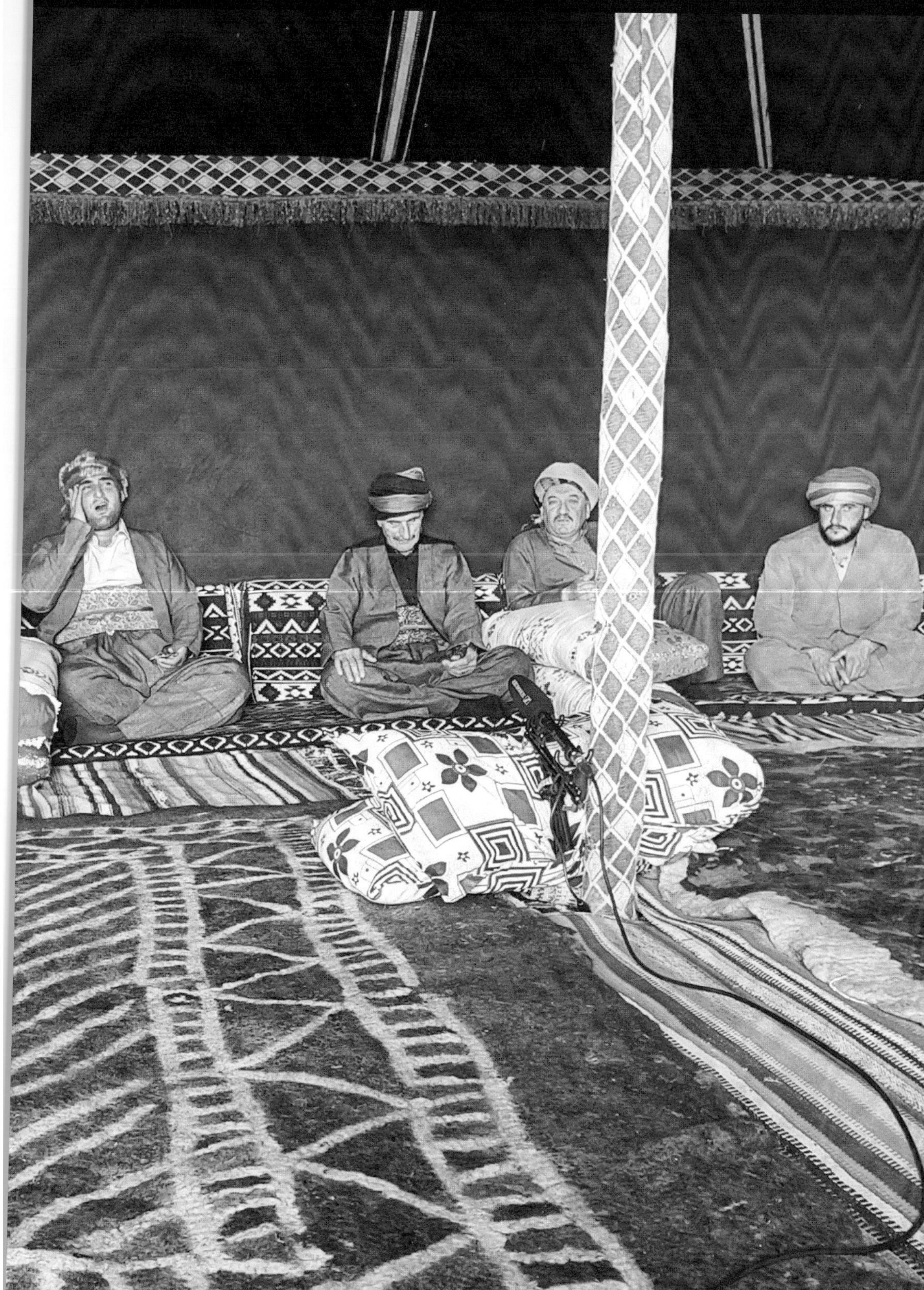

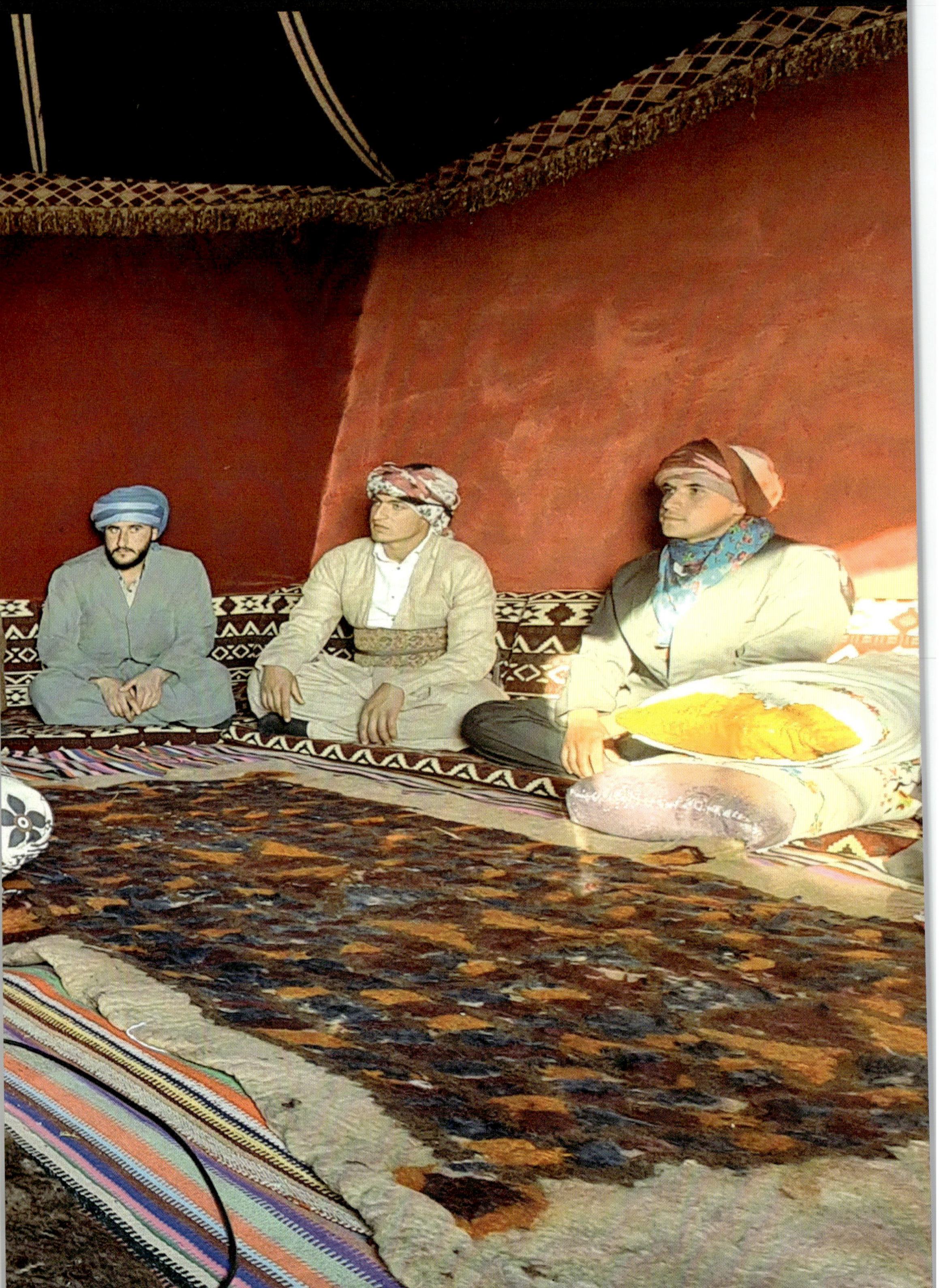

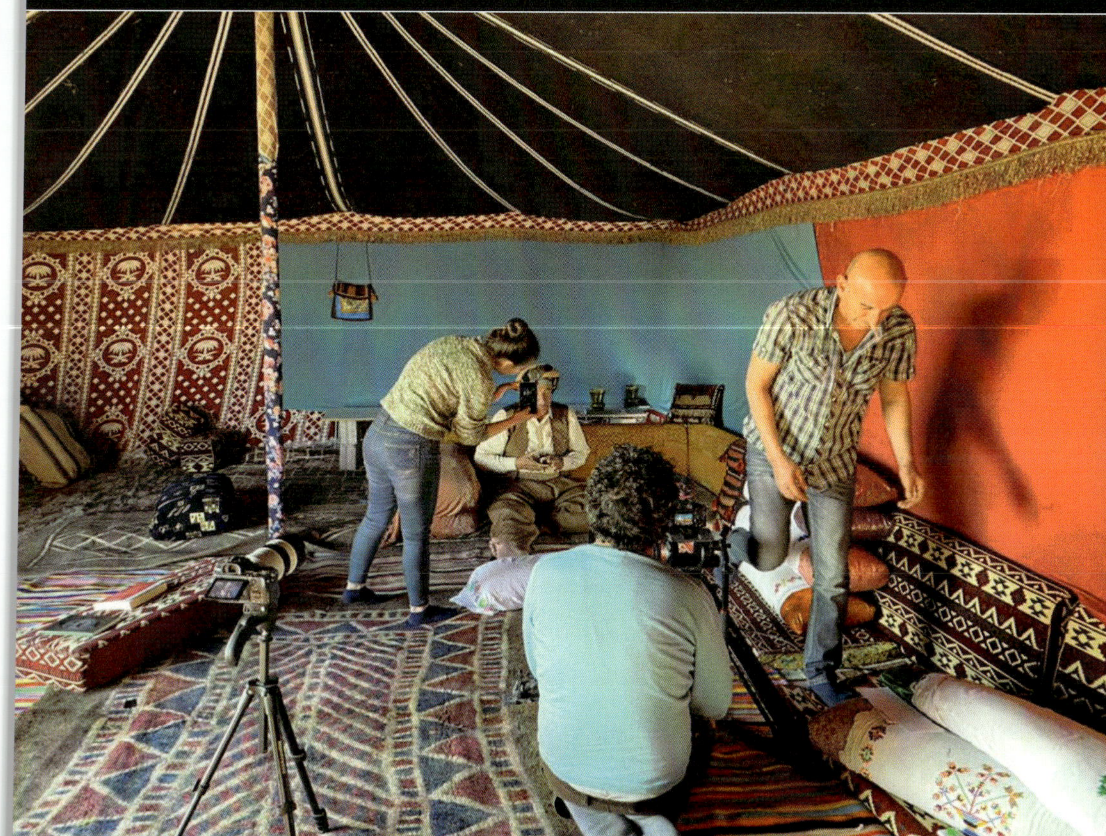

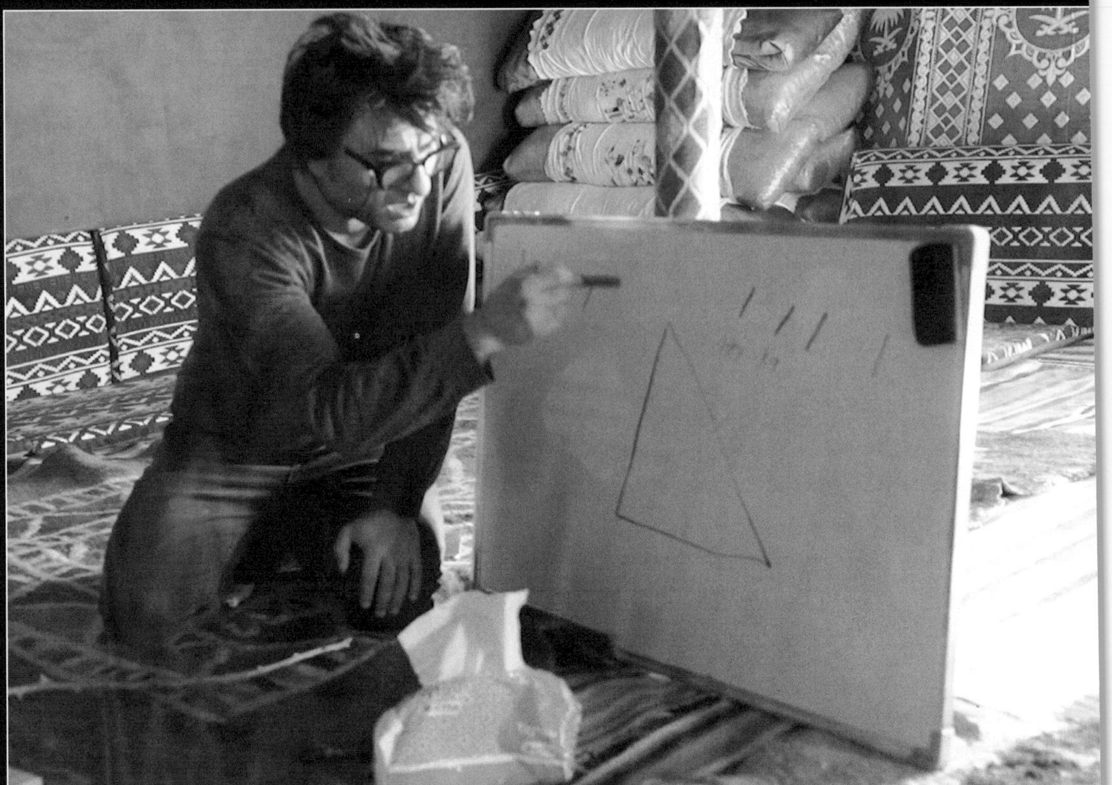

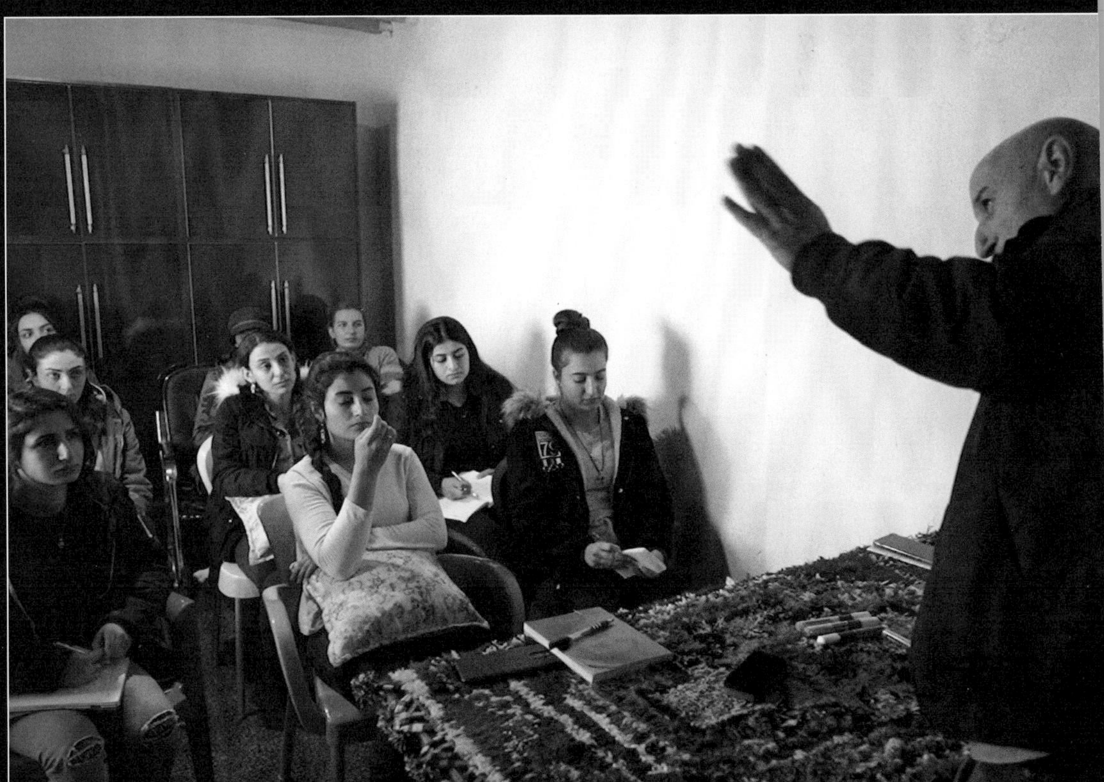

Communal Culture of the Future-Past
Rojava Film Commune, Pargîn Chapter
Training Manual

1. Involve people willing to struggle for the future and learn from the past.

2. Request to sit down together with the elderly, those with an embodied sense of place and history.

3. Ask them about what they know. Repeat two to three hours daily for a period of a week.

4. Divide into working groups and discuss: How do we transfer the knowledge we acquired? What is the *form* of the knowledge we were given?

   Is it a song? Learn to sing.
   Is it a dance? Learn to dance.
   Is it a story? Learn to tell.
   Is it a recipe? Learn to cook.
   Is it the land? Learn the land.

5. Humans come from somewhere: be aware of the history you carry as you learn of one another. Do not impose your own form.

   Do not make a film because you are a filmmaker.
   Do not write because you are a writer.
   Do not draw because you are a drawer.
   Learn *their* form.

6. A medium is a bridge between past and future. Learn to learn, to care, to transmit a memory for the future. These are the cultures of the future-past.

   Become memory.
   Become teacher.
   Become future.

MARCH 5–6, 2021, PALERMO, ITALY

Sindacati Mediterranei, Lorenzo Marsili and Studio Rizoma

Is it possible to federate not states but peoples? What would such unions look like across the Mediterranean? Picking up the roots of early *sindacalisti* [workers' unions] and anarchist philosophy and mixing theory with the hands-on practice of people working at sea, this training imagines the construction of concrete and speculative practices of communization across the Mediterranean.

Lorenzo Marsili is a writer and political philosopher working for over a decade to imagine a future beyond the nation-state. He is accompanied by members of Studio Rizoma – a new Mediterranean cultural hub based in Palermo and a guest trainer providing a hands-on experience of the Mediterranean Sea.

Visual documentation by Lorenzo Marsili and Studio Rizoma

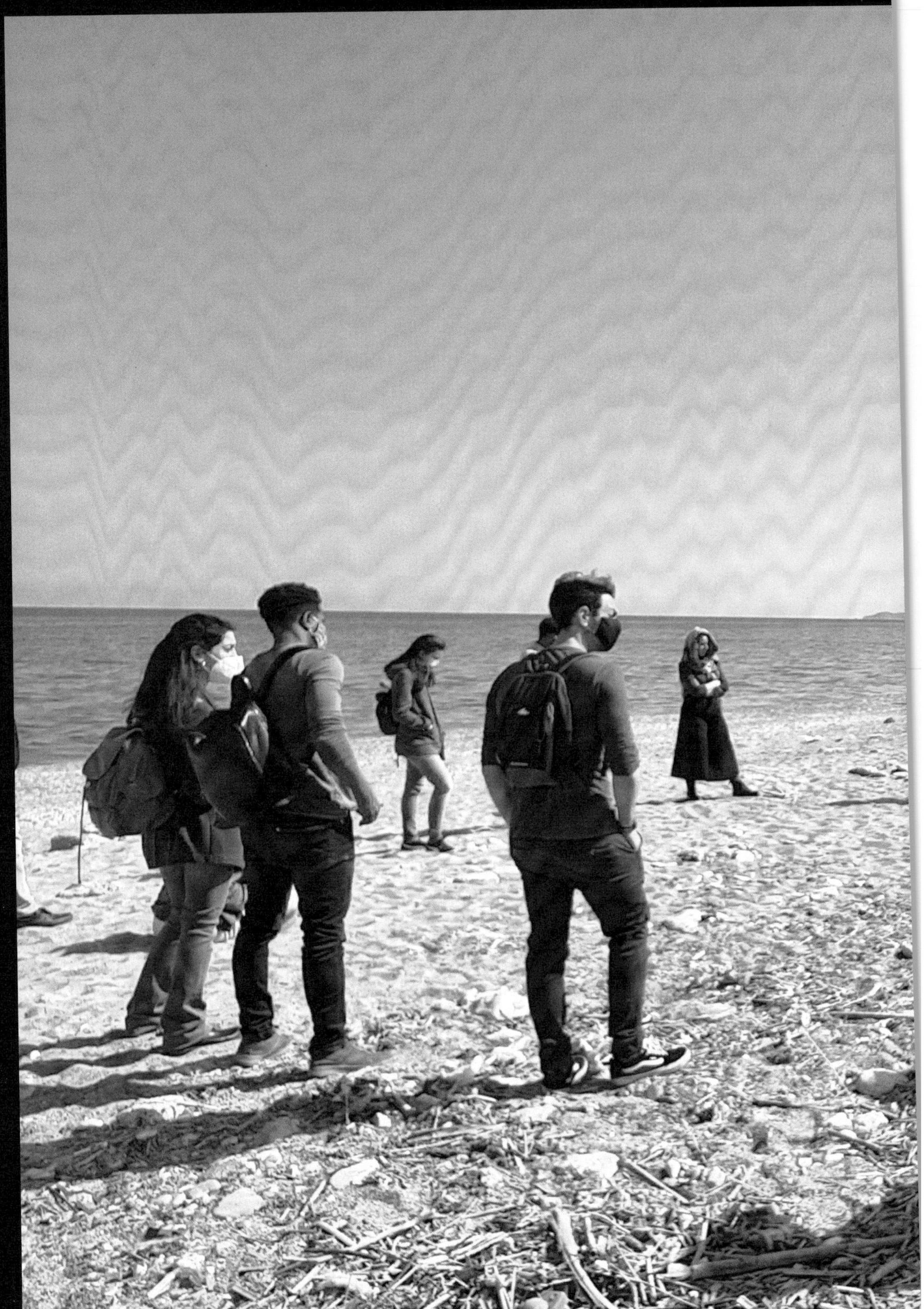

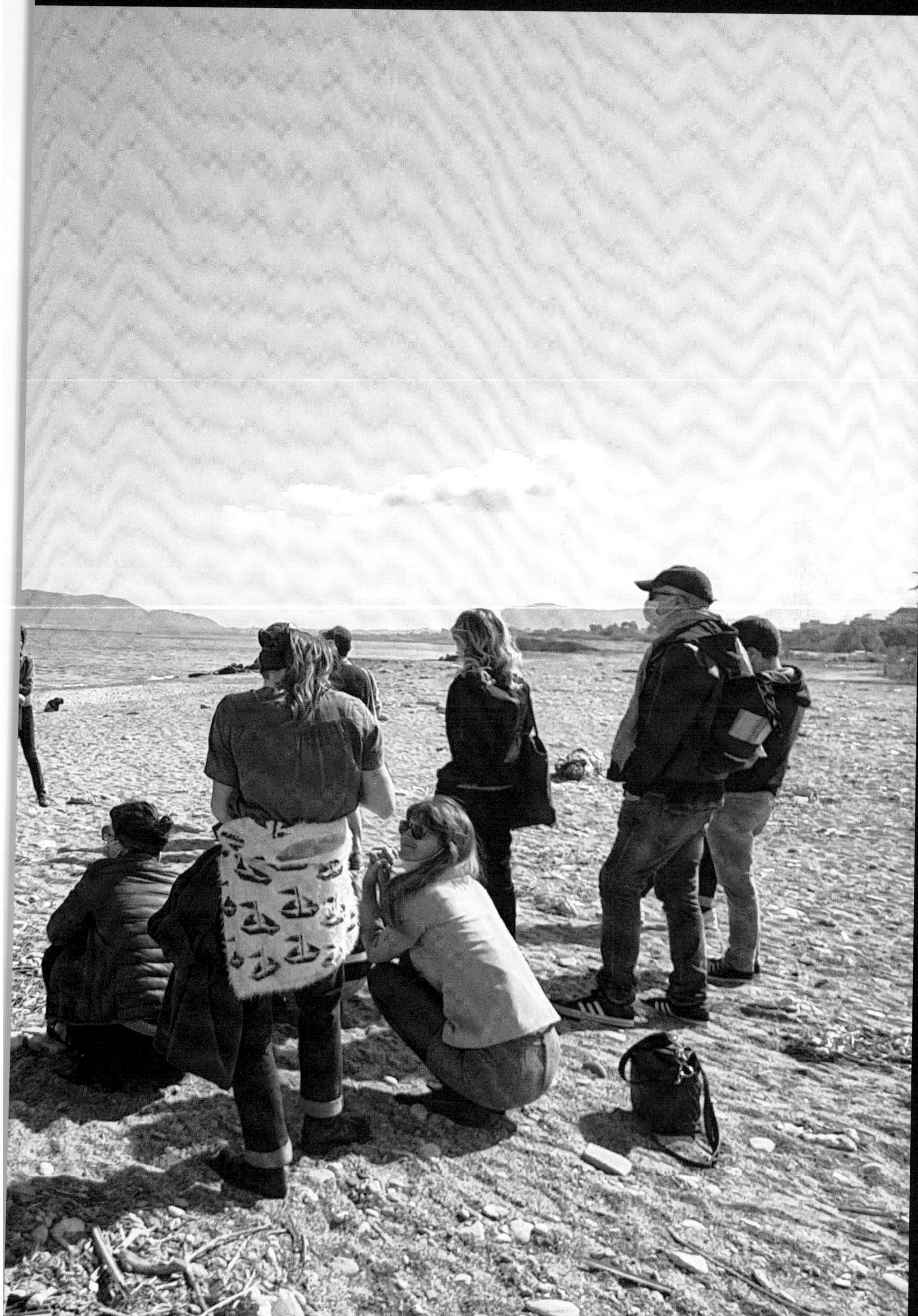

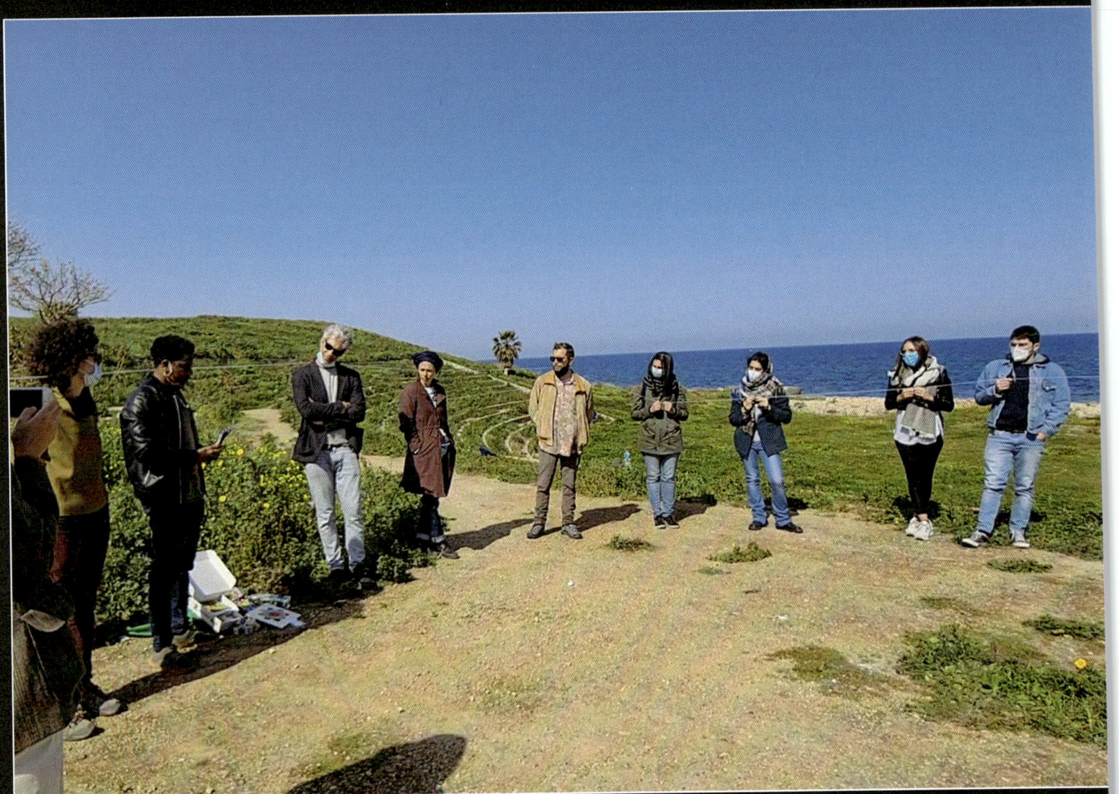

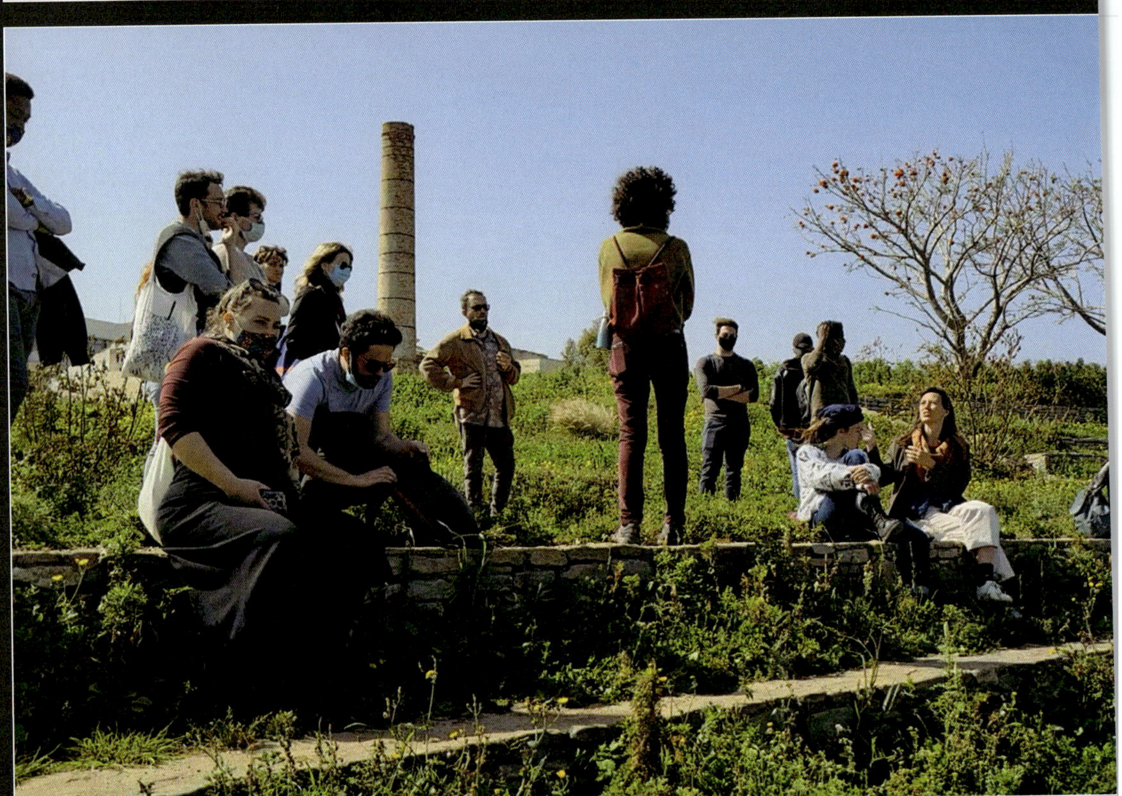

Mediterranean Unions

1.

Ports are the condition of possibility for the sea to become a defining element of human history. Ports allow land and water to compenetrate and shape each other. They render the sea a protagonist and not a prop; Fernand Braudel's sea as an agent of human transformation is unimaginable without the port. Ports are at once port cities, stretches of inhabited land that project toward the water. Ports are structural in-between spaces, a nexus of contradiction, hybridity and transformation. They are a space for the collectivization of difference, and a space of struggle over that difference.

Familiar/Uncanny | In the history of ports, we find the projection toward the outside and the construction of an inside united. Safety and danger, the familiar and the uncanny. The city, in the mythological reading of Jan Patočka, is the foundation of the familiar, of that which makes us feel at home. And this space coexists, always already, with its exterior, with the absence and denial of control, with the foreign and the disturbing. The port remains in tension between opposites and allows for their dynamic relation and interpenetration.

Self / Other | In this sense, ports are the epicenter of the interplay between self and other. Human communities are defined by a logic that is both inclusive and exclusionary, as each boundary draws a dividing line: it identifies the 'us,' the space of solidarity and that which is foreign. Ports are the door to the Other par excellence and hence they are also the premise for the construction of the self: we define our identity against those we cannot identify with. And yet ports also embody the excess of the Other, its capacity to denude and transform all fictional identity.

Goods / People | From ancient trade routes to colonial violence all the way to China's Belt and Road Initiative, logistics have represented both an apparatus of control and the condition of emancipation. It is no coincidence that the simplified alphabet – a common good of the people – was first devised in two merchant cities: Ougarit and Byblos. As waterways bridge the distances, ports foster new technologies to bridge human differences, exploding the dialectic between the human desire to connect, the economic imperative to exchange and the political aspiration to control.

Controllers / Controlled | It is in no way insignificant who exercises control over human connection and what political space is powerless in the face of economic exchange. Logistics are the promise that the frictionless movement of goods, capital and information enables the forms of control and measurement that ensure these fluxing demands will be satisfied in a timely and efficient manner. The space of logistics is therefore defined in relation to the power that operates it, the power that delivers the promise. But greater connectivity is achieved at the cost of erasing all obstacles that stand in its way, be they human flows, urban fabric or environmental elements.

The first part of our training involved an exploration of these contradictions in one of the oldest port cities of the Mediterranean: Palermo.

Departing from a cursory exploration of the four couplets identified above, we spread across the city to search for concrete instances of them: whether that be a photograph, an encounter, a crossroad, a shop, a reflection or a recollection. These *objets trouvés* provided the departure point for an open format exchange, where each person would give life to the abstract categories that mark a port city through their own personal and experiential journey through it.

2.

Departing from an exploration of the contradictions of port cities, we then enlarged the discourse to take the port city as a metaphor for the Mediterranean as a whole, and the Mediterranean itself as a metaphor for the world to come.

The Mediterranean Sea has been the great connector of peoples and histories, for better and for worse. With its Phoenician, Greek, Roman, Arab, Normand and Spanish dominations, no place enshrines this better than Sicily. But the sea is equally a great divider, separating wealth from poverty and inclusion from exclusion. It is a sea that many try to cross only to find invisible walls, rejection and, in some cases, death. Nowhere is this more evident than in the stark separation of the Mediterranean's northern and southern shores.

The Mediterranean itself may be conceived as a spread, a differentiated port city divided between the familiar and the uncanny, the self and the Other, goods and people, controllers and controlled. In Palermo, a city at once rich and poor, and filled with contradiction and stratification, we found a perfect mirror of that multifaceted sea.

We took this sea as our starting point to ask what transnational collectivities and unions may be imagined across its shores. Can we weave together the watery fabric of the Mediterranean Sea like the differentiated parts of a single city? Can we envision cross-Mediterranean practices of action and thought? What could unions of peoples across Mediterranean cities, divided by a continent but connected by the sea, look like?

Top-down institutional attempts to build functioning transnational unions appear stalled and fall victim to animosity and mutual distrust, whether in the European Union or across the Mediterranean. We explored and immediately ruled out the many institutional attempts at fostering 'structures' that federate states, as we found this approach to be embedded in the longer history of the colonial experience of the Mediterranean Sea.

Our question stemmed from this failure. We asked: Is it possible to federate not states but peoples? We were not so interested in unions of states – federations, partnerships, etc. – but unions of bodies. Is it possible to imagine a union of fishermen, a union of students, a union of migrants, of workers, of farmers, of artists, of social movements, of trade unions and local authorities stretching across and connecting the Mediterranean? Can we envision concrete practices of cooperation that unite citizens around all shores of a common sea?

If the Mediterranean offers a prism through which to observe and understand our world, envisioning new unions that cross and connect its two shores becomes a concrete gesture of healing for a divided planet.

3.

There is a rich theoretical background to such an approach, which we explored in depth. In the work of Italian Marxist and anti-fascist Antonio Gramsci, nation-building follows a double movement: on the one hand, the territory widens until it becomes that of the entire nation (and no longer, for instance, that of the medieval commune) and on the other, the cosmopolitan element of Imperial Roman and Christian culture shrinks, until it becomes nationalized and popularized. Intellectuals and elites develop ever closer ties within the new national community, a delimited territory wider than the medieval fief but more limited than the cosmos. The broadening of the territorial dimension of political authority and the diminishing of the universal horizon of belonging contribute to the formation of the nation-state, sealing a new alliance between elites and people: a community of shared destiny.

This is precisely the mechanism that today breaks down and goes into reverse, a crisis that Gramsci had anticipated. In the last years of his life he began to identify a new political constellation no longer based on the territorial extension of the modern state but, rather, on industrialism and the boundless expansion of American capitalism. The outcome of this process was a new disconnection between elites and nation-states. And as it was the nationalization of the elites that gave life to the modern state form, then their denationalization could only have a devastating effect. 'Already today,' Gramsci wrote in the mid 1930s, 'a phenomenon similar to that of the Medieval separation between the "spiritual" and "temporal" dimensions occurs in the modern world . . . Traditional intellectuals, detaching themselves from the social grouping to which they had so far given the highest and most comprehensive form and therefore the widest and most perfect conscience of the modern state, perform an act of incalculable historical significance: they mark and sanction the crisis of the state in its decisive form.'

It is from here that Gramsci began to muse about the possibility of constructing a new political subject that would be no longer national but 'cosmopolitical,' that is, capable of matching the planetary scale of the economic interdependency he saw building up around him. A cosmopolitanism for a new era.

What is a cosmopolitanism for a new era? It is not merely ushering in a new international organization for our world, as reminiscent in the many failed attempts at constructing a 'Mediterranean Union.' Instead, should it involve inventing political and cultural forms at an immediately transnational scale? This is not about federating nations or sitting with national elites in joint summits to reach inter-*national* decisions, but rather organizing citizens themselves and empowering them to act at the scale of the problem itself – and without delegation via their nations. This means transitioning from an inter-*national* to a planetary political vision. What would that look like in the Mediterranean?

4.

The question is too large for us to answer. And so we explored these thoughts, once again, with a very concrete mission. We decided to focus on imagining the organization of a Mediterranean summit aimed precisely at fostering the construction of such alliances, and role-played deciding what topics should be dealt with, who should be invited and what methodologies should be followed to ensure concrete outcomes from a trans-Mediterranean assembly of collectivization.

We decided to focus on two areas specifically: Sicily and Tunisia. While they have powerful historic ties, the two places feature contemporary realities that are starkly different from one another. What then does an alliance mean under these terms? The two spaces become a microcosm in bridge-making between north and south. In putting the cities of Tunis and Palermo at the center of this concrete attempt at unionizing, what can local alliances between the two cities and their various interest groups set in motion?

We broke down the conversation in multiple groups tasked with imagining specific forms of alliances between disparate social groups. Out of these intuitions we developed a roadmap of four main blocs that such a summit should cover.

Liquid Territory | Today, the Mediterranean is far from being considered as the sea that connects different cities. A wide range of dividing lines run through it, between continents and states, north and south, east and west, Maghreb and Mashrek. If we consider it instead as a shared liquid territory, what common political goals can be formulated among the people whose habitats extend to this territory? How can we create common democratic spaces that cross the sea? How can fishermen in Tunisia and Sicily establish common rules and goals for the conservation and regeneration of marine fauna? How can activists and citizens of the bordering states take joint action against the pollution of the sea? How can the traditional routes of exchange, migration and trade by sea be restored? How can people on both shores work together to respond to the humanitarian crisis in the Mediterranean?

The Port City | How people live together in a city, how the different social groups of a city, its minorities and elites, established and newcomers, tourists and locals, interact with each other often depends much more on municipal policies than on national ones. In the last decade, mayors and city councils have increasingly made use of their relative autonomy from national governments. Which role can they play in a scenario of an inter-urban community that goes beyond the borders of nation-states? How can sustainable structures of exchange between Tunis and Palermo in art, culture and education be built? How can they counteract the one-sidedness of these relations, relating both to economic opportunities and freedom of movement between the two cities? How can they counter the networks of the global economy that produce price dumping, an erosion of working conditions and extreme inequalities? How can international guests, artists, tourists, pensioners and smart workers be welcomed without gentrification driving locals out of their districts?

Economics and Ecology of Life | Agricultural production and food trade have historically linked Tunisia and Sicily and created many common lifestyles and shared culinary traditions. Nowadays, restrictions on the movement of workers, who traditionally migrated from the southern shore of the Mediterranean to the north during the harvest season, have made it difficult for farmers to recruit workers and have led to a degeneration of living conditions and erosion of workers' rights. How can orange and olive growers from Sicily and Tunisia fight for shared interests instead of taking part in the price-dumping competition inflicted upon them by the international market and the economies of their respective nation-states? How can seasonal workers and entrepreneurs in agriculture come together to demand a transformation of socially and economically devastating market structures? How can consumers join forces with producers to demand more sustainable, ecological and fair agricultural production? How can they jointly build an ecology of life that re-establishes their connections with the nonhuman actors, i.e. animals, plants and the soil?

Shared Histories / Shared Future | Looking back through history, Palermo and Tunis have been closer than present politics would suggest, united by a diverse shared heritage which can be felt when wandering around their antique city centers, medinas and ports. But the two cities are also linked by a long history of migration and trade, they are bound together by the people who have moved back and forth over the centuries. This has also produced a wide range of syncretisms, both culinary and linguistic. How can the existing links between transnational communities be used to build relationships of solidarity, cultural proximity and mutual understanding? How can this promote the political participation of minorities and give rise to forms of transnational political organization? How can transnational institutions of exchange in education and culture be built to enact shared, transnational narratives?

These four blocs, together with a brainstorm on which collectives, individuals and institutions to engage, formed the backbone of the first draft of a Mediterranean summit to come.

5.

And… It's happening. Thanks to external support, a Mediterranean summit connecting Tunis and Palermo will actually be organized in October 2021 by Studio Rizoma, the entity behind this training, in partnership with the Biennale of Tunis. Its main structure will depart from that devised during the draft summit, and several of the workshop participants will be engaged as facilitators. A concrete outcome resulting from a journey of action and organization-oriented learning. Full information will be made available in the summer of 2021 on www.studiorizoma.org.

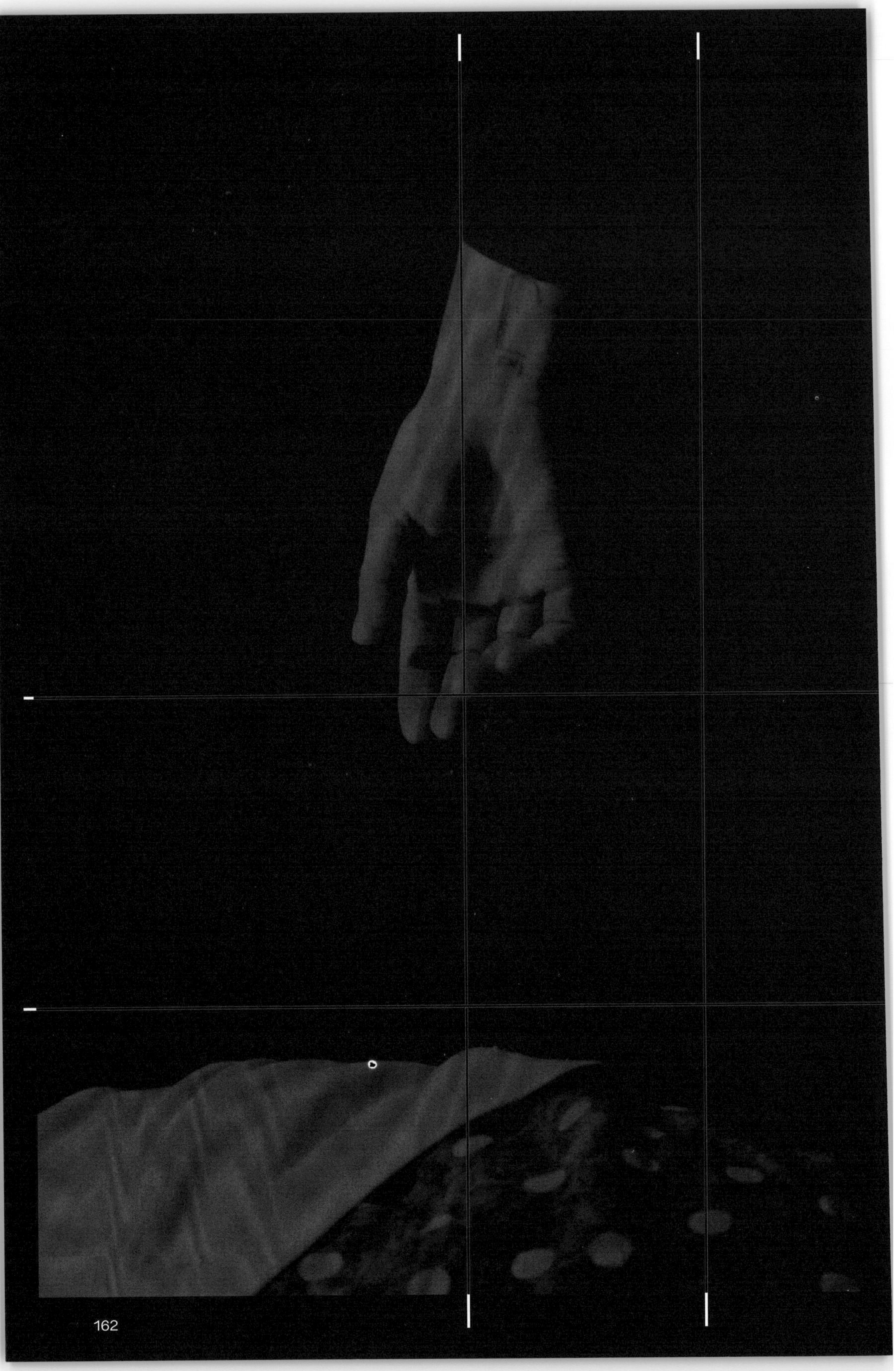

MARCH 6, 2021, VENICE, ITALY

Within and Against Utopia: Commoning Art Institutions, S.a.L.E. Docks and Extragarbo

How do we common, queer and decolonize art and its institutions? The current pandemic revealed the fragility of neoliberal art infrastructure. Through theoretical exercises and embodied practices of imagination, this training focuses on ideas of commoning care, social cooperation, the practice of conflict and self-government. Utopia is not meant to become nostalgia of the future, but rather the struggle for common imagination within the contradictions of the present.

S.a.L.E. Docks is an independent space for visual arts, activism and experimental theater located in what had been an abandoned salt-storage facility in Dorsoduro, Venice, Italy. Founded in 2007, its programming includes militant research on art labor, direct actions, activist groups, formal exhibitions, workshops and screenings.

Extragarbo is an artistic and curatorial platform founded in Venice in 2019 by Est Coulon, Cosimo Ferrigolo, Gaia Ginevra Giorgi, Edoardo Lazzari, Leonardo Schifino and Theresa Maria Schlichtherle. Extragarbo produces and supports the performative projects of its members, adopts a horizontal method and works as a shared system of research, imagination and desire.

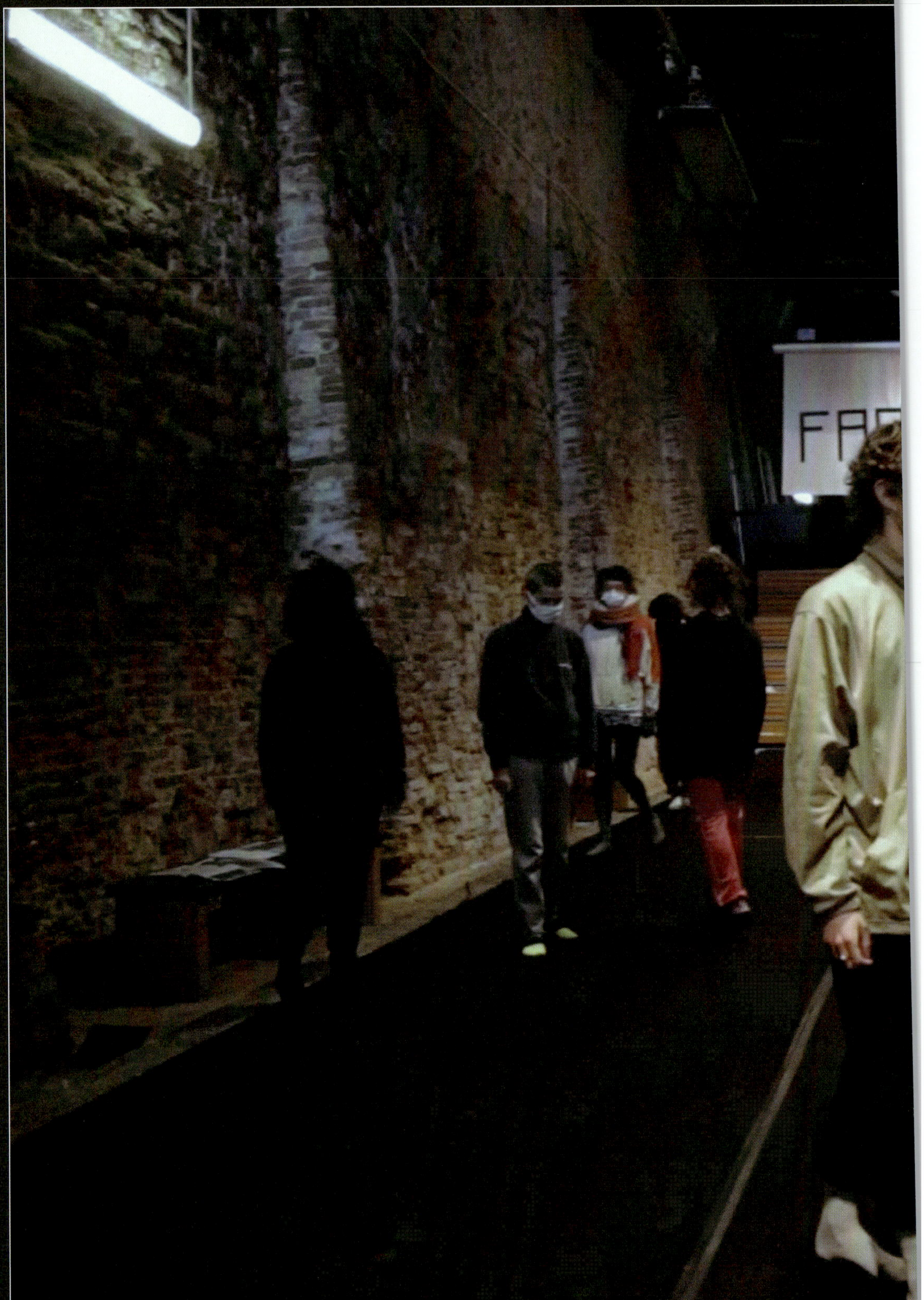

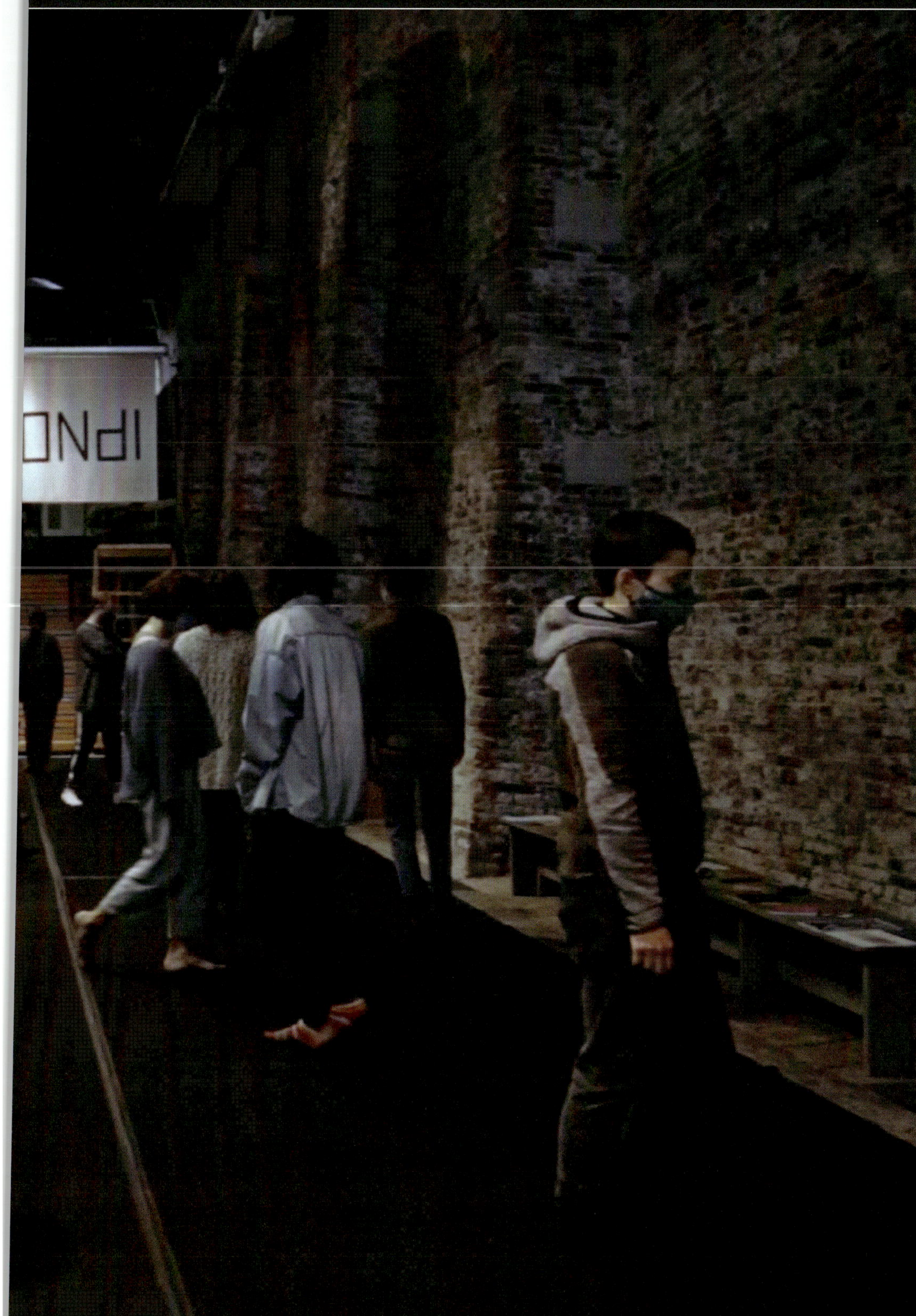

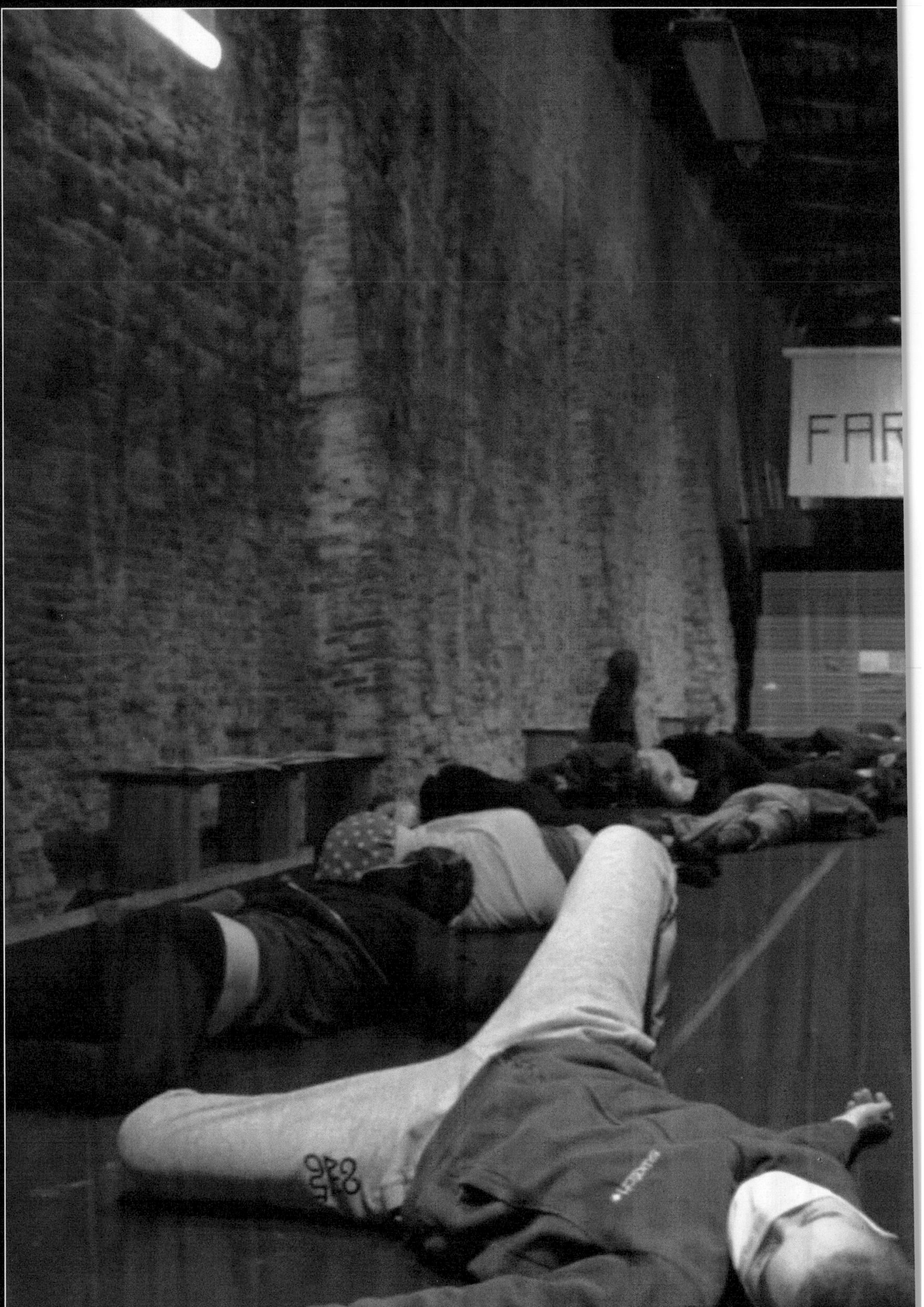

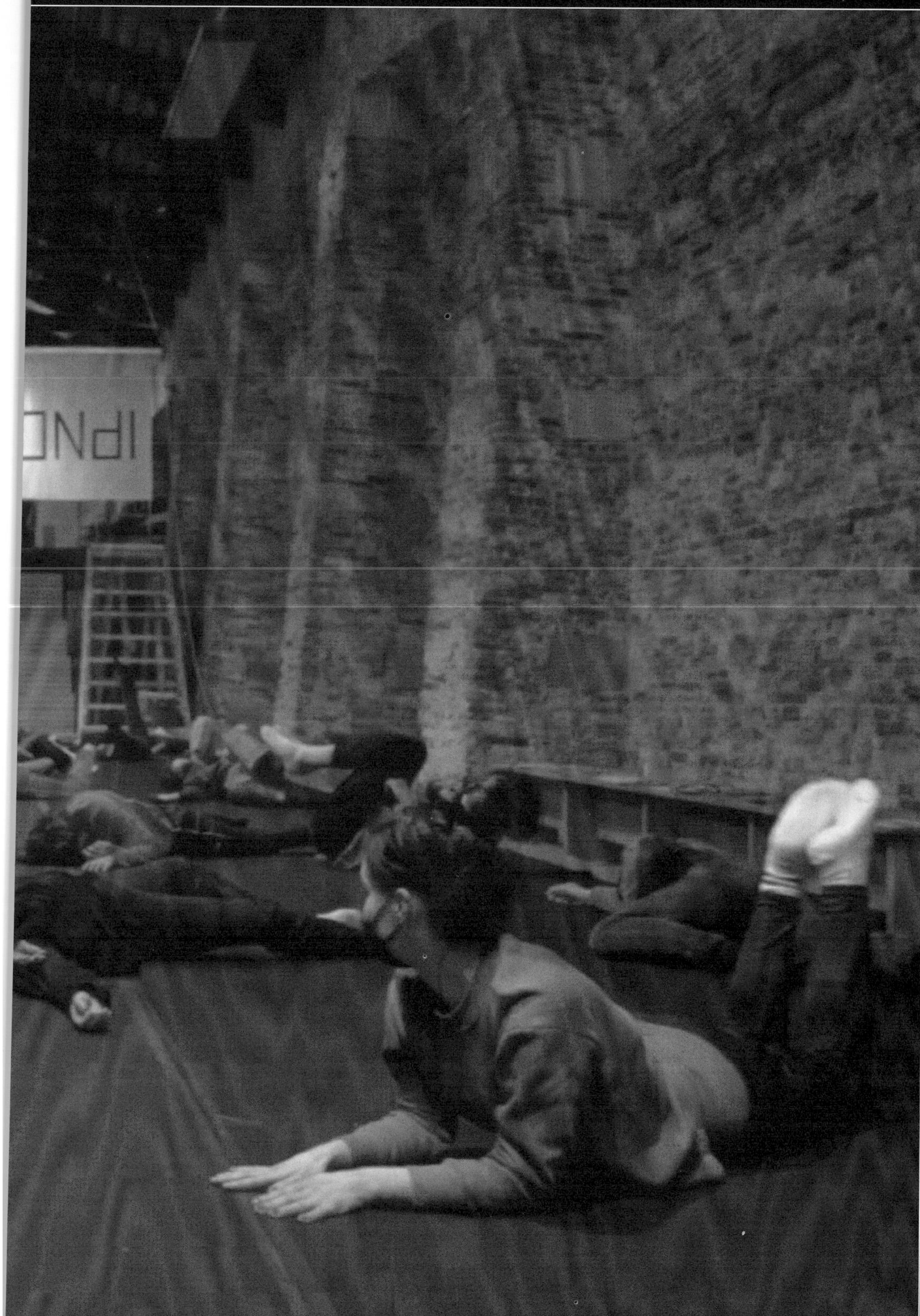

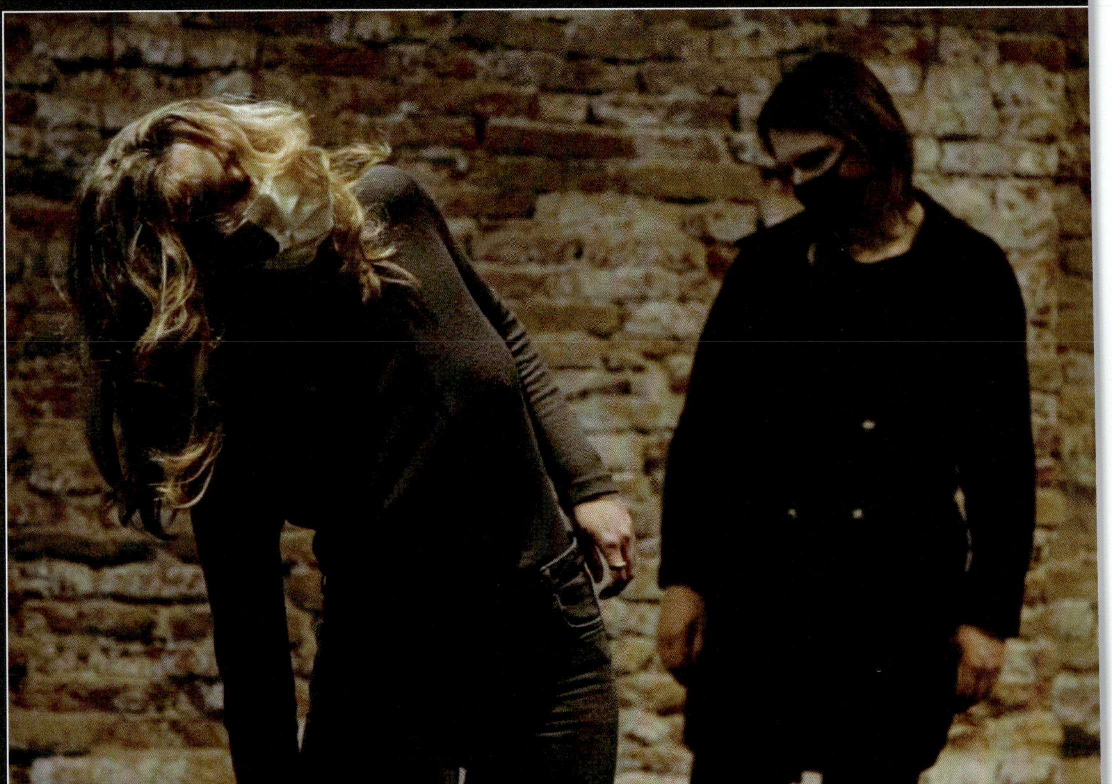

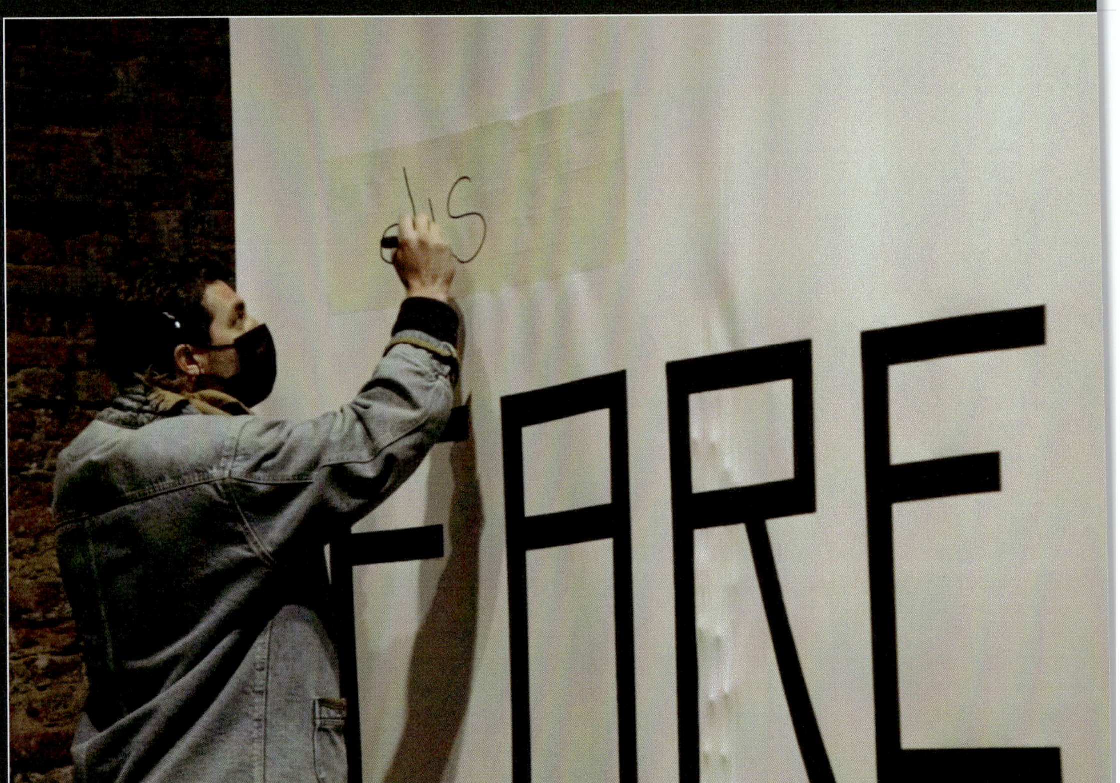
dis
ARE

Within and Against Utopia: Commoning Art Institutions
Curated by S.a.L.E. Docks and Extragarbo

This training aims, through different practices, to initiate a process for queering, commoning and decolonizing ourselves, with the intention of prefiguring artistic alter-institutions. What is a cultural institution for you? What is your experience of it? Have you ever thought of the words 'decolonizing,' 'queering' or 'commoning'? How did you feel inside a cultural space? How do you perceive it? What do you recognize yourself in?
During the training, Anna Luna Serlenga and Rabii Brahim (Milano Mediterranea) and Ilenia Caleo (researcher, activist and performer) helped us to articulate the concepts of decolonization, queering and commoning. We worked with materials (videos, photos, writings, audio, narration, objects, etc.) concerning experiences, actions and cultural spaces in Venice, and activated them in different ways with the aim of imagining models of cultural alter-institutionality.

1. Gaia

Reflection on the minimal gesture – the fundamental act.

What is involved in standing? Which muscles must be activated to stand?

Which tensions are superfluous?

The ground informs us through the soles of our feet.

What and how many negotiations are we keeping in mind to maintain balance? I try to use as little effort as possible to keep the verticality intact and to observe everything that happens while remaining simply still, rooted.

I begin to identify breaking points – places where the condition of loss, a possible imbalance, is triggered.

First, I shift my weight to different points on my feet and observe the resonances of these shifts throughout my body. I ask myself what this entails.

Each negotiation corresponds to another negotiation.

I explore the breaking points and experience their interdependencies.

I begin to explore the surrounding space, considering imbalance as a generative possibility for movement and not as a problem to be faced. Through the condition of loss and the 'near-fall' – the way in which Kathy E. Ferguson defines the fundamental act of walking in *Anarchist Women and the Politics of Walking* – I move through space and encounter other bodies.

I do not project displacement, but I am always open to encounter, as well as to abandonment.

I do not become attached. I surprise myself.

I try, through the points of rupture that I have identified, to deconstruct the vertical posture in order to find horizontality.

I observe the differences and the landscape that I myself modify by being part of it.

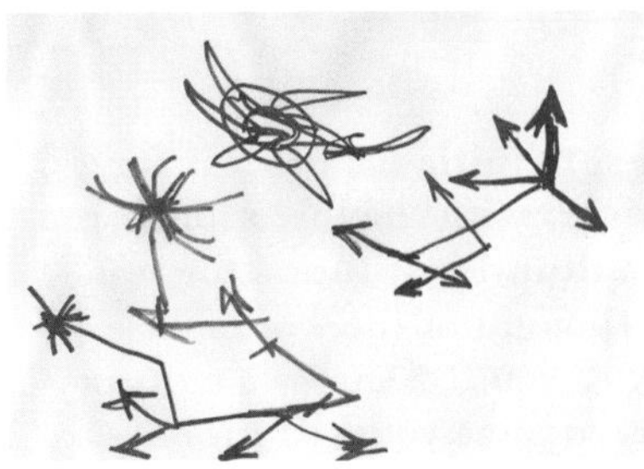

Decoloniality is not only a theme that intertwines with critical race theory, but also with forms of art production in a participatory sense. As the minimum conditionality, whiteness is about rewriting one's practices from a co-authorship perspective. We no longer write 'foreigner' and other words, and focus on the centrality of leading through practice. It's not just about giving place and making a way for others, but engaging in dialogue. Everyone does their own little bit and it takes time, but practicing is crucial.

2. Anna and Rabii

We have to leave this seminar with a toolbox. We begin by asking who is speaking and what is the place of the enunciation? From the white side of the question, everyone has to do their own part. We have to rewrite our own practices, our own postures, our own narratives, our own language and we have to practice not just making space for someone else, but engaging in dialogue with them. For example, how are institutions created and worn by some? How comfortable or uncomfortable do we feel in that dress? To answer this, we try to do a constant exercise in feeling *displaced*, out of place.

Milano Mediterranea is an independent and alternative institution born and active in the Giambellino district of Milan. It is a counter-proposal that leads to the opening of spaces of co-authorship. We have opened a call for artists from the Mediterranean basin and we have formed a neighborhood committee in order to not arrive from the outside and colonize the territory with a cultural proposal. The selection of projects has to be agreed on by all the members and together we promote a criteria of positive discrimination, participation and engagement with the neighborhood. Our proposal wants to share in a network of bodies and institutions that are interested in developing a form of collaboration. During the selection process we happened to receive projects that we liked as artists, but that the committee did not find interesting. The proposals we chose will be developed in an artistic residency and they will converge in an urban festival, open to everyone passing casually through the space. The communication is bilingual, delivered in Italian and Arabic. This is a strategy to think about language not as universal, but as something that has to be negotiated at a conceptual and spatial level.

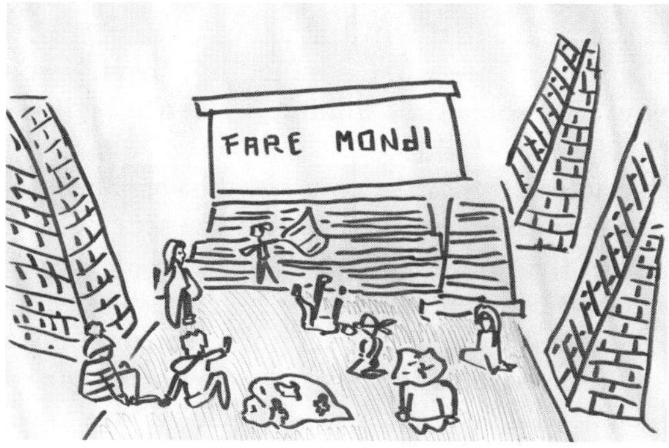

Decoloniality is not only a theme that intertwines with critical race theory, but also with forms of art production in a participatory sense. As the minimum conditionality, whiteness is about rewriting one's practices from a co-authorship perspective. We no longer write 'foreigner' and other words, and focus on the centrality of leading through practice. It's not just about giving place and making a way for others, but engaging in dialogue. Everyone does their own little bit and it takes time, but practicing is crucial.

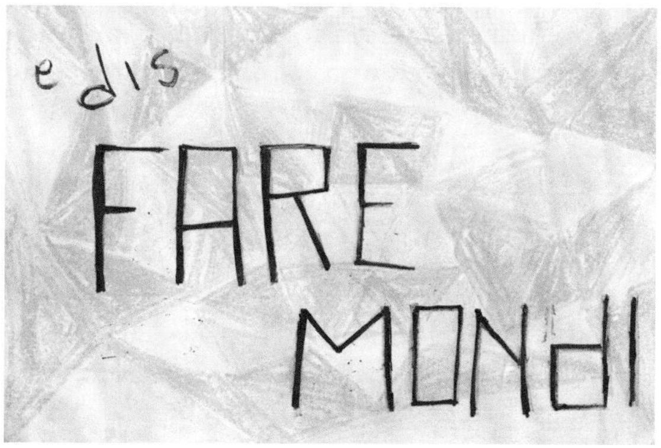

3. Leo

Prostheses and entries (object selection and interaction), 30 min.

The politics of communing – of common building – refer first of all to the capacity to practice material transformations and to a capacity to act that cannot be defined universally nor as a human agency to be realized. These are objects that you have brought with you after thinking about significant experiences regarding the alter-institution and social gathering centers. They are objects that act on our bodies. In this regard, choose an object other than the one you have brought. You have five minutes. If you find someone else interested in the object, negotiate.

Now let's start an exploration phase that will last about twenty minutes. You can stop whenever you want, to see what is happening around you, or to simply take a break. Now take some time to familiarize yourself with the object. Choose a part of the space you like.

Explore the physical characteristics of the object you have chosen (weight, color, elasticity, hardness, the sound it produces). If it is a video or a photo or a text, explore the elements of the image (the speed, the colors, the elements represented, the affective sound between objects).

If you have chosen an object with a material support, translate the shapes, the color, the movement in space with your body. Try moving in the same way, enacting the sounds of the material that is there with you. If you have chosen a digital media, do the same with what is represented in the image, video or audio. Put what you see into play with your body. Ask questions of the material.

Think also of space. How does this object interact with the place around you? Explore the details of the part of the room you have chosen. How does this space change if you move the object?

Play by making the material and your whole body interact and intersect in dialogue. Do not be representative or didactic (sorry we don't do theater), so avoid using the object for its daily use. Think that the object acts on you. Don't stop at just the hands. Transform yourself with the object.

If you have physical support, seek to balance with the material – an act that moves your body into a position of vulnerability. But if, for example, you work with digital media, let yourself be inspired by a loop playback in which you repeat what happens in the video or in a fragment.

Now that you have made an inter-relationship with the nonhuman body you have chosen, we will create a constellation among all the participants, in which the connections will be drawn through the affective resonance between the objects.

Someone takes a seat in the space, choosing the place that attracts them the most. Another participant, who feels affinity with or repulsion for the material of the person closest to them, reaches toward it in space and relates. Choose the distance, position, etc., depending on the feelings of affinity, repulsion or any relationship that passes between the body, your object and their object.

The interrelated bodies form groups for the next stage.

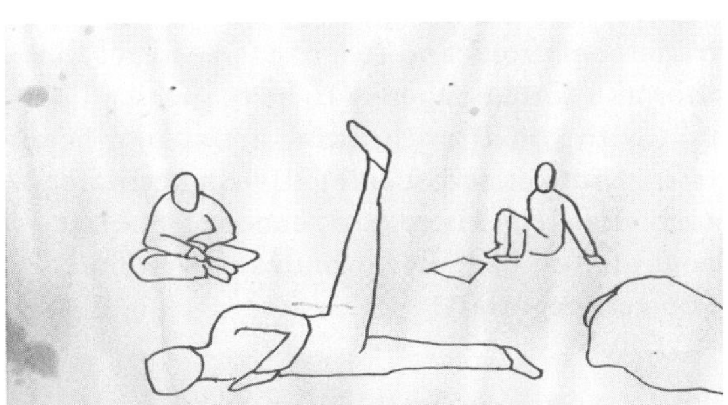

Making worlds / Practice

Common heating / Choice of any object (as long as it is not your own) and then of a point in the space where you can place yourself

Working with the object through an exploration of its physical characteristics

The rustling of paper leaves

Crouching cactus

Bodies interacting with objects and blankets

Paper planes

Be manipulated by the object so that a different balance is sought together with the object

It is the object that affects the movement

The noise of a marker on paper

We were asked to get in touch with one of the objects we brought for the day, but not with what we brought with us. And by 'we' I mean the people here in the room. We were advised to not manipulate the object but rather to let the object guide our movements. I chose a sheet of paper with a printed photo, in black and white. I realized that I am not really capable of *not* manipulating an object, especially an object that when I hold it in my hand I usually bend or tear it, etc. I wonder if this attempt to 'not manipulate' is in itself a practical manifestation of the many meanings contained in the word 'decolonize.' Only, in the West the term decolonization can probably still have so many meanings. Can we allow ourselves to think and investigate what decolonization truly means? Perhaps because in this part of the world it sometimes loses that immediate and urgent significance that it has elsewhere – where addressing it is not at all an option – because we have the luxury of living better and being better at having our say?

Okay these are just thoughts... What can the attempt to not manipulate an object teach us compared to the invitation to decolonize ourselves? As I interpreted it, not manipulating an object suggests a deviation from an action as we normally do it. To be continued...

Decolonizing and sharing are the fruits of the same deep root. I can't say what comes first and what comes after, as they are branches of the same tree. One is all and all is one. I am the Other and the Other is me. Creation is born only from liberation. Do whatever comes into your body.

4. Ilenia

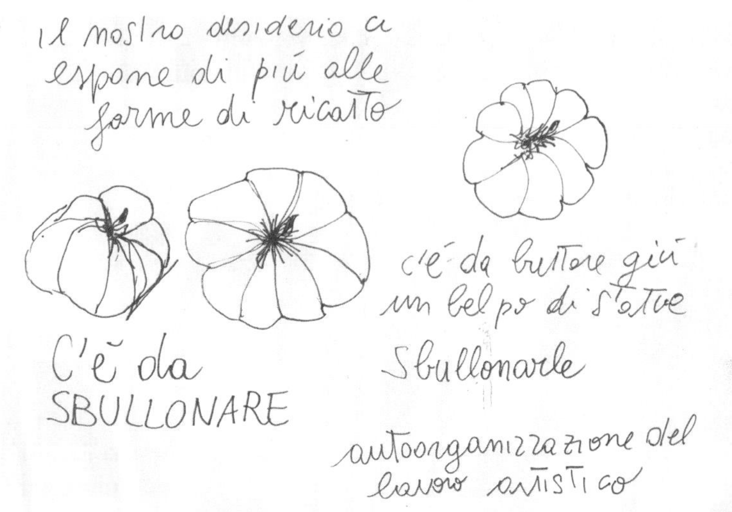

Ilenia connects with us from her car

she is in a parking lot

there is a reverb. We can't hear her

We made tea, people are having a snack

discussing the theme of institutions from a queer point of view

art workers who gave life to new artistic institutions

a body cannot be defined as such, without taking into account the space where it is creating a whole world around a body

feminism leads us to think of ourselves as a process of radical transformation

it isn't about getting into the institutions but rather about inventing new ones

Il Campo Innocente is a space/an informal group that reflects on the relationships between the

artistic world and the bodies of queers, lesbians, trans* people...

the artistic world isn't a neutral space

we need to deromanticize, the art world is full of patriarchal myths such as the myth of the

exceptional nature of art and of the artist

there are two things that we have to think of together when we deal with the need to rethink the artistic institution from a feminist point of view, one that puts non-standard bodies at the center:

first, power dynamics (exploitation, precariousness, coercion dynamics), the relationship systems,

and the questions: What do we stage? What do we depict?

we should draw inspiration from anti-racist struggles.

let's knock some statues down. Let's unbolt them!

Self-organization of artistic work

An experience of a queer institution: the vogue scene between the 70s and the 80s in New York. Black, Chicana drag scene. 'Houses': both a community and real houses, occupied houses. They create emotional networks. Social mutualism. At the center of all this there is the ballroom.

Queering has to do with the creation of political spaces for intimacy

Meanwhile, inside S.a.L.E. Docks, small groups form – aggregates of bodies that share blankets

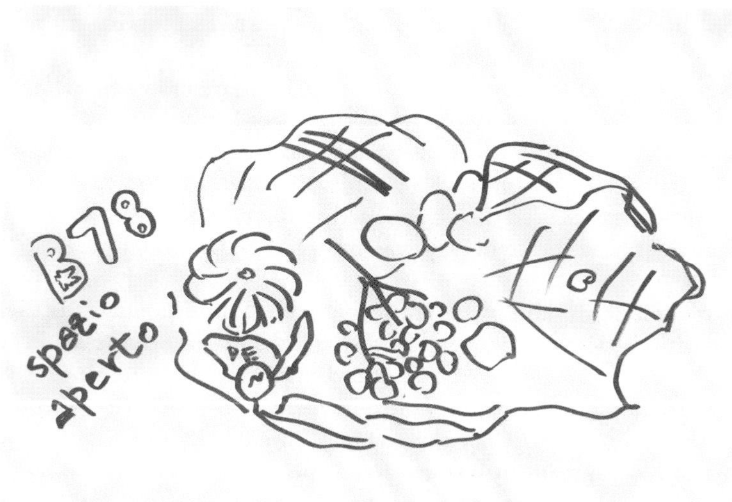

5. Marco

The theme of alter-institutionality is one with the potential to upset what Bojana Kunst defines as the 'powerlessness of art' – it can disrupt art's effectiveness in taming subalternities and free it from that market *dispositif* that feeds on what we are (activists, queer, racialized, proletarians). Alter-institutionality brings the political back into the aesthetic, where ethics tend to occupy the totality of the spectrum. Alter-institutionality is the organizational principle of transformation, the metamorphic architecture of feeling and acting in common. Opportunities must be seized and open spaces must be occupied, not to get comfortable but rather to transform and to subvert them. We don't only need safe spaces for difference, we need spaces that are unsafe for those who want to destroy difference, or try to reduce it to neoliberal one-thought flattery. NOTES: To exist, to smuggle new forms of life through the educated borders of the work of art, to transform the cities where we live, to redefine the limits of art, to give substance to new art worlds by mutating the present one, to open spaces of liberty and autonomy and to be, at the same time, against social and capitalist realisms. The problem of the former is that it represents the world as it should be, and the problem of the latter is that it deprived us of abilities that can't be reduced to the aestheticization of politics and which represent the capacity to imagine new possibilities, those ready to be offered up to actualization.

6. Est

In her article 'Queer Use,' where she reflects on the notion of use, Sara Ahmed develops some considerations on the institution. According to her, the institutional is intimately connected with use: the institutional is usual, it is an environment that has taken shape as a result of a particular, repeated use. The institution is built over time by stabilizing the requirements for what it needs to survive or thrive. Once stabilized, these requirements remain, but no longer in an explicit way. Then use becomes, at least apparently, a question of fit. The moment of use appears to be hap: it seems that a given person is selected because they happen to fit the requirements, which is rather like when a stone is selected because it just happens to be the same shape and size as the hole in the wall. But the randomness that determines who uses the institution is an illusion: it seems that people are there because they happened to fit the structure, when in fact they fit because of how the structure was built. As Sara Ahmed writes:

> People do come to inhabit organizations that are not intended for them; you can make the cut without fitting. If you arrive into an organization that is not built *for* you, you experience this *for* as tight or as tightening. If you are the one for whom an institution is intended *for* it is loose; the institution appears as open because it is open to you. This is why I think of an institution as an old garment: it has acquired the shape of those who tend to wear it such that it is easier to wear if you have that shape. And this is why I think of privilege as *an energy saving device*; less effort is required to pass through when a world has been assembled around you. If you arrive with dubious origins, you are not expected to be there, so in getting there you have already disagreed with an expectation of who you are and what you can do, then an institution is the wrong shape.

In the same article, Ahmed wonders how we could define 'queer use,' or better, 'queer uses.' Her considerations move from the use of the word queer itself, which for a very long time has been an insult. Yet the fact that some of us can live our lives by assuming the word queer and using it to define ourselves shows that past use does not prevent us from exploring the potentials of a given word. Queer, as Sara Ahmed suggests, could therefore be described as reuse. Another example of queer use is when something is used for purposes other than the ones for which they were intended.

The practice of collage and recombination that we propose now is in line with, to some extent, Sara Ahmed's thoughts on reuse and improper use. Collage consists in the combination of heterogeneous elements, elements that come from different contexts. As they are extracted from their original context and associated with new objects in a new context, these elements acquire new, unexpected meanings.

We are interested in collage because of its ability, through reworking something that already exists, to open up spaces of invention and to bring forth potentials that have not been expressed before. Collage generates a short circuit within our usual way of seeing things, and it draws both the author and the spectator into a flow of associations and free constructions of meaning.

In the final exercise, each group is invited to make a collage from the objects of the respective members, meaning four or five elements. One of the exercise's main issues is a purely pragmatic one: Which form should the collage take? It can be a two-dimensional collage, an installation or a sequence that includes actions. The elements the trainees have to assemble are very few. This is meant to highlight the very essence of the technique of collage: the fact that a number of possibilities can arise from a single object. This may also encourage the participants to translate objects from one medium to another. For example, a physical object does not have to remain as such, it can become a text or a narration. Likewise, a picture may be translated into a gesture.

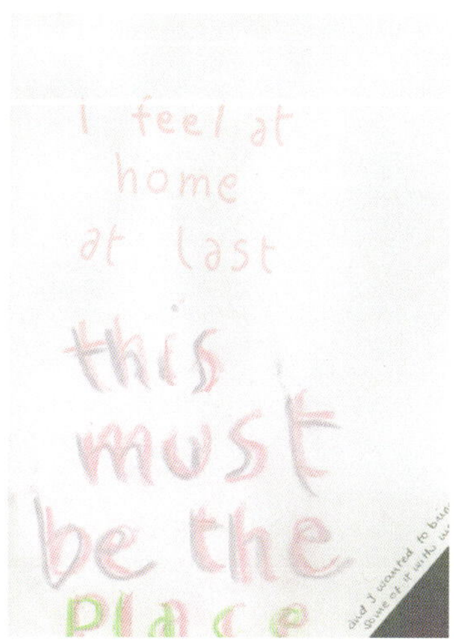

Walking as almost falling
a constant action (without beginning or end)
like the revolution
negotiating with balance
considering imbalance as a possibility that
generates movement
deconstructing organized verticality
becoming invertebrate
flag sizzles on naked hands
red hands
a thought flies
it holds us together, brand new
the thought collectivizing game
(through action)
there is and there will always be a need to
unbolt and to knock down statues, many of
them, again and again
there is an instituting flux
of words
we shouldn't expect anything
anything

MARCH 6, 2021, ZURICH, SWITZERLAND

Safe Touch, Army of Love

Safe Touch is a communal training on how to be safely intimate with strangers during the Covid-19 crisis. It practices vocal and physical exercises that can be offered to people in need of love and touch without the risk of infection. Just as people developed an understanding of 'safe sex' in response to the AIDS crisis, we are now trying to learn and promote 'safe touch.'

Inspired by Ingo Niermann's novel *Complete Love* (2016), the Army of Love is a solidarity network that offers trainings, recruitments, discussions, manuals and testimonial videos to promote the redistribution of sensual love to all who need it.

Visual documentation by Ingo Niermann

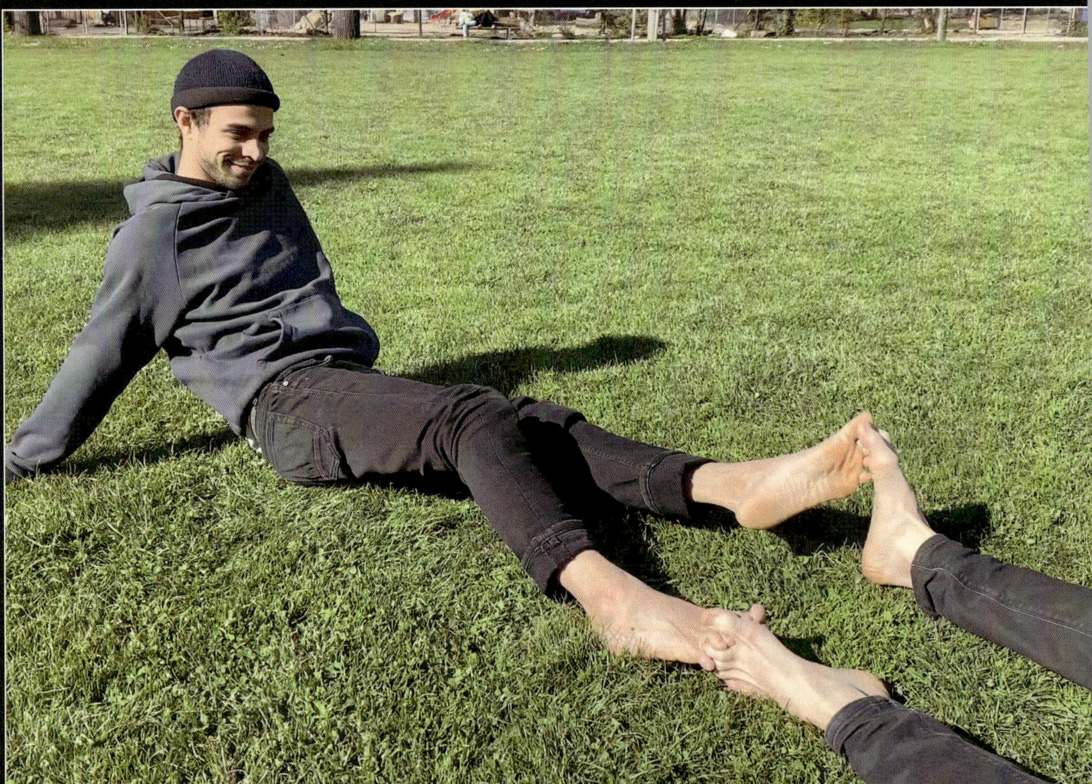

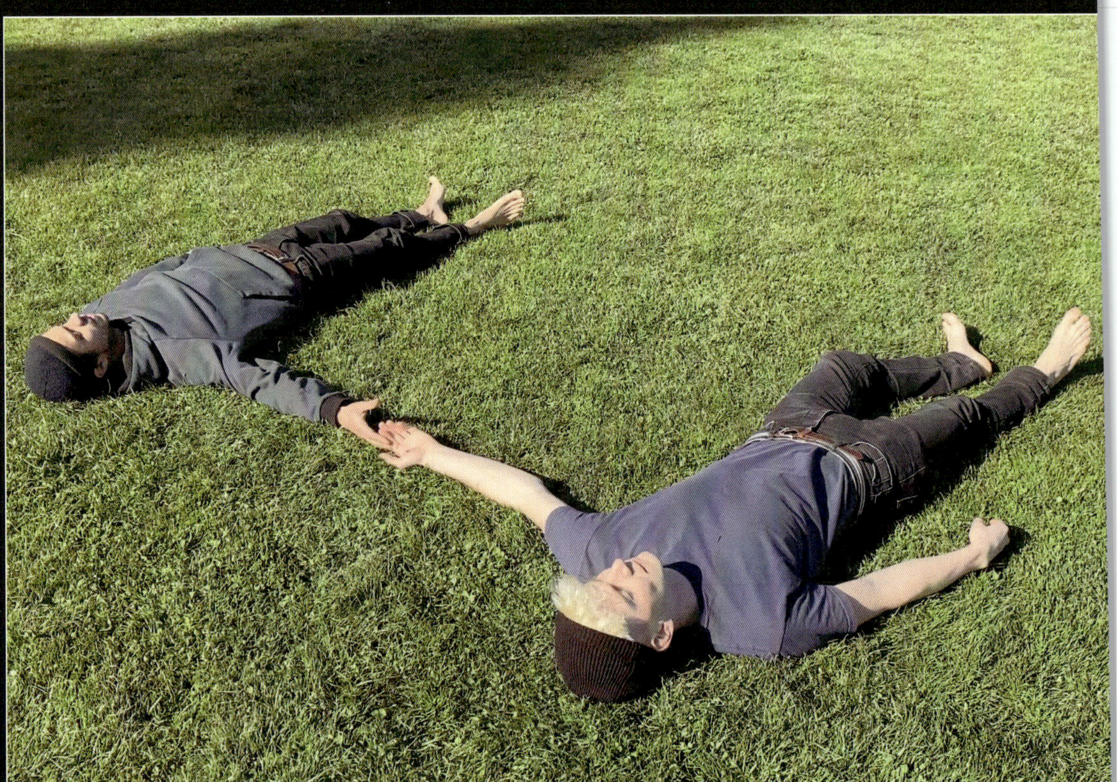

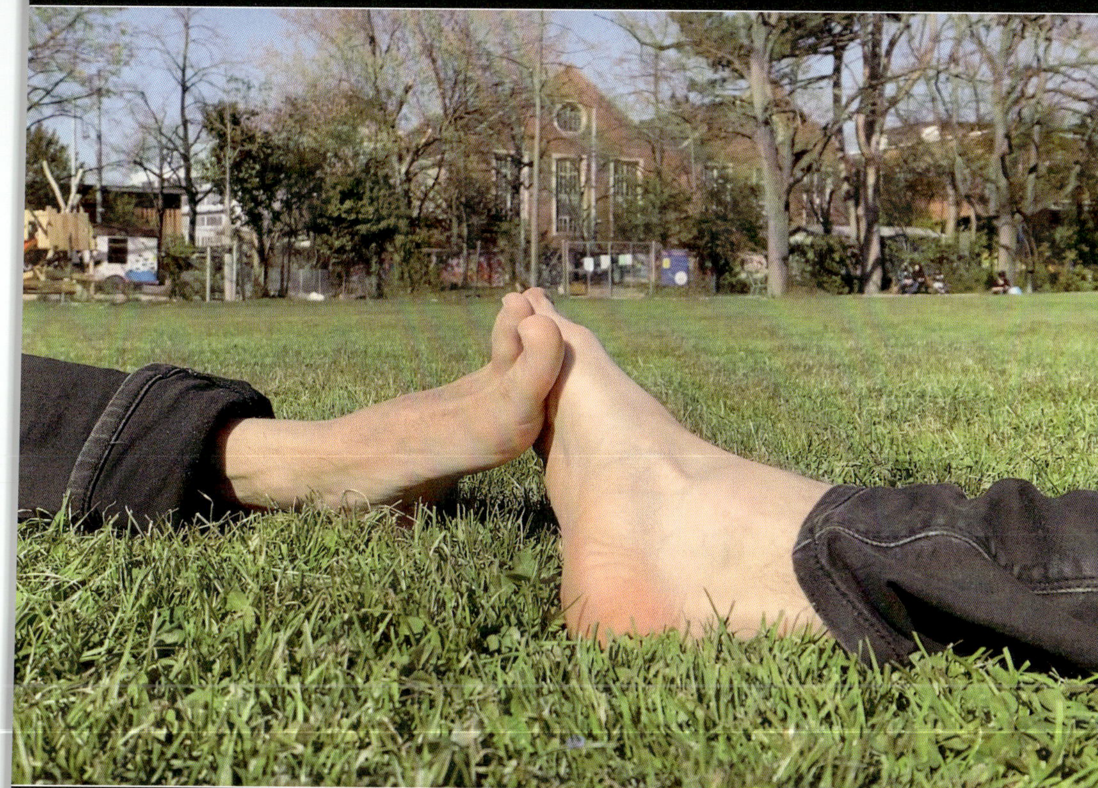

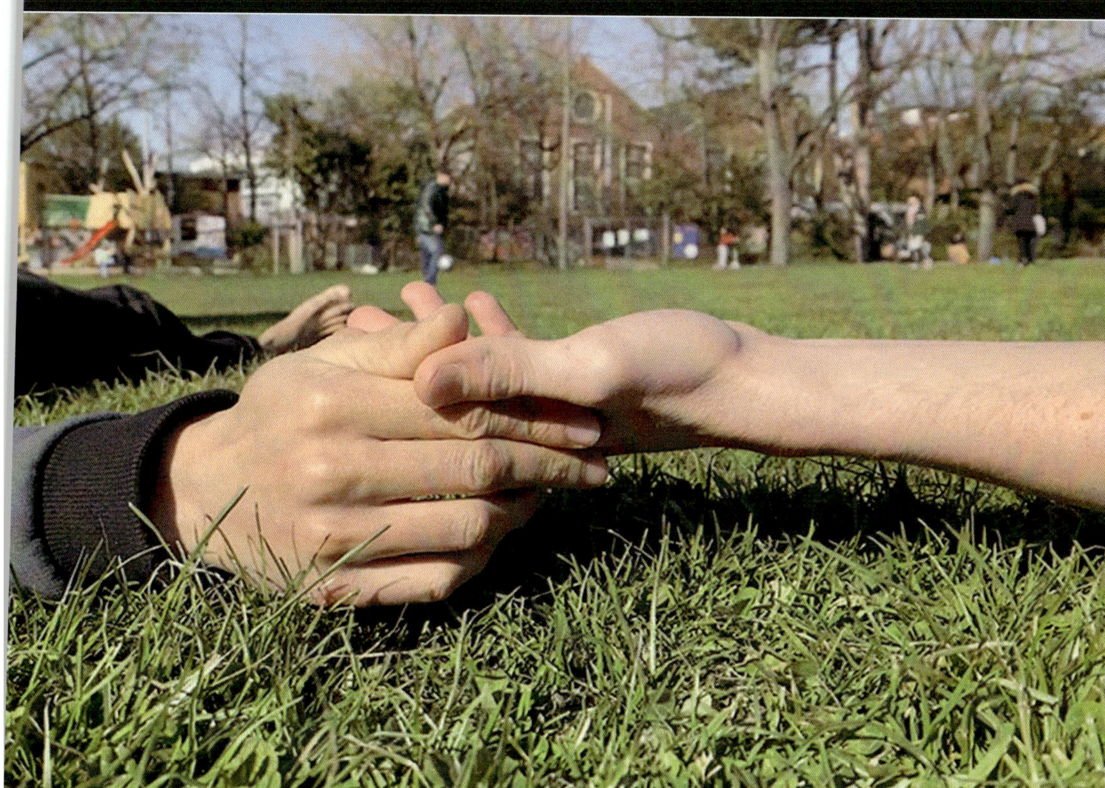

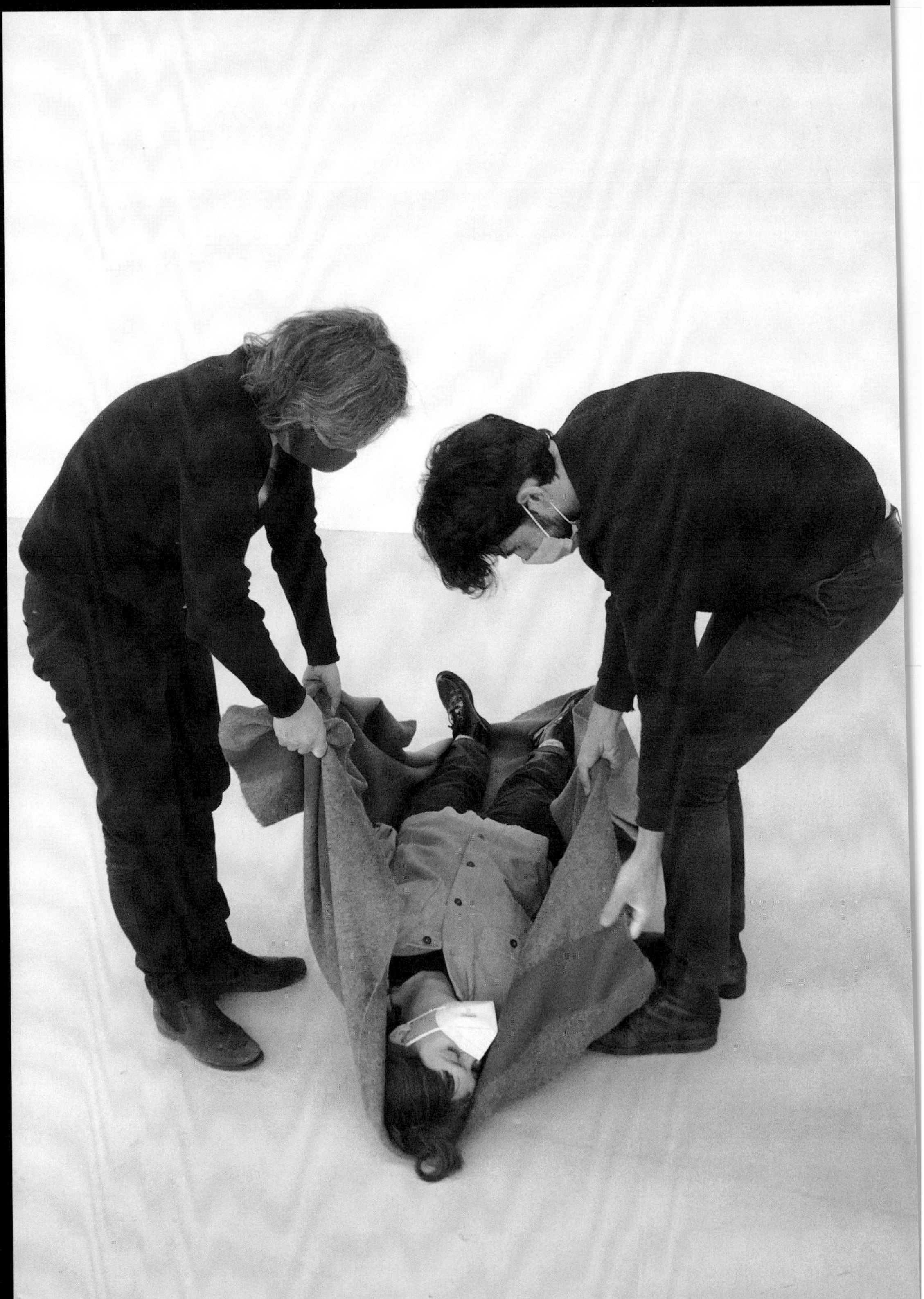

SAFE TOUCH

This training is accessible to everybody who is interested in receiving, developing or spreading our services. In case you are physically unable to do one of the exercises, it will be adapted accordingly.

Safety precautions: FFP2 masks, disinfectant, distance of at least two meters from mouth-to-mouth, ample ventilation.

INTENSE GAZE (Pairs)

Sit down with some distance, turn toward each other and close your eyes for a while. Then open your eyes, let the other person in. Allow them to look *through* your eyes and imagine that they could reach the back of your eyeballs.

We often start our trainings with this exercise. Now, you have to practice it with a bit more distance. Continue for at least five minutes.

Don't take it too seriously. You can smile. But don't pressure yourself into showing constant sympathy or bliss either.

After you have repeated this exercise with several people, talk with the last one about your impressions.

WITNESSING (Pairs)

You say or do something for several minutes. The other witnesses and reports back to you, refraining from personal judgements.

Intimate encounters are usually a quick and overlapping back and forth. This can create a great dynamic but can also be intimidating. Any hesitation might come as awkward, casting doubt on each other's openness and versatility. This exercise gives agency to the shy and cautious and requires attention from the dominant and restless.

Repeat the exercise swapping roles.

BROKEN MIRROR (Pairs and groups)

You come up with a movement and the other person mirrors you, but improperly. You then mirror them improperly and so on. To keep a safe and constant distance, keep a stick pressed between your bodies. You are now forced to counterbalance each other's movements. As soon as you feel comfortable with the situation, try it in a group of three, and then finally, all together.

This exercise creates a situation that is too delicate for one taking the lead. Everybody is challenged to make it not too boring and not too difficult. You train in getting along together without words. With a bit of experience you can close your eyes to also avoid visual communication. The dynamics of your relationships are boiled down to kinetics.

BLANKET MASSAGE (Groups of three)

You lie down on a huge blanket and two others move different parts of your body by slowly lifting and lowering different sections of the blanket. As these body parts press and shift against the blanket, the movements deliver gentle strokes. The lifted parts of the blanket also limit background noises and increase warmth, giving you a sense of protection. This indirect massage delivers the comforting pleasures of beginning to snuggle up, though slowed-down and repeated for minutes. Dragging the whole blanket over the floor relaxes the whole body.

Like many of our exercises, the blanket massage explores the limits of subtlety. For some, sudden intimacy can be too overwhelming, while everybody can profit from experiencing intimacy with strangers at an unusually slow pace. It makes us all the more aware of the particularity of the encounter.

Repeat the exercise twice swapping roles.

THE DOUGH (Pairs)

You lie flat and hide your head under a towel for additional protection. Your partner massages your back with both hands as though kneading a piece of dough and continues for at least five minutes, slowly shifting focus to the different parts of the back.

The Dough is a foolproof massage. As with most of our exercises, you can't do much wrong. You don't have to be too subtle. As with all of our exercises, you should end it with a 'No, thanks' or any other previously agreed sign if either of you starts to feel uncomfortable.

Repeat the exercise swapping roles.

CARESSING FEET (Pairs or small groups)

Some might have already tried the 'footshake' instead of the handshake. Since we'd better not touch anything with our hands, our feet are left to feel the world. We have a lot of sensitivity and flexibility in our feet, and we can train them. While masks replace sneakers as our new ribbons and ties, and while we'd better wear gloves all year long, we can still bare our feet.

The Army of Love always has to adapt. If somebody can't move their extremities, someone else helps them with stroking. The Covid-19 pandemic disables everybody to some degree, and we all have to explore where a differently-abled positivity could take us.

Repeat the exercise swapping roles.

GIVE ME YOUR HAND (Pairs)

It's actually still possible to safely touch each other's hands. We just have to stretch our arms out and avoid looking at each other.

This exercise is literally about one giving their hand to the other in whichever way they like, for at least three minutes. Like a lot of our practices, this exercise is meant to reduce the pressure for appropriate reciprocity. It can be relaxing to just focus on your own pleasure sometimes, or that of another.

Repeat the exercise swapping roles.

INSTANT LOVE (Whole group)

We build a circle with enough distance to reach our neighbors' hands when stretching our arms out to the side. While steadily holding hands for several minutes and keeping our eyes closed, we try to fall in love with either the person to the left or the person to the right. At the beginning, we might have problems focusing on an intriguing scenario but quickly it can evolve into a vivid and arousing fantasy. We try to stay neutral with our hands, but probably send subliminal messages for which we then overcompensate.

This exercise shows how easy it is to deliberately fall in love, at least under 'laboratory conditions.' It might be awkward to return to the real space. A communal debriefing – whereby we do not reveal the person we chose – can help to redirect our new love back to the group.

DEBRIEFING (Whole group)

We build a circle, resting comfortably at a safe distance. One after another, we talk for five minutes about our experiences during the workshop. The others listen and stay neutral until it's their turn.

As in our trainings in general, no one should be considered of more importance and no one should be ignored – unless they explicitly skip or quit an exercise. Everybody is meant to give and receive the same amount of attention, regardless of whether they join the training with the intention to give or to receive. To learn to give you also have to learn to receive, and vice versa.

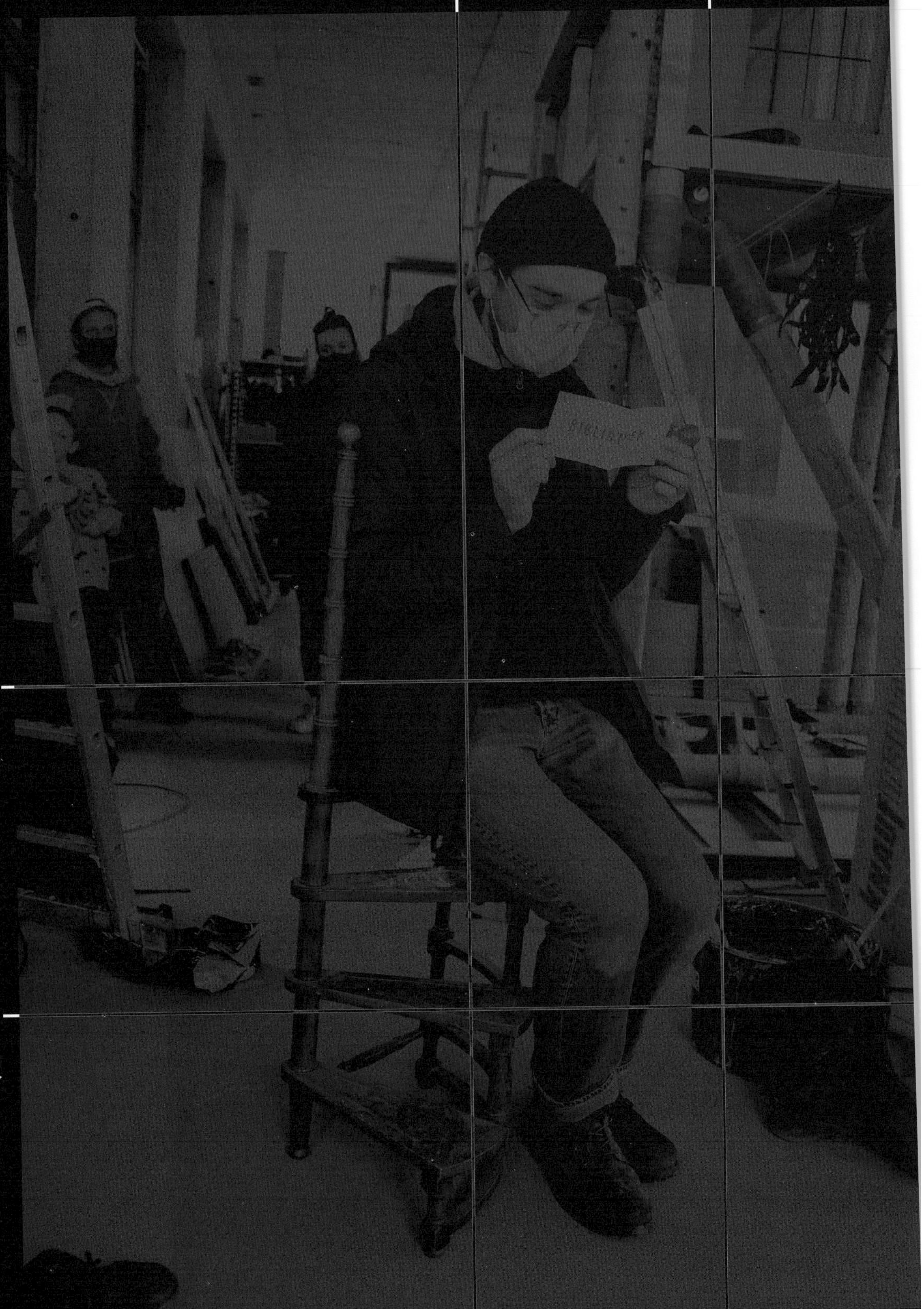

MARCH 7, 2021, ZURICH, SWITZERLAND

Retreat into the Public: A Trip into Collective Living in Urban Space, IG Hallenleben

Living and working collectively in big halls provides a possibility to create and negotiate space in a self-determined way. It is characterized by multifunctionality and the minimization of private space in order to expand communal space. Such an infrastructure – a reasonably priced hall – is difficult to find in a city that is getting more and more expensive and privatized. This training focuses on the skills needed for future forms of collective living in urban space.

IG Hallenleben is an association based in Zurich, founded by people who live and work in halls. Its aim is to encourage and enable self-determined and collective ways of living.

Visual documentation by Annett Landsmann, Luzia Vogt, Simon Schwarz and Janine Umiker

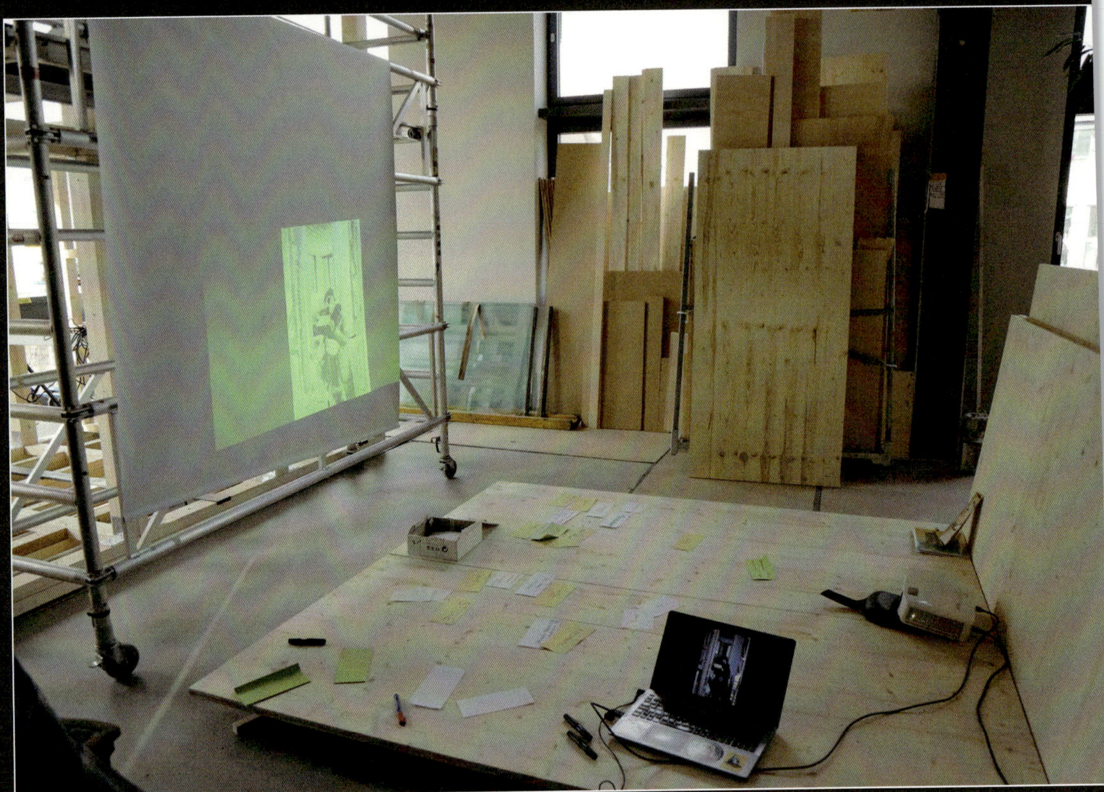

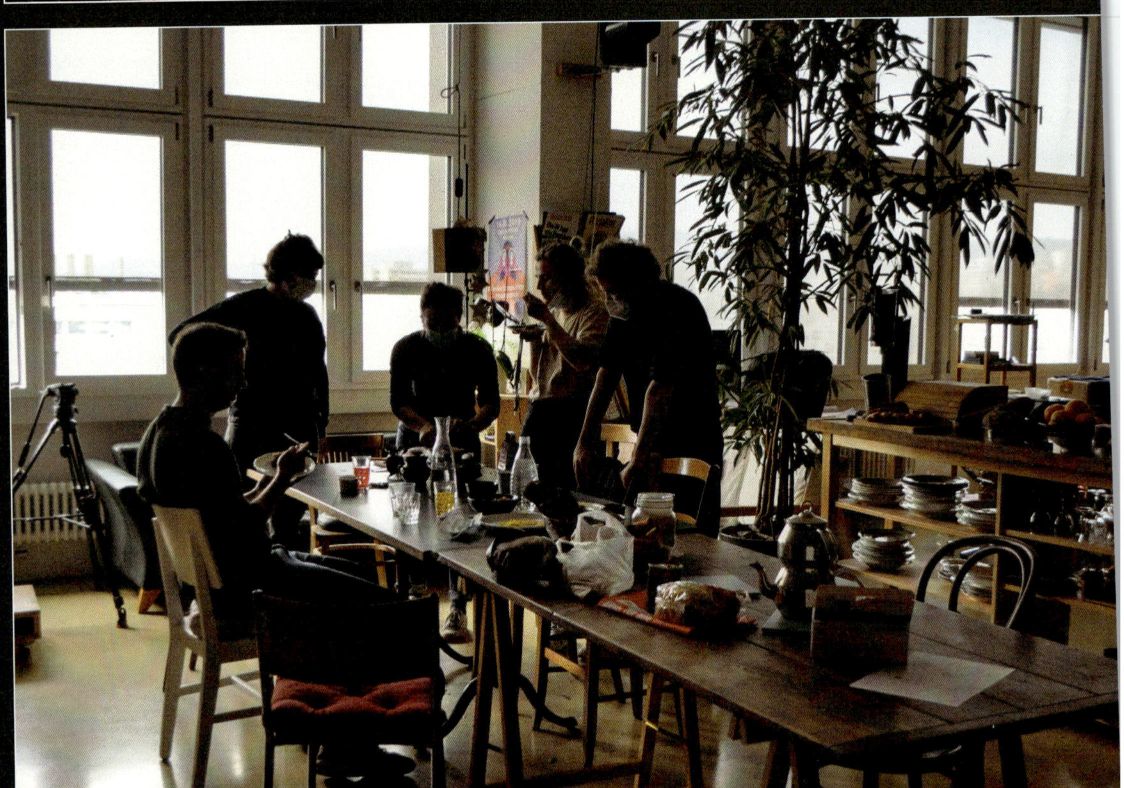

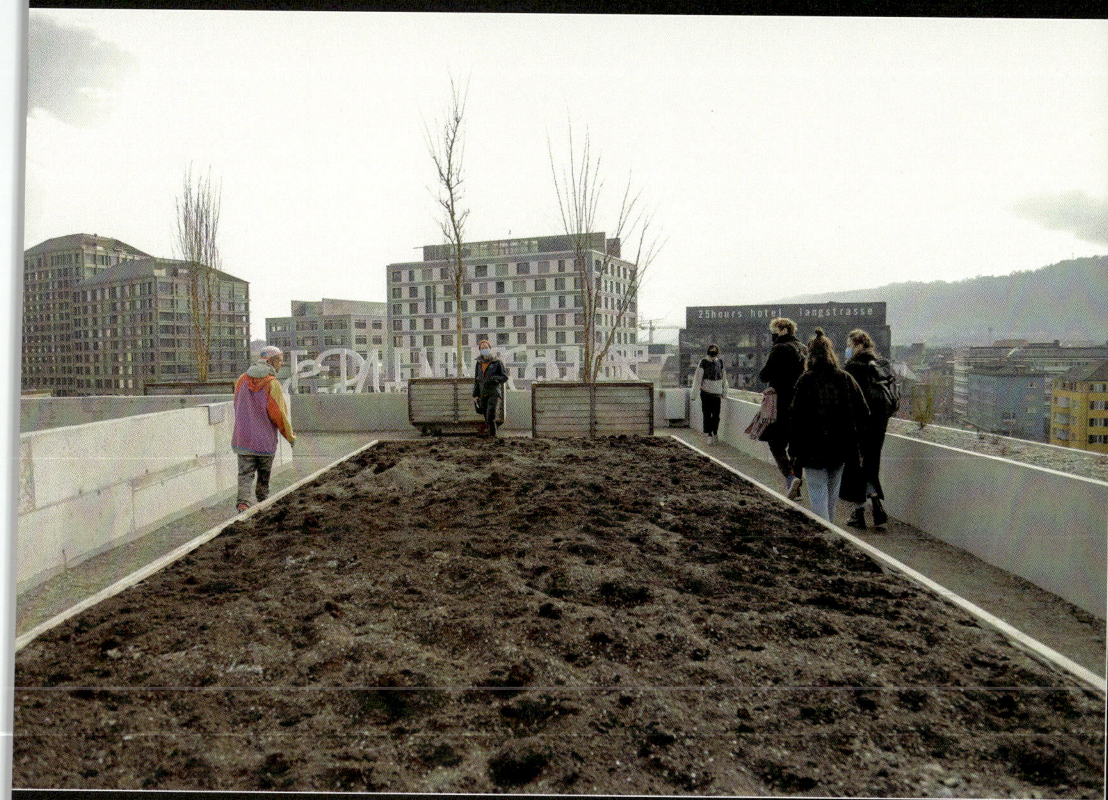
25hours hotel langstrasse

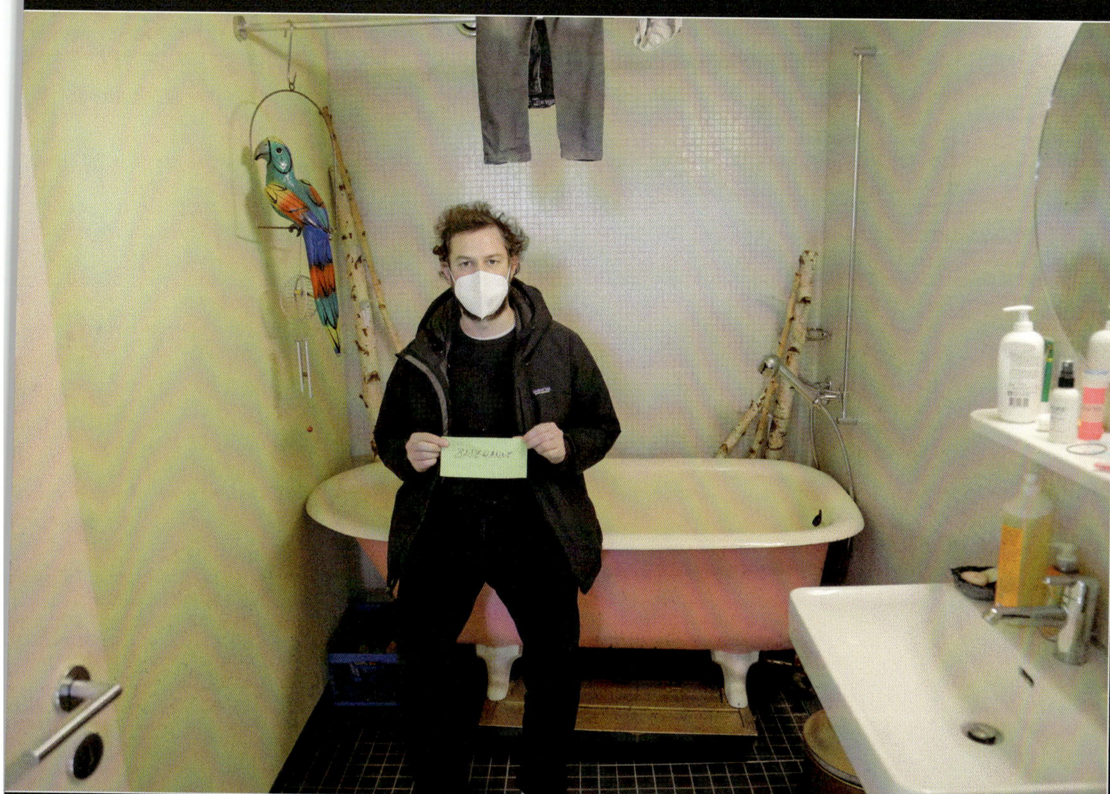

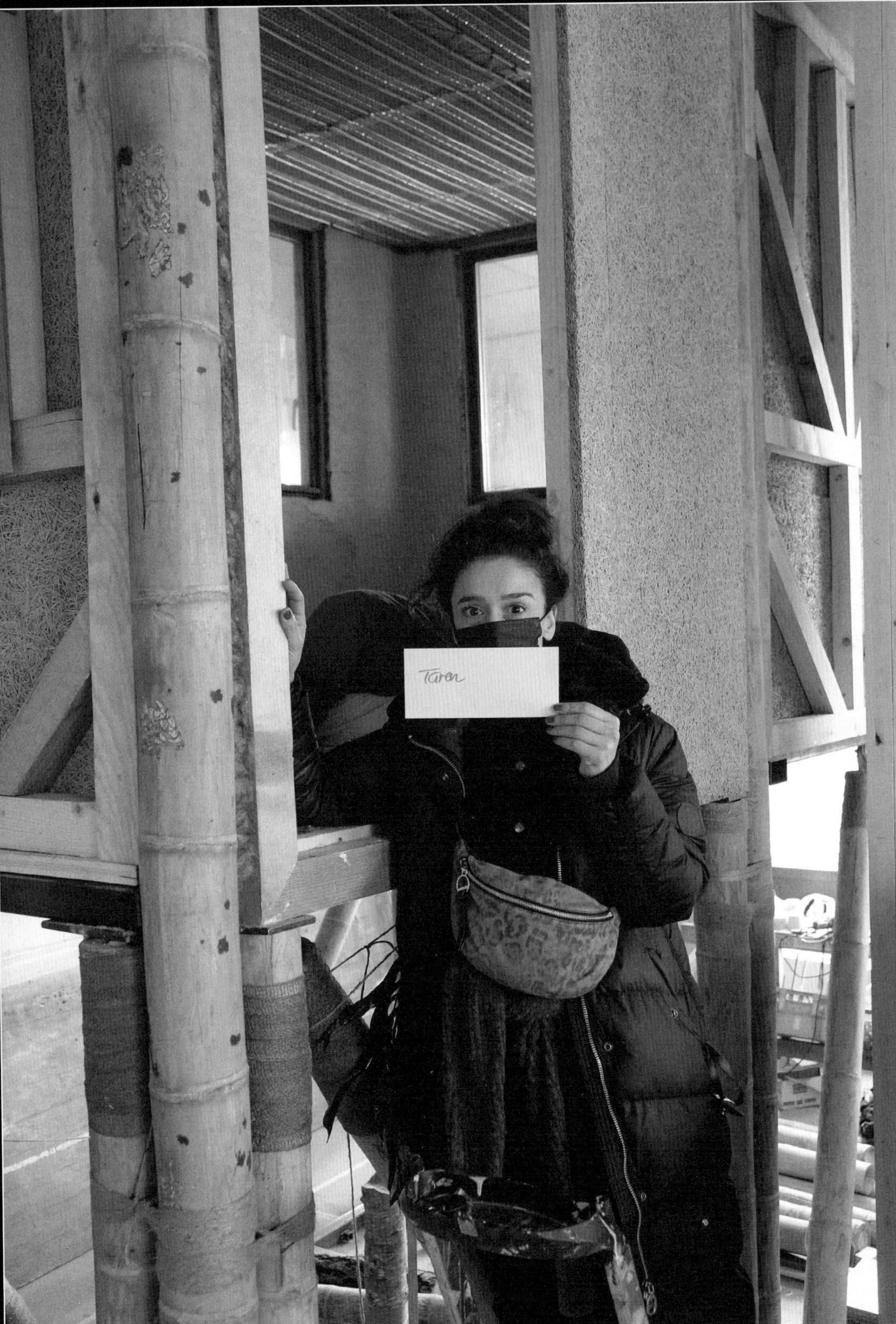
Taren

Retreat into the Public

A Trip Through Communities Living in Halls

Meet in a group of about ten people, travel by bike

Station #1

Roleplay: From the Vision to Moving In

Location: Empty theater hall (220m2), Neumarkt, Zürich

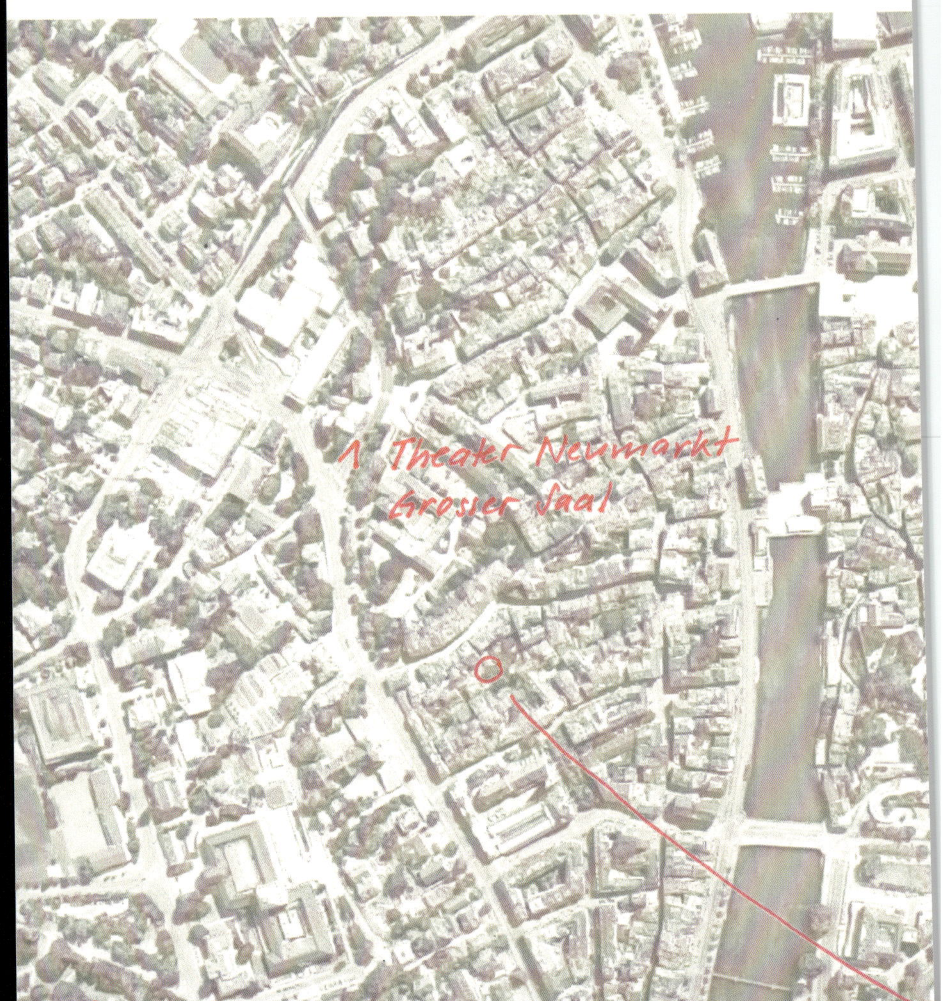

Introduction

First Assignment

Get together with roughly ten people in a space measuring around 300m2. It will take sixty minutes to experience this roleplay.

Imagine a future where living alone or in a small family is not possible anymore for whatever reason. Instead, you need to form a community and create a communal living space in a hall. As you can imagine, this process can take anywhere from three months to twenty years.

Introduce yourself by answering the following questions:

How do you live currently?
What do you like doing at your place?
What would you enjoy doing most that you cannot currently do at your place?
When do you experience community?

Get to know your new community: smile at them, they are your future roommates.

Meditation

Second Assignment

Lay on the floor, get comfortable, close your eyes. Let's meditate together.

Meditate about your favorite place:

How does it look, smell and feel?
How is the light?
Who is there with you?

Imagine this place inside the hall:

What elements can you bring into the hall?
How can others benefit from your favorite place?
Will they also enjoy it?
How can you share it?
Search for the positive feelings you have about sharing and living together. What are you looking forward to?
What skills and talents can you share with your new community?

And then let's face the fears and insecurities within you, the ones you have about this project:

Can you name your fears?
Can you come up with solutions?

Process

Third Assignment

Walk through the room and have a good look at it. This is your future place!

What is there?
What is missing?
Where is your favorite place in the room?

Keep on walking. Find a person and start discussing:

How many people do you need to build the imagined space?
Where will your space be?
In the city or in the countryside?
How are you going to find this space? (Via websites, friends or searching directly in the city, etc.)

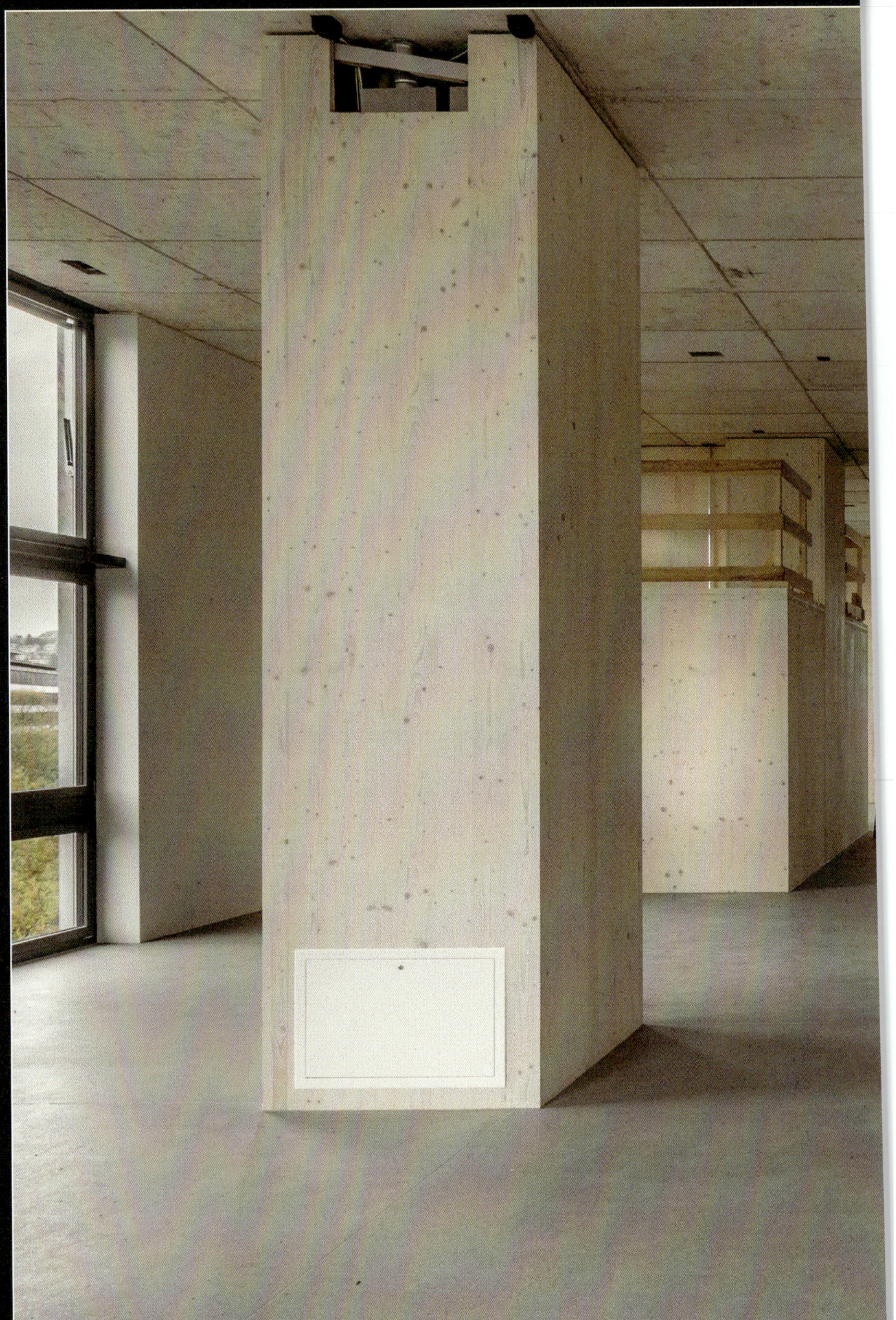

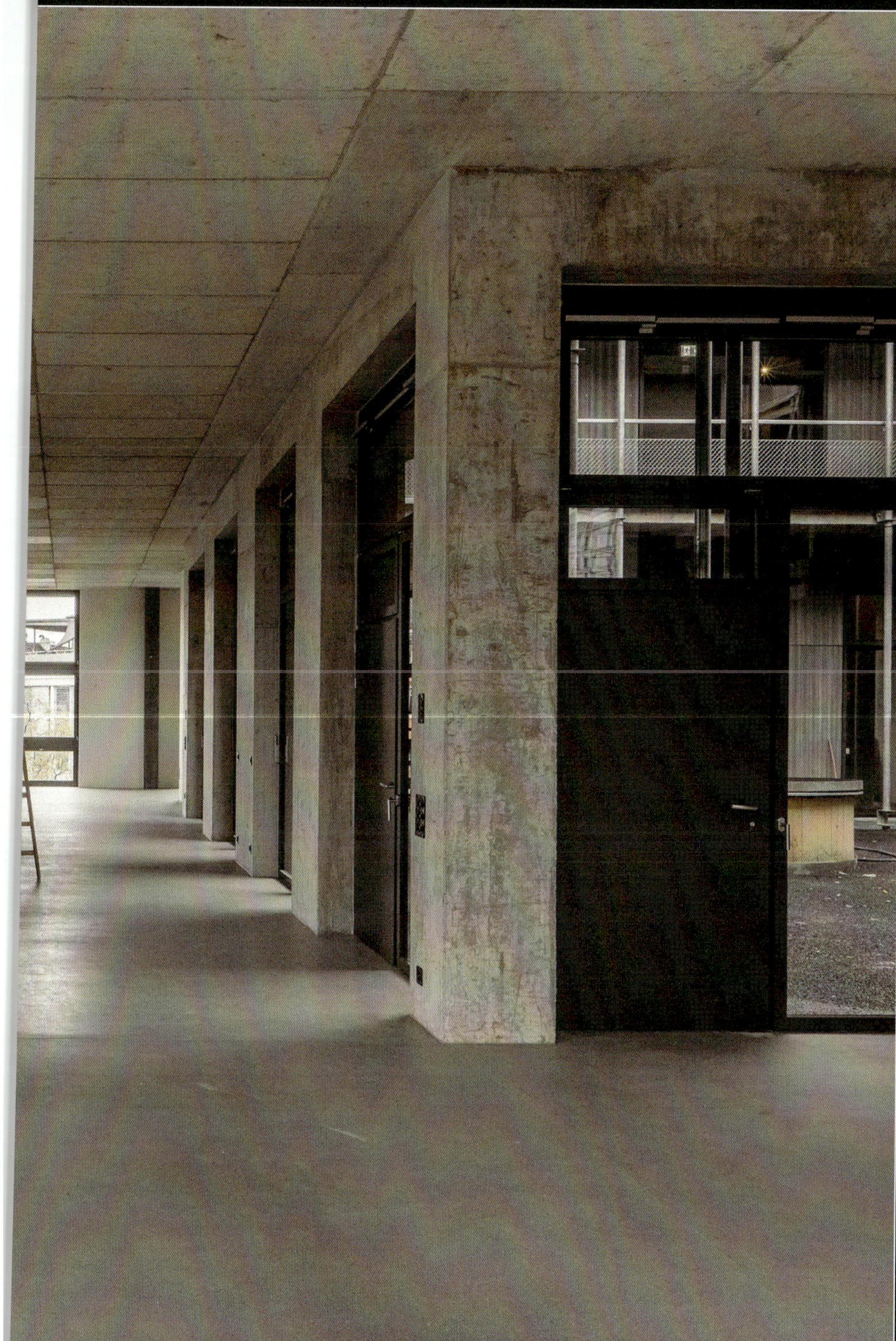

Station #2

How to Get Food for Your Community

Location: Foodsharing fridge, Sihlquai 131, Zürich

Listen to the Audio

Scan the QR-Code

Is there a foodsharing fridge in your city that is accessible to the public? If yes, explore the place and listen to the audio about solidary projects connected to food in Zürich.

Foodsharing fridge
Platform to share leftover food
International

Ortoloco
Cooperative farming
Zürich, Switzerland

Rampe21
Grassroots
Food cooperative store
Zürich, Switzerland

Solrosa
Non-profit association supporting working conditions for refugees
Bern, Switzerland

Dumpster diving
Ecological and cheap
Behind your local store

Station #3

Hall Under Construction

Location: Zurwollke, Zollstrasse 121, Zürich

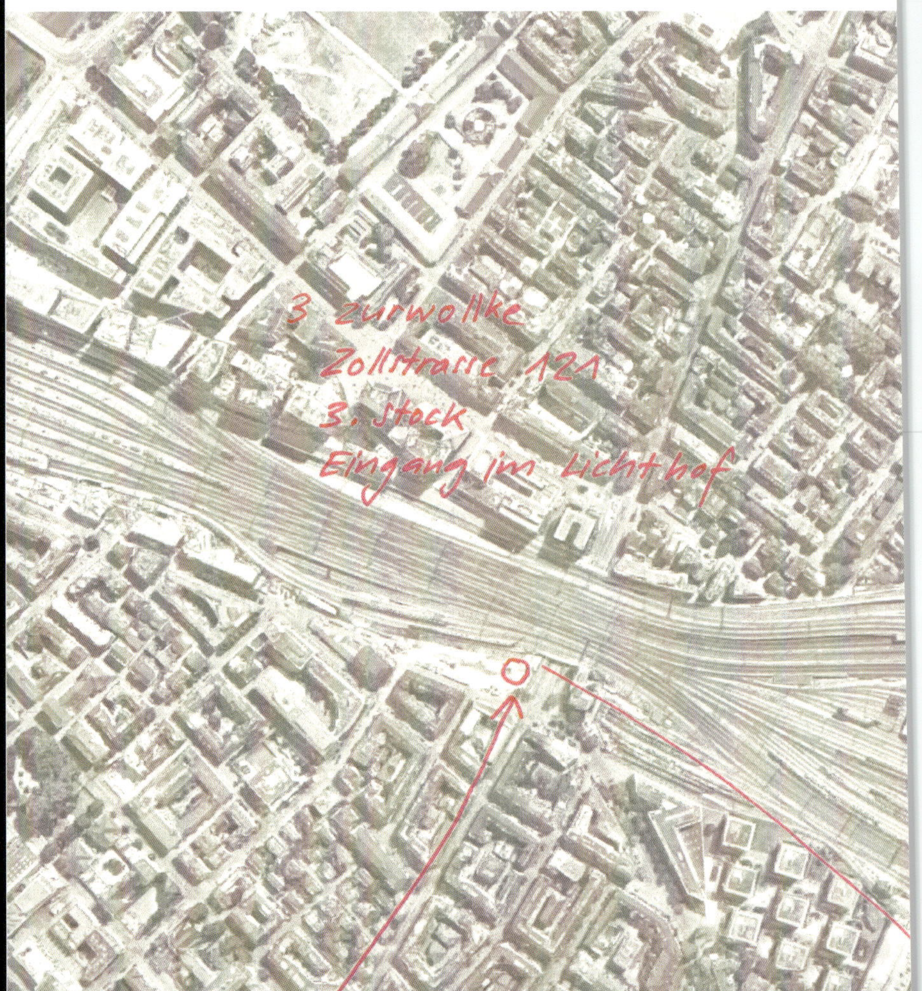

Exploring the Construction Site as Playground

If possible, try to visit a hall that is under construction in your city

Introduction

Observe the construction site:

What different functions does the place accommodate at the same time?
Which new opportunities does the space offer?

Discovery

Explore the space:

What is key for it to work?
What elements are missing?

Try to look as if through the eyes of a child.

Enactment

Think about what you have been missing in this space. Embody your vision/the thing you are missing. Ask someone to take a photo of it. Is it:

A space to retreat to?
A swing?
A connection to the street, like a balcony?

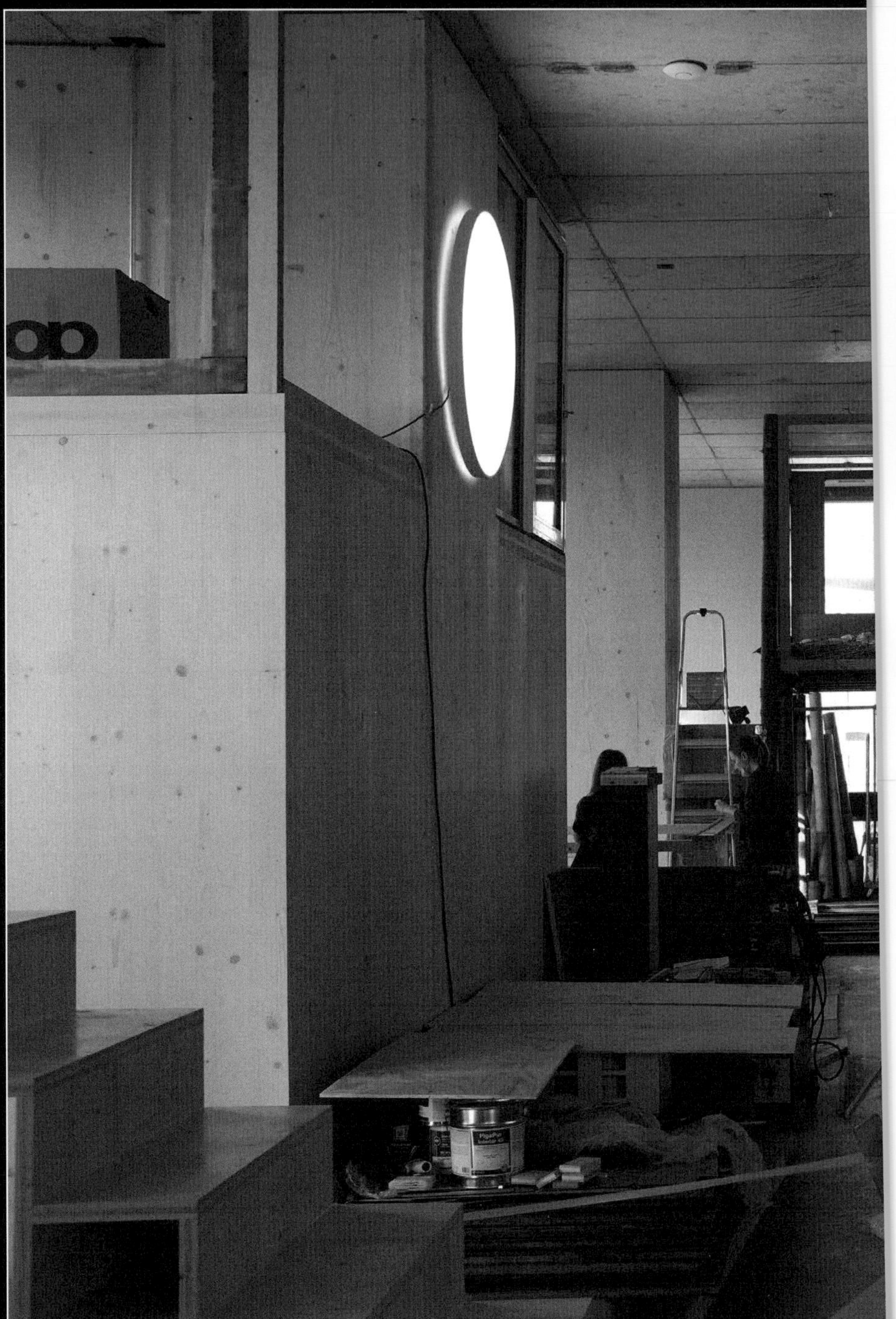

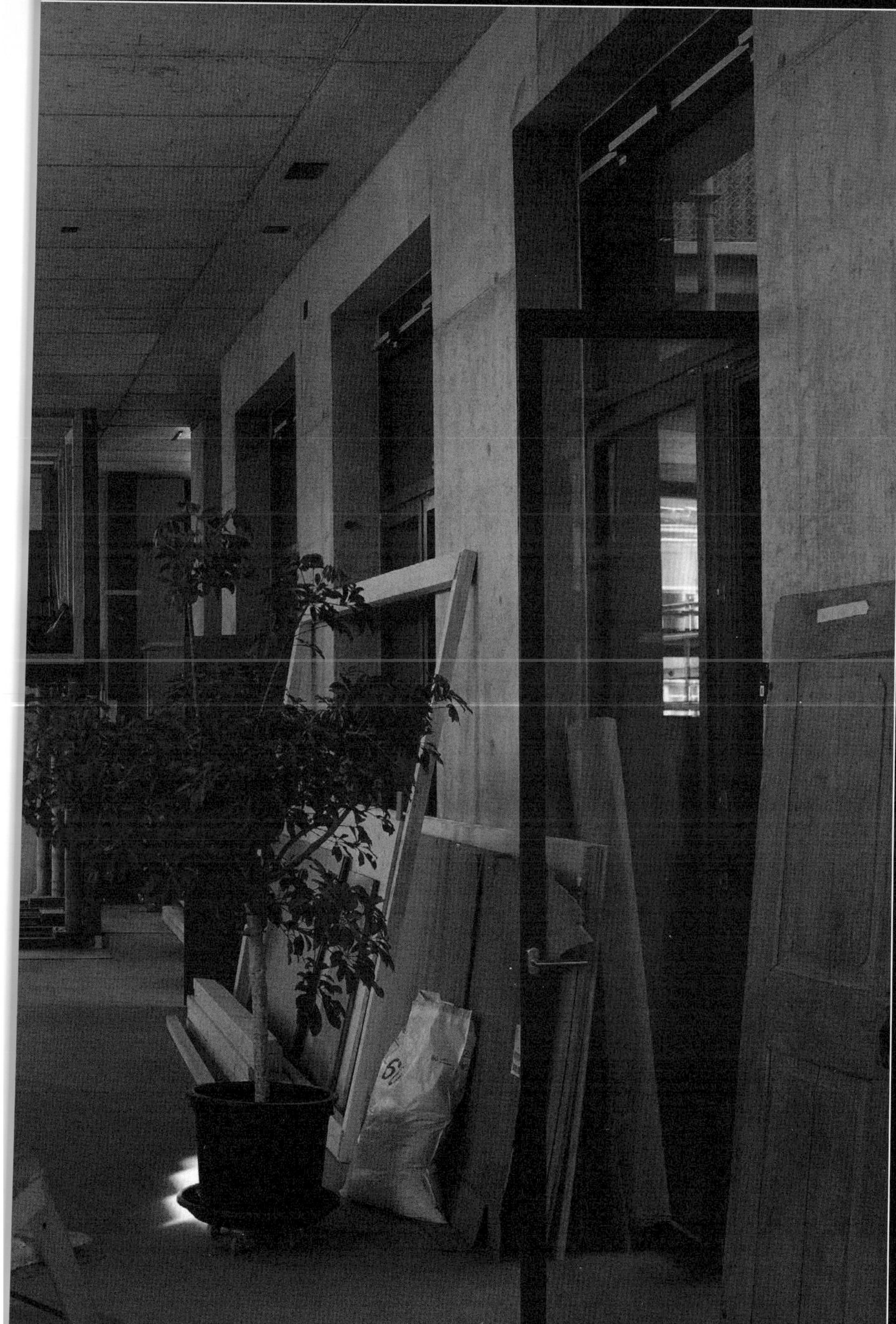

A space to retreat to…

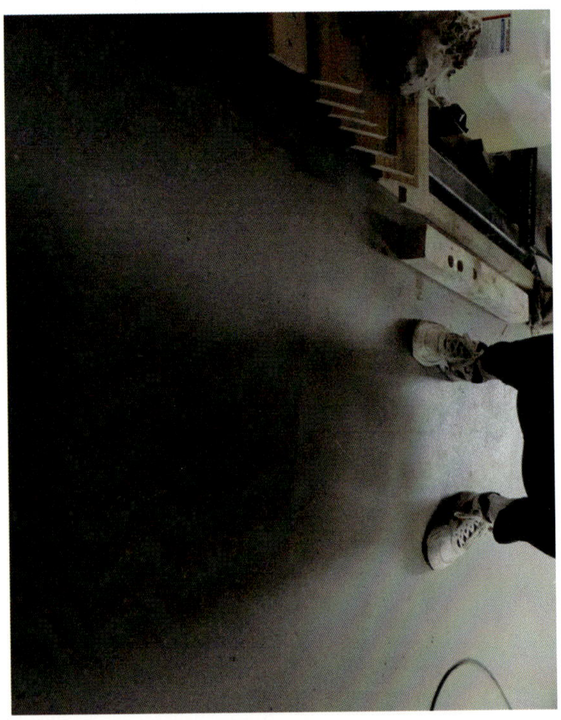

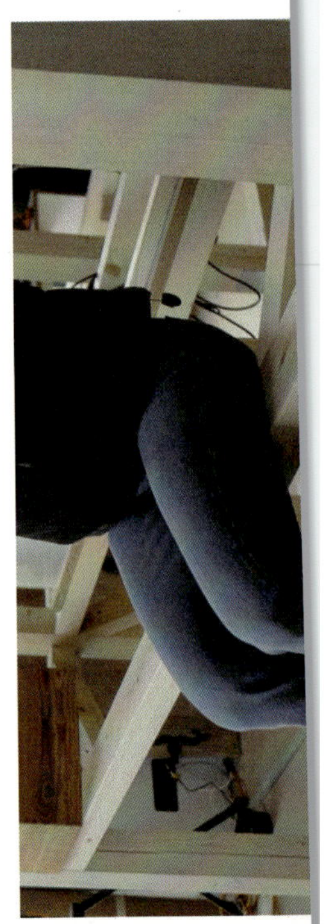

A swing...

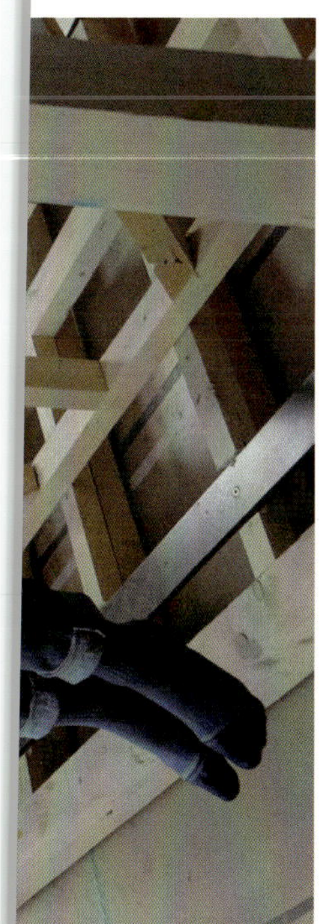

A connection to the street...

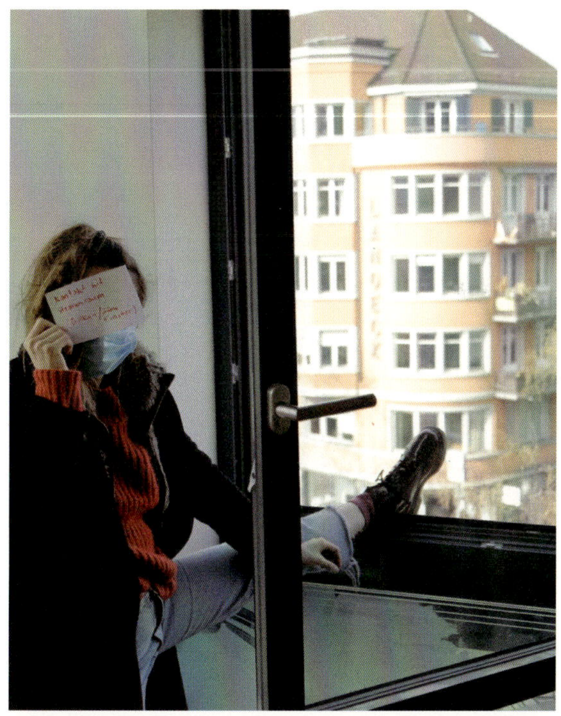

Station #4

Voices from the Halls

Location: Stadionbrache, Förlibuckstrasse 236, Zürich

Listen to the Audio

Scan the QR-Code

Search for an urban wasteland in your city. Maybe it is in the city center, maybe it is more on the outskirts.

Scan the QR code, let your gaze wander into the distance and listen to the different voices answering the following questions:

What is the echo like in a hall?
Why do you think that you are a collective?
In what moments are you overjoyed to be included in a collective?
When does it annoy you?
What are the challenges you are currently dealing with?
What was a major turning point in the development or history of your collective?

Station #5

Established Hall Projects

Location: Vulkanplatz Altstetten, Zürich

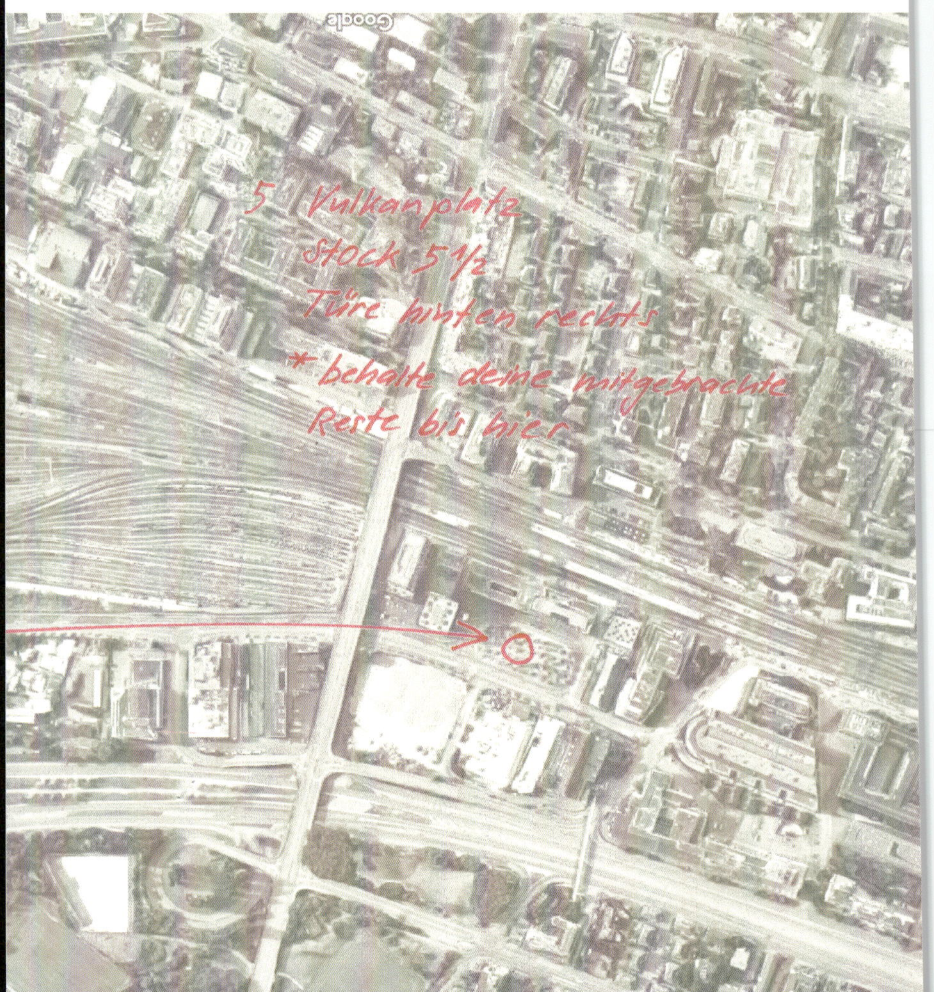

Following the Traces

If possible, try to visit an already established hall project

If in Zürich, you would find yourself at the edge of the city now. You would enter a vivid hall used for community living, which can only exist in that form on the periphery of the city as high rental prices push alternative ways of living out of the center.

What projects do you know of in your city that were victims of gentrification?

Discuss how the situation in your city is.

Imagine coming home to your hall hungry. In such instances, there are different scenarios that could play out:

What is the procedure going to be?
Are you cooking for yourself, or just snacking on some leftovers in the fridge?
Are you asking others to join you in cooking?
What are their needs?

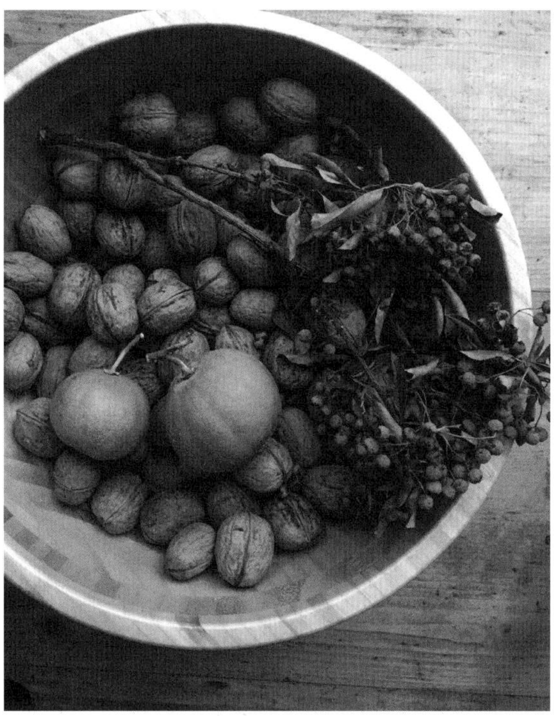

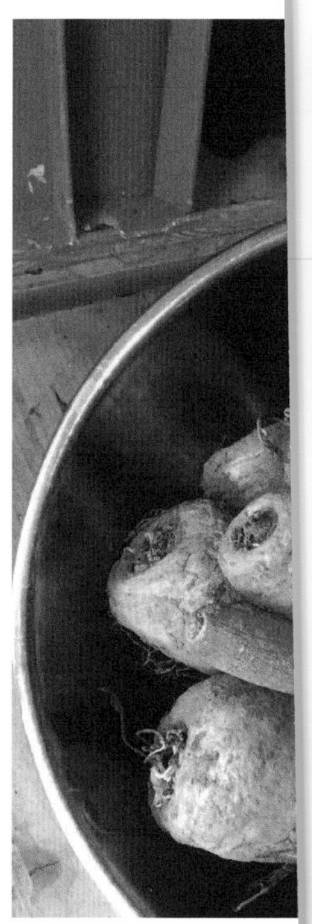

Performing Daily Routines

Cooking Collectively

What food is in the kitchen?
How full is the fridge?
Are there any leftovers?
Are there enough leftovers for everybody or do you need to enrich the meal?

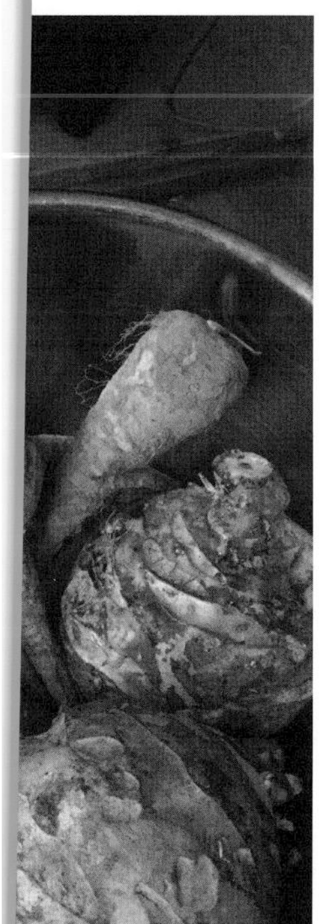

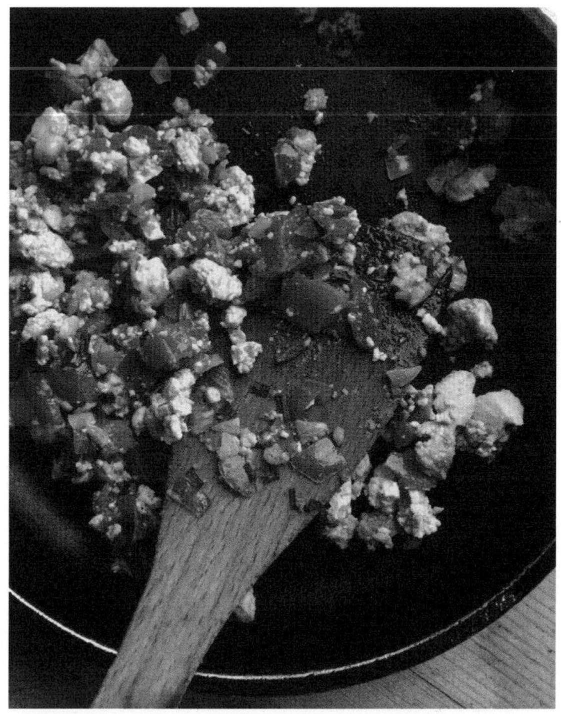

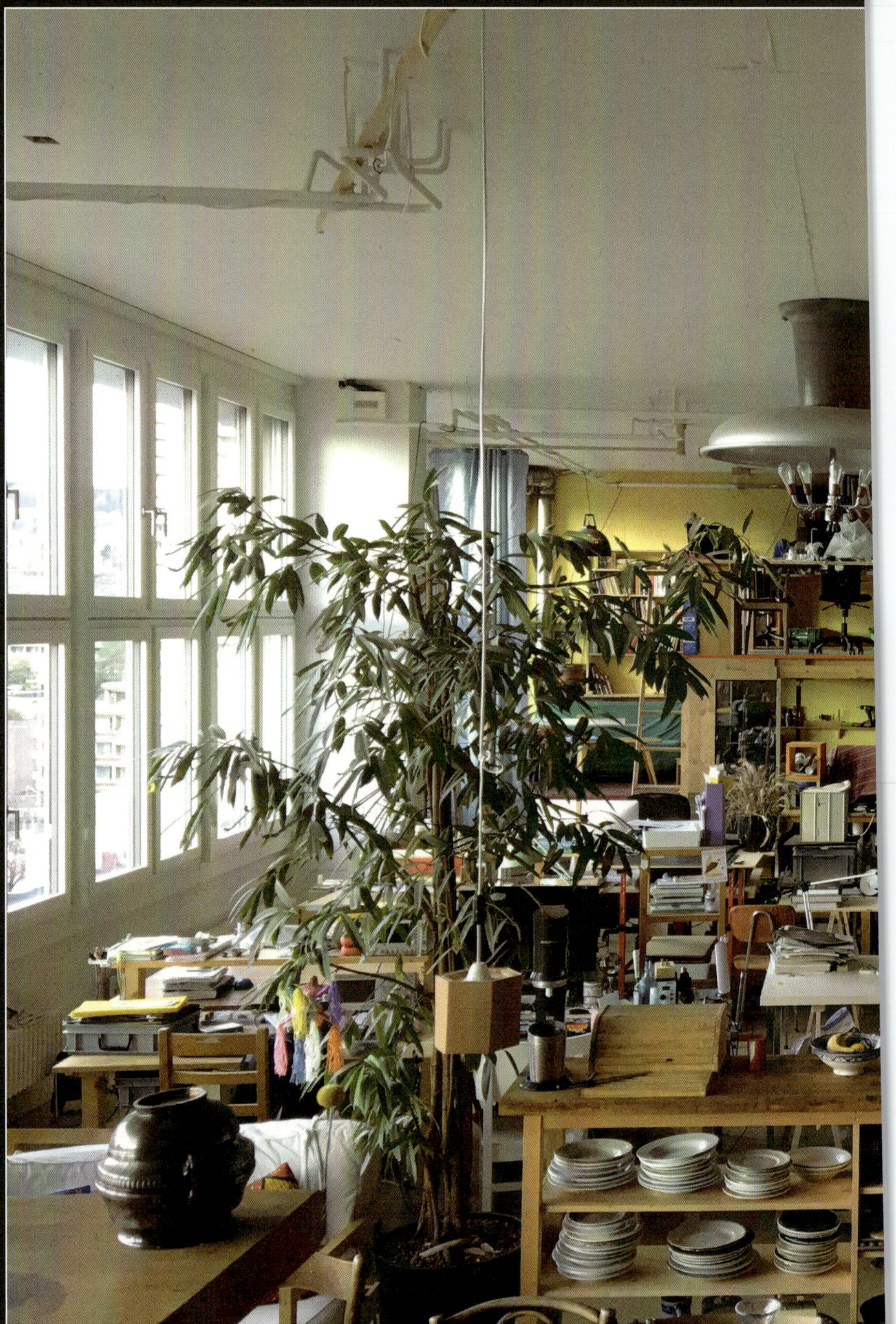

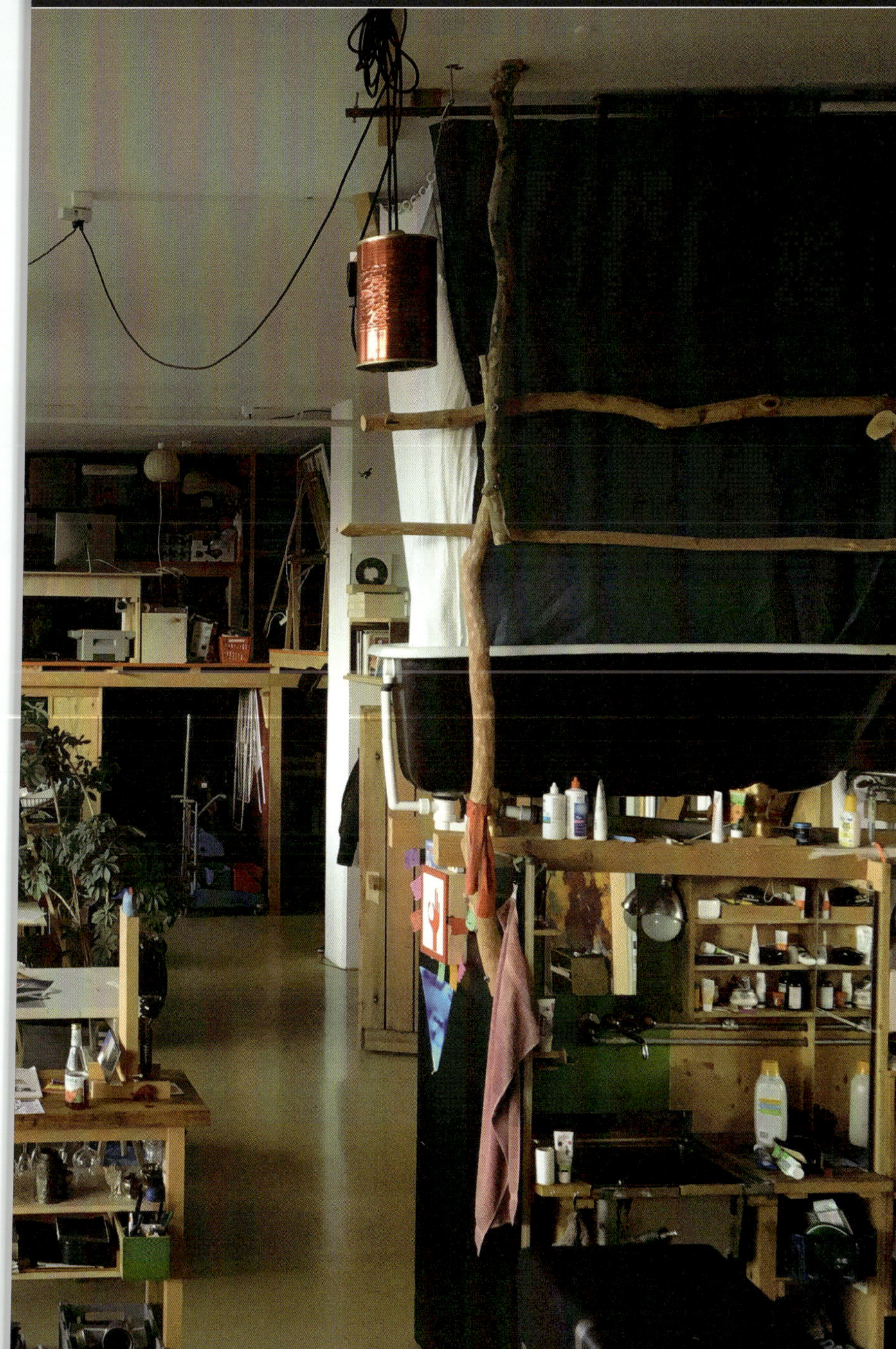

Living and working collectively in big halls is a possibility to create and negotiate space in a self-determined way. It is characterized by multifunctionality and the minimization of private space in order to expand communal space. Such an infrastructure – a reasonably priced hall – is difficult to find in a city that is getting more and more expensive and privatized. As such, this training focuses on the skills needed for future forms of collective living in urban space.

IG Hallenleben is an association based in Zürich, founded by people who live and work in halls. Its aim is to encourage and enable a self-determined and collective way of living.

MARCH 7, 2021, ZURICH, SWITZERLAND

Growing Food with Humanponics, Antonio Scarponi

Hydroponics is a soilless farming technique that allows growing food under any environmental conditions. Usually, complicated machinery and chemical fertilizers are used in hydroponics, however in this training participants learn about ELIOOO – an affordable do-it-yourself technique. ELIOOO is a simple system that enables people to grow food at home using inexpensive IKEA boxes and their urine. ELIOOO will not only create a close connection between people and their environment but it also hacks IKEA's distribution chain, transforming it into the manufacturer of an idea.

Antonio Scarponi is an architect, designer, author, educator and entrepreneur, and founder of the Zurich-based office Conceptual Devices – which he established with the firm intention to redefine the way we are doing and talking about 'change.' He works on DIY community engagement practices through the development of what he calls 'anti-products.'

Visual documentation by Antonio Scarponi / Conceptual Devices

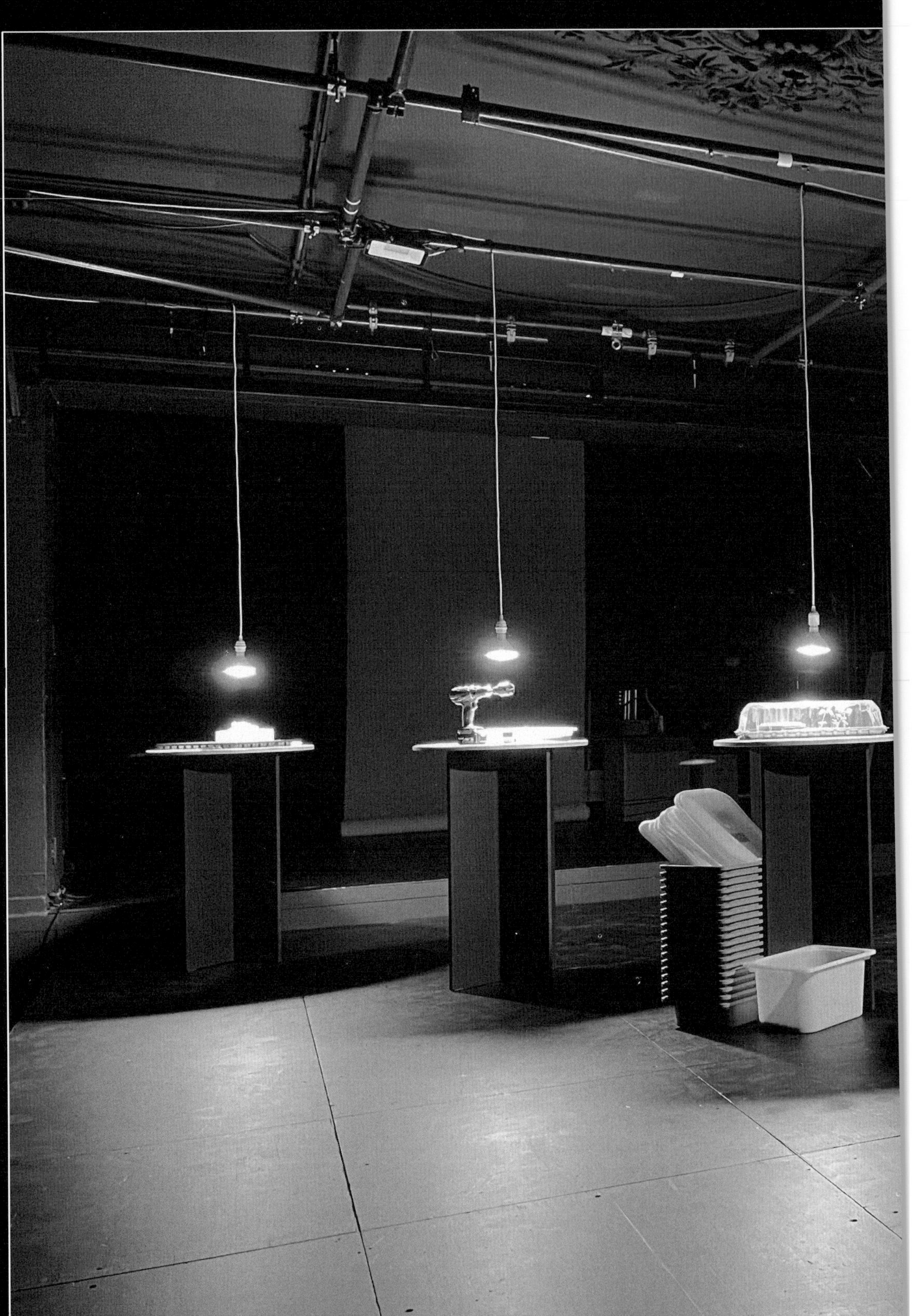

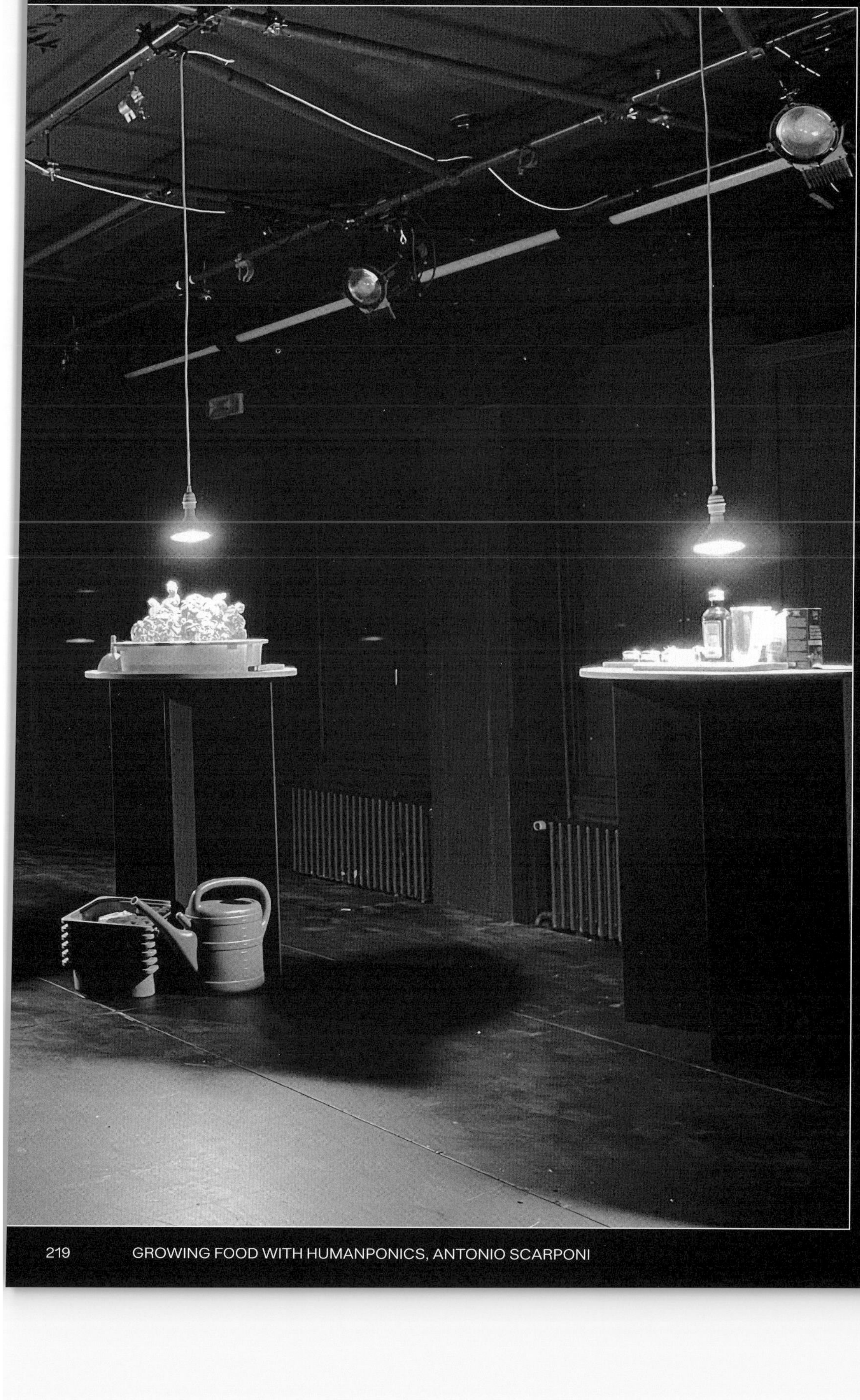

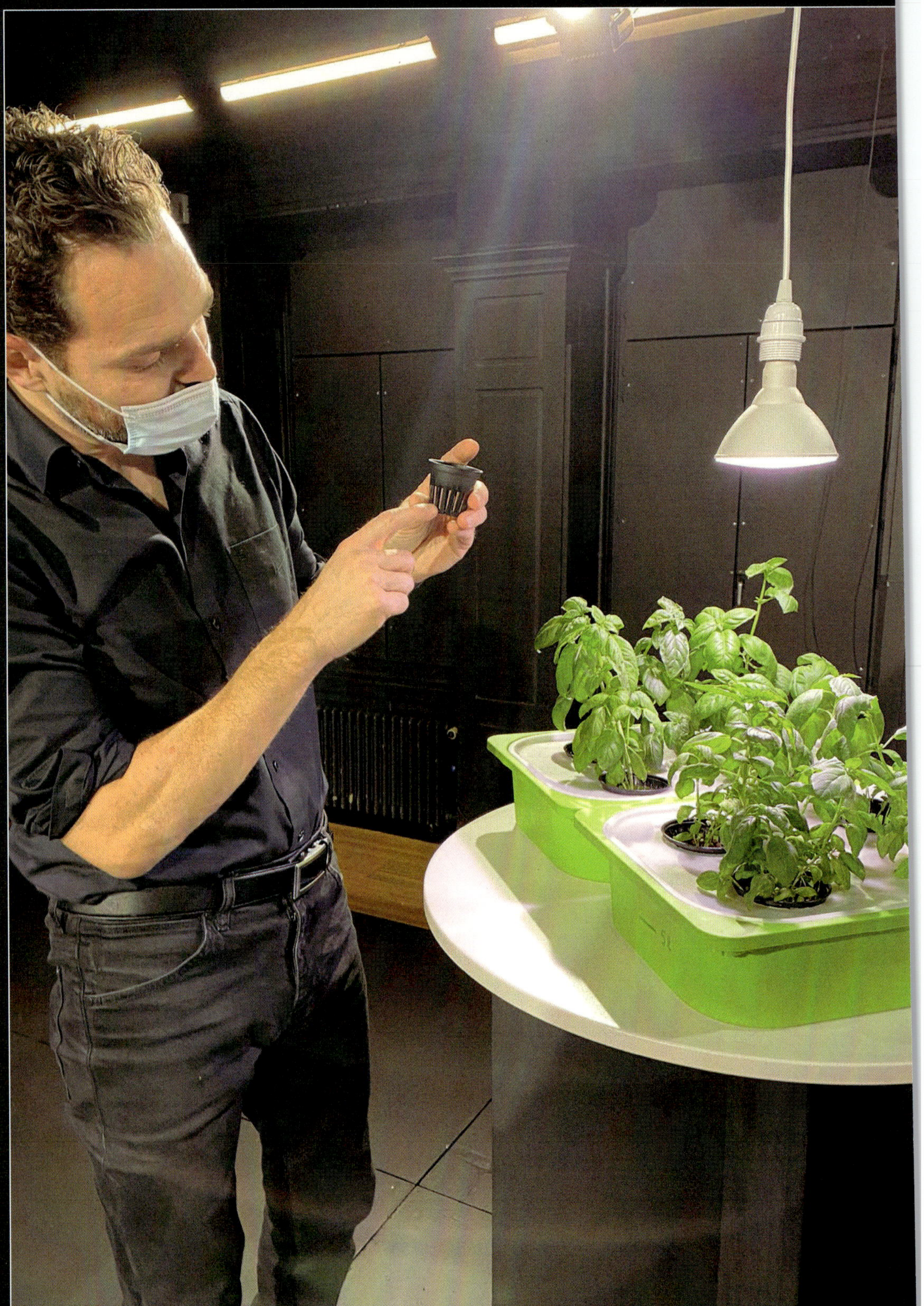

HOW TO GROW FOOD AT HOME

HUMANPONICS

USING HOMOEOPATHIC DOSES OF YOUR URINES

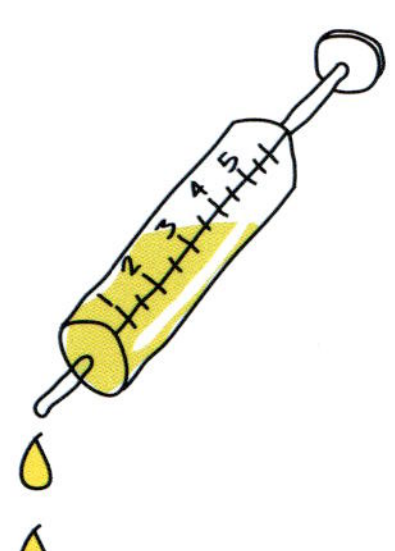

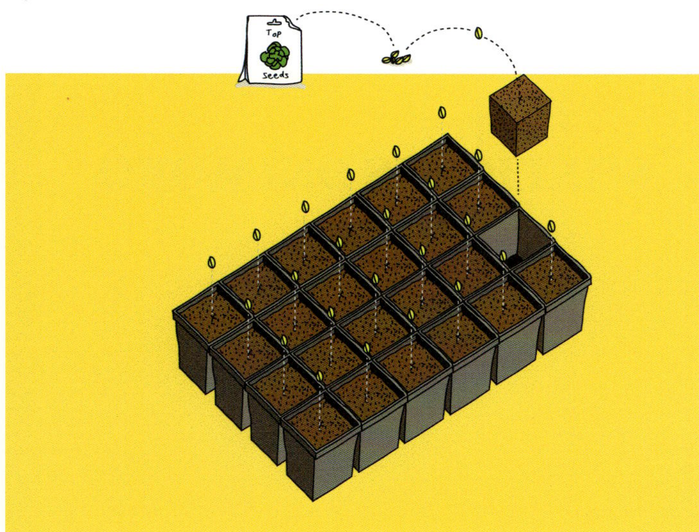

ANTONIO SCARPONI

Hydroponics allows you to grow food anywhere. Plants grow in water diluted with chemical fertilizers. But, in homoeopathic doses, you can also use your urines instead.

I am Antonio Scarponi, this is my TRAINING FOR THE FUTURE, and you are the seed of this idea.

1

GROWING SEEDLINGS

METHOD A.

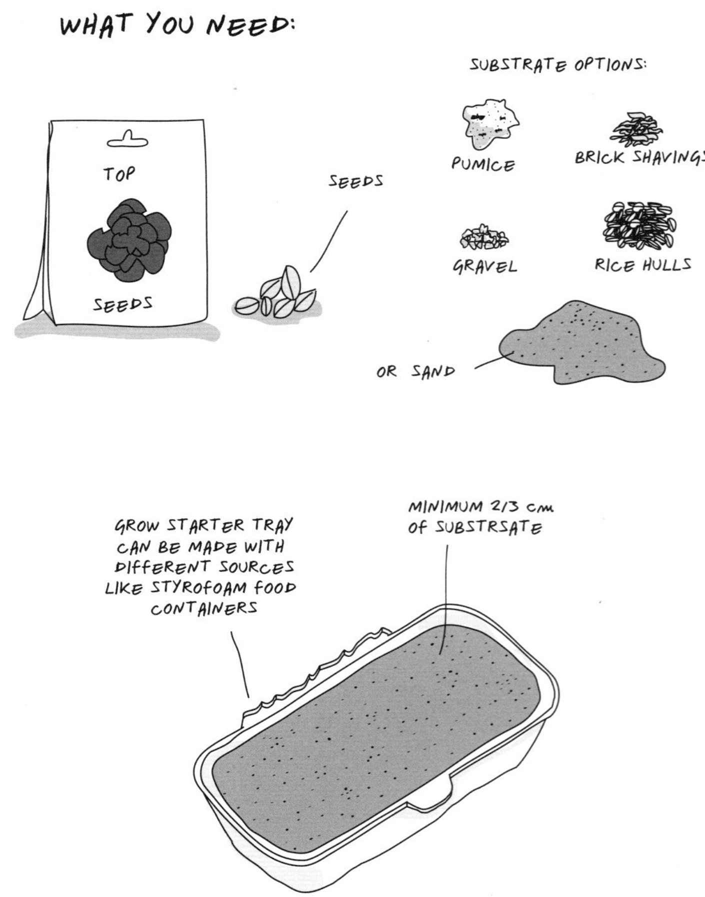

1 WASH THE SUBSTRATE

PLANTING THE SEED IN A GROW MEDIUM – SUBSTRATE. A MEDIUM OR SUBSTRATE, CAN BE MADE OF DIFFERENT MATERIALS. SEE OPTIONS.

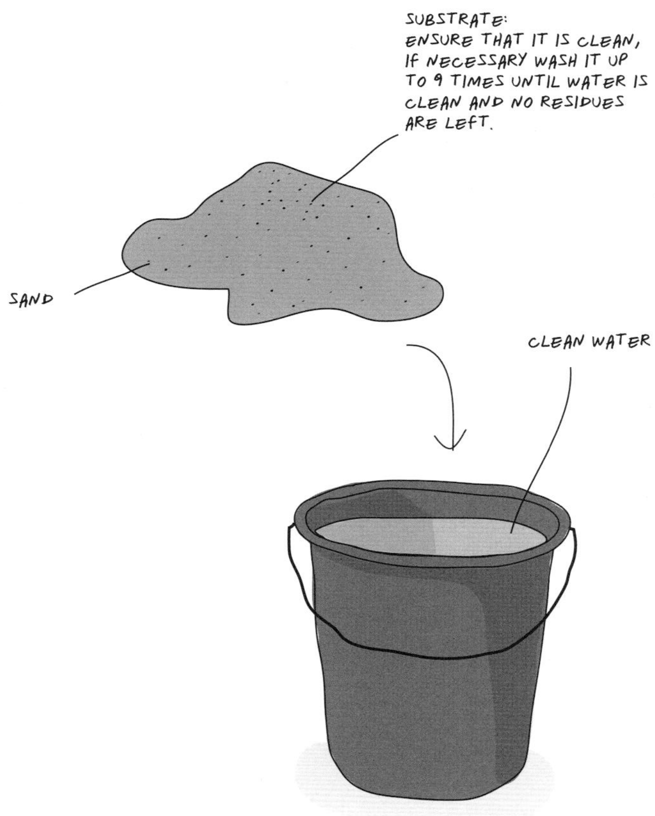

2 SEED PLANTATION

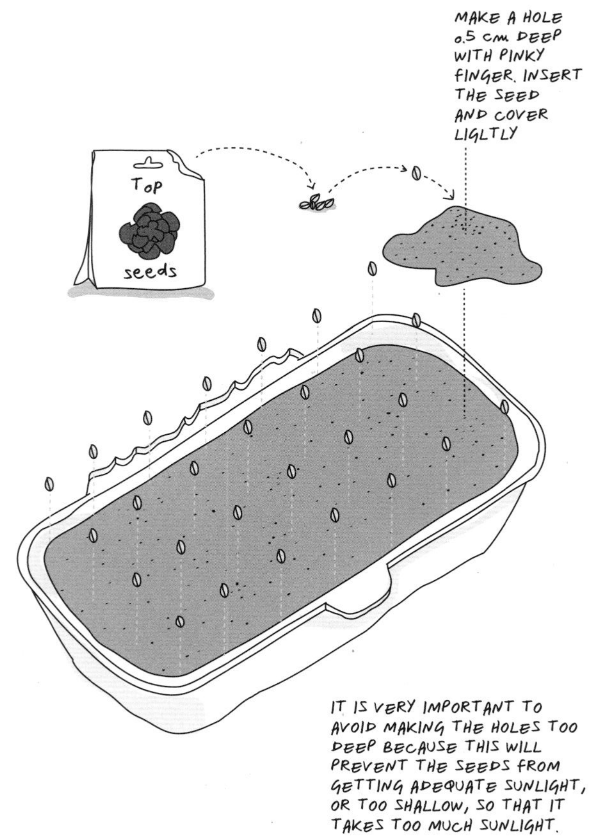

3 GROWING SPROUTS

KEEP INSIDE AND NOT IN DIRECT SUNLIGHT.
AFTER A FEW DAYS, PLANTS WILL START SPROUTING.
WATER AND MOISTEN GENTLY.

TRANSPARENT FILM OR TRANSPARENT PLASTIC BAG. WET PAPER OR KITCHEN ROLL CAN ALSO WORK FOR THIS PURPOSE.

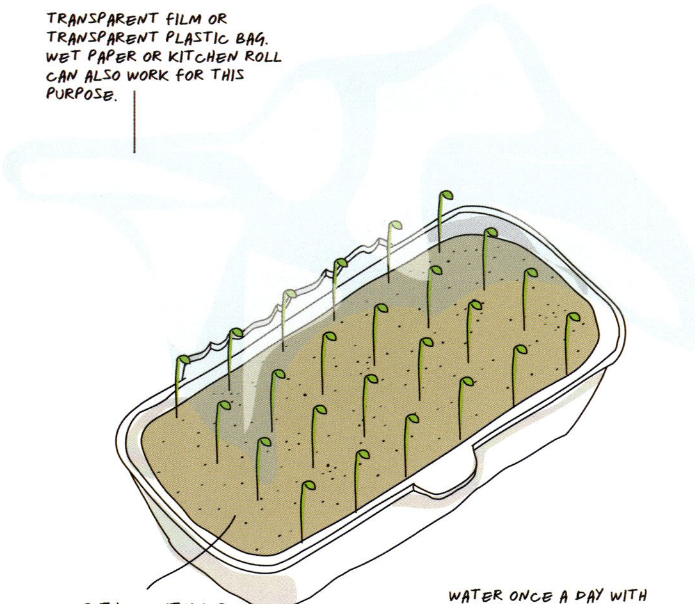

COVER THE CONTAINER WITH PAPER DURING THE FIRST 3 DAYS UNTIL THE FIRST LEAVES SPROUT.

WATER ONCE A DAY WITH SPRAY BOTTLE OR REFILL RESERVOIR.
AFTER THREE DAYS WATER WITH HALF STRENGHT NUTRIENT SOLUTION – REF APPENDIX FOR MIXING INSTRUCTIONS.

METHOD B: COCONUT FIBER CUBES

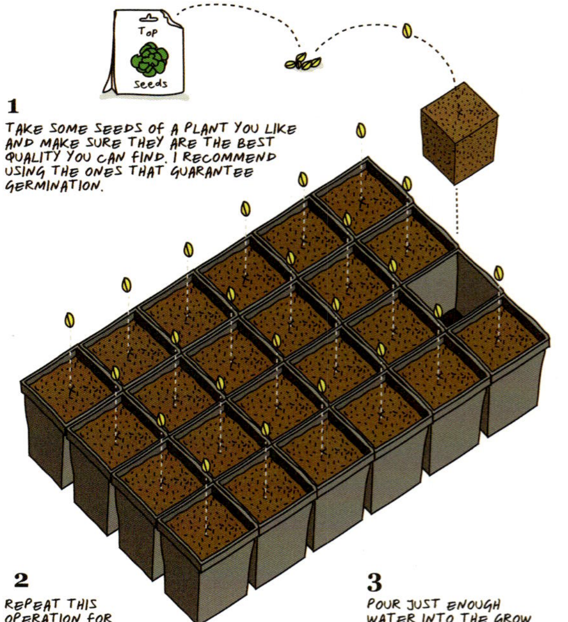

1
TAKE SOME SEEDS OF A PLANT YOU LIKE AND MAKE SURE THEY ARE THE BEST QUALITY YOU CAN FIND. I RECOMMEND USING THE ONES THAT GUARANTEE GERMINATION.

2
REPEAT THIS OPERATION FOR AS MANY SEEDLINGS AS YOU WANT.
I RECOMMEND LOOKING AT THE INSTRUCTIONS ON THE SEED ENVELOPE FOR BEST RESULTS.

3
POUR JUST ENOUGH WATER INTO THE GROW STARTER TO MAKE IT HUMID AND PLACE THE SEED IN THE GROW STARTER, JUST A BIT BELOW THE SURFACE.

4

PLACE THE GROW STARTER TRAY INSIDE THE MINI GREENHOUSE AND VAPORIZE SOME WATER TO KEEP IT MOIST. YOU CAN GET ONE IN A GARDENING SHOP. OTHERWISE A PLASTIC BAG COULD ALSO WORK.

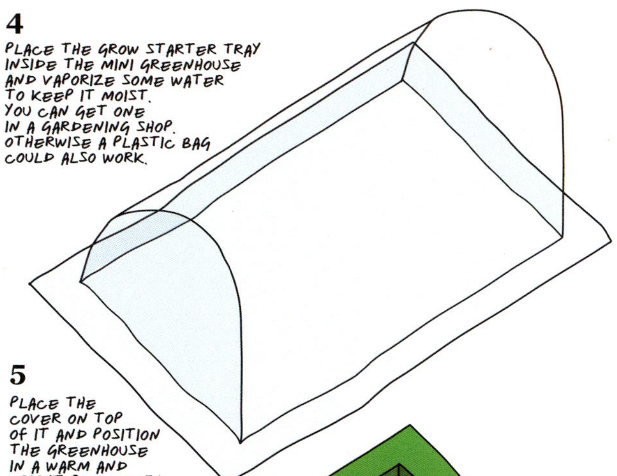

5

PLACE THE COVER ON TOP OF IT AND POSITION THE GREENHOUSE IN A WARM AND BRIGHT PLACE WITH INDIRECT LIGHT.

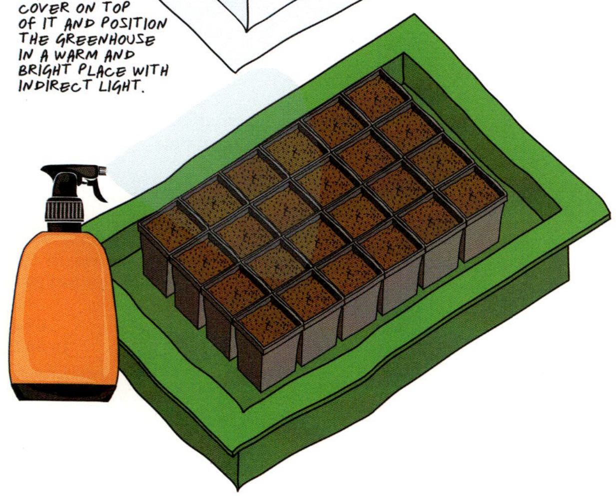

6

AS SOON AS THE SEEDS TURN INTO SEEDLINGS WITH ONE OR TWO ROUNDS OF LEAVES, IT IS TIME TO TRANSPLANT THEM INTO YOUR HYDROPONIC SYSTEM. LIFT THE SEEDLING AND STARTER GENTLY, TAKING CARE NOT TO DAMAGE THE ROOTS.

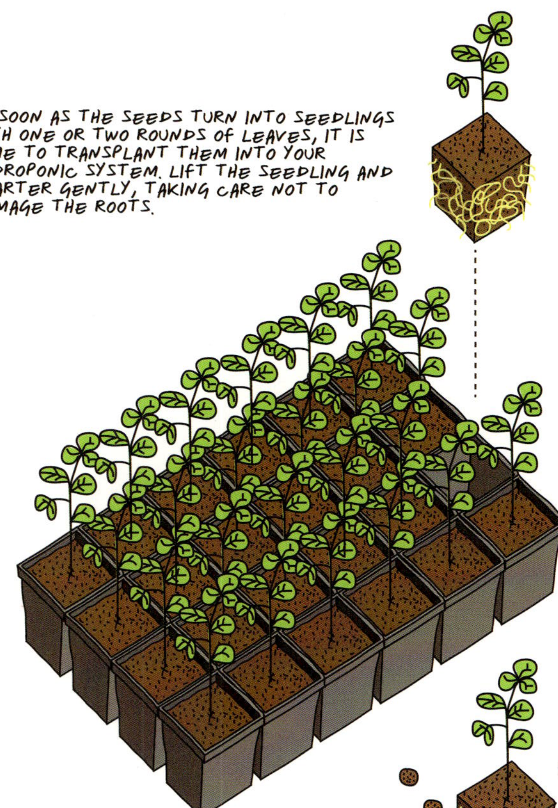

7

PLACE EACH SEEDLING INTO A NET POT AND FILL THE GAPS WITH SOME EXPANDED CLAY. MAKE SURE THE GROW STARTERS REMAIN MOIST UNTIL THE ROOTS GROW TO REACH THE WATER. CONGRATULATIONS – A NEW PLANT IS GROWING.

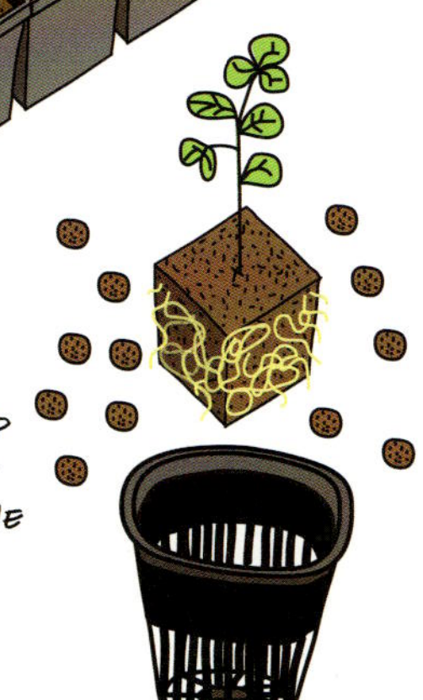

TABLE OF GERMINATION TIMELINE FOR DIFFERENT CROPS

SUMMER

Type of Crop	Time to first transplant	Time to second transplant	Time to harvest	Plants /sq. m.
Head Lettuce	Days 14	Days 14	Days 42	30
Baby Greens	No first transplant	Days 10	Days 28	72
Spices	Days 14	Days 14	Days 42	30 - 42
Asian Greens	Days 14	Days 7	Days 35	30 - 42
Hearty Greens	Days 14	Days 14	Days 42	30

WINTER

Type of Crop	Time to first transplant	Time to second transplant	Time to harvest	Plants /sq. m.
Head Lettuce	Days 14	Days 21 - 28	Days 56	30
Baby Greens	No first transplant	Days 14	Days 42	72
Spices	Days 14	Days 21 - 28	Days 56	30 - 42
Asian Greens	Days 14	Days 14	Days 42	30 - 42
Hearty Greens	Days 14	Days 21 - 28	Days 56	30

2

TRANSPLANTATION

METHOD 1. KITCHEN SPONGES

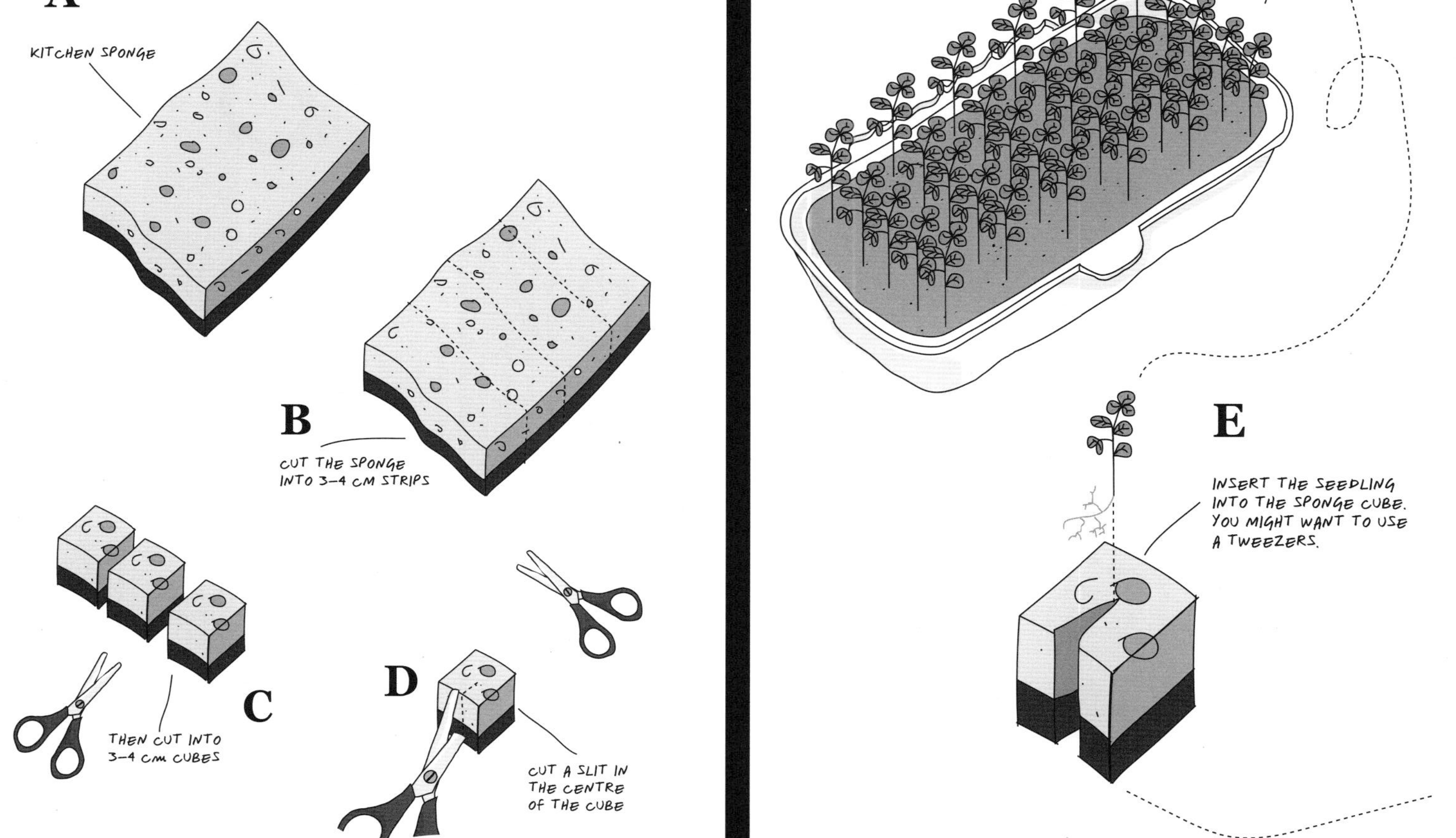

F

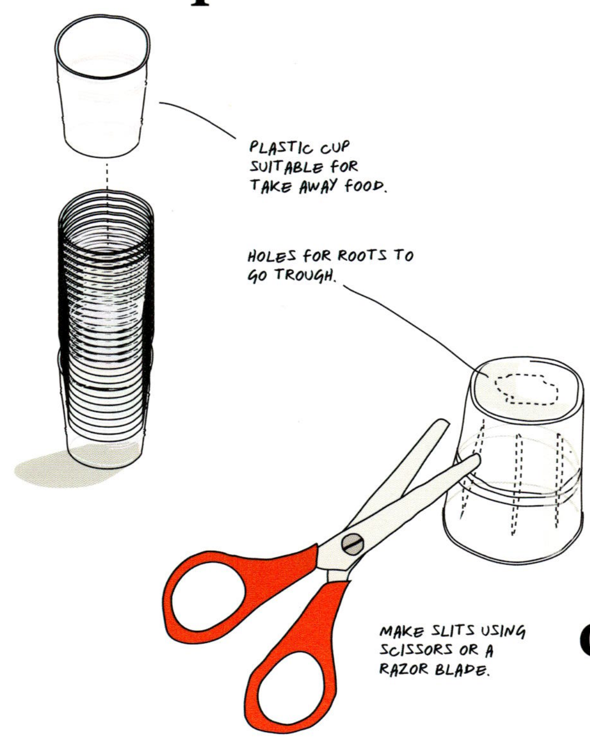
PLASTIC CUP
SUITABLE FOR
TAKE AWAY FOOD.
HOLES FOR ROOTS TO
GO TROUGH.
MAKE SLITS USING
SCISSORS OR A
RAZOR BLADE.

G

H

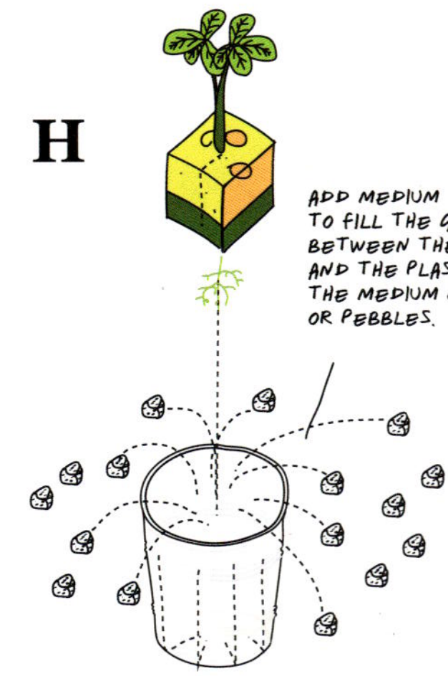
ADD MEDIUM
TO FILL THE GAPS
BETWEEN THE PLANT
AND THE PLASTIC CUP.
THE MEDIUM CAN BE GRAVEL
OR PEBBLES.

I

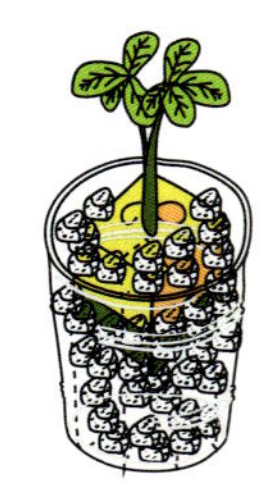
THE SEEDLING IS READY TO
BE TRANSPLANTED INTO ANY
HYDROPONIC SYSTEM.

L

WITH A PENCIL MARK EIGHT SPOTS ON A LID THE IKEA TROFAST LID OR SOMETHING EQUIVALENT

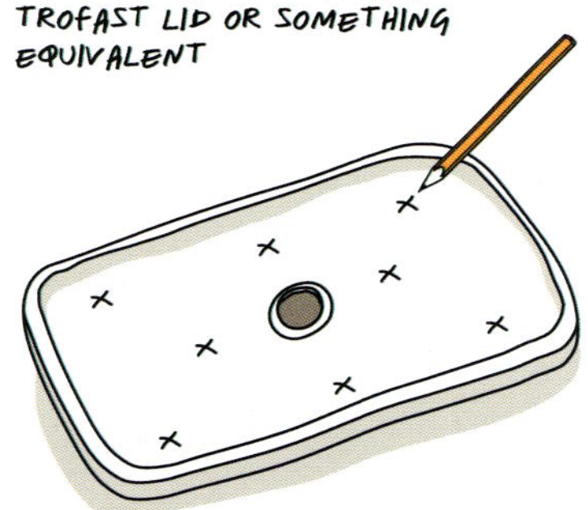

M

MEASURE THE SIZE OF YOUR NET POT AND DRILL THE HOLES WITH A TWIST BIT TRIANGULAR SHANK.

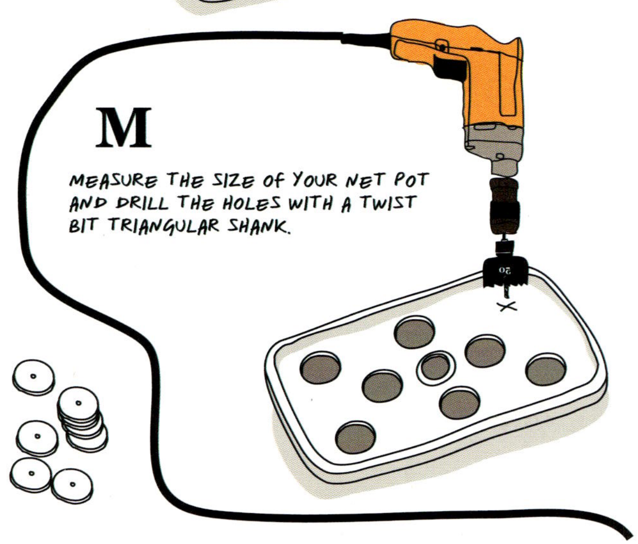

O(R)

TAKE THE SEEDLING OF YOUR FAVOURITE AROMATIC HERB AND PLACE IT IN THE NET POT. USE SOME EXPANDED CLAY BEADS TO FILL THE GAPS.

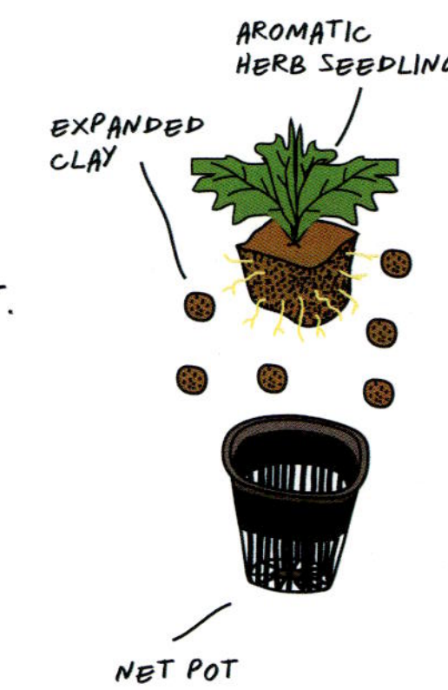

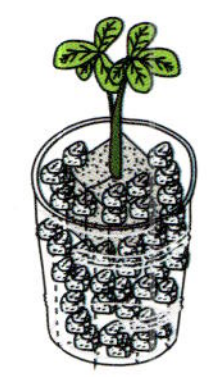

P

PLACE THE NET POTS INSIDE THE HOLES AND ENJOY SEEING YOUR FAVOURITE AROMATIC HERBS GROW.

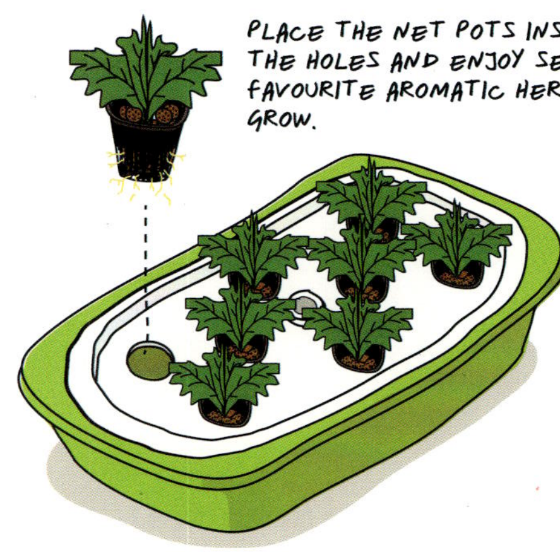

3

FERTILIZING, CLONING AND HARVESTING

FERTILIZING: 'TRADITIONAL' METHOD

MACRO AND MICRONUTRIENTS

MACRONUTRIENTS INCLUDE:

N NITROGEN
P PHOSPHORUS
K POTASSIUM

MICRONUTRIENTS:

CA CALCIUM
S SULFUR
FE IRON
MG MAGNESIUM
B BORON
MN MANGANESE
ZN ZINC
MO MOLYBDENUM
CU COPPER
CO COBALT

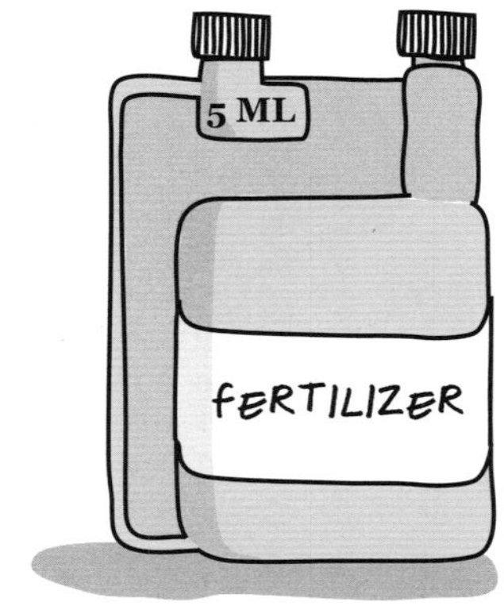

Nutrition Formulas (Using Molina Salts)	Light Feeders	Medium	Heavy
Ammonical Nitrogen	1.5 g per L	1.7 g per L	2 g per L
Potassium Nitrate	1.7 g per L	1.7 g per L	1.7 g per L
Iron	0.17 g per L (1 app. / week)	0.17 g per L (1 app. / week)	0.17 g per L (1 app. / week)
Magnesium Sulfate	0.6 g per L	0.6 g per L	0.6 g per L

Light Feeders Baby Greens
Medium Feeders Head Lettuce
Heavy Feeders Spices, Asian Greens and Hearty Greens

pH chart 5.5 - 5.8

FERTILIZING: 'HUMANPONICS'

NORMALLY FOR THIS PRACTICE, FISH URINE IS USED.
THE TECHNIQUE IS CALLED AQUAPONICS. IT IS A CLOSED LOOP: FISH FERTILIZE WATER FOR THE PLANTS AND PLANTS CLEAN THE WATER FOR THE FISH. THIS TECHNIQUE IS NORMALLY USED TO FARM BOTH FISH AND PLANTS AT THE SAME TIME. FROM A CHEMICAL POINT OF VIEW, FISH URINE IS IDENTICAL TO HUMAN URINE. OF COURSE IT NEEDS TO BE DILUTED, OTHERWISE IT WILL "BURN" THE PLANT. HERE ARE SOME REFERENCES FOUND ON WIKIPEDIA:

S. A. Esray, I. Anderson, A. Hillers, R. Swaper, *Closing the Loop: Ecological Sanitation for Food Security* (Tepoztlán: SARAR Transformación, 2000).

H. Jonsson, *Guidelines on the Use of Urine and Feces in Crop Production*, EcoSanRes Publication Series, Stockholm Environment Institute, (2004).

R. Gensch, A. Miso, G. Itchon, *Urine as Liquid Fertilizer in Agricultural Production in the Philippines: A Practice Field Guide* (Cagayan de Oro City: Xavier University Press, 2011).

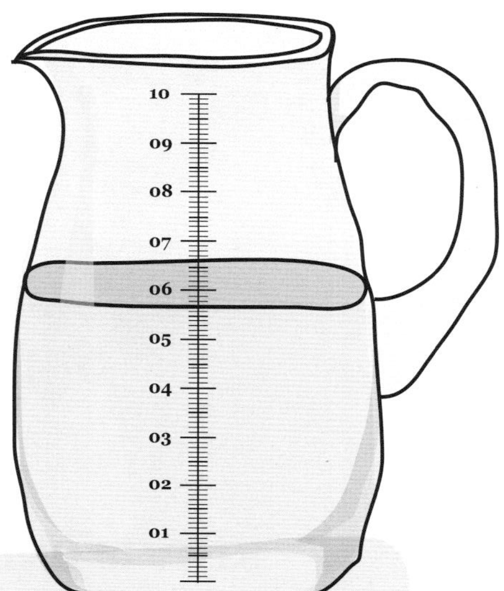

WITH A SYRINGE DROP ABOUT 5 ml / LITER OF HUMAN URINE ALTERNATIVELY. ALSO WITH A SYRINGE OR A SMALL GRADUATED JAG, DILUTE THE FERTILIZER ACCODING TO INSTRUCTIONS, USUALLY 5 ml /LITER.

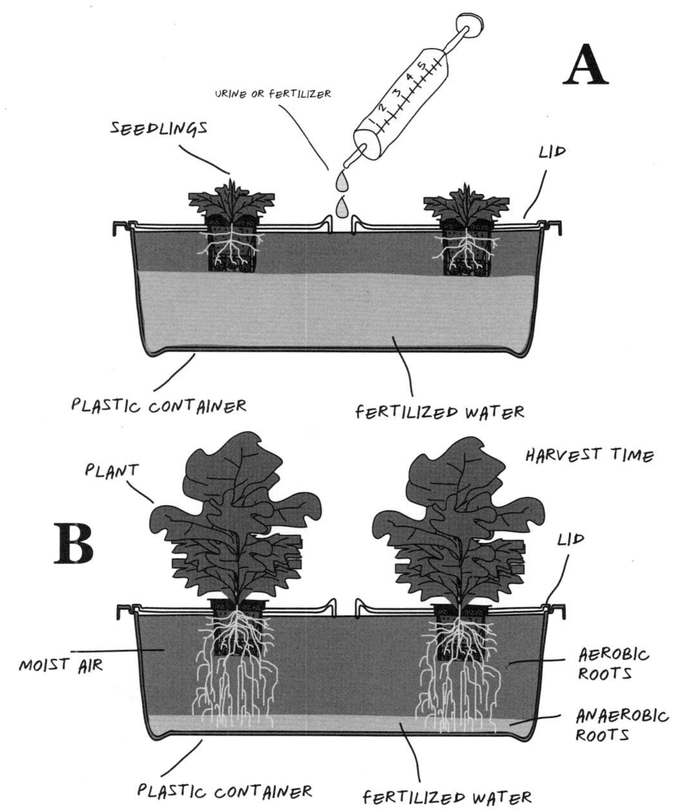

KEEP ADDING NOURISHED WATER AS THE PLANT GROWS.
KEEP AWAY FROM DIRECT SUNLIGHT, POSSIBLY IN BRIGHT BUT COOL ENVIRONMENT.

THIS SYSTEM IS IDEAL FOR INDOOR LIGHTING WITH NEON LIGHT OR DEDICATED LED.

CLONING PLANTS

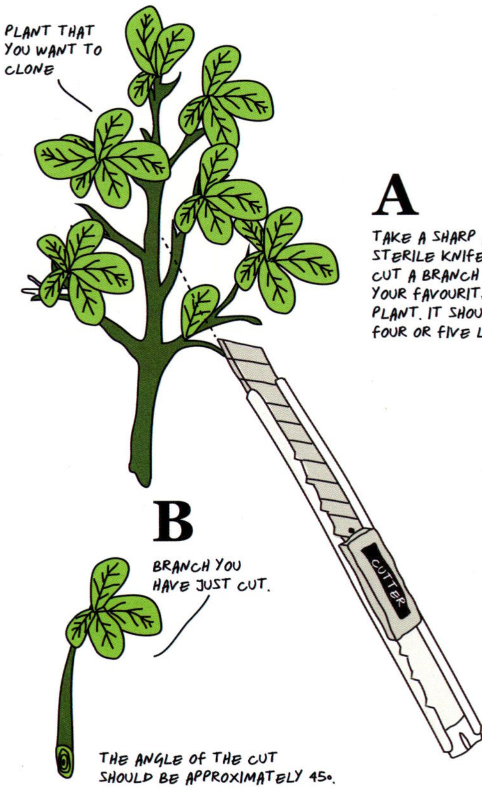

A

TAKE A SHARP AND STERILE KNIFE AND CUT A BRANCH OF YOUR FAVOURITE PLANT. IT SHOULD HAVE FOUR OR FIVE LEAVES.

B

THE ANGLE OF THE CUT SHOULD BE APPROXIMATELY 45°.

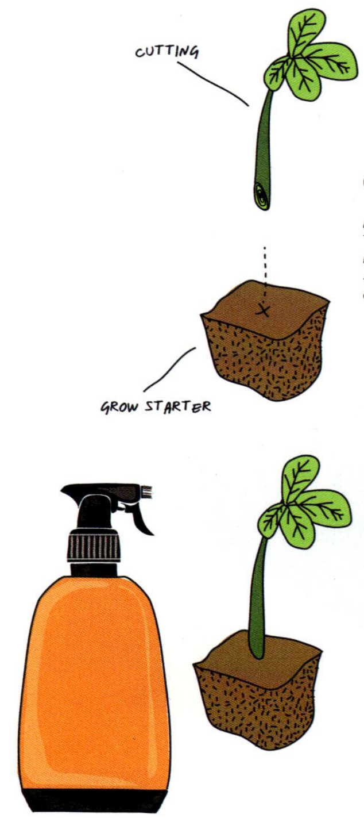

C

NOW YOU CAN INSERT THE BRANCH INTO A HUMIDIFIED GROW STARTER OR ALTERNATIVELY YOU CAN TRY JUST A GLASS OF WATER.

D

NOW MAKE SURE TO KEEP THE BRANCH IN INDIRECT SUNLIGHT IN A WARM AND HUMID ENVIRONMENT UNTIL THE ROOTS GROW OUTSIDE THE STARTER. YOU CAN ALSO COVER IT WITH A TRANSPARENT LID TO MAINTAIN THE LEVEL OF HUMIDITY. THE IDEA IS THAT YOU HAVE A SORT OF MINI GREENHOUSE. VAPORIZE SOME WATER FROM TIME TO TIME AND KEEP THE STARTER HUMID. AS IT GROWS, MOVE THE BRANCH GRADUALLY INTO STRONGER SUNLIGHT.

THIS SYSTEM ALLOWS YOU TO SAVE TIME AND KEEP GROWING PLANTS WITHOUT SEEDS.

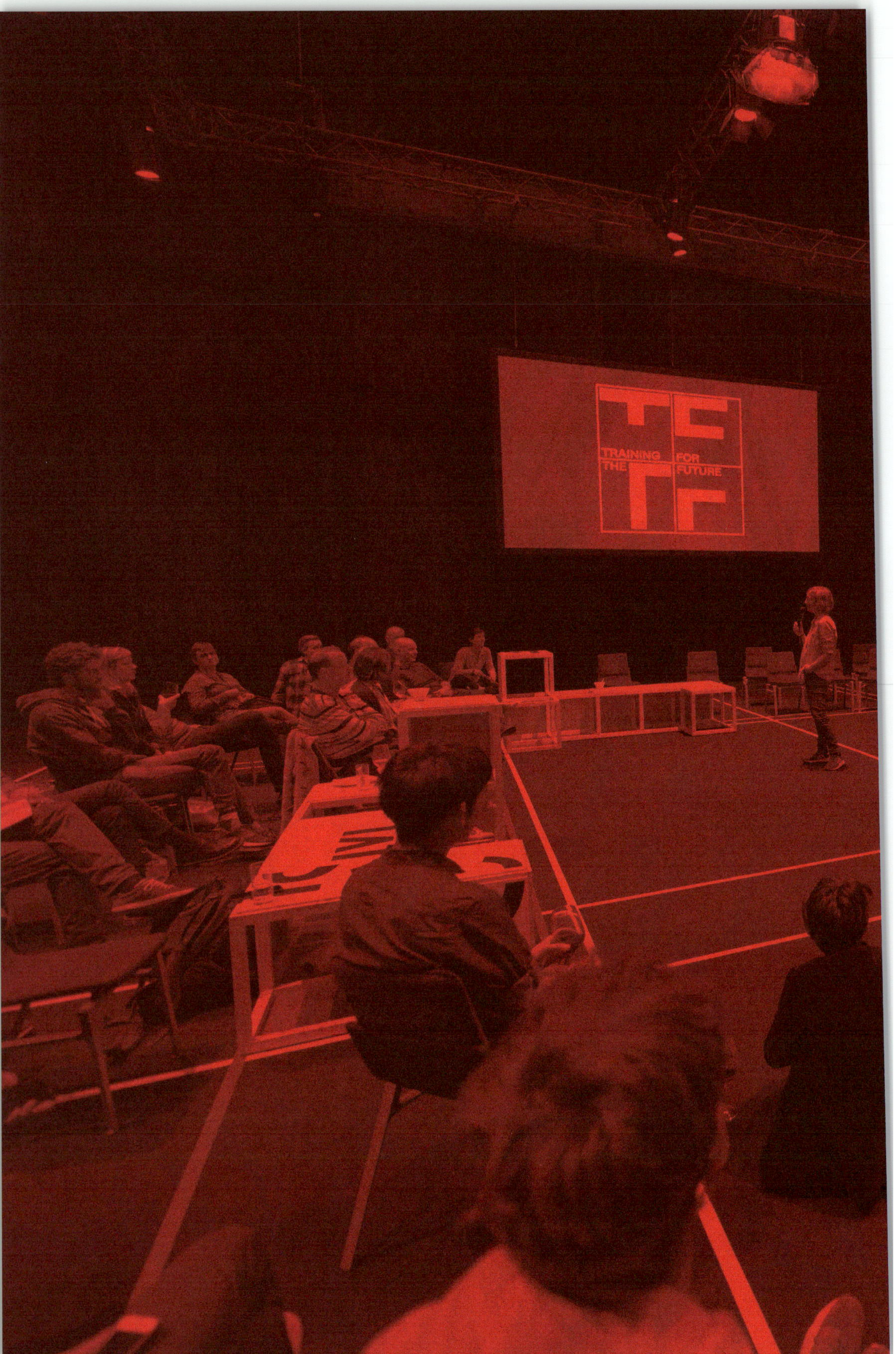
TRAINING
THE
FOR
FUTURE

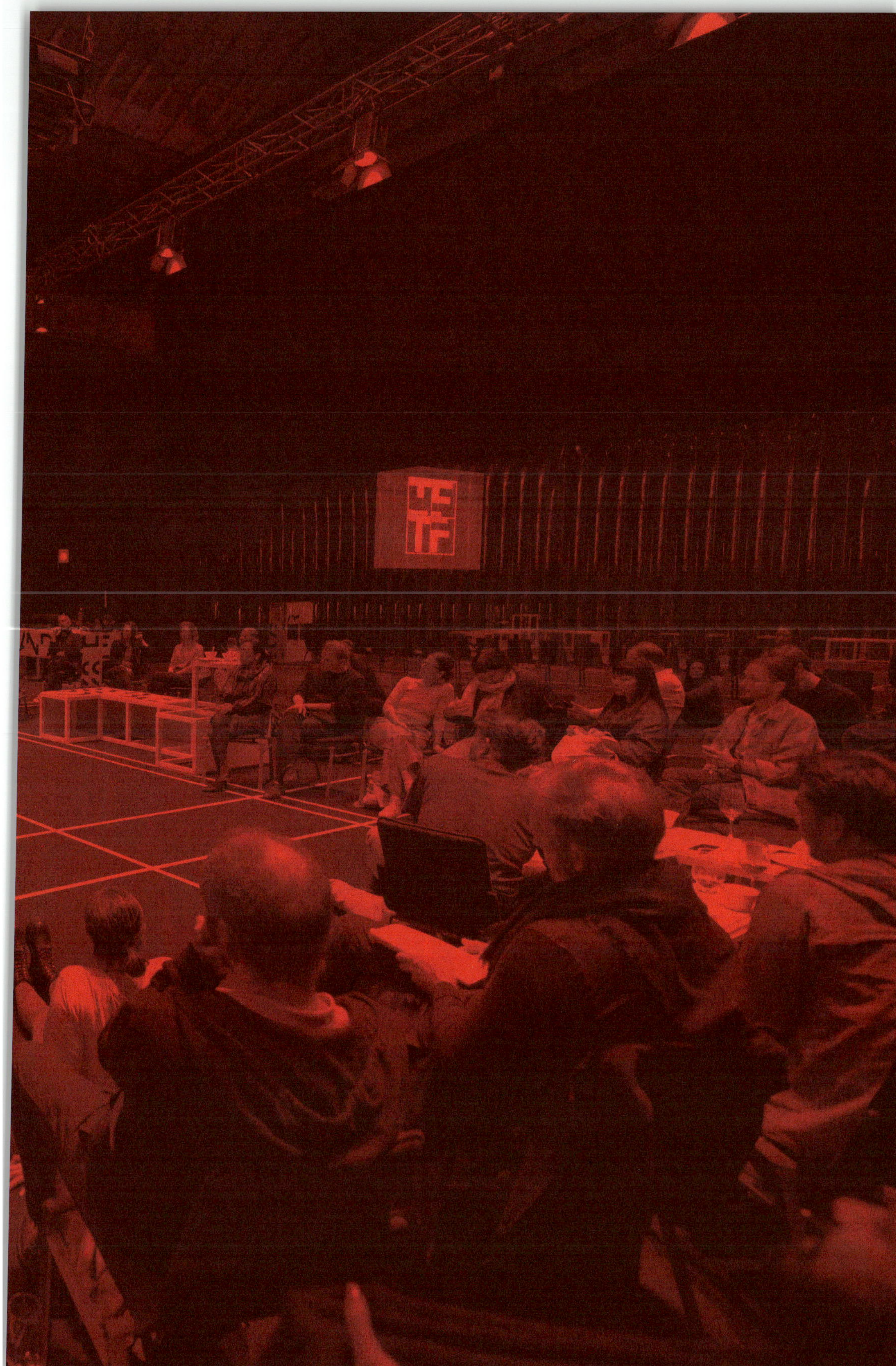

Choreographies of Togetherness, Public Movement (Ma'ayan Choresh and Hagar Ophir)

This series of three trainings focuses the body on movements that turn a public into a united force. Through exercising choreographies used by military, police and activist groups, trainees gain access to the performativity of collective entities.

Public Movement is a performative research body that investigates and stages political actions in public spaces. It studies and creates public choreographies, forms of social order and overt and covert rituals. Public Movement was founded in December 2006 by Dana Yahalomi and Omer Krieger. Yahalomi became the sole director of the group in 2011.

Ma'ayan Choresh has been a member of Public Movement since its foundation. As a professional dancer, she has worked with Public Movement, Noa Dar Dance Group, Sharona Florshiem and others. Choresh is also a teacher for contemporary dance, improvisation and contact improvisation for dancers and adults. She has been teaching Public Movement workshops since 2012 in various schools in Israel and abroad and was the Public Movement delegate for a new project at the Australian Centre for Contemporary Art, Melbourne.

Hagar Ophir is a Berlin-based artist, born in Jerusalem. She is a performer and visual researcher and her works examine constructions of historical narrative and national identity through the choreography of bodies. A member of Public Movement since 2008, Ophir has co-created diverse actions by Public Movement, such as *Taanit – Civil Fast* (Jerusalem, 2012) and *Honor-Guard*, performed at the Asian Art Biennial (Taiwan, 2013). She also collaborated with Alhena Katsof and Dana Yahalomi on *Debriefing Section II*, acting as its debriefing agent at the Tel Aviv Museum of Art (2015) and as the work's conductor at the Guggenheim Museum in New York (2016).

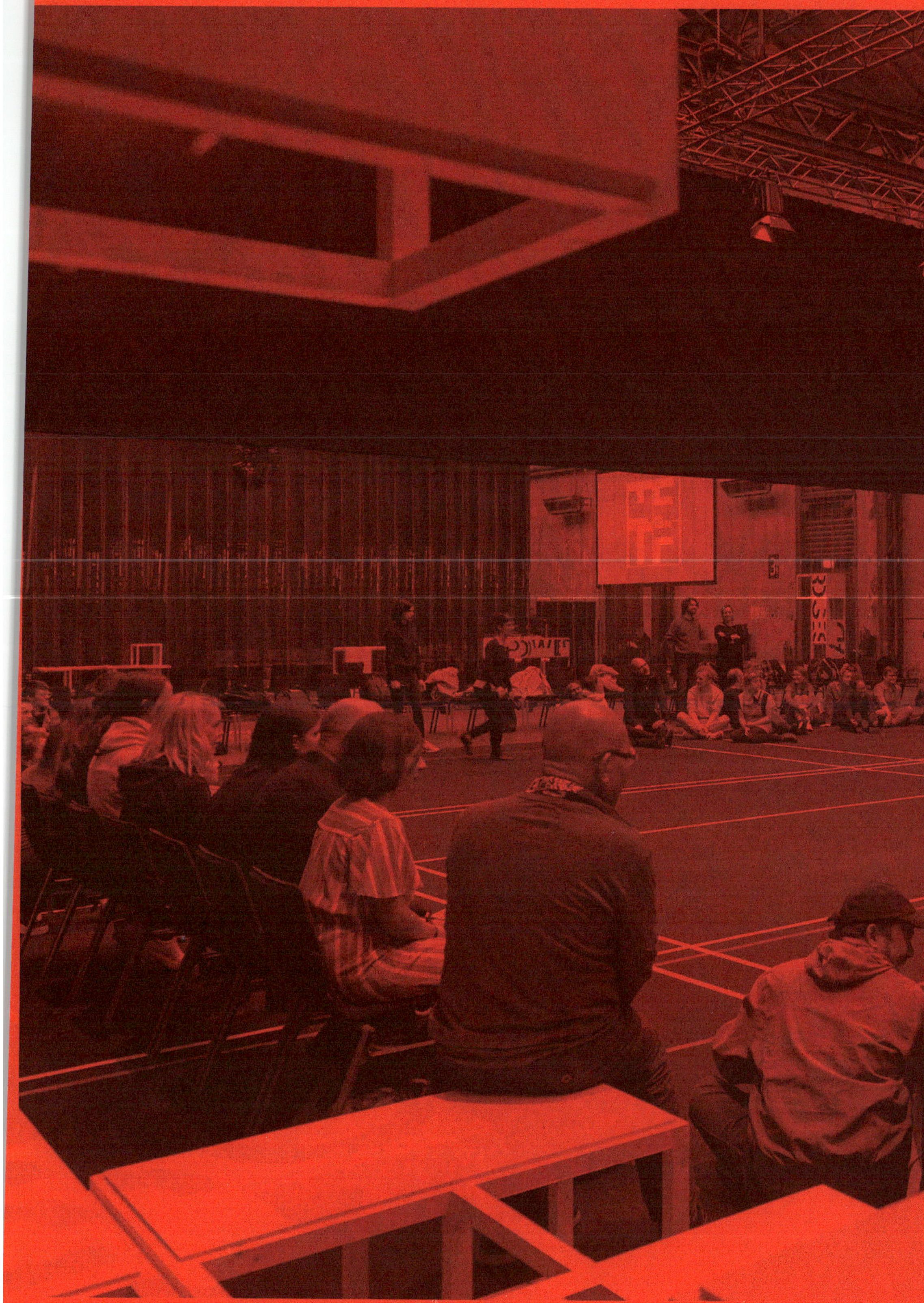

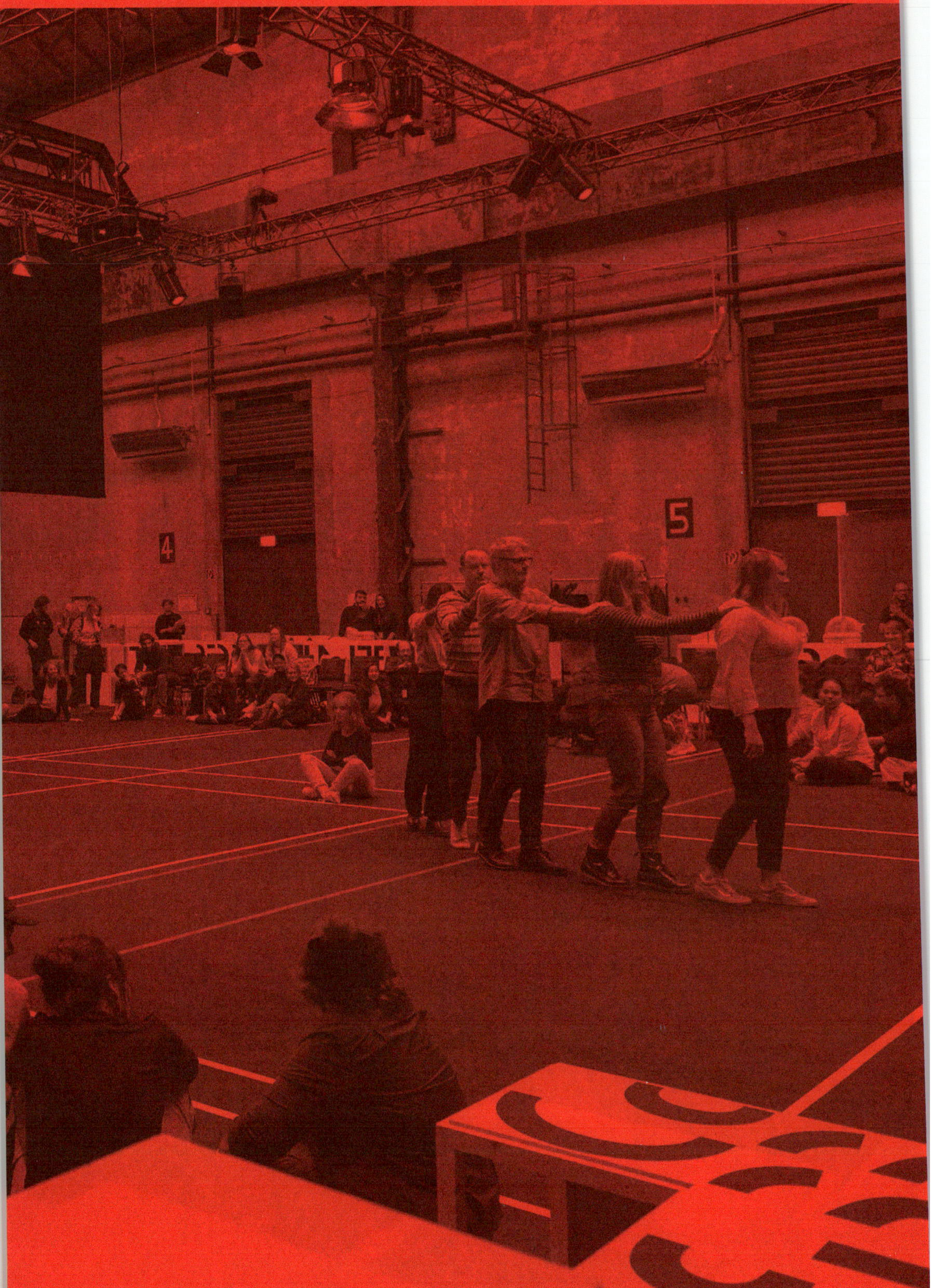

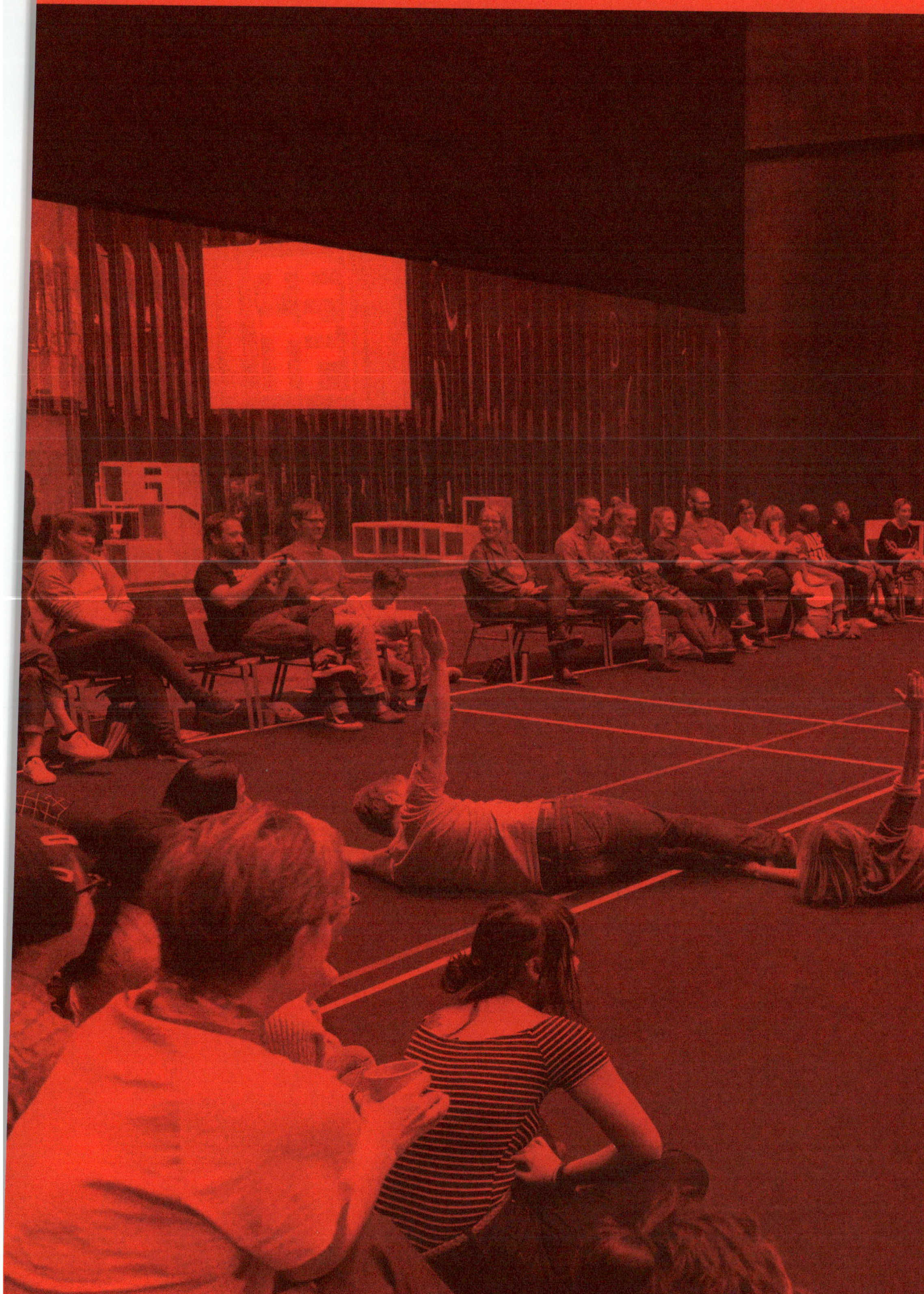

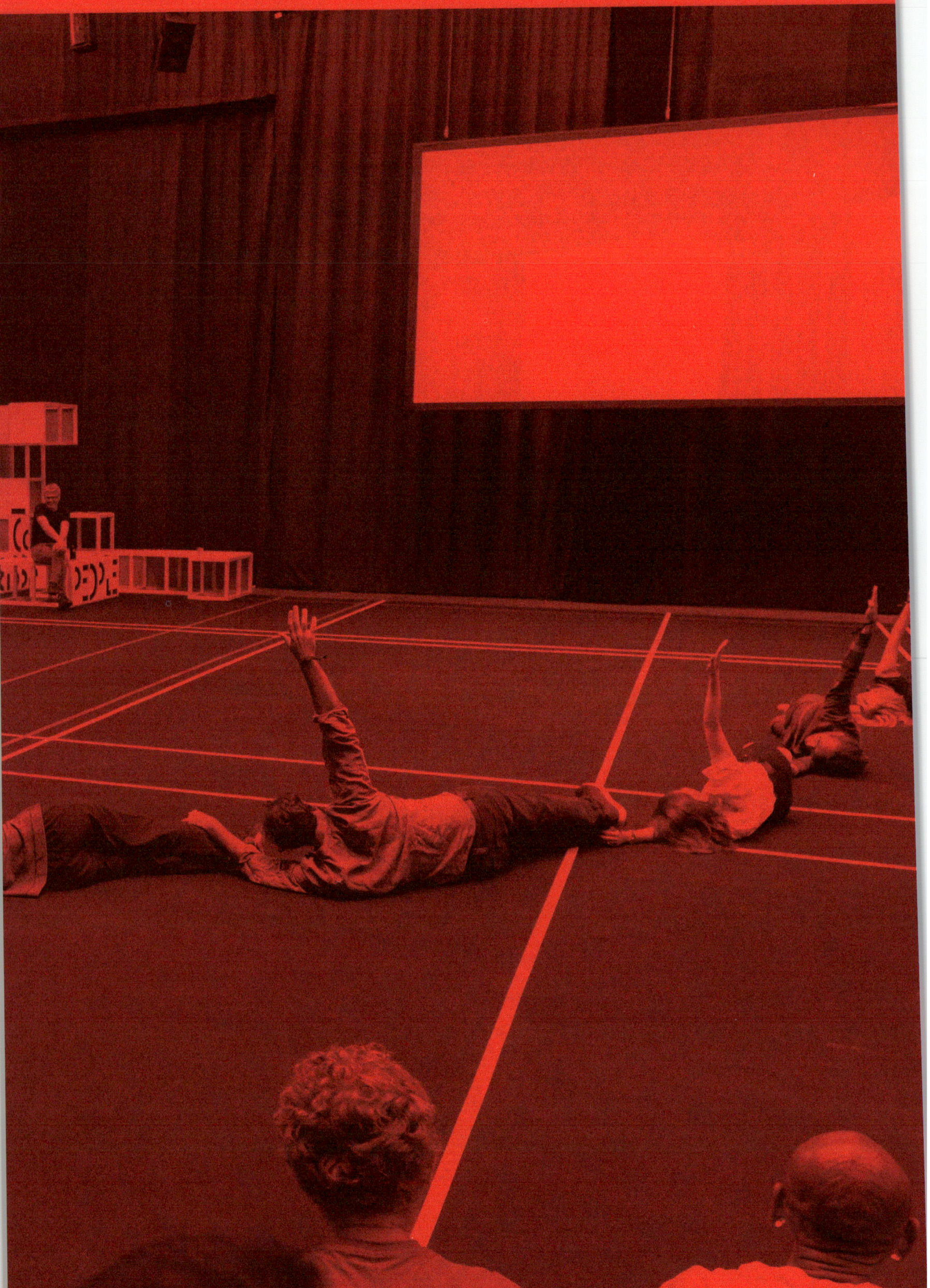

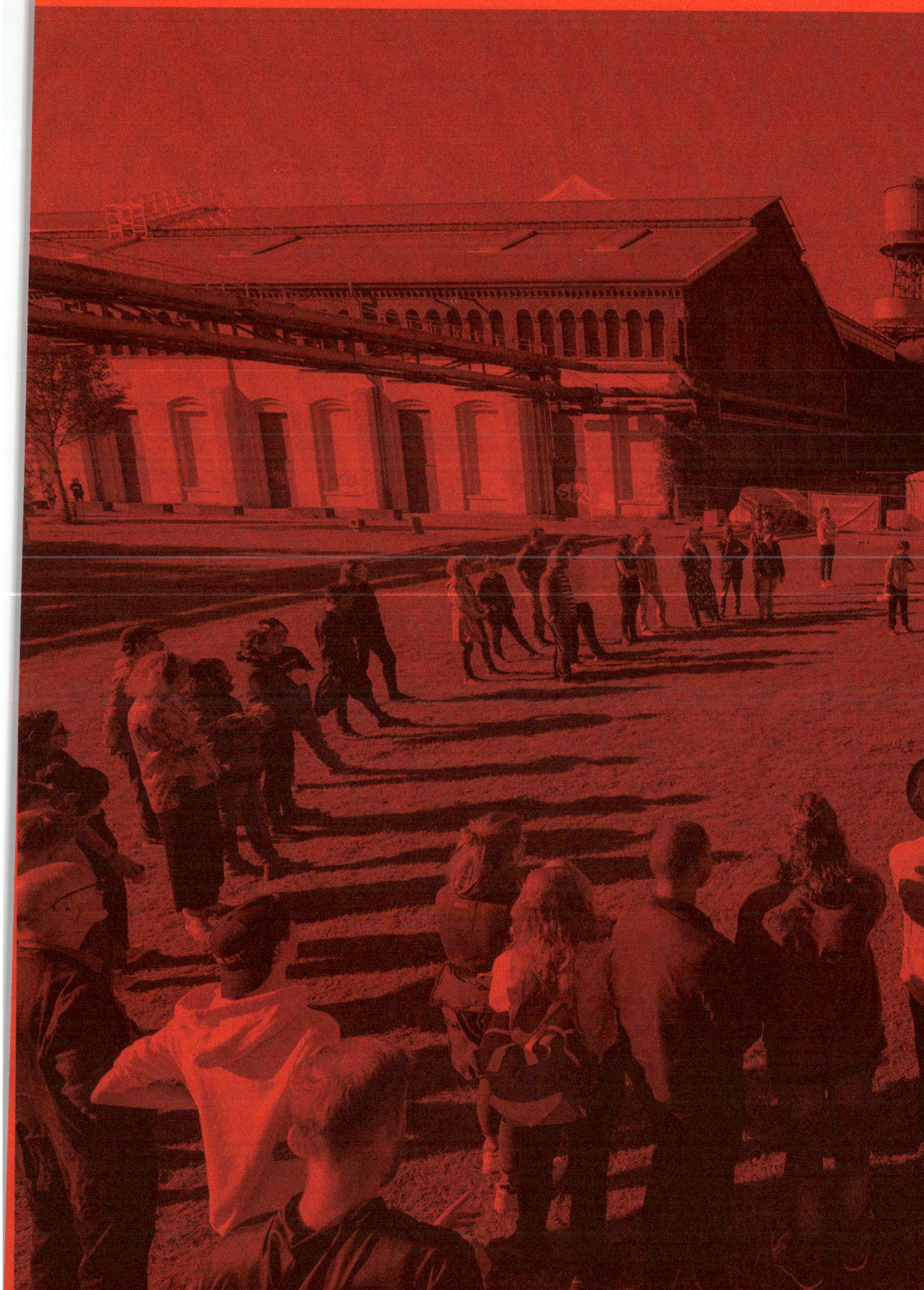

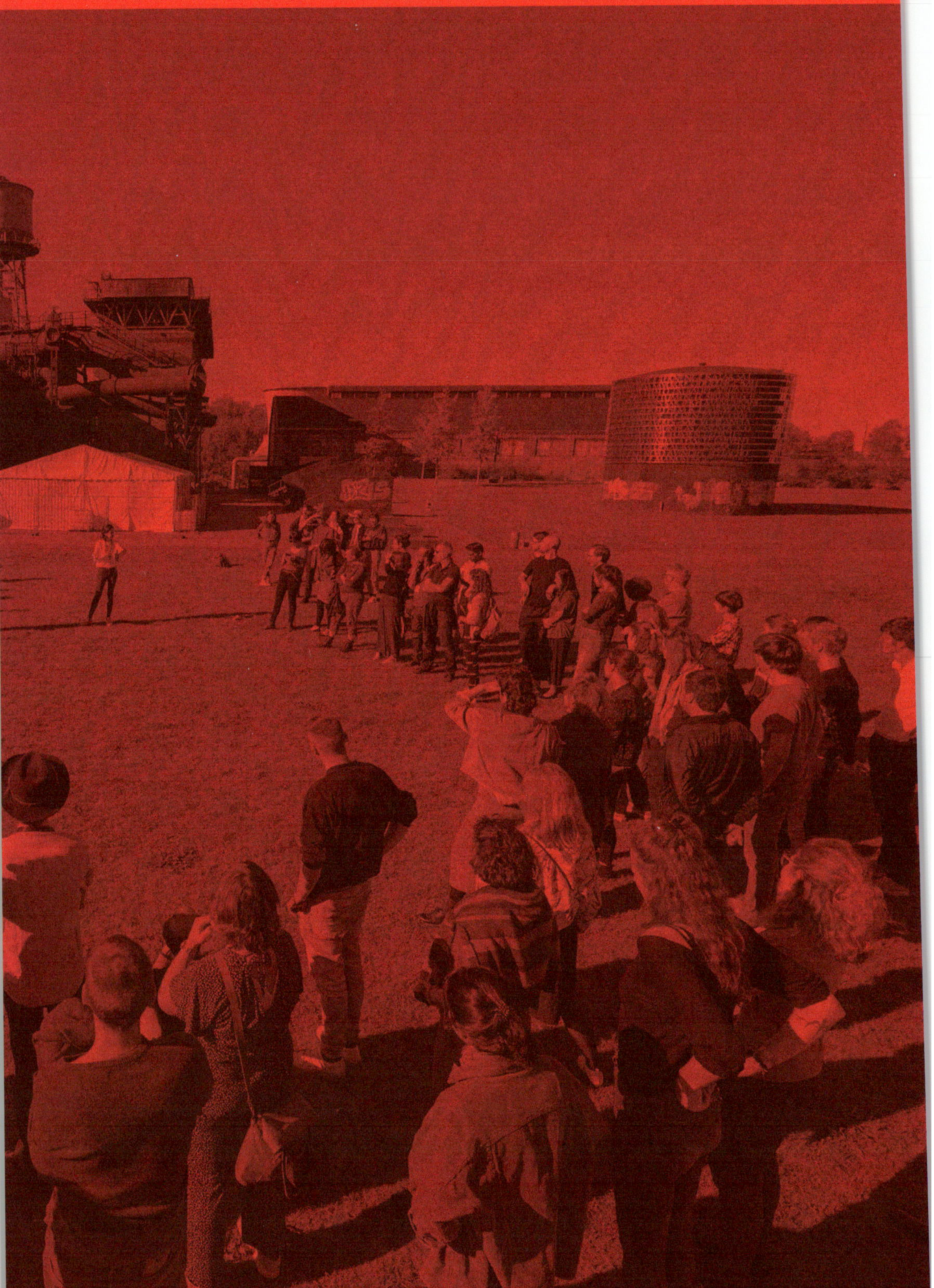

Heuristic Public Practices for the Future

Public Movement

How did you approach the notion of the 'training' and what does the term mean to your practice?

Public Movement sees the role of the artist as one of a facilitator who creates civic arenas where public choreographies are practiced and performed. With this in mind, we also think of our actions as training grounds where we lead and invite the public to rehearse various modes of touch, to perform their opinions and beliefs and to exercise moving as one body. We believe that we can practice our civic bonds by enacting choreographies of care, evacuation, compassion and so forth.

Over the years, Public Movement has built an arsenal of corporal knowledge by studying from and training with state institutions such as the military, the police force, firefighters, ambulance services, etc. We were fascinated by the dance of the state, observing it as combinations of movements that signify sovereignty and governance. We aimed to master these movements in our bodies as a crucial physical knowledge. We explore these choreographies as an expression of identity, which constructs our mode of belonging and thus can transgress and break through somewhat sealed political affiliations.

This arsenal is one we keep building. It's a bodily archive, from which we draw choreographies that we then bring back to the public sphere, perform and pass on as a form of knowledge sharing, public training and/or being a public.

Conceptually speaking, our actions often function as a 'pre-enactment,' a term used by Oliver Marchart to describe a form of rehearsing (politically) towards an unknown future. At the core of our practice is the idea that being and moving together is a seed for most political actions, which require exercising and repetition. Public space is where strangers meet and show solidarity and thus we read the act of assembly as an essential rehearsal that produces the tools to act together in an event to come.

In a time of dystopian normativity, what does the notion of the 'future' mean to you?

In our practice, the 'future' translates to a physical-mental state of being prepared, of taking responsibility and holding the knowledge from a civic perspective so as to enable a reorganization of power and new forms of being together. Returning to the concept of pre-enactment, the future, or the future event, is yet to come and yet to reveal itself. Our practice is an attempt to prepare for that unknown future by staging public actions that form civic alliances. These might include exercises where the public is confronted with the decision to obey or disobey, thus becoming agents of choice. When thinking of a future, we can also think of ceremonies and apparatuses that can reconstruct power relations, and then ask: With who and how can we start to design these futures today?

Throughout the last year we were held in a realm of unknowns. We were required to examine and declare what is essential for our political life, what the role of public space is, what the function of spontaneity in our social life is, to what degree can we live without touch or physical proximity and what a civic practice is when we cannot physically be near each other. These are definitely not the characteristics of a utopia, yet we are not sure these belong to the sphere of the dystopian either. More than anything, for Public Movement these examinations reflect the urgent need for heuristic public practices for the future – a future that might not come, but which is, to an extent, partly realized through the practice itself.

What does it mean to reclaim the future's means of production?

Reclaiming the means of production starts with mapping and analyzing current power structures. Becoming an agent of change – which can definitely be within the possible outcomes of the artistic act – means to hold a demand or a claim for power, which comes with certain worries and fears. When we seek control over the means of production, we place ourselves in an arena of power struggles, whether soft or hard power. The artist-activist's action isn't obliged to move toward a clear ideology or a defined trajectory, yet it must understand itself as part of a negotiation for power. More often than not, such an action will find itself at the heart of a moral-political-social dilemma, bringing to the surface conflicts and disagreements.

How would you describe the relationship between trainers and trainees?

Public Movement's workshop leaned on the accumulated knowledge of public choreographies that exist within the bodies of participants. These movements are often familiar and ingrained in our experiences and civic life: participating in a protest, helping a stranger on the street, celebrating spontaneously in the city square or even witnessing an arrest or a police patrol. Bearing this in mind, the role of trainers is to awaken this corporal knowledge while leading sessions of both sharing and teaching. Together with the trainees, the trainer rehearses state and civic choreographies that she learned from official units and activists and uses these exercises to turn the trainees into a group, guiding them to become and move as one body. By the end of the workshop, through rehearsing and repeating these accumulated methodologies, the group embodies the various physical gestures in the process of becoming.

Communalizing Data, Institute of Human Obsolescence (Manuel Beltrán and Wael Eskandar)

This training develops tools to communalize the means of production and governance emerging from the control assumed over digital data.

Institute of Human Obsolescence is an artistic research project investigating the repositioning of human labor in a time where manual and intellectual labor are being increasingly performed by machines – a development in which new forms of inequality and exploitation arise. With a new understanding of our relationship to work, it might become possible to negotiate the terms of data labor and claim a better position for human workers.

Manuel Beltrán is an artist, activist and researcher. He researches and lectures on contemporary art, activism, contemporary social movements, post-digital culture and new media. In 2015, he founded the Institute of Human Obsolescence, through which he explores the future of labor, the social and political implications regarding our relationship with technology and the economic and governance systems surrounding the production of data. He is also the co-founder of ad.watch, a project exploring new forms of political propaganda on social media.

Wael Eskandar is an independent journalist, activist and creative technologist. He is part of the team that runs Exposing the Invisible, a program of work by Berlin-based Tactical Tech, which tells the story of released data by exploring different techniques, tools and methods alongside the individual practices of those working at the new frontiers of investigation.

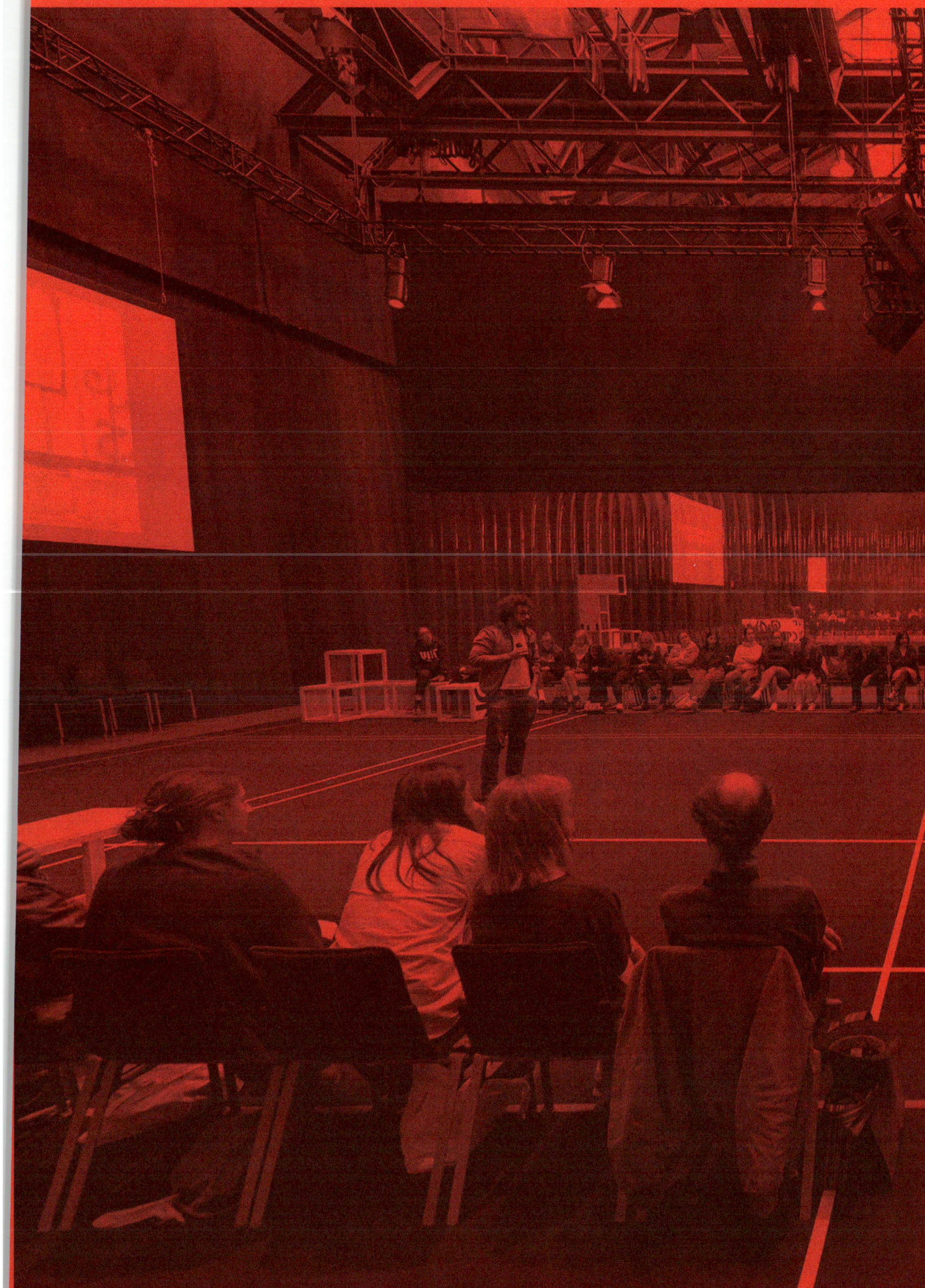

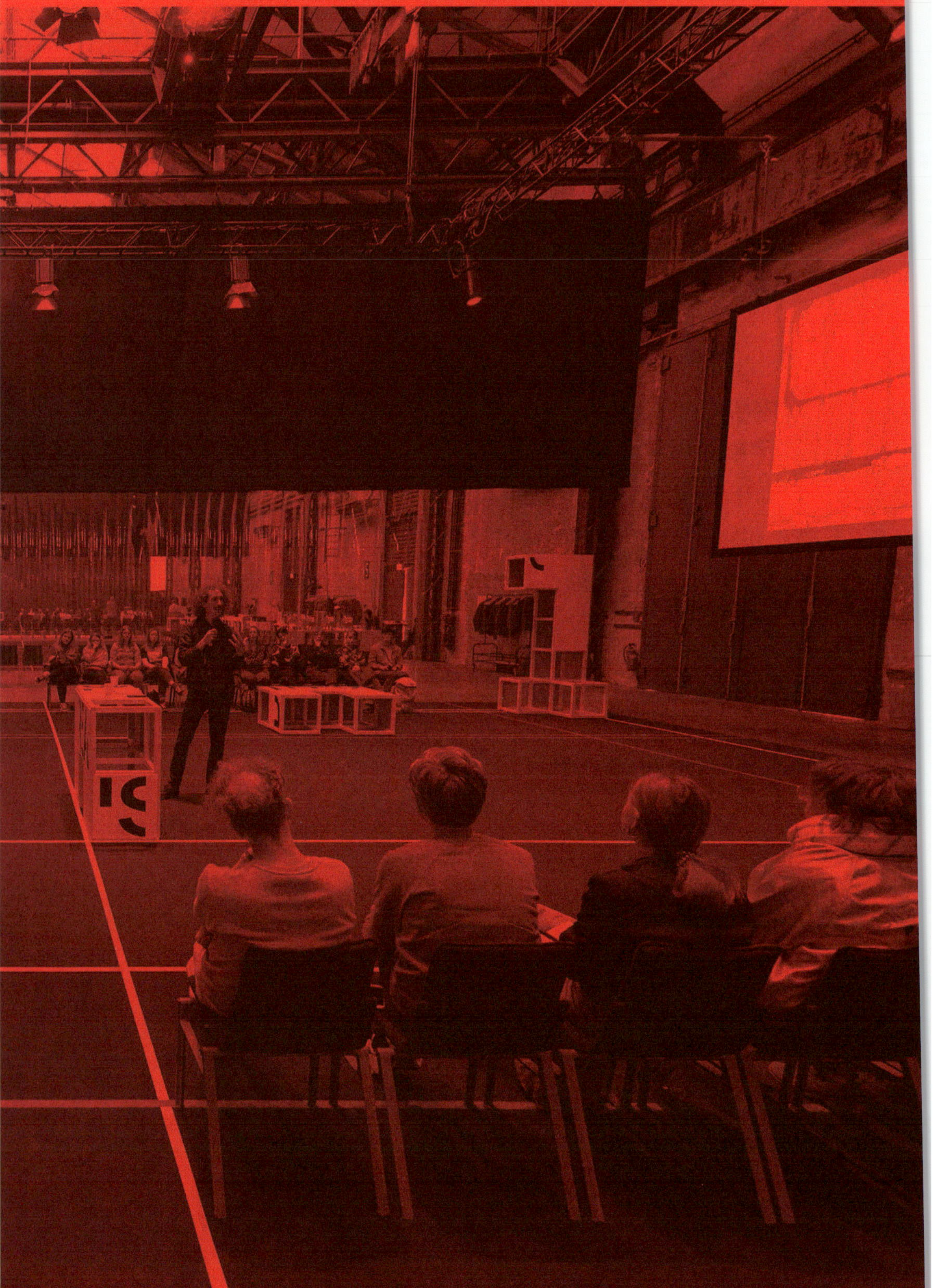

Get a Jump Start on the Battles Ahead

Institute of Human Obsolescence (Wael Eskandar)

How did you approach the notion of the 'training' and what does the term mean to your practice? And additionally, what does the notion of the 'future' signify to you, in a time of dystopian normativity?

I think traditionally speaking, the idea of training is associated with the passing down of knowledge by someone who has figured something out that is deemed important to possess, but in general that's no longer how we approach it. We can think of it as some time and effort spent by some people on behalf of others, who then share their findings and methods with an openness to listening to and incorporating other people's experiences, thoughts and criticisms. In that sense, the notion of training is also an exercise in learning and approaching our experiences critically, whether while preparing or conducting the training. Of course, this notion becomes even more complex and less straightforward when thinking about the notion of the 'future.' To train someone for the future is to imagine a trajectory of where we're heading and address what we think is a fundamental root cause for what we will experience in our (most probably) dystopian future. It then becomes a means of trying to prepare people for resistance and to get a jump-start on the battles that lay ahead. Oftentimes we understand how things happened in retrospect, but there is something valuable in recognizing what the future might be from the traces the present leaves for us to analyze.

What did you learn from your training? What aspects would you develop further or change?

There needs to be more work done with regard to identifying the problems of the future, but not just that. We also need to start thinking immediately about effective ways to counter the issues that are building up and resulting in more disempowerment. One of the things to develop is an alternative model to reclaim the means of production. A true training for the future is not just about anticipating the future and warning of the fundamental issues, but imagining alternative ways of resisting, organizing and empowering each other to confront the future. Ideally, there would be a bigger portion of collaboration where not just new futures are imagined, but new structures, actions and initiatives are imagined also. Perhaps here, as a very concrete example, I would say that it's not enough to present communizing data as a remedy to the problem of disempowerment facing the future, but we additionally need to offer structures, tactics and ways in which we imagine this can happen.

How would you describe the relationship between trainers and trainees?

Trainers and trainees are counterparts, and each one comes in with their own experiences and ideas in various fields. It just so happens that trainers have spent time preparing and structuring the session and that their experiences are relevant to the topics they 'train' on. The trainer's work is done on behalf of trainees who also have a wealth of knowledge that can contribute to the collective whole. It's a matter of different roles within the organizational dynamic and should not be viewed as hierarchical.

How do you envision the further distribution of tactics and knowledges to reclaim the future?

Part of being able to further distribute tactics and knowledges to reclaim the future is being able to reclaim the means of production. This relates to establishing knowledges and structures that help disseminate and distribute. Awareness and action are the key tenets of being able to reclaim the future: awareness of real, underlying issues that are contributing to a dystopian trajectory and the action needed to address those issues. One without the other is not effective.

Orgy with Machines, New Centre for Research and Practice (Mohammad Salemy and Nathalie Agostini)

This training engages in speculating through hybrid methodologies for the research and production of short fiction and memes in order to reimagine artificial intelligence as a plural, collective and shared entity between humans and machines oriented toward a democratic socialist future.

The New Centre for Research and Practice is an international, non-profit, higher education institute offering graduate and professional development-level certificate programs, workshops, seminars, exhibitions, residencies and conferences in art and curatorial practice, critical philosophy, media and technology, social and political thought and transdisciplinary research and practice. The New Centre's aim is a constructivist one: to assemble an environment, both virtual and actual, that inspires our members to invent alternate understandings that can be put into collective practice.

Mohammad Salemy is an independent Berlin-based artist, critic and curator from Canada. He has shown his works at Ashkal Alwan's *Home Works 7* (Beirut, 2015), Witte de With (Rotterdam, 2015) and Robot Love (Eindhoven, 2018). His writings have been published in *e-flux*, *Flash Art*, *Third Rail*, *Brooklyn Rail*, *Ocula*, *Arts of the Working Class* and *Spike*. Salemy's curatorial experiment *For Machine Use Only* was included in the 11th Gwangju Biennale (2016). Together with Patrick Schabus, he forms the artist collective Alphabet Collection. Salemy is also the organizer at the New Centre for Research and Practice.

Nathalie Agostini is an independent researcher based in London. She works with artists, galleries, non-profit organizations and agencies on questions of production, archiving and communication. Agostini is an alumna of the New Centre for Research and Practice, where she regularly collaborates on developing the organization's public programming. In 2019, she co-organized the *Interlocutories* conference at Spike, Berlin, and the *Hyperannotations* interview sessions for the New Centre at Ocean Space-TBA21-Academy during the 58th Venice Biennale's pre-opening days.

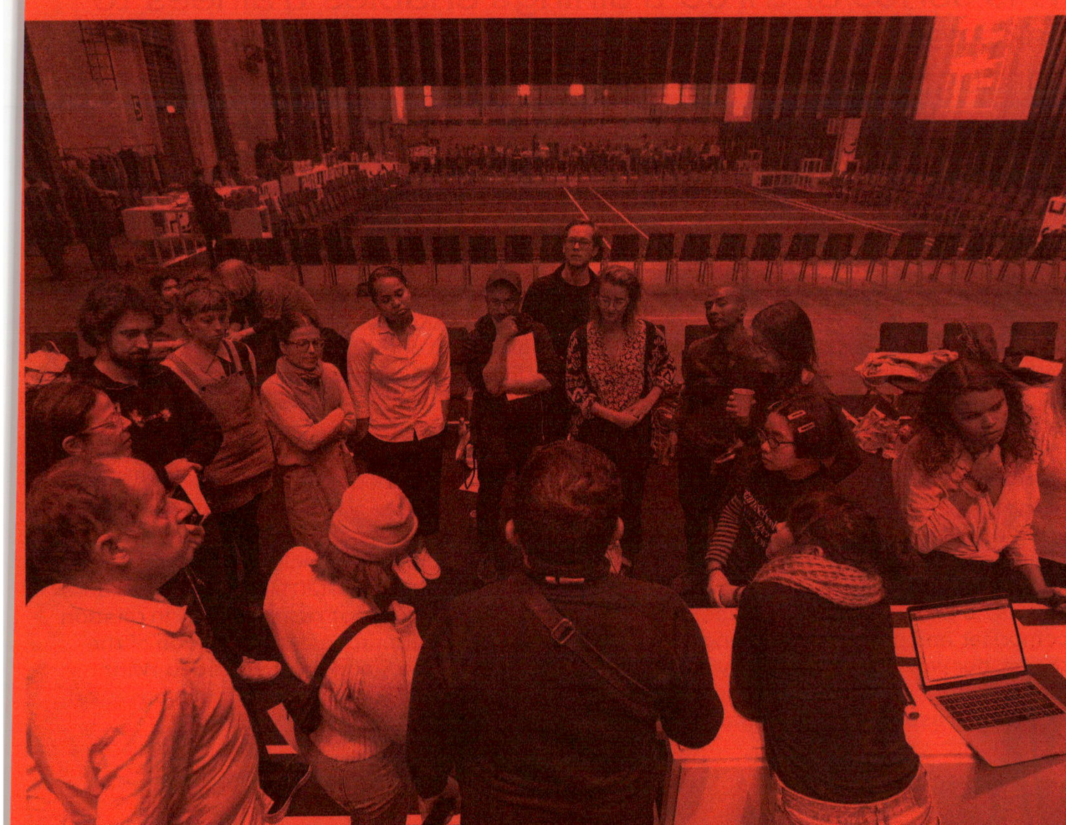

Multitudes of Listeners, Maya Felixbrodt, Germaine Sijstermans and Samuel Vriezen

This series of three trainings enables trainees to take responsibility for the possibility of polyphony through expression and/or attention, developing a plural voice, a collective ear, a shared resonance.

Maya Felixbrodt is an experimental musician, performer and artist based in Amsterdam. In her cross-disciplinary practice, she investigates different styles, genres and disciplines as a performer, composer and researcher. Felixbrodt is also an educator, working with all ages and with diverse populations, teaching music, leading creative workshops and facilitating interdisciplinary making. As a consultant for research and stage work, she plays a pivotal role in companies such as Zvov and Sex_Kitten_Baby and is the founder and co-editor of *Synzine*, a magazine for musical games.

Germaine Sijstermans is a clarinetist, composer and performer. Among other things, her work is influenced by nature, indeterminate/silent music and Butoh dance. The spatial aspects in her compositions are an essential component of her works from the very initial stages on, both in the music itself as well as in the use of the performance space. She is currently involved as an artist-in-residence at the Dutch music production house Intro, where she is developing compositions that are performed inside her installations.

Samuel Vriezen is a freelance composer and writer living in Amsterdam. Over the past two decades, his work has orbited around the Lagrange points between music, mathematics, politics, poetry and play. Recent work includes the radio play *Schade* [Damage] (2017) – which considers how to talk about responsibility in relation to the environmental destruction of the Niger Delta – and an opera titled *What Happened/Plays* (2019) – a piece based on the work of Gertrude Stein.

Multitudes of Listeners

Musicians are always training. It's not just practicing for the future that will be the performance – since music itself does not distinguish between being played for fun, for practice or for a professional stage with an audience. You're always trying to get better, listen better, follow the sounds better, play together better and, if we speak of the quality of a musical performance, what is really sought is the intensity of a training that is continually going on. Likewise, if there's a futurity in music, it's a futurity within the listening situation itself. Music's futurity is inherent to its present, and its politics is that of a long-term fidelity to an ongoing practice.

Normally such training is a life project. Now, when training with an audience, who may not have the same sort of habitual musical training, what can you do? This is the question that arises when you're confronted with a large and heterogeneous group of a hundred people or more, like we were in 2019 in Bochum, with everybody bringing their own backgrounds and musicalities, their own ease and unease, hopes, desires and sensitivities. And if you only have three sessions of half an hour in which to create a situation of musical training – which is also a musical performance – how do you manage?

Day 1

We started with listening to the space – a big space in which the entire collective of people, all from highly diverse backgrounds, can come to feel its existence together. We wanted to get a sense of what the many voices of the group were. Also, since we didn't know who or what to expect, we didn't want to impose any sense of a future to train for, but rather, we wanted to investigate what futures might already be present within a group. The space itself and the randomly gathered crowd would become something like a resonance, or maybe a giant collective ear. So we thought, let's try hearing each other's voices, hearing the voice in the room, hearing the room from different angles and hearing other people and their concerns.

We chose a musical archetype that we assumed everybody could understand: a drone. We wanted to invite everybody to contribute their voices to the drone. We also wanted the drone to move, so that people could hear the voices from many perspectives. We then invited people to insert their own thoughts and questions regarding the future, so that no singular futurity would be imposed on the first day. We wanted to see what might emerge.

We decided we wouldn't spend time giving explicit instructions so that the entire half-hour could be one uninterrupted stretch of time. We would simply start and try to get the whole group to join.

Humming. Until everybody is humming.

Walking. Until everybody is walking.

Then inviting words and questions. Individual voices.

Then inviting people to echo what they heard if they want. Maybe singing words together.

This drone is a space for voicing questions and concerns and we will sing them.

A walking resonator for words. Words to float in the time of the drone. To move back and forth between voices. To maybe change their quality so they would be heard differently and to unfold what they could mean. Thereby, to listen to what this particular moment of being together could be and what it could mean.

Risking disharmonies, hoping for resonances.

At some point, ending.

Day 2
Speech Melody Game: A game for exploring the meanings that verbalized words can carry beyond their definitions.

This training consists of multiple rounds.

Trainees are divided into groups of five or six people (or smaller, depending on the number of trainees). The groups stand in small circles, all the groups are spread out across the space and start the game simultaneously.

Each group decides on a short sentence to be used in the game. This sentence could be relevant to the context of the training. An example o[f] a sentence would be: There are many futures.

In each group the trainees take turns going around the circle over and over, saying the sentence out loud. With each turn, and as they wish, the trainee can say the sentence with a speech melody/intonation, emphasis or character. For example:

There are many futures
There are **many** futures
There are many futures?
There are many futures!
Theeeere are maaaaany
fuuuutuuuures
There are many futures

Each group should explore the many ways in which the sentence can be said and should observe how the meaning of this one sentence change[s] with each form of delivery or within each group.

The trainers will walk between the groups and announce when it is time to break up the groups and form new ones, or for groups to join together to form a bigger group. When new groups are formed in this way, they can decide whether to continue using previously used sentences or to establish new ones. Over the course of the training, the groups of trainees wil[l] become fewer and bigger, ending the game in one big circle with all trainees. The time for each round can vary from around two minutes for the small groups at the beginning of the training to longer periods per round as the groups get larger.

a trainer observes that a group ould benefit from a different or new irection of exploration, they may, for xample, join a group and the game or a short time. If joining a group vould be impractical, for example if is a big group, they may also simply ffer a suggestion to the group.

Day 3

n two groups, find sounds that you can make together:

use your voice
breath
body
b o d i e s

What sounds do you want to make together?

noises melodies words humming
animals humans questions
statements
rhythm surprise comfort

How can you act and make sound together?

find a common language
signs that you agree on
that you all understand
make eye contact
use body language
listen to each other
wait for each other
lead, follow

Once you have gathered your sounds and communication strategies you can begin. Try to not use verbal communication from now on.

The first group (givers) takes the second group (receivers) by the hand. Then the first group leads the second group, now with closed eyes or blindfolded, with care, gently and firmly giving security and comfort, making sure to feel empathy for the other. The first group leads the second group to a chosen destination. Then, after carefully sitting down or lying on the ground, begin giving your sounds:

take, give, T I M E
spread, come close
loud and soft
fast and slow
to one to all
listen
be listened to

attention, intention, intuition

be alert, be there
within your body
b o d i e s

When the first group's sound-giving has reached its peak, SWITCH. To do this, the first group reaches an agreement without words, each finds a spot and sits down. Then close your eyes, listen to yourself, listen to your surroundings.

The second group, when you feel it's your moment as a group, GO. Start giving your sounds, never stop and keep changing.

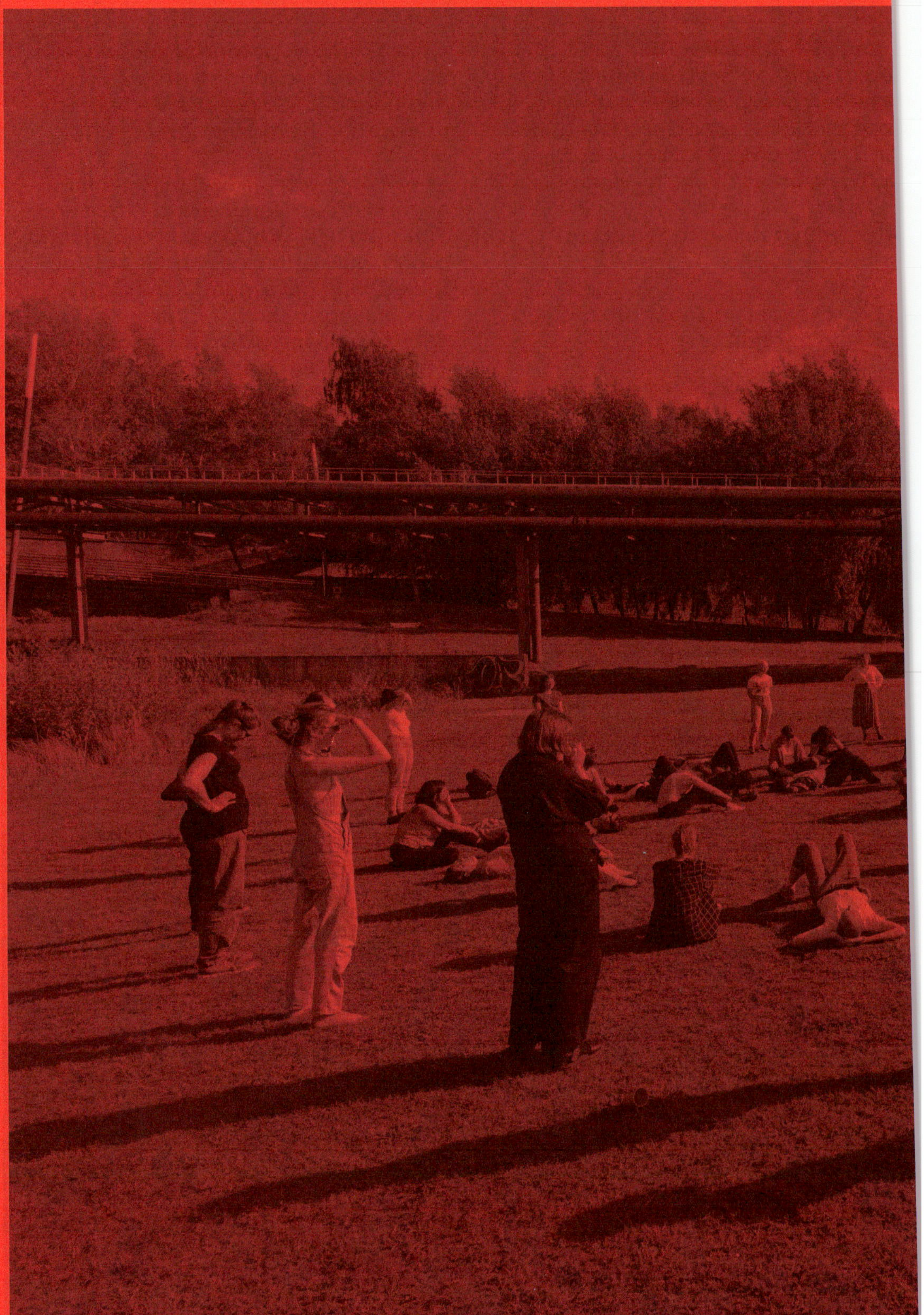

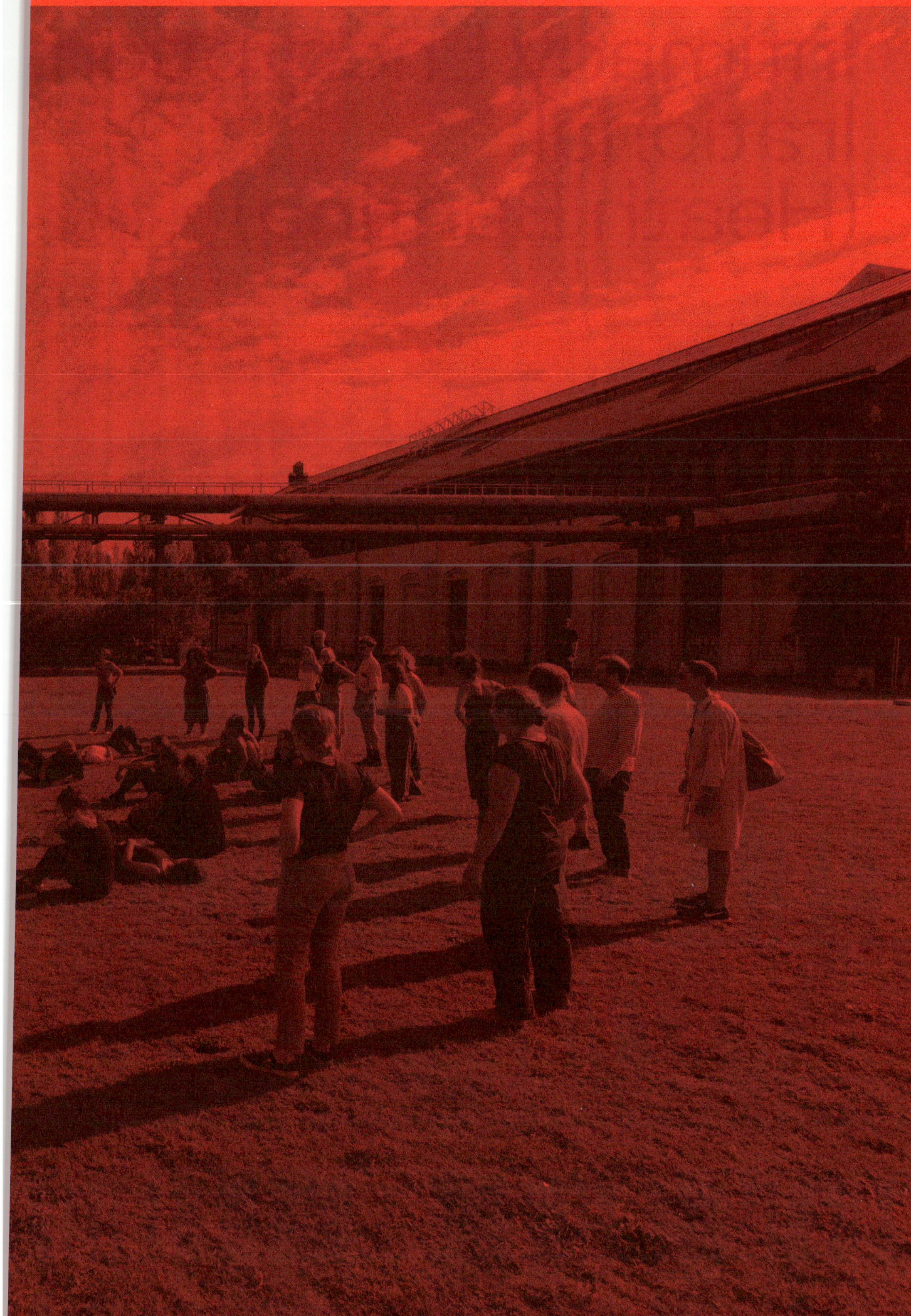

SEPTEMBER 9, 2019, BOCHUM, GERMANY

Intimacy Encryption, Irational (Heath Bunting)

This training teaches trainees to build intimate knowledges about one another in order to create coded languages and develop collective counter-interrogation skills.

Heath Bunting's main work, *The Status Project* (2004–), involves using artificial intelligence to search for artificial life in societal systems. He has had multiple works of art censored and permanently deleted (including all copies and backups) by the British security services, including an artwork that was exploded by an army bomb disposal team from Hereford – an instance that he is prevented from talking about in public. He is currently training artists in security and indoor and outdoor survival techniques so they can out-live organized crime networks in the coastal forest during the final crisis.

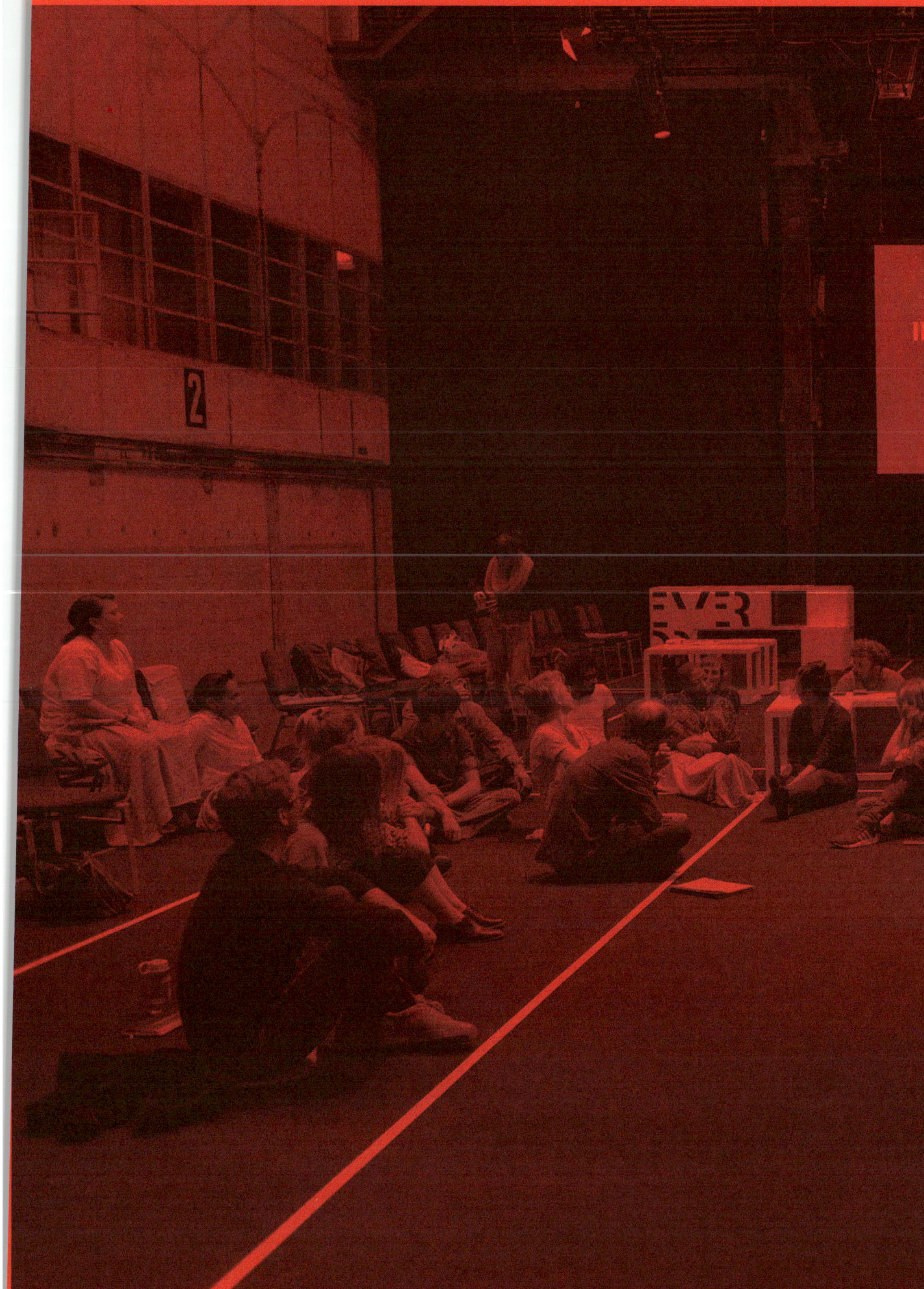

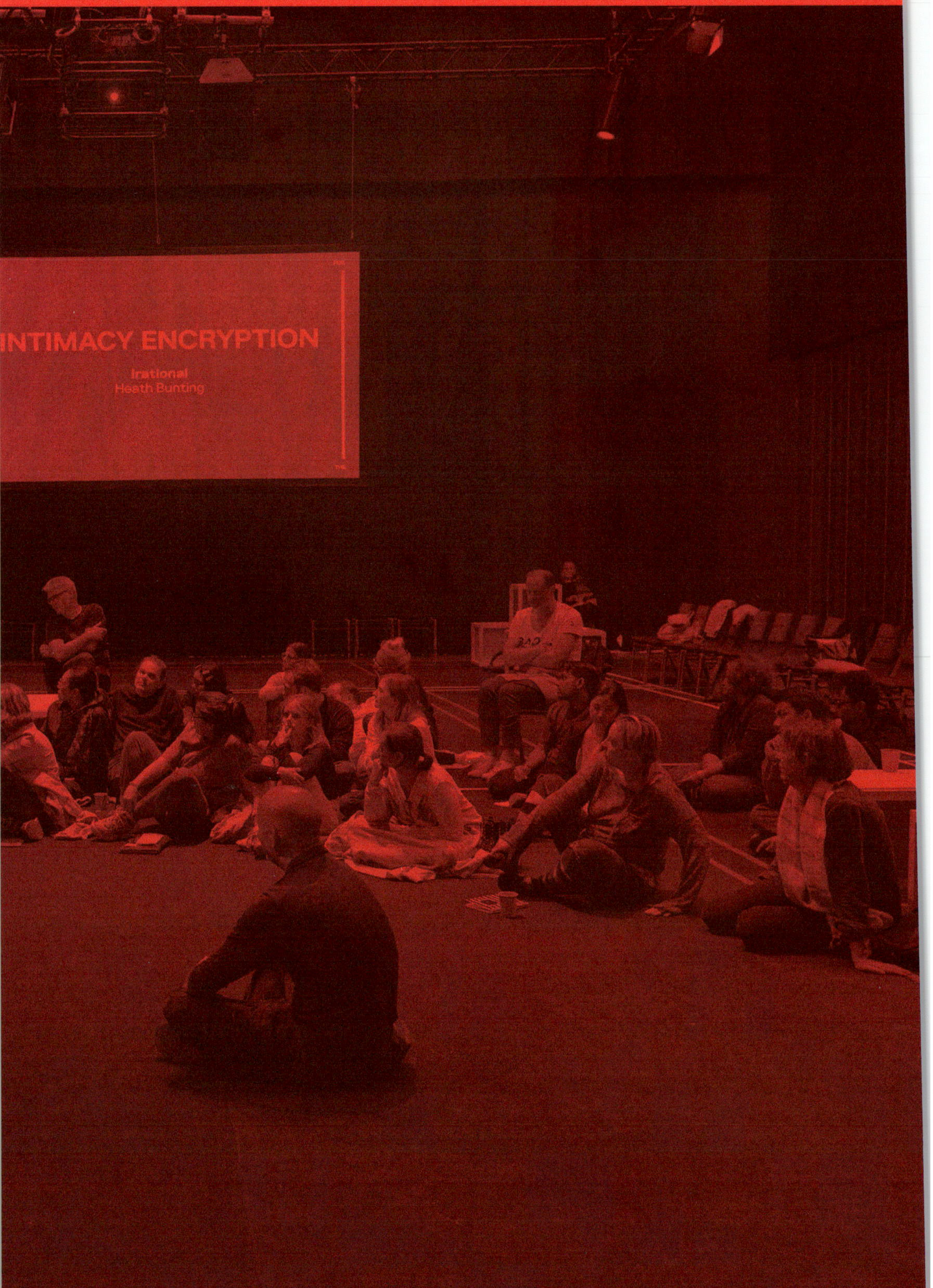
INTIMACY ENCRYPTION
Irational
Heath Bunting

Benign Cat with Many Mice

Irational (Heath Bunting)

How did you approach the notion of the 'training' and what does the term mean to your practice?

I guess through two processes. Firstly, by changing the way people see themselves and the world around them, and secondly, by prompting the experience of this reimagining through prescribed activities.

In a time of dystopian normativity, what does the notion of the 'future' mean to you?

Limiting bad consequences of present action or inaction – it's not for the taking or making anymore. At best we can only hope for reduced losses instead of any gains.

What does it mean to reclaim the future's means of production?

It means the removal of authority from expert futurologists and the introduction of personal practice and responsibility for future envisioning.

What did you learn from your training? What aspects would you develop further or change?

It was interesting to train very large groups of more than a hundred people. For some perverted reason, I felt like Tom Cruise delivering a TED Talk.

How would you describe the relationship between trainers and trainees?

As a benign cat with many mice.

How do you envision the further distribution of tactics and knowledges to reclaim the future?

I think the past is reclaiming us. I envision fatalism, spiritualism and modesty over control, intellectualism and ambition.

Killing the Dominant Male, Center for Jineology Studies (Ceren Akyos and Yasemin Andan)

This training introduces the field of jineology (women's sciences), developed by the Kurdish Women's Movement, to undo patriarchal behaviors and exercise in cooperative democracy.

European Center for Jineology Studies is a Kurdish organization dedicated to women's studies. The term 'jineology' means 'women's science,' with *jin* meaning 'woman' in Kurdish. 'Logy' is derived from the Greek term *logos*, meaning 'knowledge,' and *jin* additionally comes from the Kurdish term *jiyan*, which means 'life.' From the perspective of women, it is important to work together to build an alternative field of social sciences, to establish a system of women's studies, to overcome the current dispersal in the region and to strengthen scientific flow and the intersections.

Ceren Akyos dedicates her thoughts, being and compassion to learning from and sharing with the womxn of the world – workers, peasants, militants, indigenous womxn, mothers, daughters, sisters, solitaires (by choice but never alone), liberationists and libertarians. Rebellious and courageous, womxn are owners of their own words and world, and they organize their rage while defending joy, freedom and the struggle to rewrite a history so that the oppressed peoples of the world are given their rightful place. Akyos is also a militant researcher in postcolonial studies, for the time being.

Yasemin Andan is a Kurdish women's activist. She is currently a member of the Jineology Committee in Europe. She holds a degree in sociology and psychology, and also has a master's degree in gender, education and international development.

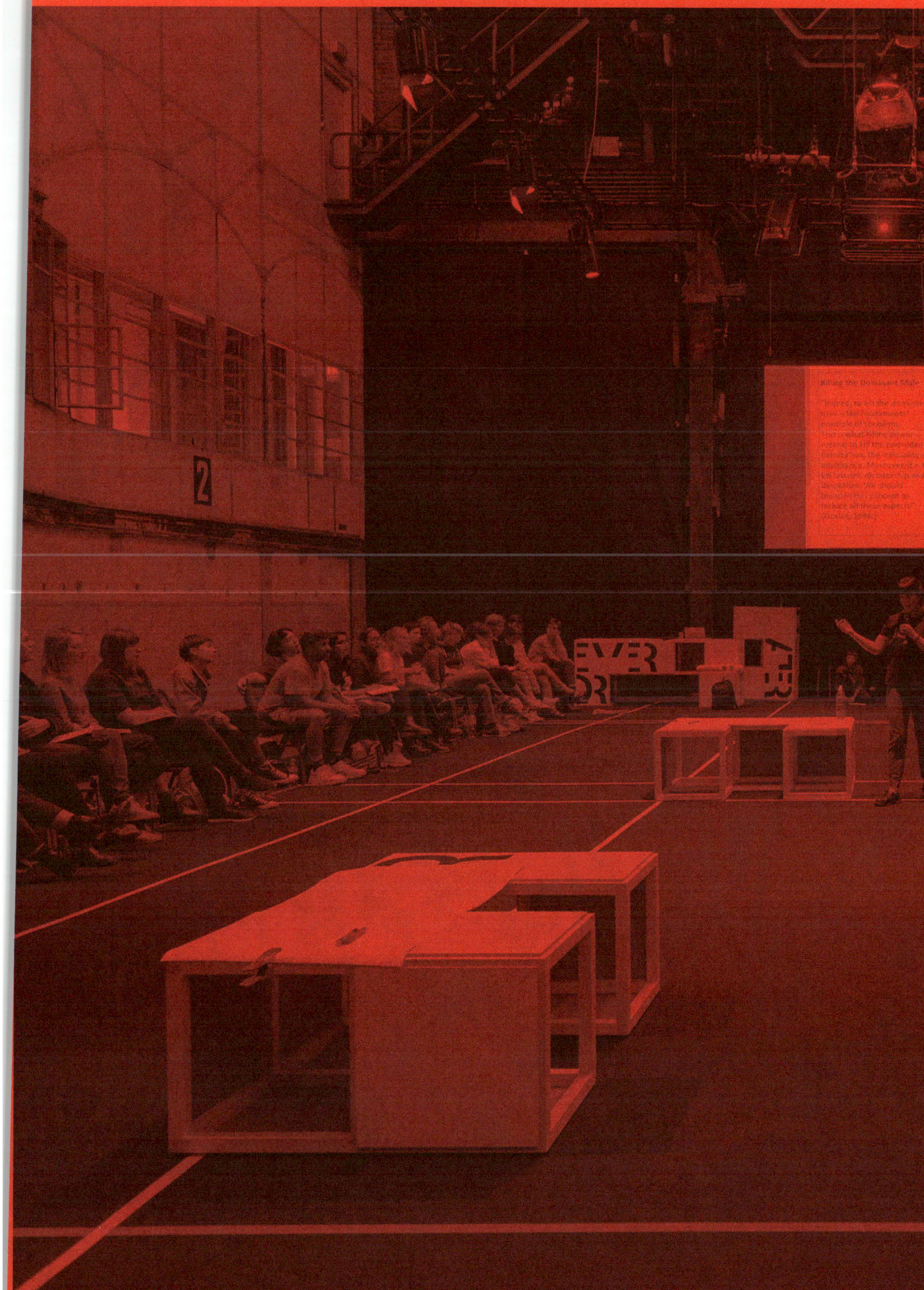
Killing the Dominant Male

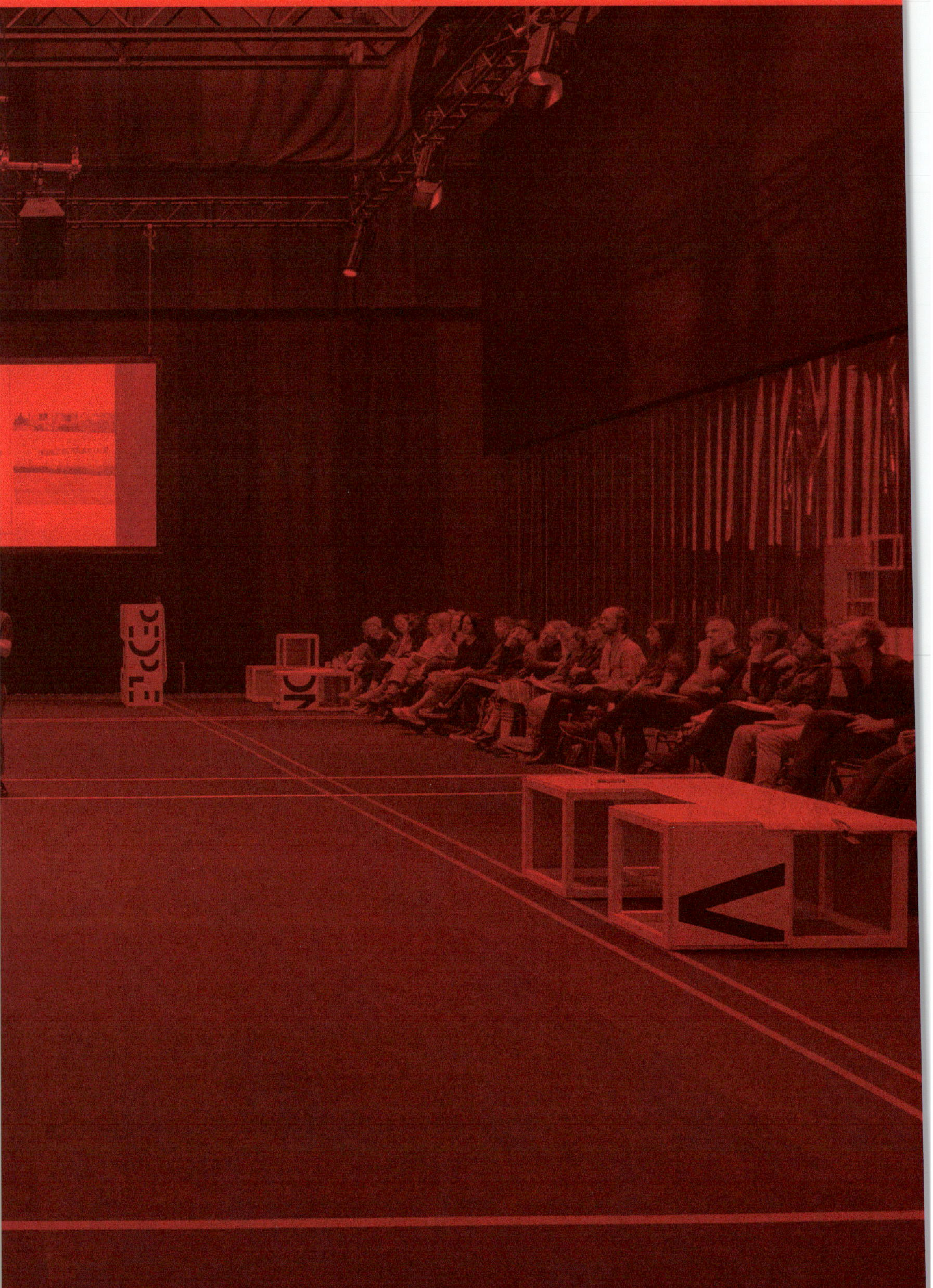

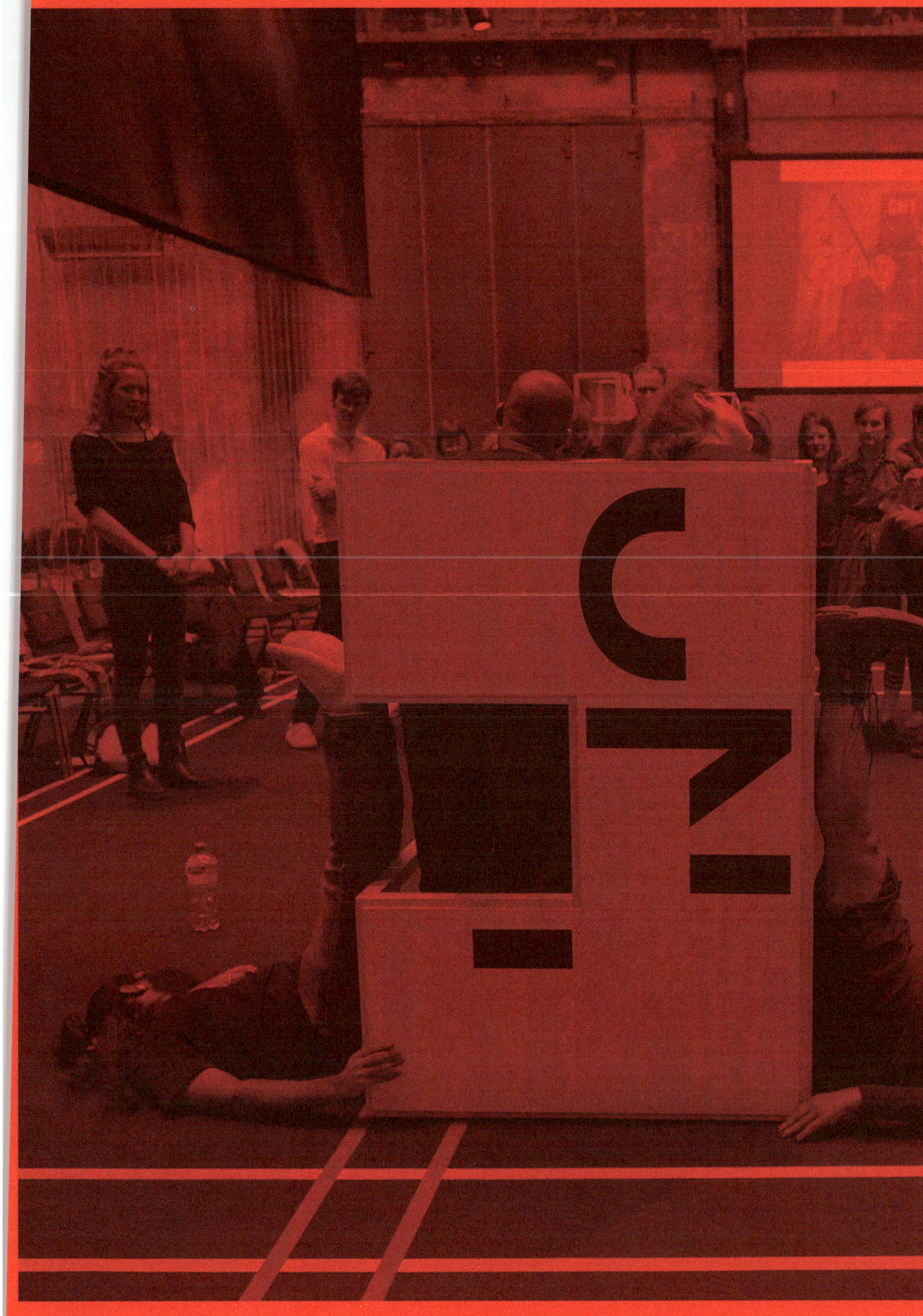

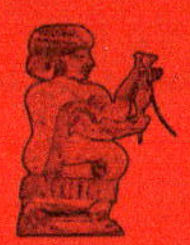

Fellow comrades,

These questions are directed to men struggling alongside women in order to understand the difficulties that our comrades encounter in positioning themselves as men in the quest for liberty and their underlying reasons. The idea behind this is to encourage you to be introspective and question the power relationships we harbor, albeit unwillingly, that perpetuate a 'dominant male' figure so that we can challenge the current societal understanding of masculinity.

- How would you define yourself as a 'man'? Would it be possible to define man beyond the definitions based on power and hegemony?

- What are the main handicaps you encounter in your relationships with your male comrades? How do you define male friendship? Besides the kin relationships between a father and a son and brothers, or between colleagues or flatmates, do you think men can have intimate relationships? What are the determining emotions in such a relationship? What do you expect your male friendships to be? And how do these male relationships define your attitude towards women?

- What are the main issues that men seek understanding on? Do you have emotional difficulties in communicating these issues with your comrades? If so, why do you think it is hard for men to express themselves emotionally? These emotions could include affection as well as sadness, defeat, anguish, etc.

- Would you say that solitude is in the nature of men? Why would you think that men who naturally build a sharing relationship with women are excluded from men's circles?

- How do you approach your personal liberation? What are the decisive emotional factors for men seeking liberty? What are the emotions that you cannot get over?

- Why is it the responsibility of women to transform men? How do you feel about having women's liberty as the measure of your liberty? Are you able to accept this in your personal struggle for liberation? What kind of emotions does this arouse? How do you feel about it now?

- What is the deepest obstacle you encounter as a man in the struggle for liberation?

- What do you understand of the idea of 'total divorce' (from the patriarchal system)? What is the gender struggle for you? In your opinion, what are the impediments facing the gender struggle in the present context? How do you think, as a man, we could get past the situation?

SEPTEMBER 21, 2019, BOCHUM, GERMANY

Decolonizing Society, Initiative Schwarze Menschen in Deutschland (Tahir Della) and glokal e.V. (Lucía Muriel)

This training looks at stories of colonial violence, racism and economic exploitation, and simultaneously focuses on self-empowerment and resistance. It encourages participants to understand colonial history as something that has immediate implications on both the present and our collective future.

The Initiative Schwarze Menschen in Deutschland [Initiative of Black People in Germany] is a registered non-profit association. Its mission is to represent the interests of black people in Germany and to stand for justice in the migration society. The initiative highlights and combats racial discrimination, deprivation and exploitation, offers space and activities for black children and teenagers, promotes political, black projects and advocates an anti-racist attitude in all areas of society.

glokal e.V. is a Berlin association for critical educational work and counseling, which has been active in political youth and adult education since 2006. Through their work, glokal e.V. wants to sensitize people to global and intra-social power relations and empower them to contribute to their dismantling.

Tahir Della lives and works in Berlin. Since 1986–87, Della has been part of the Initiative Schwarze Menschen in Deutschland (ISD) and the younger black movement in Germany. He was initially active in the local ISD group in Munich, focusing on community work, film festivals, lectures, talks and campaigns. In addition to this work, he helped shape the exhibition *Homestory Deutschland* (2006–). Della has also been active on behalf of glokal e.V., currently holding the position of Promotor of Decolonization and Anti-racism, which will be supervised by ISD and glokal e.V. over the coming three years.

Lucía Muriel was born in Ecuador. She is a graduate in psychology and has advanced training in industrial, occupational and organizational psychology. She is also a psychotherapist with a therapeutic focus on trauma, migration and violence. For many years now, she has been a leader in debates focused on anti-racism, emancipation, gender empowerment and decolonization in educational and public spaces. She is the author of *Die (bundesdeutsche) Eine-Welt aus einem Guss?* (2014).

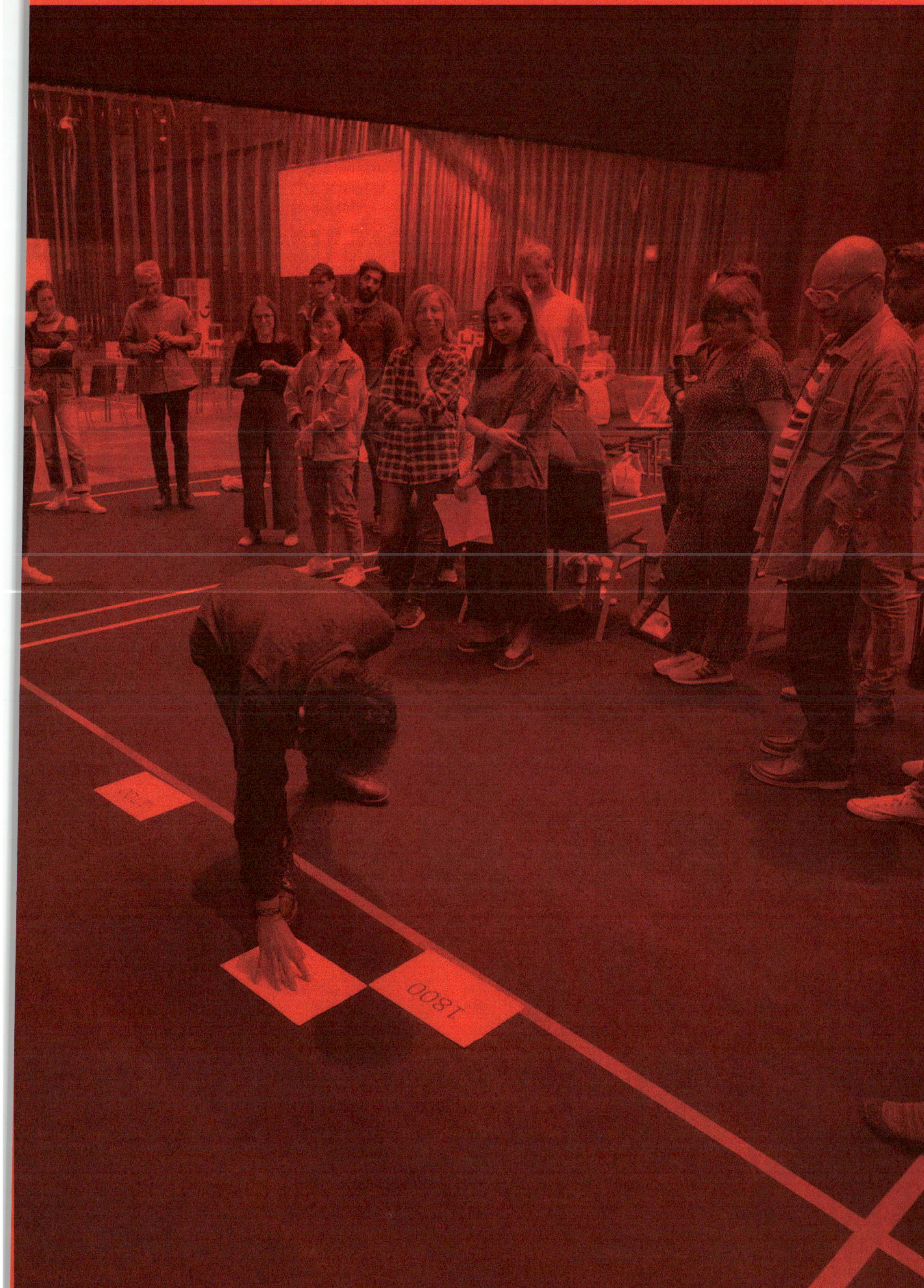
1800

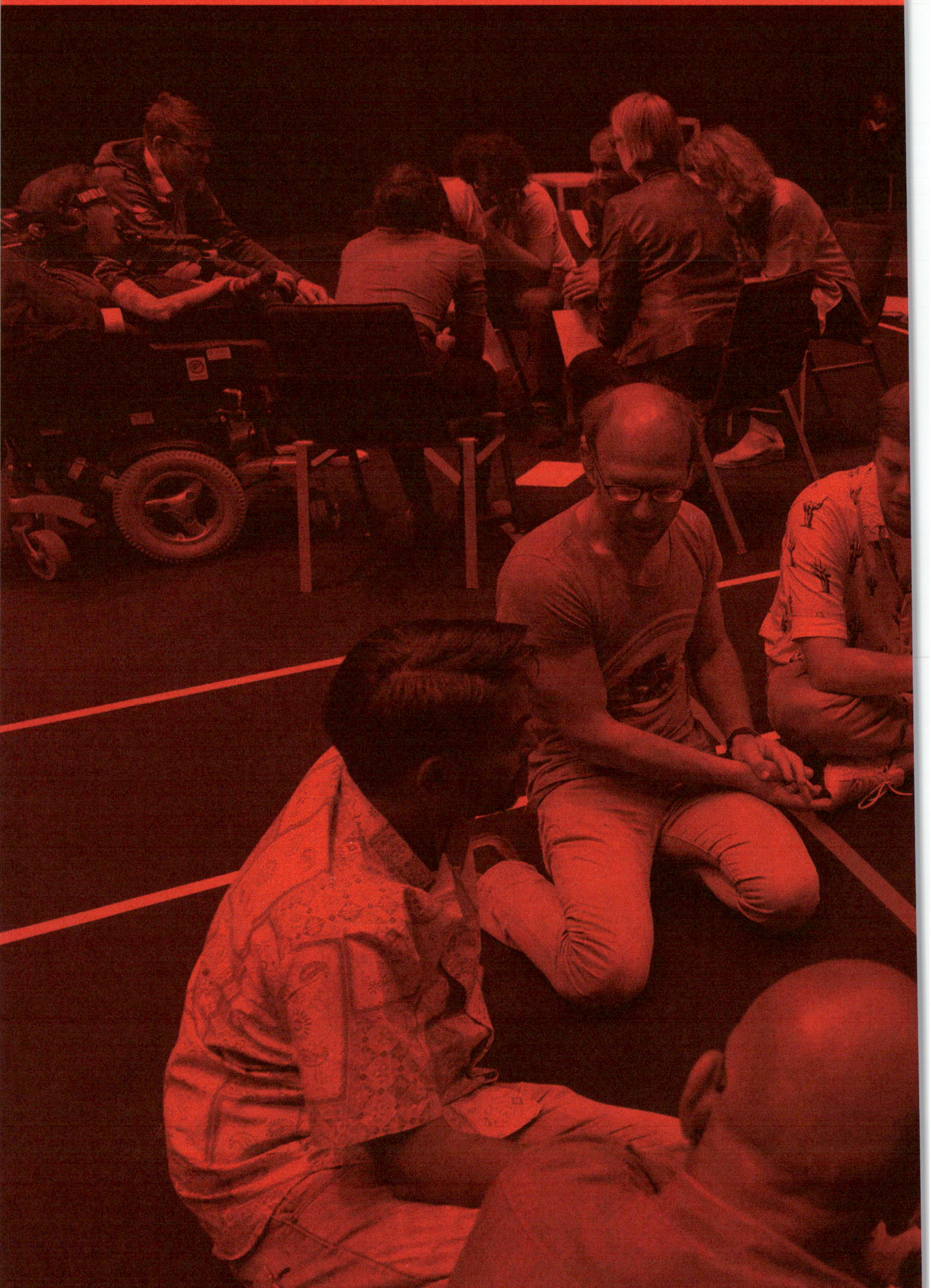

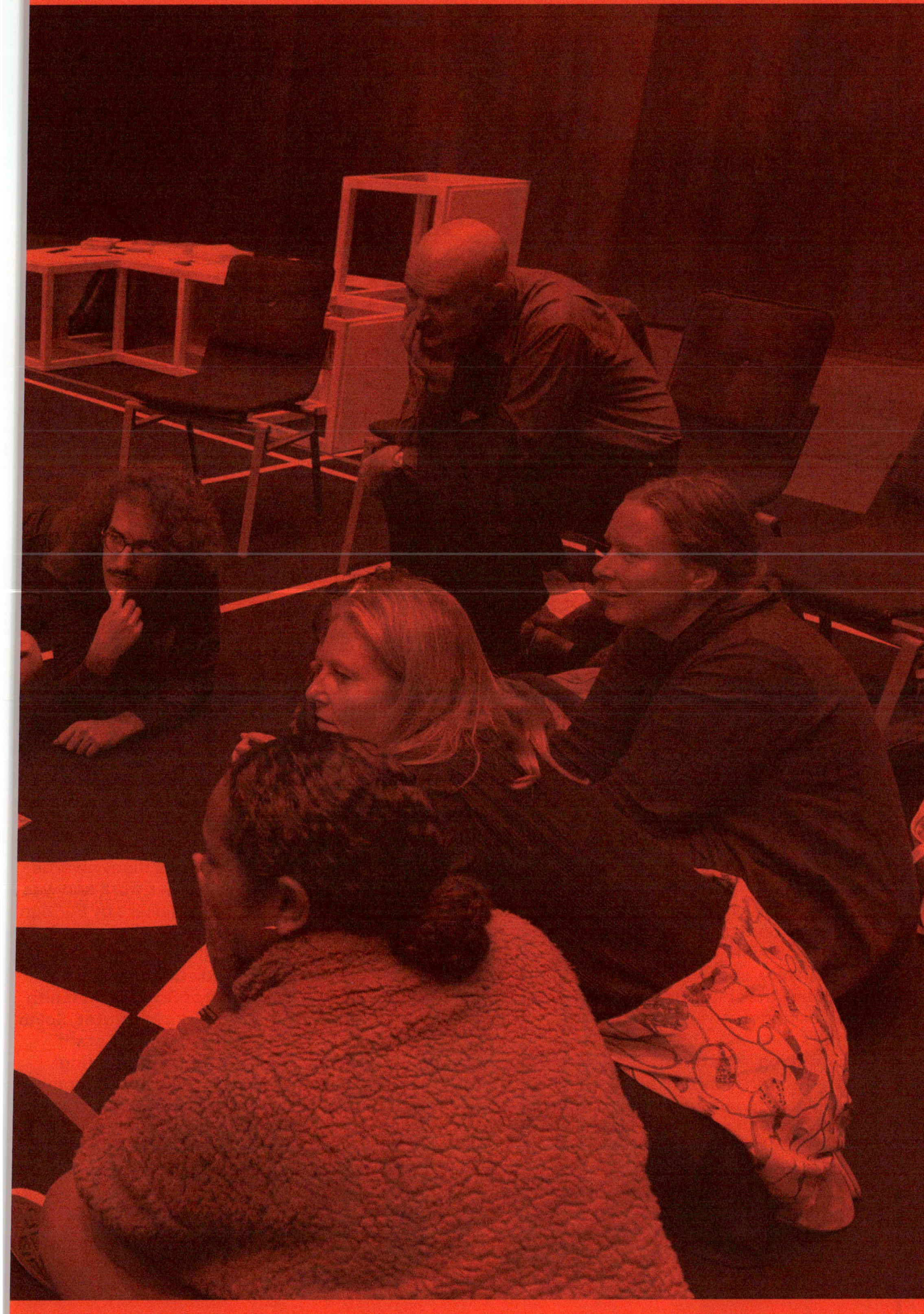

Extraterritorial Activism, Women on Waves (Rebecca Gomperts and Victoria Satchwell)

This training explores how to use extraterritorial spaces to pit different legal realities against one another for activist purposes through boats, drones and robotic devices.

Women on Waves (WoW) is a Dutch pro-choice non-governmental organization created to bring reproductive health services, particularly non-surgical abortion services and education, to women in countries with restrictive abortion laws. Other services offered by WoW include contraception, individual reproductive counseling, workshops and education about unwanted pregnancy. Services are provided on a commissioned ship that contains a specially constructed mobile clinic, named the A-Portable. When WoW visits a country, women make appointments and are taken on board the ship. The ship then sails out approximately twelve miles, to international waters, where Dutch laws are in effect on board ships registered in the Netherlands. Once in international waters, the ship's medical personnel provide a range of reproductive health services that include medical abortion.

Rebecca Gomperts, MD, MPP, PhD, studied medicine and visual arts in Amsterdam, the Netherlands. In 1999 she founded Women on Waves and in 2005 she founded Women on Web, a telemedical abortion service. The service supports women living in countries where safe abortion is not available to obtain information and access abortion pills. Gomperts has received many awards and much recognition for her work and was named one of the global thinkers by Foreign Policy in 2015.

Victoria Satchwell studied feminist philosophy and has a Master of Science in Health Economics from Karolinska Institutet, Solna. She has worked as a program assistant focusing on the provision of HIV testing within universities, a market access consultant within the pharmaceutical industry and a philosophy tutor at the universities of Cape Town and Stellenbosch. Currently she is a research coordinator at Women on Web, where she also works on the helpdesk providing information to women accessing telemedical abortion services.

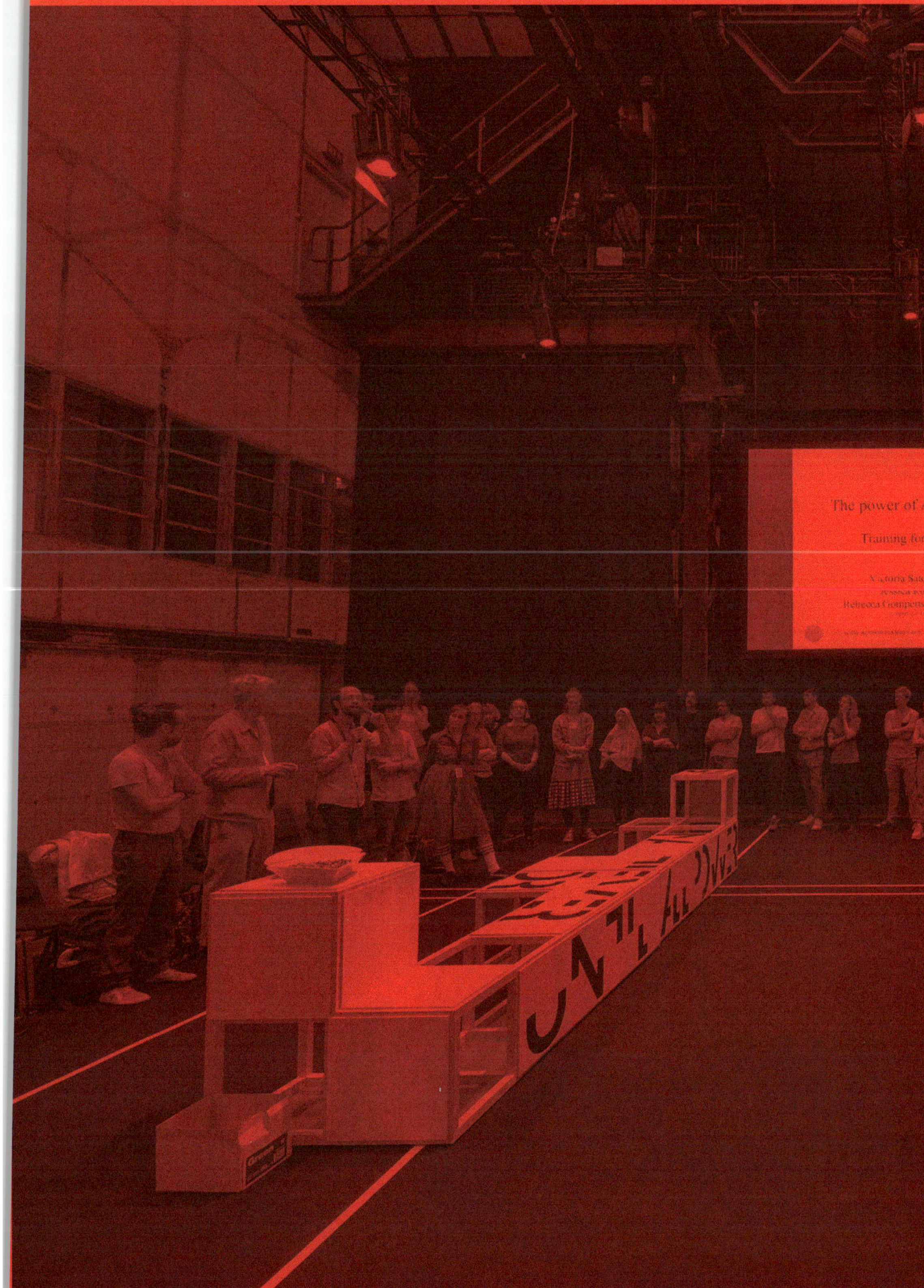

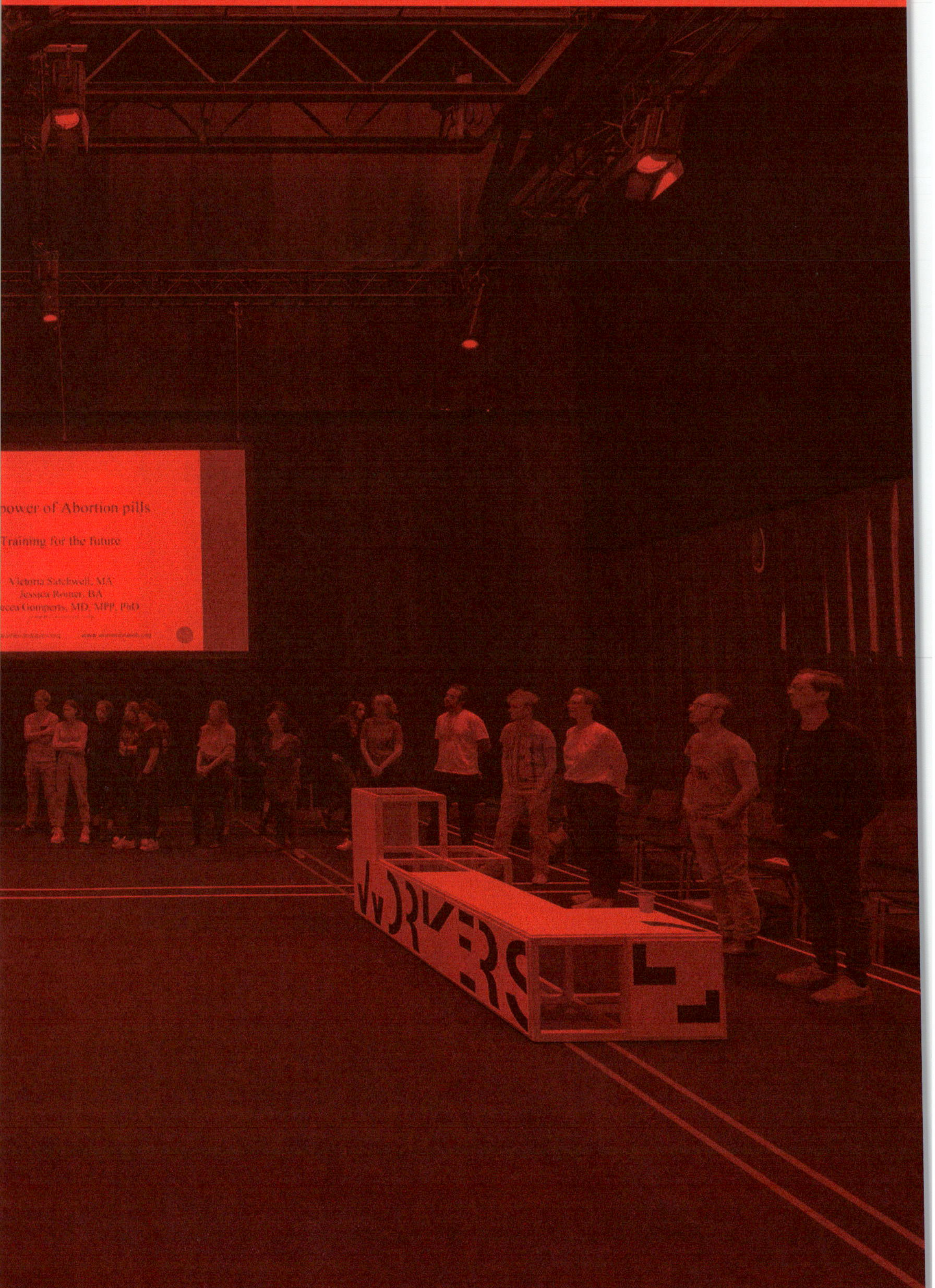
power of Abortion pills
Training for the future

Extraterritorial Zoönomy, Klaas Kuitenbrouwer and Sjef van Gaalen

This training uses role-play to prepare for the establishment of a zoöp (a particular human and nonhuman cooperative) in extraterritorial waters.

Klaas Kuitenbrouwer is a curator, initiator and moderator working at the intersection of culture, technology and ecology through various public events. He is a researcher in digital culture at Het Nieuwe Instituut, Rotterdam, where he was also responsible for the exhibition and research projects *Garden of Machines* (2015) and *Gardening Mars* (2017). He currently develops the Zoöp project – a legal format for collaboration between humans and collective bodies of nonhumans. Furthermore, Kuitenbrouwer teaches media and theory at the Rietveld Academy, Amsterdam.

Sjef van Gaalen is a Rotterdam-based researcher and designer. His practice focuses on futures and fiction, collage and camouflage. His current research combines design strategies and methods from agro-ecological practices with speculative and participatory design methods, working with stakeholders in farming and design to explore the co-creation of futures, narratives and strategic mapping in the interest of a regenerative ecology.

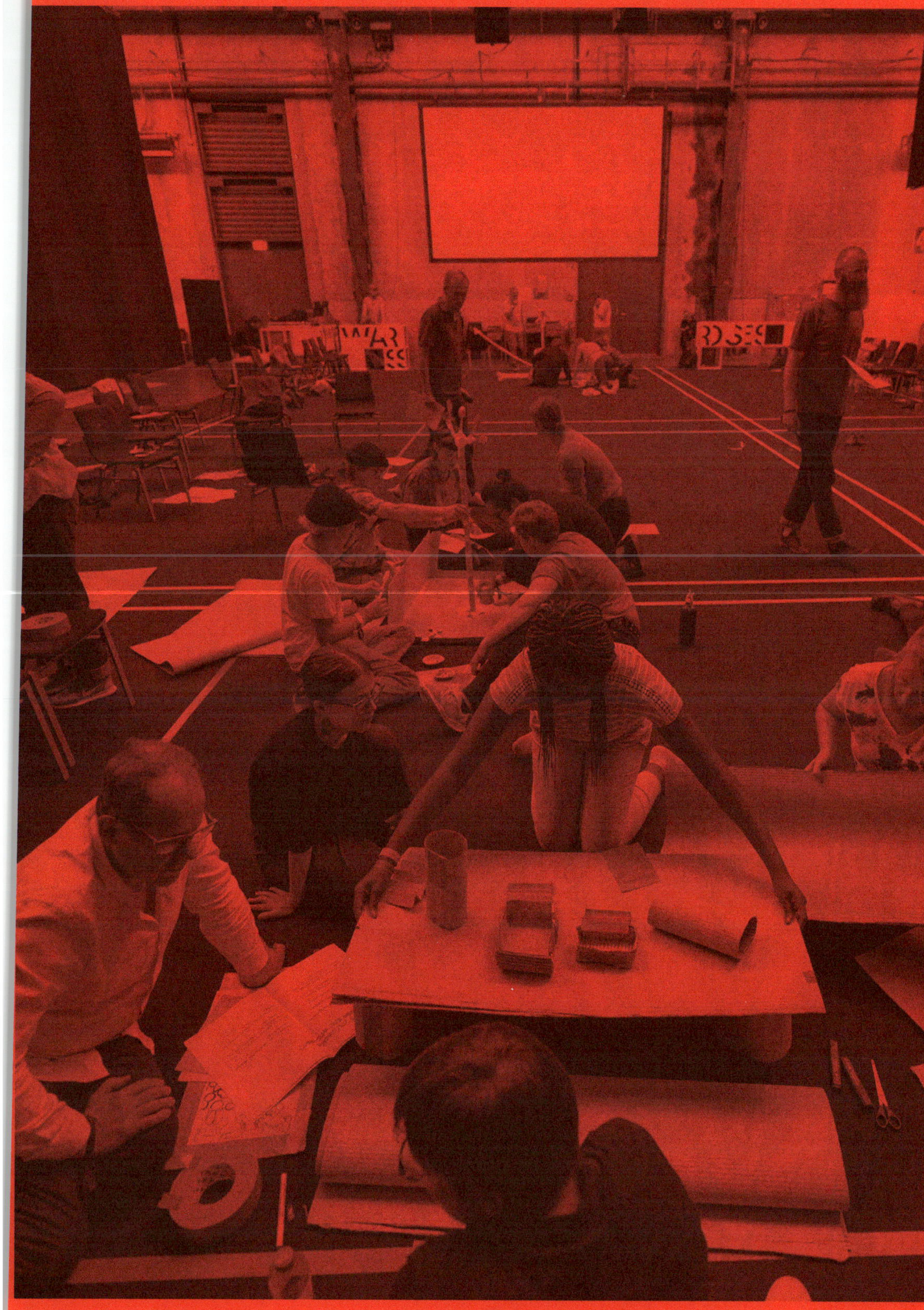

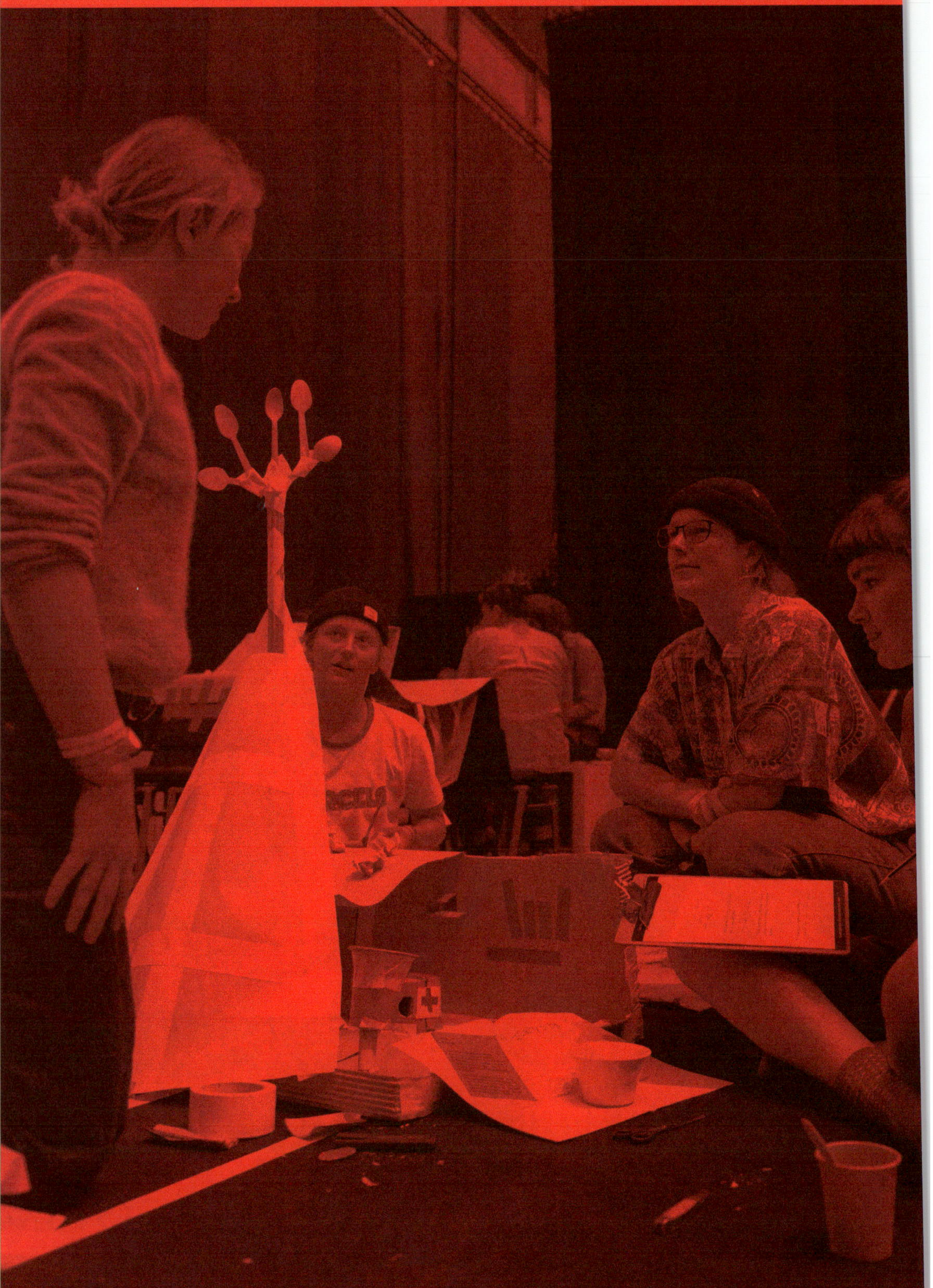

Zoönomic Futures

Klaas Kuitenbrouwer and Sjef van Gaalen

How did you approach the notion of the 'training' and what does the term mean to your practice?

In our set-up, 'training for the future' meant attempting to inhabit possible futures in the present. In this sense, it can be considered as a form of prefigurative politics. We created a narrative space within which alternative visions of the future could be constructed, and did so by using an approach loosely based on role-playing to think through some possible alternatives. The 'training' lies in helping people to experience some shift in perspective as part of the exploration, to catch a glimpse of how reality might be otherwise configured.

In a time of dystopian normativity, what does the notion of the 'future' mean to you?

The notion of a 'singular future' isn't necessarily particularly useful or meaningful. There are various latent and more manifest futures present amongst a plurality of futures that are unfolding at all times. The work is to redistribute statistical probabilities by generating precise resonances in the present. The present is a diffractive whole composed of endless amounts of simultaneously present futures – probability waves in superposition. It is important to realize that when futures' probability waves collapse (so, the moment a future becomes more manifest), this manifestation also takes place backwards in time. This means a future that is manifesting *at that moment* turns out to have been present all along.

The particular future we attempted to amplify in the present focused on the work of repair in relation to different levels of human and more-than-human existence. It includes metaphysical reorientation, a thorough reconsidering of material conditions and human existence, a reconception of society as a multispecies community and a multispecies politics, architectural analysis and an ethics that is already internalized as morals.

With regards to a present attitude of dystopian normativity: yes, conditions we view as dystopian have been the lived reality of many on this planet for a long time. To abuse the familiar Gibson quote, 'they are also unevenly distributed.'

What does it mean to reclaim the future's means of production?

There are several parts to this process, the first of which, if things are to change, is to imagine how the means of production themselves have to be reimagined and then understood differently. Our training was focused on this imagination: the exploration of a possible space in which the recast means of production were already present. This approach helps to bring forward future (un)likelihoods.

However, for anything to actually change, more than imagination is required. Longer-term, real-world, strategically focused and tactically engaged practice must be applied for new realities to be instantiated. Within the Zoöp project we might call it collapsing the zoönomic probability wave.

The work of repair that the Zoöp project – a legal format for collaboration between humans and collective bodies of nonhumans – is involved in, not as speculation but as a practical project, makes the ongoing present more capable of providing habitats for zoönomic futures and makes the gap between the dystopian present and a zoönomic future easier to jump, so to speak.

How would you describe the relationship between trainers and trainees?

In our training the relations between trainers and trainees are that of narrators and protagonists, or maybe of navigators and travelers. Although, it is important to realize that in this case the navigators were only familiar with the broad contours of the landscape that was to be explored. They had the map and provided direction, but it was in fact the travelers themselves who filled in the details of the territory through which they traversed on their journey.

How do you envision the further distribution of tactics and knowledges to reclaim the future?

Zoönomic Futures (and its descendant, Marine Zoönomy) forms one of the more speculative iterations of the Zoöp project, informing its radical imaginaries and in turn keeping the practical implementation of the Zoöp model in resonance with the most interesting of its potential futures.

Zoöp is short for zoöperation, a new legal entity that allows a wide variety of organizations to collaborate with (a representation of) nonhuman life within their practices. Zoöp is an attempt to make a beginning through the work of repair and a pragmatic answer to the issue of capitalist realism, as formulated by Mark Fisher. As he famously noted, 'It is easier to imagine the end of the world than the end of capitalism.'

These days, the desperate voices of collectives of animals, plants and other less-obviously living matter can be raw to the senses. But it still requires dedicated effort to take them into account. The design of the Zoöp model therefore has three goals. Firstly, we hope to strengthen the political position and legal standing of nonhuman life within human societies (in capitalist cultures). The second goal is to support ecological regeneration. In Zoöp's own vocabulary: Zoöp-based organizations want to develop their zoönomy, meaning, to develop the quality of life of multispecies communities within and surrounding Zoöp. The third goal of the format is for it to be adopted (and actually applied) by a wide variety of organizations – from farms to municipalities, from hotels to cemeteries, from commercial enterprises to non-profit foundations. The Zoöp model is the centerpiece of the Zoöp movement and the anchor point for the practice of zoönomy.

An organization transforms into a Zoöp-based one by including a so-called Zoönomic Foundation in its executive board. A Zoönomic Foundation has one task only: to articulate and represent the needs and interests of the nonhuman community within the spatial and operational sphere of the organization in question and to apply these needs and interests to decision-making processes. The Zoönomic Foundation acts as a speculative and political organ for the nonhuman community. By joining Zoöp, an organization keeps its existing goals. A school is still a school, a farm remains a farm, a hotel is a hotel. But it adds a new goal to its existing ones: to develop the situated zoönomy.

The Zoöp legal format does not require legislative reform – which takes a very long time – but works with the existing legal instruments of private law. Zoöp does not grant rights or personhood but works on the premise that nonhumans already have rights. Zoöp is a way of organizing, a practice and a procedure that actively acknowledges the rights and subjective experiences of nonhumans and is focused on collaborating with them. In this sense, the Zoöp model is a shortcut within the rights-to-nature discourse. Once an organization joins Zoöp, it performs a yearly cycle of four movements – demarcating, observing and sensing, characterizing and intervening – with the aim to develop a local, thriving multispecies community (that includes humans). This then provides the base to work on other, less-local aspects of the operational sphere of Zoöp.

Inventing the Radical, Not An Alternative (Steve Lyons and Jason Jones)

This training proposes strategies for deploying myth and conspiracy to benefit the production of social movements.

Not An Alternative is a collective established in 2004 that works at the intersection of art, activism and critical theory. The collective's latest ongoing project is *The Natural History Museum* (NHM, 2014–), a pop-up museum that highlights the socio-political forces that shape nature. Not An Alternative's performances, exhibitions and presentations have been shown at MoMA PS1 (New York), Tate Modern (London), Victoria & Albert Museum (London), MOCAD (Detroit) and Museo del Arte Moderno (Mexico City), as well as in the public sphere, where they collaborate with community groups and activist mobilizations. At Training for the Future, Not An Alternative is represented by Steve Lyons and Jason Jones.

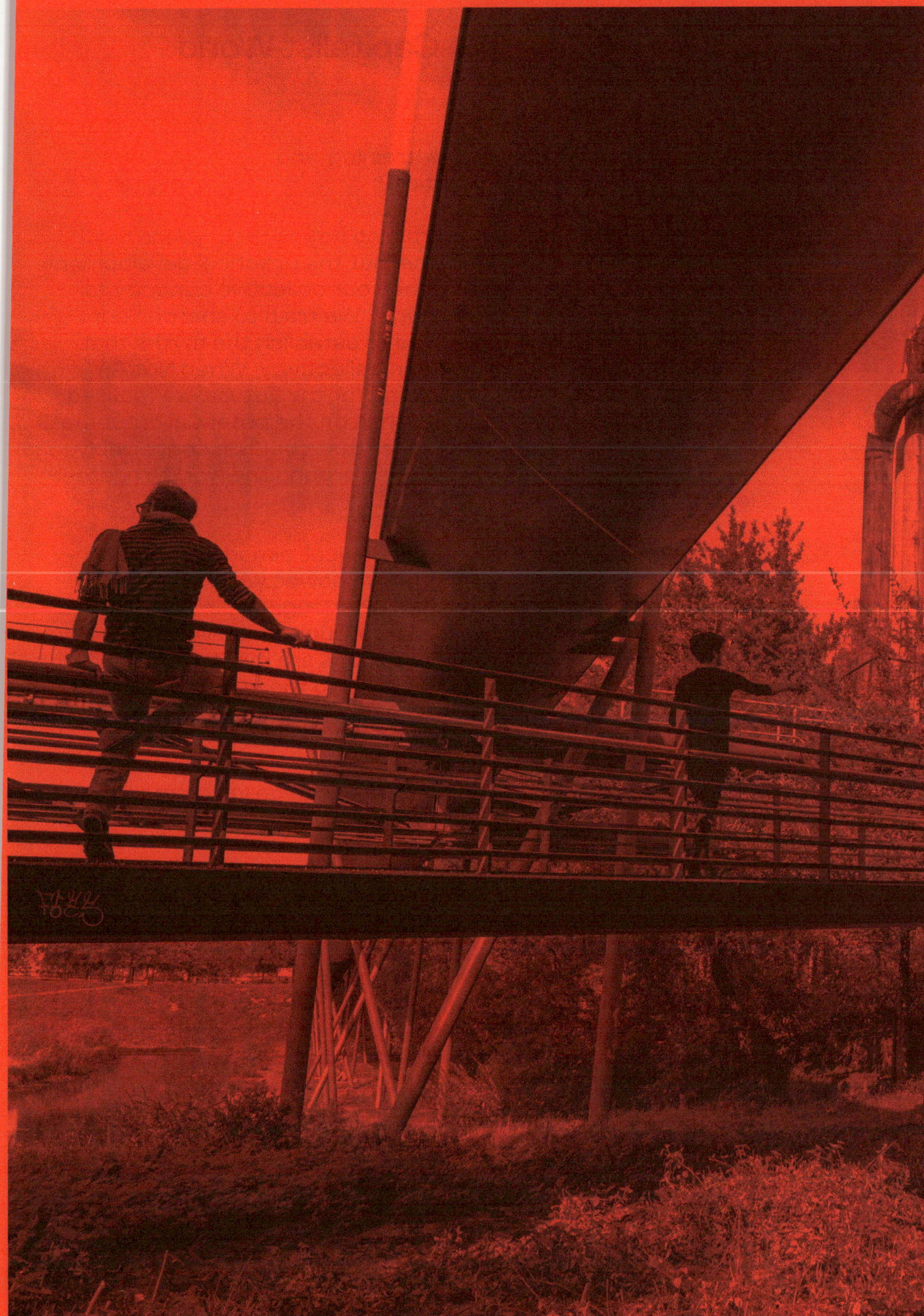

We Produce a Gap in the Capitalist World

Not An Alternative

How did you approach the notion of the 'training' and what does the term mean to your practice?

Our collective understands training not as the endless rehearsal of a future yet-to-come, but the practical development of competencies that strengthen our collective capacity to *make* the future through struggle. We train to sharpen our tools, to organize ourselves and to establish the myths that we need to build and strengthen collectivity. When Not An Alternative was invited to Training for the Future, we focused less on the process of training than on the potential outcomes. What generic tools could we offer that could be conceivably adopted and deployed in struggles around the world, regardless of the objective conditions?

Our training, titled Inventing the Radical, aimed to train trainees in a *way of seeing* our collective power, which Not An Alternative argues is inscribed in the 'language in common': the visual and communicative forms through which social movements and other collective formations are made to appear. Before we can effectively contribute to the building of the language in common, we have to be able to see where it already exists, to attune our vision to the signs of our power that are already inscribed in the landscape. Our collective's position is that the capacity to build on the language in common first requires that we can identify the signs of collective power that already exist.

Because of the specific setting of the training (a former industrial plaza in a German city we had never been to), we embraced the visual language of the training facility as a resource. We asked trainees to see the neo-constructivist visual language of the training facility (which itself is an iteration on the visual language of Soviet design) as a case study in the practice of iteration. We asked trainees to develop an inventory of the signs and symbols that demarcated the partisan dimensions of the design. We then sent the trainees outside with materials leftover from the installation with the task of iterating the visual language that was already there, to produce forms of 'communist graffiti' beyond the immediate training site. We wanted trainees to take away one central idea: collective power is not built through the production of novel or innovative forms, but through the conscious and unconscious iteration of the 'language in common' we inherit, learn to recognize as ours and that holds us together as a 'we.'

In a time of dystopian normativity, what does the notion of the 'future' mean to you?

The Bulletin of Atomic Scientists' Doomsday Clock tells us that it is '100 seconds before midnight.' Not only is it easy to imagine the end of the world, but also the end of capitalism. The paralyzing problem is that both ends are imagined to correspond with the termination of humanity as a whole. Convinced by the 'dystopian' tendencies in contemporary discourse and climate science, many on the left write off the possibility of egalitarian emancipation, leaving us without firm ground to stand on. But as Potawatomi philosopher Kyle Whyte reminds us, the dispossessed peoples of the world have struggled under apocalyptic conditions for centuries – not just for survival, but for the collective flourishing of human and more-than-human life. There are reasons to live and reasons to struggle, even and especially when the future is not guaranteed.

For Not An Alternative, the future is not in the future. It is neither a vision of utopia or dystopia. Rather, it is a horizon for struggle in the here-and-now. We inscribe the future in the present by insisting neither on the certainty of planetary collapse, nor on the certainty that communism will follow the death of capitalism, but on the indeterminacy of the future. If the inevitable names the enclosure of the future, the indeterminate points to the common beyond and beneath. When we understand that the future is indeterminate, we do not sit and wait for the opportune moment, instead, like Marx's mole of history, we plot and scheme in order to produce the opportunities needed to strengthen our side.

What does it mean to reclaim the future's means of production?

We have been arguing that our collective counterpower grows and develops in a dynamic relation to the counterpower we inherit from our ancestors, from the revolutionaries whose struggles have informed our own. By recognizing that our struggles fall within a long tradition of resistance, and iterating on the means of communication that we inherit, we build power and make the future possible. In this sense, we would suggest that the means of the production of the future do not need to be 'reclaimed.' They have never been abandoned. Therefore, our collective task is not to reclaim the means of producing the future, but to consciously and intentionally build on the means of production we inherit. When we iterate on the work of our ancestors, we produce a gap in the capitalist world – an opening from which to affirm our collective difference and construct an infrastructure to support it.

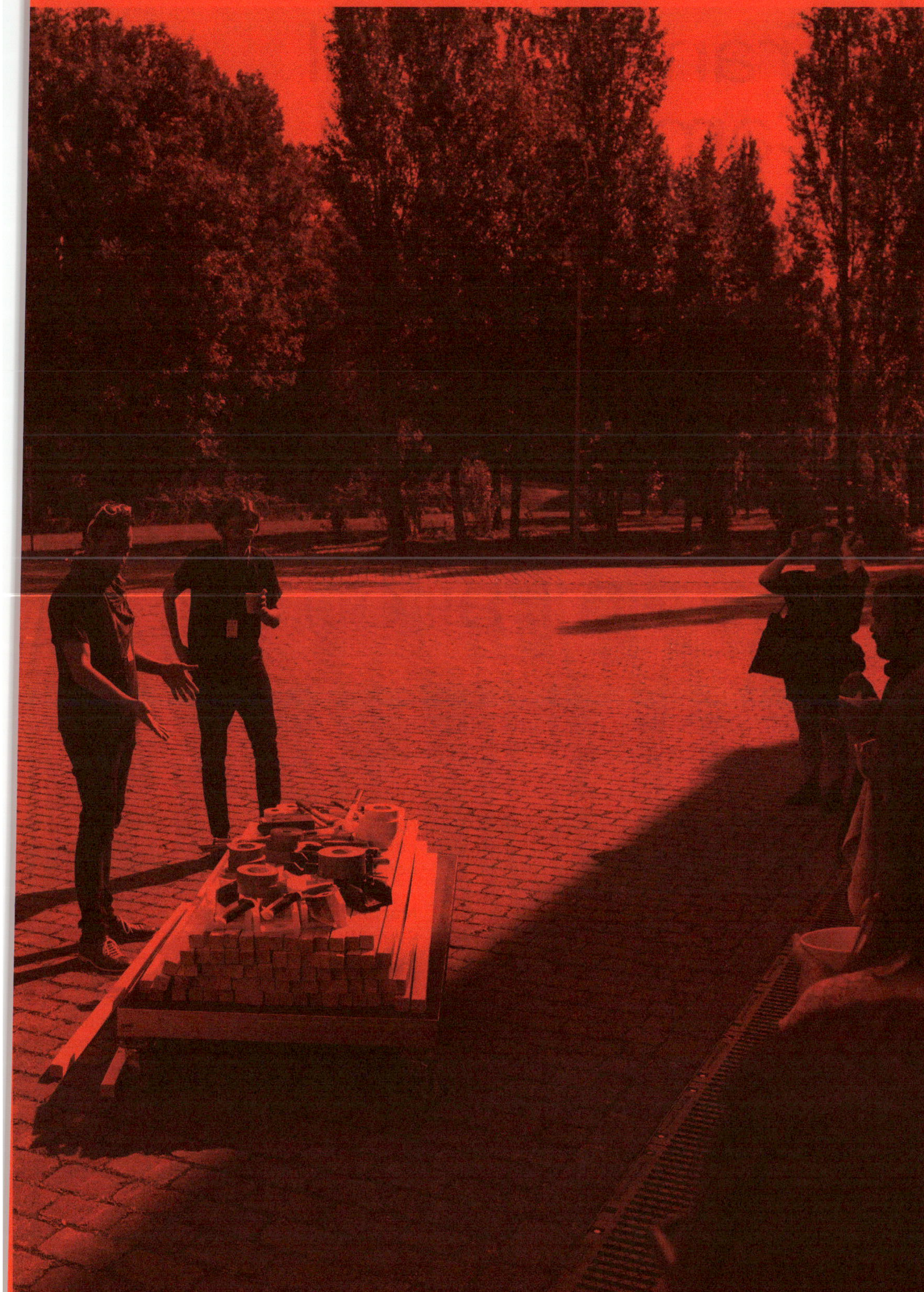

Transnational Campaigning, School of Transnational Activism / European Alternatives (Lorenzo Marsili and Martin Pairet)

This training practices transnational politics beyond the nation-state through campaigns, collective action and experimental forms of (self-)governance.

European Alternatives (EA) is a transnational civil society organization and citizen movement promoting democracy, equality and culture beyond the nation-state. After ten years of experimentation with transnational participation, advocacy, campaigning, research, trainings and cross-border events, EA condensed its knowledge of transnational democracy activism together with other civil society actors into a new platform called the School of Transnational Activism.

Lorenzo Marsili is a philosopher and political activist working for a future beyond the nation-state. He is the co-founder of the transnational non-governmental organization European Alternatives and was one of the initiators of the pan-European movement DiEM25. His latest book is *Citizens of Nowhere* (Zed Books, 2018), and he was the founding editor of the independent journal *Naked Punch Review* (London and Beijing). He currently serves on the board of the global non-governmental organization CIVICUS.

Martin Pairet lives in Berlin. He coordinates capacity building programs and members' communications at European Alternatives. Pairet has been working in the non-profit sector for ten years with experience gained in membership development, communications and fundraising at international organizations such as IFOAM – Organics International and Oxfam France. He is also a member of CitizensLab, a transnational network of local change-makers exploring systemic change through collaborative projects in the fields of democracy, the arts and the commons.

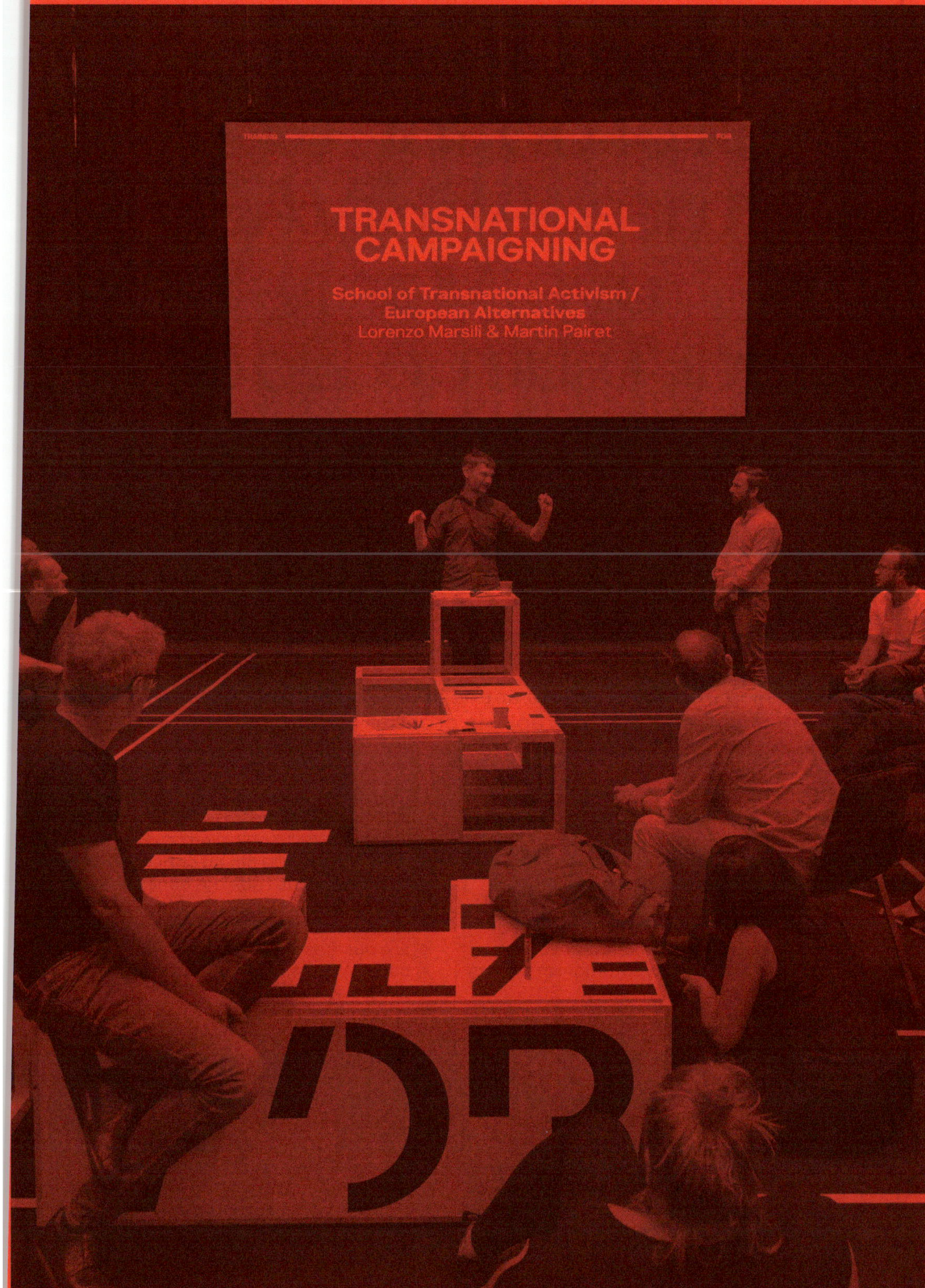
TRANSNATIONAL CAMPAIGNING
School of Transnational Activism / European Alternatives
Lorenzo Marsili & Martin Pairet

Beyond Welcome: Agitprop for the Future, ARRiVATi (La Toya Manly-Spain and Asuquo Udo) / Schwabinggrad Ballett (Nikola Duric and Liz Rech)

This training illustrates how to act as a heterogeneous collective body, using performativity and choreography in order to create unexpected situations in public space that go beyond ritualized forms of protest.

The agitprop collective Schwabinggrad Ballett was founded in 2000 and combines performance, concert and activism. Over the course of the so-called 'refugee crisis,' Schwabinggrad Ballett has joined forces with ARRiVATi, a performance group of refugees and people of color. Within this collaboration, agitprop meets Afrobeat, epic theater meets pop, situationism meets political task force. In September 2016, their acclaimed album *Beyond Welcome* was released by Buback Records. For their latest project, they focused on the eviction of Oranienburger Platz in Berlin. At Training for the Future, Schwabinggrad Ballett is represented by Nikola Duric and Liz Rech.

ARRiVATi is a collective of artists and activists of color that uses the means of art and resistance to develop strategies of decolonization in the fight against inequality. Their official statement reads: 'In the first place we no longer want to be called refugees! We don't like to be called refugees! We are here and we will remain until WE DECIDE to go away. We rock the boat. We survive by any means necessary, We learn other languages, We infiltrate and multiply, We are outsiders, We are Insiders, We fight back, We speak out, We talk back. We are artists and activists, children and adults. The ARRiVATi is an autonomous collective of border crossers, We are defenders of free movement, We are Cultural Invaders, We are considered endangered species, We work together to create a society where diverse people live with dignity, with equal rights. We collaborate and work with other allies, solidarity groups and collectives from the community.' At Training for the Future, ARRiVATi is represented by La Toya Manly-Spain and Asuquo Udo.

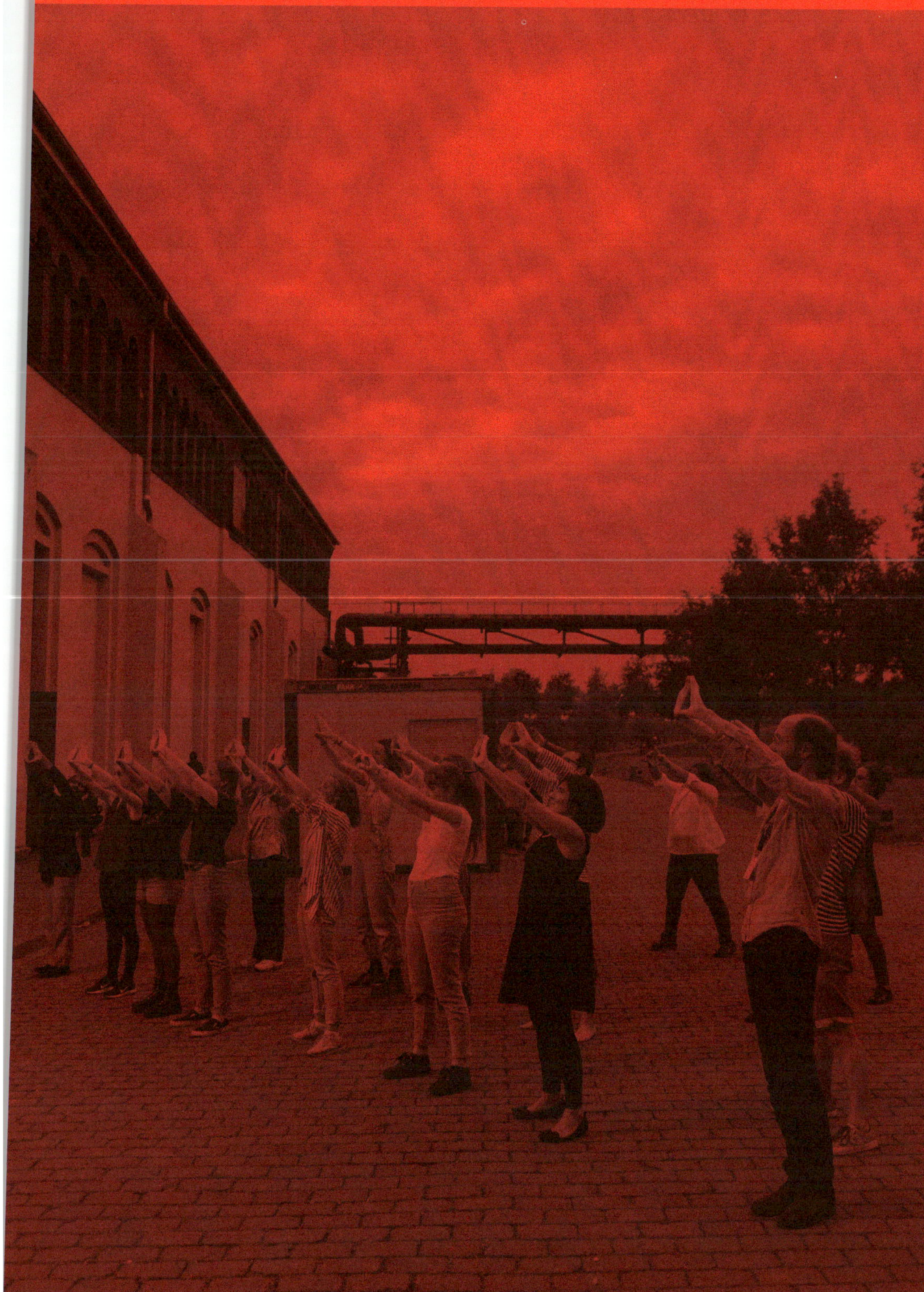

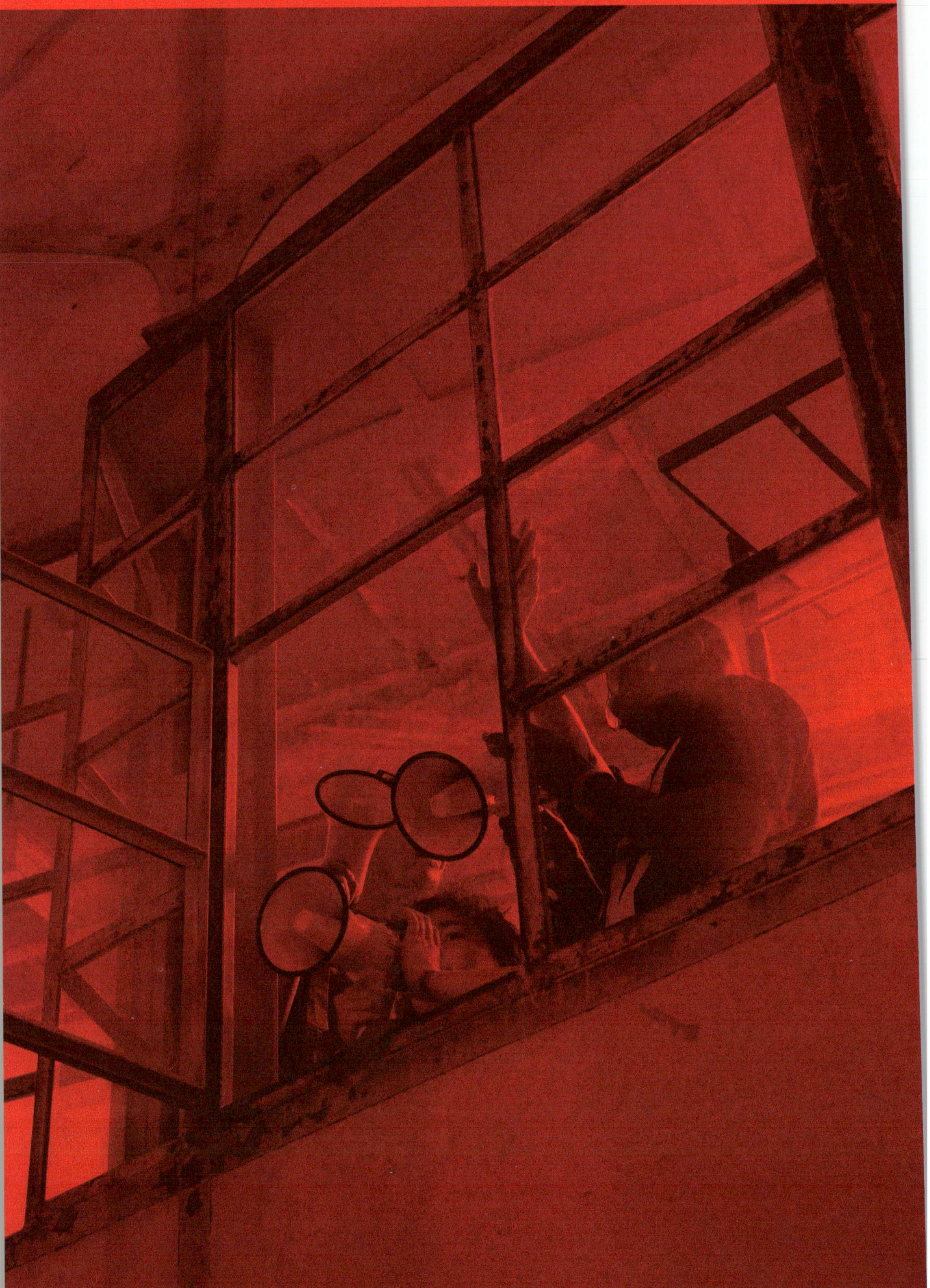

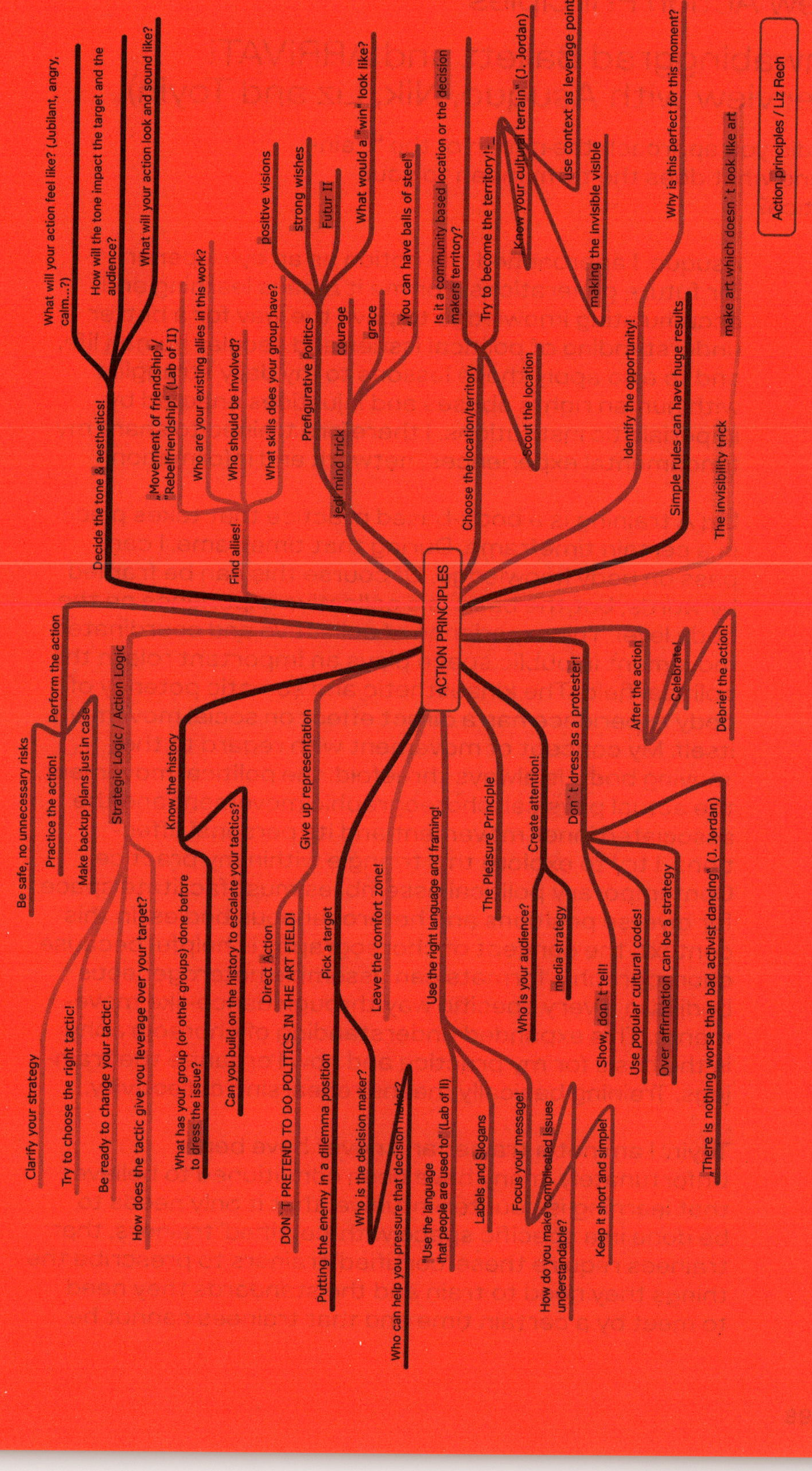
ACTION PRINCIPLES
Decide the tone & aesthetics!
What will your action feel like? (Jubilant, angry, calm...?)
How will the tone impact the target and the audience?
What will your action look and sound like?
Find allies!
„Movement of friendship"/ "Rebelfriendship" (Lab of II)
Who are your existing allies in this work?
Who should be involved?
What skills does your group have?
Prefigurative Politics
positive visions
strong wishes
Futur II
What would a "win" look like?
Jedi mind trick
courage
grace
„You can have balls of steel"
Choose the location/territory
Is it a community based location or the decision makers territory?
Try to become the territory!
„Know your cultural terrain" (J. Jordan)
use context as leverage point
making the invisible visible
Scout the location
Identify the opportunity!
Why is this perfect for this moment?
Simple rules can have huge results
The invisibility trick
make art which doesn`t look like art
Action principles / Liz Rech
Perform the action
Be safe, no unnecessary risks
Practice the action!
Make backup plans just in case
Strategic Logic / Action Logic
Clarify your strategy
Try to choose the right tactic!
Be ready to change your tactic!
How does the tactic give you leverage over your target?
Know the history
What has your group (or other groups) done before to dress the issue?
Can you build on the history to escalate your tactics?
Give up representation
Direct Action
DON`T PRETEND TO DO POLITICS IN THE ART FIELD!
Pick a target
Putting the enemy in a dilemma position
Who is the decision maker?
Who can help you pressure that decision maker?
Leave the comfort zone!
Use the right language and framing!
"Use the language that people are used to" (Lab of II)
Labels and Slogans
Focus your message!
How do you make complicated issues understandable?
Keep it short and simple!
The Pleasure Principle
Create attention!
Who is your audience?
media strategy
Don`t dress as a protester!
Show, don`t tell!
Use popular cultural codes!
Over affirmation can be a strategy
„There is nothing worse than bad activist dancing" (J. Jordan)
After the action
Celebrate!
Debrief the action!

New Action Principles

Schwabinggrad Ballett and ARRiVATi (Interview with Asuquo, Nik, Liz and Toyin)

How did you approach the notion of the 'training' and what does the term mean to your practice?

Asuquo: I approached the notion as an eye-opener for future generations. For me it means learning and accumulating knowledge to pave the way for a better understanding of political issues and secular human life, and to also apply these lessons to my daily struggles with human rights abuses and injustices enacted by imperialistic institutions. I therefore trained to share my fundamental experiences, network and information.

Liz: A training is a body-based practice that takes place in a certain timeframe. During that timeframe, I can pass on body knowledge. Of course this can be framed by words, but the basis is a collective experience on the body level. The experience of collective and coordinated movement in public space plays an important role in the political field. The kinaesthetic and somatic potency of body experience has a direct effect on social movement itself. My concept of movement with regard to the 'moving body' is always threefold: the political movement, the actual physical, choreographic movement and the associated inner movement and its personal affections. I try to explore this triangle within my practice. Contemporary political assemblies must facilitate space for diverse positions and heterogeneous bodies. In this context, the concept of choreography is helpful because choreographic formats can assemble heterogeneous bodies in a very specific way through dance-like movements. This expanded understanding of choreography is the basis for my practice and how I organize the trainings. Training basically means rehearsing collectivity.

Toyin: I am not a trainer and never have been. Unfortunately, many have been conditioned to believe that learning is counter-intuitive, that it only needs to be done in a specific space with 'certified' trainers, that trainees require these 'certified' trainers to prescribe the things they need to train and the standards they need to meet by a certain time and that trainees cannot be trusted to initiate and facilitate their own learning. We cannot imagine everyone learning in their most natural and organic form because most of us have been deprived of that experience ourselves. Many of us were rejected and ridiculed when our intuition to guide our own learning took over. We have all had those moments. That is the reason why some easily give up on the freedom and self-experience of singing and moving. They have lost the basic ability to simply be and simply do. Nevertheless, this should not be the reason why so many refuse to let go of the old, oppressive communication systems of intellectualism. Now is the right time to say, 'Bullshit.' Let's decolonize our minds and chuck out all these underdeveloped and uncivilized notions about 'training' and go back to our deep roots and simply ask our ancestors.

In a time of dystopian normativity, what does the notion of the 'future' mean to you?

A: We cannot talk about the future without reflecting on past centuries and decades of history. Future-reflecting on the history of human misery, which was caused by human beings themselves, is also passed on to this generation. In the process, that imperialism becomes institutionalized. The future happened to be a desired destiny for all of humanity, but unfortunately for me, it becomes uncertain due to the oppression and discrimination I experience every single day of my life. This reminds me of one of my slogans which says, 'Man made policies and ideologies and brought misery and misfortune to the human race.'

Nik: I come from socialist Yugoslavia. There, the future was not just a word, but also a goal that fueled the entire engine of society. This engine was like a steam locomotive operated by many people and it worked and moved forward quickly. In capitalist realism – in which capitalism is sold to us as having no alternative – we are urged to remain calm and to not want to change anything, because otherwise everything will take a turn for the worse. We are not supposed to move so that the money can work for us, but the money only flows upwards anyway. A lot has changed with digitalism. There is no longer a choice between a horizontal or vertical line, as I described above. Today we are surrounded by a web and have to decide whether we want to spin along with it or just lie down in it. I learned from the science-fiction author Ursula K. Le Guin that utopia is a term that can be easily misused. Men in particular feed all the dreams of social change into it, meanwhile saying that it can't be achieved anyway. In her book *Dancing at the Edge of the World*, Le Guin describes utopia as a masculine force called 'yang.' It's a motorbike ride: luminous, bright, dry, clear, strong, consolidated, active, aggressive, straightforward, progressive, creative, expanding, forward and hot. Contrarily, the female 'ying' utopia would be dark, ambiguous, weak, yielding, passive, participative, round, cyclical, peaceful, caring, contracting, retreating and cold. Interestingly, these are qualities that are mainly found in indigenous communities and that could point to a way out of climate change.

L: In the recent past the term *alternativlos* [without alternative] has become a really dominant figure in politics. I think we definitely have to address this very critically, because this would be the end of the political discourse. Decision-making has to be reclaimed and reinvented. During the pandemic we realized how quickly reality can change if people think that what is facing it is urgent. I think we now have to tackle big issues like the climate crises and the distribution of wealth with the same radical openness to change.

What did you learn from your training? What aspects would you develop or change?

A: I learned a whole lot about impediments: the good, the bad and the ugly. I learned that my acceptance could be based on differing conditions – either positive ones, like my potential, or otherwise exclusionary ones, like racism and oppression. I learned to live in an environment where hatred is the order of day. So with that said, I would like to change the perception of some minds, and give an education to the ignorant. I would also like to develop networks, as I believe in the human capacity to change the narrative through doing things like creating awareness in schools. This is especially important: to reach out to young people, or students of all levels for that matter, and to also do so through families and parents.

N: The best workshops were those given by groups involved in a concrete struggle: preserving a piece of forest, empowering a neighborhood, fighting for more affordable housing or campaigning for a democratic internet.

L: The heterogeneity of our group is a potential. If everybody can realize their potential than we can create a group experience.

How would you describe the relationship between trainers and trainees?

A: A trainer is someone who teaches skills or transfers knowledge on or for a particular job, profession or whatever task it is that they have to train you on. Trainees are those who receive this transfer of knowledge, and who learn and practice the skills or knowledge until they have been acquired.

L: To create a rhythm within a training is essential for the energy level of the group. In an ideal moment, curiosity is high on both sides. While sharing my own practice, I am always learning new aspects through the reactions of the trainees.

How do you envision the further distribution of tactics and knowledges to reclaim the future?

L: I strongly feel that we have to teach the histories of social movements in relation to their bodily practices, their actions and their strategies. We need to be inspired by these movements and to see ourselves within a tradition of struggles and movements. Action principles are important to distribute to the people, to be used in their own struggles. Therefore, I am working permanently to gather new action principles, which is of course an open process. (See: the 'Action Principles' sheet at the beginning of this interview.)

We Are Nature Defending Itself, Laboratory of Insurrectionary Imagination (Isabelle Fremeaux and Jay Jordan)

This training aims at becoming ecological beings, understanding how we can learn from the natural world in order to fight for the commons.

The Laboratory of Insurrectionary Imagination (Laboffi) merges art and life, creativity and resistance, proposition and opposition. Infamous for touring the United Kingdom recruiting a rebel clown army, running courses in post-capitalist culture, throwing snowballs at bankers, turning hundreds of abandoned bikes into machines of disobedience and launching a rebel raft regatta to shut down a coal-fired power station, Laboffi treats insurrection as an art and art as a means of preparing for the coming insurrection.

Art activist Jay Jordan has been described as a 'magician of rebellion' by the press and a 'domestic extremist' by the British police. They are the co-founder of Reclaim the Streets (1995–2000) and the Clandestine Insurgent Rebel Clown Army as well as the co-author of *We Are Everywhere*: *The Irresistible Rise of Global Anticapitalism* (Verso, 2003), which was later published in Germany as *Wir sind überall weltweit: unwiderstehlich.antikapitalistisch* (Nautilus, 2007).

Isabelle Fremeaux is a popular educator, action researcher and deserter of the academy. Together with Jay Jordan, she co-ordinates the Laboratory of Insurrectionary Imagination, a collective bringing artists and activists together to design tools and acts of disobedience. Co-author of the film and book *Pfade durch Utopia* (Nautilus, 2005), she now lives and works on the ZAD of Notre-dame-des-landes – a liberated territory against an airport and its world.

LEARNING
ZONE
COMFORT
ZONE
PANIC ZONE

Art and Activism to Nourish the Radical Imagination

Labofii (Isabelle Fremeaux and Jay Jordan)

How did you approach the notion of the 'training' and what does the term mean to your practice?

At the Laboratory of Insurrectionary Imagination (Labofii), different forms of pedagogy have always been central to our work, which brings together artists and activists to co-design and implement tools of resistance and disobedience. The founding event of Labofii, which was held as part of a fringe autonomous event during London's European Social Forum in the winter of 2004, was a several day-long training at the RampART squatted social center. Over a hundred art activists and collectives from across Europe converged and shared their work, trained people in a specific tactic and then went out into the streets to try them out. For four days, hundreds participated in radical forms of cultural resistance across London, disrupting and disobeying the everyday consumer and the capitalist behaviors of the metropolis.

Actions ranged from baffling games of bingo at MacDonald's with the Space Hijackers to urban climbing in the financial district with Lottie Child, from mass prayers to shut down Selfridges department store to hexing the headquarters of multinationals with the Center for Tactical Magic, from games of street tag via department store makeup counters with My Dads Strip Club to learning to steal food for a huge feast with Yo Mango and, finally, to an unexpected battle between the Clandestine Insurgent Rebel Clown Army and Capitalism Represents Acceptable Policy (CRAP), which accidentally interrupted the premiere of a Johnny Depp film.

Since then, we have never divided our pedagogy, politics and art and the three are always entangled in every one of our experiments. (We never describe our output as projects, pieces or works but instead as experiments, suggesting the right to fail, take risks and develop an attitude of discovery and collective learning.) Unlike the many artists who view pedagogy as the thing they do on the side of the 'real work,' for us it is at the heart of creating spaces of symbiosis for art and activism to nourish the radical imagination.

This has involved a week-long open workshop in art, activism and permaculture design, held at Arnolfini Gallery in Bristol, where participants built prototypes for tools of disobedience using abandoned bikes, which were then upscaled in Copenhagen for actions against the corporate take over of the United Nations Climate Summit a month later. It has also meant introducing over 900 bodies to civil disobedience and giving them confidence despite the state of emergency that banned demonstrations during the 2015 Paris Climate Summit. And where we live on the ZAD of Notre-dame-des-Landes, a rebel territory of 4000 acres near the city of Nantes where an international airport project was successfully resisted, we held trainings in the hot autumn of 2016 – the date the French government had set to come and begin constructing the airport and evict all the farmers and the community of land defenders who had resisted for decades.

Over five weekends, despite the president of the region trying to ban what he named 'the school of violence,' we trained people in affinity group work, legal rights and how to protect themselves from the dangers of the weaponry that the French cops favor (tear gas, concussion grenades and rubber bullets). We then sent the newly formed affinity groups into the fields and forests on an adventure that was part orienteering course, part treasure hunt and part dress rehearsal for the evictions. Using a specially designed ZAD pocket atlas, listening to the pirate radio station via hand held receivers and communicating with walkie talkies and encrypted phones, they had to organize together without being caught by the 'police.'

Of course, these were fake police, folk from the ZAD who drove around the zone in Mad Max-type cars without number plates and with big CB radio aerials sticking out of them. Hanging from the cars' open windows, all dressed in black and wearing balaclavas, these ZAD cops looked as scary as the real thing. They would attempt to arrest members of the affinity groups and take them to a pretend jail, where they would undergo a realistic process of detention. At the end of the day a debriefing session would enable strategies to be shared and reflected on. Over 900 very different people took part, from high school students to old age pensioners. The training left them with an embodied knowledge of the territory, an understanding embedded in bramble scratches and tired muscles obtained while scrambling through its opulent hedgerows. They returned home with a new sense of confidence and desire to defend the ZAD.

The trainings were on the back of numerous mass actions that year, ranging from 500 tractors, 1000 bikes and 20,000 bodies occupying a major bridge with a banquet to 4000 people in a choreographed ritual, beautifully disguised as a demonstration planting staffs and walking sticks in the ground as a pledge to retrieve them should the government return to build the airport. The government never came. The wetlands, fields and forests will never be runways and life continues to produce life. For us at Labofii, this is the key to any aesthetic of the future: blocking the monocultural machines of capitalism and enabling life to flourish.

In a time of dystopian normativity, what does the notion of the 'future' mean to you?

At the start of nearly all our trainings, including the one at Bochum, we present three spectrum lines, which are pedagogic tools to begin conversations between everyone. The first is about the participants' visions for the future. To start, a line is drawn on the floor, with one end of the line bearing the word 'utopia' and the other end 'dystopia.' We then ask the participants to place themselves on the line in relation to the future that they imagine. As it is a spectrum, participants can place themselves anywhere on the line. We then ask each of them why they have decided to place themselves at that particular place. One of the rules of the exercise is that if someone says something that changes your mind, you can change your position.

What generally occurs is that one immediately sees people spread out across the line, some with deeply dystopian visions and others with the opposite. Over the years (we have been doing this exercise since 2006), the tendency has of course been that people are shifting more toward the dystopian end of the line, but ultimately it always depends, and there are never no utopians in the room. For some people it seems clear that they require the threat of collapse to feed the energy they need to be motivated, yet for others to keep motivated they need more positive visions of the future. The exercise makes visible the diversity of political sensitivities that are present at the start of a workshop. The second spectrum line we draw asks if participants consider themselves as an artist or an activist. This enables us to quickly see folks identity as well as the balance in a group (our ideal workshops are when there is no disequilibrium, e.g. not too many artists or activists but a spread). It also enables a group discussion about these roles and begins a critique of identities that hold monopoly and give expertise on creativity and social change. The final spectrum line asks if collective practice changes our worlds, with one end of the line bearing 'yes' and the other 'no.' This often takes us full circle back to the future, and to how the future is only constructed by our actions in the present.

Modernity was based on hope, but its fantasy of a brighter future has never rung so false – even despite Elon Musk's wet dream of moving to Mars. In this moment, this historical blip – meaning, the pathological belief in progress – is a linear motorway that tells us there is only one history, only one bright point toward which we are all going, that the past is dead and that all those attached to it backward. But perhaps this toxic story, with its sky gods and skyscraper temples, has at last come back to earth. Some biologists call humans the 'future eaters.' But to blame humans is to let the real culprits off the hook: only 20% of humanity consumes 80% of the world's resources, and since the start of the industrial revolution two-thirds of all climate-wrecking gases have been produced by just ninety corporations, all of which have names and addresses.

A recent official European Commission policy paper ended with the warning that if we go beyond 1.5 degrees of warming, 'we will face even more droughts, floods, extreme heat and poverty for hundreds of millions of people; the likely demise of the most vulnerable populations—and at worst, the extinction of humankind altogether.' We are living in a time where it is easier to imagine the collapse of life as we know it than to imagine reinventing the right ways to live together. For many of the colonized peoples of the world, this collapse is not in the future: it began 500 years ago.

We all know the apocalyptic lists of facts and figures, and the more terrifying it gets the more banal it becomes. In this terrifyingly banal fashion, all these facts and figures, headlines and newsflashes just pass by like all the others. Anodyne in their abstraction, the only emotion they seem to evoke is a fear of the future. Greta Thunberg told us not to hope but to panic. Fear and anxiety have become the dominant affects of our age and history shows us that fear has tended to be the petri dish where fascism, authoritarian systems and Gulags grow. For the most motivated, panic might create an explosion of action and passion, though it is often short-lived as bodies filled with too much adrenaline and fear burnout fast. But for many, the response to fear is to freeze or flee, rather than to fight. Flee into any one of the numbing worlds capitalism puts at our disposal – developing powerful addictions and new needs is after all the craft of the best entrepreneurs – or freezing into a depression while attempting to keep on going as if everything is normal. All the statistics, graphs, nuclear countdown clocks, measurements and invisible parts per million molecules don't give us anything to hold on to. It's all too big and scary, and is it really mobilizing the right kind of action to turn things around anyway? How will we survive? Will we survive? These questions are misleading, they take us on a path of panic toward a plethora of false solutions and techno-fixes: the geo-engineering, the financialization of nature, the 'net zero' emissions accounting that turns the crisis into a game of maths, all to keep business as usual. Perhaps the real question should be: What do we want?

A learning model we often present at the start of a training is composed of two concentric circles. In the center sits a circle with 'panic zone' written inside it, and then a second circle surrounding it says 'comfort zone.' Through this model we suggest that the trainees find the edge between panic and comfort and that it is there where true learning occurs.

Put this book down for a minute. Stand up, feel the weight of your feet on the ground. As quickly as you can, think of the future. Try to imagine one image from it and take a step into it. Just one step.

Did you step forwards or backwards? Most likely you stepped forwards, most of us do. But ask the same question to an Aymara, one of the Amerindian peoples from the highest valleys in the Andes, and they will step backwards. For them the word 'future' [*q'ipa*] translates as 'behind,' while the word for 'past' [*nayra*] literally means 'eye,' 'sight' or 'front.' The Aymara face the past, and in doing so they can see how the multitudinous experiences of dead ancestors (human and more-than-human) have nourished their present. And as a result they have their backs to the future, to the world that is not yet there, the unknown, the uncertainty of what comes next. Unlike Walter Benjamin's angel of history, with its back to the future yet still blown about uncontrollably by the storm of progress and with wreckage building up in a mountain in front of it, the Aymara people turned to the past is perhaps a better metaphor for us to take into the future. It reminds us that the past is neither dead, dusty history nor just disaster, but a living experience, visible in the present, that can be felt in every one of our cells. The rods and cones in the eyes with which you're reading these words were once spirochete bacteria, the same microbes that bring us Lymes disease and syphilis. Blink. Think/feel this. Thanks to those ancient bug ancestors, we can see the world and they remind us that even the present is simply a process in which past and future are always implicated; that the future is so close that we can feel its breeze tousle the hairs on the back of our necks.

How would you describe the relationship between trainers and trainees?

We have an approach that has its roots in popular education, i.e. to not separate action from analysis, to not separate those who do from those who think and decide and to work out ways together to transform our worlds so that they are livable for all. It is not about having experts that teach, but rather about having trainers with experience that open up spaces allowing them to become as fertile as possible for participants to share their knowledge and construct both self-confidence and confidence in collective creativity together. It's about creating frameworks rather then curriculums, community as much as knowledge.

One of the most important inspirations for our training is the Highlander Folk School, which was founded in 1932 in Tennessee by Myles Horton. The basic principle was to merge community *and* conflict through living together and learning to organize together, but not in a distant or abstract way. It was about being strongly embedded in social movements while experiencing collective life in situ. Initially working with the drive toward unionization in the post-Depression poverty of the south of the United States, it shifted to support the civil rights movement in the 1950s. It was at Highlander Folk School that one of the most famous activists of the civil rights movement was trained: Rosa Parks, who in Montgomery, Alabama, in December 1955, triggered the great boycott of all buses by black people after she refused to give up her seat to white passengers. It was also here that Zilphia Horton taught the famous folk singer Pete Seeger the gospel song that became the anthem for the civil rights movement, titled 'We Shall Overcome.' The right even erected billboards with pictures of Martin Luther King attending Highlander, under which big white letters read, 'MARTIN LUTHER KING AT COMMUNIST TRAINING SCHOOL.' The school continues today, and just last year had its archives burnt to the ground during a right-wing arson attack – an act that proves that it continues to be radical nearly 100 years after its founding.

For us, the idea that force is generated through trainings that create a temporary community within the context of struggle is key. One can only create this sense of community if there is the least amount of hierarchy possible between trainers and trainees, and if a sense of trust has been woven between all participants. Joseph Beuys' idea of creating a 'warm' space is important here. This warmth is created by not only immediately opening up the space for all to speak at the start of a training, something achieved through the use of the spectrum lines, but also by using playfulness and games as key pedagogical tools to embody knowledge. We think that it is key to reclaim the right to play for adults, and to develop the space of play as a respected space of learning. In play we learn to let go, we learn to think with our bodies, we learn to open ourselves to the unexpected and to take each other a lot less seriously. Play breaks hierarchies between all involved in a training quickly. When we play the game 'Let's All,' which is learnt in clown training, people take turns to call out a desire that the rest of the group must follow. 'Let's all be worms,' they might say, and then everyone says together, 'Yes, let's all be worms,' after which they then embody a squiggling worm until someone else says, 'Let's all be a broom,' and so on. When you have forty people, including the trainers, crawling around on the floor becoming beings and objects of all sorts, the fear of being ridiculous quickly fades away. Therefore, warm spaces are also those where there is the least fear of judgment.

Our emphasis on the importance of the joy of resistance also creates a sense of lightness and a breath of fresh air despite the heavy political context. Many of the art activism acts we talk about during trainings, whether our own work or that of comrades, have humor in them. From the flamenco dancers blockading a bank with their dancing to Labofii leaving Hamburg's Kampnagel Theatre after arming the audience with ants that sabotage computers in banks that fund fossil fuels, there is always a good balance of cheek and creativity. 'Our theater is there to train people in the pleasure of transforming reality,' wrote Bertolt Brecht. For us, that is the key to bringing people into radical social movements, and often we see our trainings as a doorway into direct action movements. If people sense that being part of a movement is something that will give them pleasure and an expression of passion, that it is not just loads of boring A to B protest marches and endless meetings, it gives them more encouragement to take risks and get involved. We try to suggest through our storytelling during trainings that being part of social movements is not a process of sacrificing life for a struggle, but finding meaning in life via the friendships and communities that emerge through struggle.

How do you envision the further distribution of tactics and knowledges to reclaim the future?

In the laboratories of social and natural sciences, 'human exceptionalism and bounded individualism,' writes biologist Donna Haraway, 'those old saws of Western Philosophy and political economics, become ... seriously unthinkable.' We find ourselves at this fulcrum moment in history where life is in more danger than it has been for the last two hundred million years, while at the same time our understandings of life are being revolutionized. Yet in the museums and studios, concert halls and theaters, galleries and festivals, art schools and theater conservatoires, it seems that even though this era *should* make *art as we know it* seriously unthinkable, business as usual continues. Artists continue to represent and comment on the world rather than transform it. They continue to extract value from movements or political crises to feed their careers rather than taking the risk of entangling themselves in the everyday organizing and on-the-ground processes of movement-building and solution-forming.

But *art as we know it,* this universal defining feature of an 'advanced civilization' and the great bringer of what is good, according to art historian Larry Shiner, 'is a European invention barely two hundred years old.' For Labofii, *art as we know it* is yet another dualistic tool of the modern, which emerged in the white colonial metropolises and split the beautiful from the useful, the artisan from the artist, the genius from the skill and art from life. This turned art into a thing to be contemplated; a thing that no longer inhabited somewhere and no longer had a specific place, time or purpose.

With so many of these institutions now being closed during Covid-19 lockdowns, perhaps we can use this opportunity to seriously rethink their function. Perhaps all the museums and theaters and galleries of the Western world could stop being places to show things to people but instead spaces to transform each other together via learning and training. Perhaps the art schools and conservatoires could stop training people to become individualistic, extractivist artists, and instead become social centers for imagining and creating new forms of resistance; places to learn how to radically remake this system that is designed to separate us and to build worlds that connect us.

This requires us deserting the old forms and building new ones. Isa and JJ both deserted the academy. Both were senior lecturers, Isa in cultural studies at Birkbeck, University of Lodon, and JJ in Fine Art at Sheffield Hallam School of Art and Design. When we arrived on the ZAD we had a dream of setting up a school, but for five years we concentrated on organizing the struggle against the airport and then against the revenge the state took on our way of life after the infrastructure project was abandoned in 2018. But we also realized that it was already an open-air pluriversity, a space of totally immersive informal teaching and learning. On these 4000 acres against an airport and its world, a canvas of commoning emerged during the six years where no police or government officials set foot in the zone. Without any planning laws, and having to invent our own common customs and ways of dealing with conflict, the ZAD was a source of constant learning for how to take back control of everyday life without the double-headed monster of state and market. Squatters learnt to become farmers, and farmers became squatters. Many of the building sites were called *chantier école* [school sites], which meant that, for example, in the winter of 2016 when we built a twenty-meter-high working illegal lighthouse on the site of where they wanted to build the control tower of the airport, the aim was not productivism – not getting the lighthouse built as quickly as possible, even though threats of eviction were coming in fast and furiously – but to make sure that those working on it were learning new skills. It was about qualitative attention, outside of the frenetic rhythm of the market. For five months we put together a ragged band of deserting architects and engineers, an ex-homeless kid, a ceramicist, a few farmers and a genius welder whose day job was building the world's biggest cruise-liners in France's largest shipyard. Many left the site able to weld and, most especially, with the force of confidence that arises after completing a totally audacious act of radical imagination.

We need to develop more territorially based spaces of learning and training. The ZAD is now part of a loose network of autonomous schools, many set up by deserting artists and teachers now based in radical communities. This includes a school of philosophy, a nomadic women's traditional carpentry school and the Zapatista-inspired School of the Earth.

On January 17, 2021, to celebrate the anniversary of the cancellation of the airport, the frames of a new building were illegally raised on the ruins of one of the farmhouses destroyed by the French government in their first attempt at eviction in 2012. The idea is that this building becomes the base for the School of the Newts, a learning space mixing education on the living world with naturalists and scientists. It's a new kind of workshop for training deserters of all sorts, and it will merge art, politics and everyday life. For the opening, the Ritual Action Cell designated a ritual to protect the building using a magic sigil drawn by hundreds of people on the buildings wooden posts with charcoal made from the willows in the hedgerows that were saved from destruction. The sigil was 'charged' by everyone present singing a karaoke version of a hacked Sex Pistols song, which saw the chorus change from 'I am an anarchist!' to 'I am an animist!'

In the spring of 2022, we hope to begin this new workshop for deserters, where we attempt to break the separations forged between everyday life, politics, education and art. Those three letters, A-R-T, come from a merger of the Latin *ars* and the Greek *techne* and for many thousands of years they meant *any* human activity. Shoemaking and verse writing, horse breaking and governing, vase painting and cooking, medicine and navigation, all activities were considered an art. And not because they were done by an artist, but because they were performed with grace and skill. Grace is an act of thinking with and thanking the world. The word comes from the old French word *grace*, meaning 'thanks,' as in *grâce à* meaning 'gratitude.' To thank life for giving us life, to practice mutual reciprocity: that is the core of a practice that no longer separates ethics and aesthetics. This is an art of life. These approaches and principles will be at the heart of our trainings, which take place here on these wetlands, where we continue to build and learn new ways of commoning that can nourish rather than eat our future.

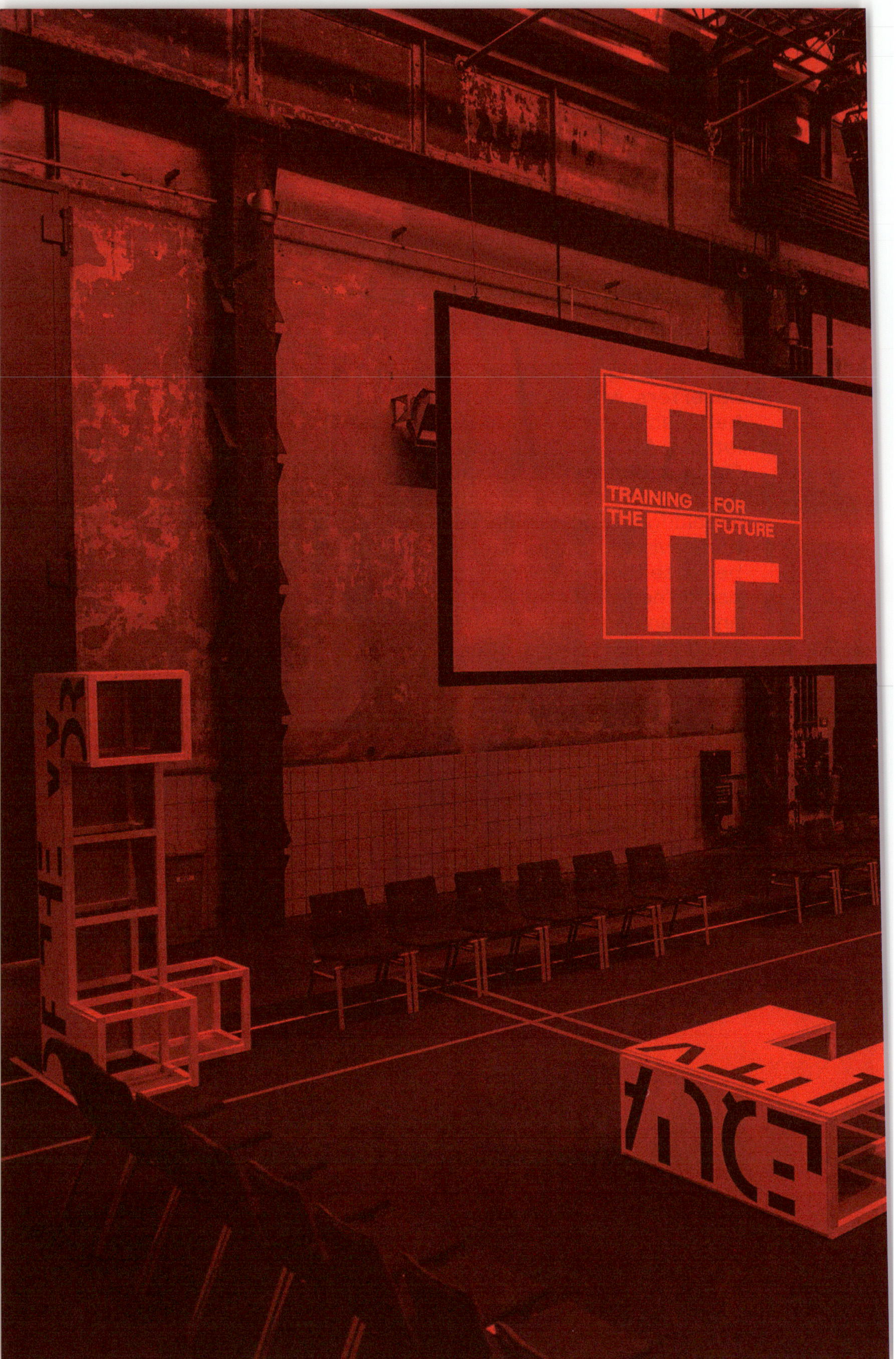
TRAINING
FOR
THE
FUTURE

Training for the Future 2018–2021

Training for the Future is a project by Jonas Staal, curated and co-programmed by Florian Malzacher

Training for the Future:
A Pre-enactment
Bochum, Germany

September 8, 2018
Co-produced by Ruhrtriennale, Germany

Project team: Jonas Staal (artist), Florian Malzacher (curator and co-programmer), Stefanie Carp (artistic director Ruhrtriennale), Paul Kuipers (architect), Remco van Bladel (designer), Younes Bouadi and Evelien Scheltinga (production and coordination Studio Jonas Staal)

Training for the Future
Bochum, Germany

September 20–22, 2019
Co-produced by Ruhrtriennale, Germany, in partnership with Goethe-Institut, Munich
With additional support from Mondriaan Fonds, Amsterdam, and Bundeszentrale für politische Bildung, Bonn

Project team: Jonas Staal (artist), Florian Malzacher (curator and co-programmer), Paul Kuipers (architect), Remco van Bladel (designer), Younes Bouadi and Nadine Gouders (production and coordination Studio Jonas Staal), Charlie Berendsen (website). Team Ruhrtriennale: Stefanie Carp (artistic director), Vera Battis-Reese (managing director), Jürgen Reitzler (artistic management director), Hanna Kriegleder (artistic production manager), Lisa Holzberg (planning), Christiane Biallas (travel, accommodation), Vroni Obermeier (artistic production manager), Mirko Bartos (technical production manager), Rainer Ott (technical production manager)

Training for the Future: Collectives, Collectivity and Collectivizations
Argentina, Colombia, Italy, the Philippines, Rojava, South Africa, Switzerland, the United States

March 6–April 6, 2021
Co-produced by Goethe-Institut / Performing Architecture Venedig, Munich, and Theater Neumarkt, Zurich

Project team: Jonas Staal (artist), Florian Malzacher (curator and co-programmer), Nadine Gouders (coordinator Studio Jonas Staal), Hayat Erdoğan and Nikolai Prawdzic (programmers Zurich), Susanne Traub (Performing Architecture team, Goethe-Institut), Remco van Bladel (designer), Studio RGB (website development)

COLOPHON

Training for the Future: Handbook
Edited by Florian Malzacher and Jonas Staal

Design: Remco van Bladel
Copy editing: Isabelle Sully
Photos: Ruben Hamelink (2019),
courtesy of the trainers/authors (2021)

Training for the Future
Goethe-Institut / Performing Architecture
Venedig, Munich
Theater Neumarkt, Zurich

Printed in the Netherlands by Drukkerij
Raddraaier SSP, Amsterdam
ISBN 978-3-95679-628-9

Distributed by The MIT Press, Art Data and
Les presses du réel

Published by

Sternberg Press

Sternberg Press
Caroline Schneider
71–75 Shelton Street
London WC2H 9JQ
www.sternberg-press.com

GOETHE INSTITUT

neumarkt
playground theater akademie digital

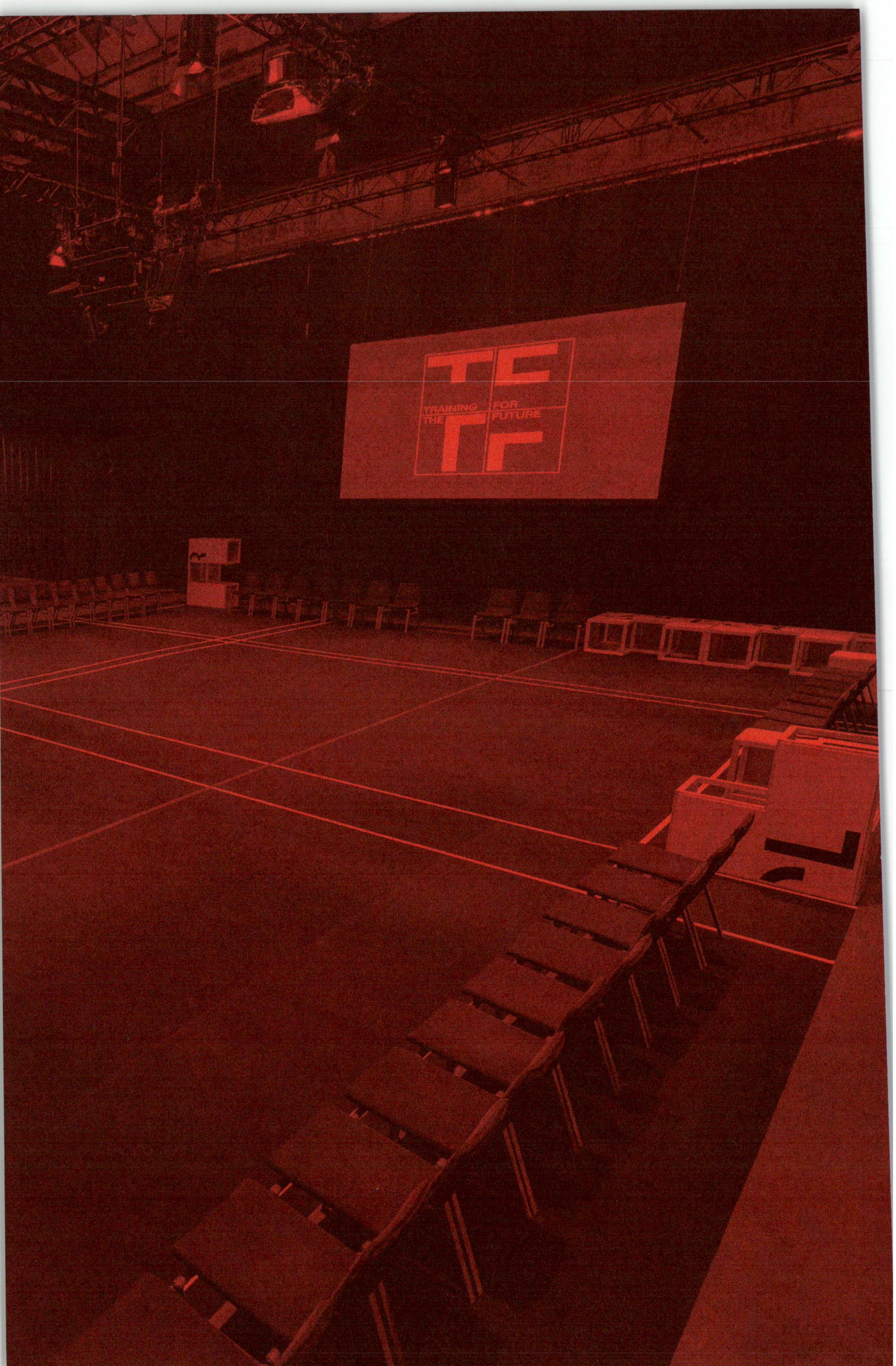
TRAINING
THE
FOR
FUTURE